The Woodworker's PROBLEM SOLVER

The Woodworker's

PROBLEM SOLVER

512 Shop-Proven Solutions to Your Most Challenging Woodworking Problems

TONY O'MALLEY, *Editor*

Rodale Press, Inc.
Emmaus, Pennsylvania

Editor: Tony O'Malley
Contributing Editors: Ken Burton, Kevin Ireland
Cover and Interior Book Designer:
  Marta Mitchell Strait
Cover and Interior Illustrator: Graham Blackburn
Photographers: Mitch Mandel,
  W. Curtis Johnson (page 18), John McKay (page 294),
  Dennis Slabaugh (page 20)
Cover Photographer: Mitch Mandel
Photography Editor: James A. Gallucci
Layout Designer: Dale Mack
Copy Editor: Sara Cox
Manufacturing Coordinator: Patrick T. Smith
Indexer: Diane Benison
Editorial Assistance: Jodi Guiducci, Lori Schaffer
Rodale Design Shop: Fred Matlack

On the cover: illustration from "Rebuilding a Profiled Edge," page 288

Rodale Home and Garden Books

Vice President and Editorial Director:
  Margaret J. Lydic
Managing Editor, Woodworking Books: Kevin Ireland
Director of Design and Production: Michael Ward
Associate Art Director: Carol Angstadt
Studio Manager: Leslie M. Keefe
Copy Director: Dolores Plikaitis
Book Manufacturing Director: Helen Clogston
Office Manager: Karen Earl-Braymer

Library of Congress Cataloging-in-Publication Data

The woodworker's problem solver : 512 shop-proven solutions to your most challenging woodworking problems / Tony O'Malley, editor.
      p.   cm.
Includes bibliographical references (p.) and index.
ISBN 0–87596–773–6   (alk. paper)
  1. Woodwork—Amateurs' manuals.   2. Workshops—Equipment and supplies—Amateurs' manuals.
3. Woodworking tools—Amateurs' manuals.
I. O'Malley, Tony.
TT185.W6593   1998
684'.08—dc21   97–33810

Distributed in the book trade by St. Martin's Press

2 4 6 8 10 9 7 5 3   hardcover

RODALE PRESS

HOW OUR WOODWORKING BOOKS BEGAN

Twenty years ago, a group of creative editors at Rodale Press decided to put together a book of great yard and garden projects and offer it to the loyal readers of Rodale's *Organic Gardening* and *Prevention* magazines. They had a gut feeling that other people just might love woodworking as much as they did. It turned out they were right. Over 800,000 people bought that first book, and that was the beginning of what has become the most successful woodworking book business in the country.

There were no rules to follow in those early years. The editors would come up with enough projects to fill a book or two a year, and they would cover everything from fences and decks to cold frames and chicken houses. But even then, they knew that it was important to get all the instructions and dimensions right. So, they would test every project by building it in the company shop.

Today, Rodale is known as the publisher of some of the best-selling woodworking books of all time, including the *Workshop Companion* series (over 1.4 million copies in print), *Cabinetry* (over 600,000 copies in print), and the critically acclaimed *Understanding Wood Finishing*. We publish seven to ten new books a year, filling each one with carefully designed projects, detailed woodworking techniques, and dozens of time-saving tips. And though we still rely on the ideas of the skilled woodworkers on our staff, we also reach out to some of the best woodworkers in the country, including the dozens of professional craftsmen we meet each year and readers like you.

Yes, we're bigger now, but we still believe in doing things the right way. Our editors still love woodworking. And we still test everything we write about to ensure that your time in the shop will be satisfying, productive, and fun.

If you ever run into a problem with one of our books, please contact us. We're always glad to help. And if you're ever in Emmaus, stop by. We'll be pleased to share our woodworking war stories with you and show you our shop.

Kevin Ireland

Kevin Ireland
Managing Editor
Rodale Woodworking Books

CONTENTS

INTRODUCTION   viii

Using This Book   ix

DESIGN AND LAYOUT SOLUTIONS   2

Improving Proportions   3

Avoiding Structural Problems   10

Enhancing Design Details   15

Drawing Plans and Laying Out Parts   21

Shop Math and Geometry   30

Working with Figure and Grain   33

MATERIALS SOLUTIONS   36

Choosing Materials   37

Working with Materials   46

Dealing with Blemishes and Defects   50

Storing and Drying Lumber   55

STOCK PREPARATION SOLUTIONS   60

Jointing Stock   61

Planing Wood   67

Resawing Thick Stock   72

Working with Veneer   75

CUTTING AND SIZING SOLUTIONS   78

Ripping Lumber   79

Crosscutting Lumber   84

Cutting Sheet Goods   94

Other Sizing Problems   96

BENDING AND SHAPING SOLUTIONS   98

Routing and Cutting Profiles   99

Creating Shapes   105

Bending Wood   114

JOINERY SOLUTIONS   120

Improving Corner Joints   121

Making Better Miters   130

Frame Joinery Solutions   135

Mortise and Tenon Solutions   138

Doweling and Drilling Solutions   148

Handling Case Joinery   151

Making Edge Joints   155

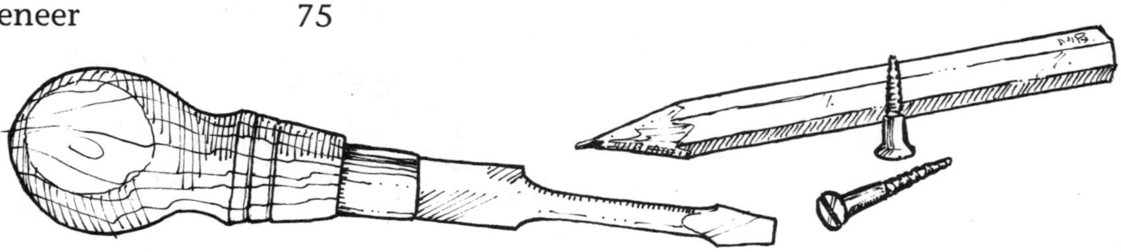

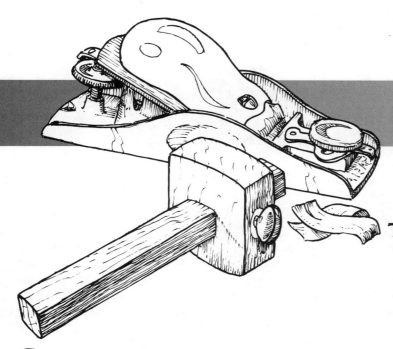

GLUING AND ASSEMBLY SOLUTIONS   158

Gluing and Glues   159

Gluing Up Solid
Wooden Panels   164

Assembling Cabinets
and Furniture   169

Assembling Doors,
Drawers, and Frames   175

Installing Doors, Drawers,
and Hardware   179

Clamping Difficult Assemblies   187

Using Fasteners   193

Installation Solutions   197

SANDING SOLUTIONS   200

Using Sanding Tools   201

Smart Sanding Strategies   208

FINISHING SOLUTIONS   216

Prepping for Finish   217

Staining Wood   220

Applying Finishes   226

Fixing Finishes   241

Painting Wood   246

TOOL MAINTENANCE AND SHARPENING SOLUTIONS   248

Table Saw Solutions   249

Band Saw Solutions   253

Jointer Solutions   258

Other Stationary Machines   260

Router Solutions   262

Hand Tool Solutions   265

Sharpening Solutions   269

REPAIR SOLUTIONS   274

Fixing Dents and Gouges   275

Solving Gluing Problems   280

Dealing with
Structural Problems   282

Repairing Twist and Warp   291

Fixing Imperfections in Wood   294

Repairing Finishes   296

SOURCES   298

CONTRIBUTORS   300

INDEX   304

INTRODUCTION

Early in my career as a full-time woodworker, I built a set of tall bookcases for a customer who lived in a high-rise apartment. I planned the project carefully, measured everything twice, and got through the job without any major hitches. Then after all of those hours of work, I showed up at the apartment loading dock ready to deliver the project, anxious to get paid. Within a few minutes it became clear that I'd overlooked one little detail: The cabinets were about 2 inches too tall to make it into the elevator. Did I mention that the customer lived on the 17th floor?

After about an hour of fretful deliberation in which a circular saw figured prominently, I got on the phone and cajoled a buddy to help bail me out of the jam. The pain of carrying those bookcases up 17 flights of stairs was relieved only by the certainty that it was the best solution to the problem at hand.

Since then I've discovered over and over again how woodworking is all about solving problems. It challenges you to work around puzzles and predicaments as they arise, and when you solve one, you feel pride in beating an adversary. In a big way, overcoming the diverse challenges that woodworking presents is exactly what makes it such an enjoyable activity.

That's the premise for *The Woodworker's Problem Solver*. This book is filled with over 500 clever solutions that dozens of skilled woodworkers developed during all their satisfying hours in the shop. Like you, they sometimes get stuck along the way toward completing a project. The solutions they have come up with are sure to help you out of a jam too.

To gather the solutions in this book, we contacted professional and amateur woodworkers from across America and asked them to give us their best ideas on everything from design and layout to finishing and repair. (The "Contributors" list, beginning on page 300, shows what a diverse and talented group they are.) Then we polled the editors here and at our sister publication, *American Woodworker* magazine, to gather the very best solutions developed in-house over the years.

Finally, to make sure we didn't overlook anything, we also spent hours on the Internet checking on the types of problems woodworkers were posting on the message boards there. The result is a mix of material that is sure to give you good, solid solutions to all sorts of woodworking predicaments, whether you're a beginning woodworker or a pro.

As you explore this book, you'll find that it works at three levels. First, when you're stumped by something, the book will quickly show you methods to overcome the problem. Whether you need to find the radius of an arc, joint the face of a wide board on a narrow jointer, or stain different colored woods to the same tone, you'll find the answers here. So you'll want to keep the book close at hand in the shop. On another level, *The Woodworker's Problem Solver* will help you avoid problems before they happen, like designing shelves so they don't sag, choosing the best wood for a specific project, or cutting joints exactly right the first time. There's also an entire chapter on solutions you'll use after you thought the job was all done—creating an invisible patch in a gouged tabletop, flattening a twisted door, or repairing a broken spindle.

Woodworking problems are often related to your particular circumstances—your lineup of tools, the size of your shop, or your level of skill and experience—and solving them involves figuring out how to best make do with what you have. But just as often they are intrinsic to the work—choosing the right joinery, gluing up panels that are flat and frames that are square, applying a dust-free finish—basic stuff that you've just not had to do before. Each step of the way, *The Woodworker's Problem Solver* will help you get it right the first time or get you out of a jam when you don't. And make no mistake about it, solving problems is just as important for the pro who's making high-end furniture as it is for the hobbyist who's building humble kitchen cabinets. More experienced woodworkers don't encounter fewer problems, they just get better at solving them.

Using This Book

The Woodworker's Problem Solver is designed so that you can pick it up and quickly locate a good solution to any woodworking problem you encounter. The table of contents shows all of the main subject categories within each chapter. Then the opening page of the chapter lists each entry by page number. Additionally you'll find many entries with cross-references to related solutions. Finally the comprehensive index lets you locate all of the entries that mention a particular word.

The majority of the entries in The Woodworker's Problem Solver are presented in standard problem/solution format. Mixed in throughout the book you'll find "Quick Tips," which are smaller nuggets of information that help you avoid particular problems; "Against the Grain" boxes, which offer an unconventional or slightly offbeat approach to solving a problem; and "Shop-Made Solutions," which show you how to make a jig or fixture that will solve or prevent a whole array of problems. There are also tables that will help you select, for example, the best finish for your project, or the right size to make a dining table to seat six. You'll also find a list of "Sources," beginning on page 298, for unusual or hard-to-find materials mentioned throughout the book.

The Woodworker's Problem Solver is a book you'll reach for again and again as you enjoy the best part of woodworking: Finding the best solutions to the predicaments you encounter. The more you use it, the better you'll be at woodworking.

Tony O'Malley
Editor

DESIGN AND LAYOUT
SOLUTIONS

IMPROVING PROPORTIONS

Making Scale Models 3

Good Looks Start with the Proportions 4

Quick-Change Proportions on Drawings 5

Sizing Cabinet Doors 5

Standard Furniture Dimensions 6

Modifying Designs 8

AVOIDING STRUCTURAL PROBLEMS

Mocking Up Key Joints 10

Avoiding Sagging Shelves 11

Maximum Shelving Spans 12

Wood Movement as a Design Factor 12

Avoiding Bad Miter Joints 13

Designing Site-Built Projects 14

ENHANCING DESIGN DETAILS

Sketching Alternative Designs 15

Locating Knobs and Hinges 15

Creating No-Show Hinges 16

Alternative Drop-Leaf Table Edge 17

Using Repetition and Contrast
to Spice Up Your Designs 18

Adding Molding to Enhance
Plain Projects 19

Applying Molding to Conceal Simple
Construction 20

DRAWING PLANS AND LAYING OUT PARTS

Making Drawings from Photos 21

Avoiding Inaccurate Layout Lines 21

Scribing Accurate Lines with a Pencil 22

Determining Odd Frame Angles 23

Erasing Lines with Alcohol 23

Enlarging, Transferring,
and Reversing Patterns 23

Sign-Making Layout Simplified 24

Laying Out Curves 24

Drawing an Ellipse or Oval 25

Avoiding Measurement Mistakes 26

Laying Out Polygons 28

SHOP MATH AND GEOMETRY

Dividing a Line
into Equal Segments 30

Determining Stave Angles 30

Dividing a Cylinder into Equal Segments 31

Finding a Center for Routing an Arc 32

Finding the Radius of an Arc 32

WORKING WITH FIGURE AND GRAIN

Grain Contrast in
Book-Matched Panels 33

Arranging Boards for Best Grain Match 33

Inlaying Wood across the Grain 34

Laying Out Right on the Wood 34

Improving Proportions

Making Scale Models

PROBLEM: *A project I just completed looks much different than I anticipated, based on the drawings. Is there a way to tell how a piece will really look when built?*

SOLUTION: Project designs that look perfect on paper often look disappointing when you build them. They may seem too top-heavy or not deep enough for their height. That's because drawings don't allow you to see the true relationship between all the dimensions and all the elements in a piece of furniture. So once you're happy with a design on paper, I recommend that you preview it by constructing a three-dimensional model.

Full-sized models will give you the truest reading, but you can use scaled-down models for convenience—just reduce all the parts by the same factor (half, quarter, etc.). The model does not need to be elaborate or carefully made, as long as you adhere to the dimensions on your plans. If the piece of furniture will be a uniform color, use only one material throughout the model. If it will have contrasting woods or colors, then use contrasting light and dark materials in the model.

You can make models from heavy-gauge paper, cardboard (large appliance boxes are great), hardboard, plywood, particleboard, medium-density fiberboard (MDF), or wood. To attach parts, use staples, packing tape, hot glue, screws, or nails.

Models like these are easy to make, and they allow you to change proportions, joinery, and details before starting to build a project.

Hardboard is a premier model-building material. It comes in 4 × 8-foot sheets in 1/8- and 1/4-inch thicknesses, and its dark brown color gives a good wood effect.

Model making is easy for pieces with straight lines. Just cut and assemble the parts. Use inexpensive wood like 2 × 4 scraps for thick pieces like legs. To simulate frame-and-panel doors, use a piece of sheet material the size of the door and then attach strips to the sheet to mimic the stiles and rails. Hot glue or double-sided tape will hold the parts securely. A piece of sheet material attached to the middle of the panel will give the effect of a raised panel. Crown molding can be simulated with a flat piece attached at a 45-degree angle.

To simulate a curved case, saw several struts from wood or plywood and attach a flexible sheet, like paper or cardboard, to it.

If you like what you see, then you're ready to cut the material for your project. If not, then experiment with the sizes of the different elements until you get the effect you want.

Ben Erickson
Eutaw, AL

Good Looks Start with the Proportions

PROBLEM: *I recently built a tall chest of drawers with all the drawers the same size. It seemed like a good idea at the time, but now something about the piece looks "off." Where did I go wrong?*

SOLUTION: I suspect you've run into the thing that's at the root of many design problems: the issue of proportion. Whenever you look at a piece of furniture, your mind subconsciously compares the relationships between the dimensions of the various parts. If the proportions are random or poorly planned, the piece will lack the harmonious character that would make it enjoyable to look at.

There are several systems for proportioning parts, but the one I find particularly satisfying is the Golden Section. In this mathematical system, the parts are laid out so that the shortest dimension relates to the intermediate dimension by the same ratio as the intermediate dimension relates to the longest dimension. See below left. This ratio is 1:1.618, or about 5:8. Applying the Golden Section to your cabinet, you would have ended up with drawers that increased in size along a progression like this: 3 inches, 5 inches, 8 inches, 13 inches, and so forth. You can apply the ratio to other dimensions of a project as well, as shown below left. Furniture that conforms to the Golden Section will be more attractive than furniture that does not.

Another system for generating mathematically related dimensions is the Hambridge Progression. To use this system, begin with a square, and draw its diagonal. The length of this diagonal is equal to the long side of a related rectangle, as shown below right. The diagonal of the new rectangle is the same length as the long side of the next related rectangle, and so on.

W. Curtis Johnson
Corvallis, OR

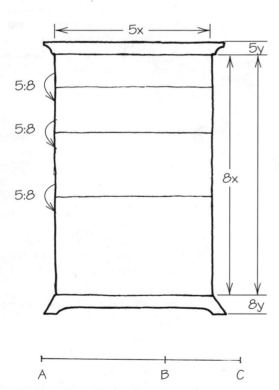

The line (*above*) shows the Golden Section: Line B-C is to line A-B as line A-B is to line A-C. The cabinet shows the ratio applied from drawer to drawer, from the width of the cabinet to the height, and from the weight of the top to the base.

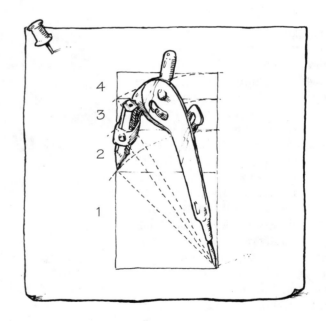

Step 1. To employ the Hambridge Progression, start with a square and use a compass to measure its diagonal.

Step 2. Use this measurement to create the long side of a rectangle; then draw the remaining sides.

Steps 3–4. Continue the process to create a progression of related rectangles.

Quick-Change Proportions on Drawings

PROBLEM: *I'm building a project from plans, and I want to change some of the overall dimensions. How can I tell what the piece will look like without redrawing the plans?*

SOLUTION: You can get an idea of how a scale drawing will look with different dimensions by folding it so that it appears narrower or shorter. To make the piece look wider or taller, cut the drawing and add a section of paper. Then connect the lines to complete the drawing. If the drawing is small enough to fit on a copying machine, tape the cut drawing to a blank piece of paper and copy it. Then connect all the lines to get the larger drawing of the piece. A photocopier lets you see your modified drawing on a single sheet of paper, which is easier to use than the cut and taped original.

Ben Erickson
Eutaw, AL

You can easily manipulate dimensional changes on a drawing by folding it or cutting it.

Fold to make narrower or shorter.

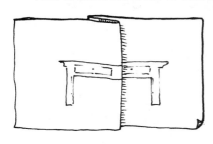 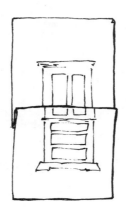

Cut and reconnect lines to make wider or taller.

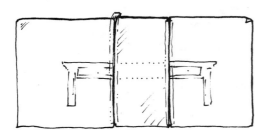 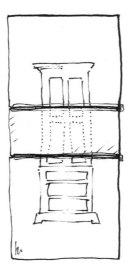

Sizing Cabinet Doors

PROBLEM: *I'm designing a set of kitchen cabinets. Are there guidelines for the minimum and maximum width of cabinet doors?*

SOLUTION: For standard kitchen cabinets, keep the width of doors in the 12- to 20-inch range. Making frame-and-panel doors narrower than 12 inches is impractical, and machining short rails for very narrow doors can be unsafe. Doors wider than 20 inches look too square. Also, if the doors are frame-and-panel construction, the extra width can lead to excessive wood movement, as the panel expands and contracts between winter and summer. End panels, which are commonly made to look like the doors, and tall doors for pantry cabinets often need to be wider; if they're over 24 inches, divide the door panel in half vertically by adding a center stile.

Furniture pieces, such as entertainment centers or secretary desks, usually are narrower than 40 inches, so you can use pairs of 20-inch-wide (or smaller) doors. But for wardrobes, which tend to be from 4 to 5 feet wide, you'll need to make a pair of 24- to 30-inch-wide doors. The extra width is balanced visually by the height of these doors. When making wider doors, I usually use plywood for the panels because it is dimensionally stable, and it will not shrink and expand like solid wood. You can use hardwood plywood that matches the door frame, or you can veneer the panels yourself, using inexpensive plywood or medium-density fiberboard (MDF) as the core stock.

Ben Erickson
Eutaw, AL

STANDARD FURNITURE DIMENSIONS BY NICK ENGLER

The dimensions shown for the following tables are averages. They are intended as guidelines, not absolutes. Use them as a jumping-off point in designing your own furniture.

DINING TABLES

SHAPE	NUMBER OF SEATS	HEIGHT	LENGTH	DEPTH OR WIDTH
Square	2	27"–30"	24"–26"	24"–26"
	4	27"–30"	30"–32"	30"–32"
	8	27"–30"	48"–50"	48"–50"
Rectangular	2	27"–30"	30"–32"	24"–26"
	6	27"–30"	66"–72"	30"–36"
	8	27"–30"	86"–96"	36"–42"
Round	3	27"–30"		30"–32" dia.
	4	27"–30"		36"–39" dia.
	5	27"–30"		42"–45" dia.
	6	27"–30"		48"–52" dia.
	7	27"–30"		54"–58" dia.
	8	27"–30"		62"–66" dia.
Oval	4	27"–30"	42"–48"	28"–32"
	6	27"–30"	60"–66"	32"–36"
	8	27"–30"	72"–78"	48"–52"

OCCASIONAL TABLES

USE	HEIGHT	LENGTH	DEPTH
Coffee table	15"–18"	30"–60"	22"–30"
End table	18"–24"	18"–24"	18"–24"
Hall table	34"–36"	36"–72"	16"–20"
Nightstand	24"–30"	18"–20"	18"–20"
Side table	18"–24"	24"–28"	18"–20"
Candlestand	24"–32"	15"–24"	15"–24"

Table Sizes and Capacities

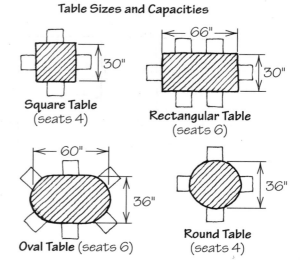

Square Table (seats 4)

Rectangular Table (seats 6)

Oval Table (seats 6)

Round Table (seats 4)

SPECIALTY TABLES

Use	Height	Length	Depth
Child's table	20"–22"	26"–30"	18"–22"
Computer table	25"–28"	36"–60"	22"–30"
Drafting table	32"–44"	31"–72"	23"–44"
Dressing table	29"–30"	40"–48"	18"–22"
Game table	29"–30"	30"–32"	30"–32"
Typing table	25"–28"	36"–42"	16"–24"
Writing table	28"–30"	36"–42"	20"–24"

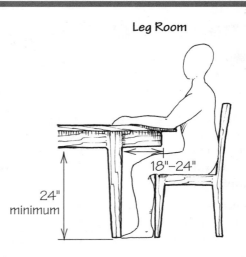

Leg Room

24" minimum

18"–24"

DESKS

Type of Desk	Work Surface Height	Overall Height	Overall Width	Overall Depth
Lap desk	4"–6"	4"–6"	20"–24"	12"–18"
Slant-front desk	28"–30"	40"–42"	36"–42"	18"–24"
Secretary	28"–30"	78"–84"	36"–42"	18"–24"
Writing table	28"–30"	28"–30"	36"–40"	20"–24"
Table desk	28"–30"	38"–68"	30"–48"	20"–30"
Pedestal desk	28"–30"	28"–30"	48"–72"	24"–30"
Rolltop desk	28"–30"	40"–48"	48"–72"	24"–30"
Typing table	24"–28"	24"–28"	36"–42"	16"–24"
Computer desk	24"–28"	24"–58"	24"–60"	20"–30"
Children's desk	20"–22"	20"–22"	24"–30"	18"–20"

KITCHEN CABINETS

Type of Cabinet	Height	Width	Depth
Base cabinet	36"	12"–96"	24"–25"
Wall cabinet	30"–42"	12"–96"	12"–13"
Tall cupboard	60"–84"	12"–96"	12"–25"
Base cabinet doors	26"	18" maximum	
Drawers	Top drawer: 5"–6" others: up to 10"	Matches door width for same size cabinet	

Sources: Dining, Occasional, and Specialty Tables: Reprinted from Nick Engler, The Workshop Companion: Making Tables and Chairs (Emmaus, PA: Rodale Press).

Desks: Reprinted from Nick Engler, The Workshop Companion: Making Desks and Bookcases.

Kitchen Cabinets: Reprinted from Nick Engler, The Workshop Companion: Making Built-In Cabinets.

MODIFYING DESIGNS

The appeal of a specific furniture design is a subjective thing: One person will find pleasing what another finds unattractive. But you don't have to abandon entirely a design that's not working.

Instead, try to figure out what works in a design and what does not. Get in the habit of modifying designs to make them more appealing to your eye. Here are some elements I watch for when working from project plans or photographs or even copying other pieces of furniture.

PIECE APPEARS BOTTOM-HEAVY

Raising a piece off the ground by adding feet or a base can provide the necessary lift. Feet can be simple square blocks set in a little from each corner. They can be left plain or can be shaped to match a molded element elsewhere on the piece. There are also bun feet, which are turned pieces that are doweled or screwed to the bottom of the case. Bracketed feet are made from two or more mitered pieces that are applied with screws and glue blocks.

One of the easiest ways to lift a piece from the ground is to add a plinth. Plinths are typically made of two sides and a front that are mitered or dovetailed at the corners. The front may be solid or may be cut out. The cabinet sits on the plinth, and the joint is concealed with molding, as shown below. Because it supports the weight of the whole piece, a plinth must be sturdy.

TOP LOOKS TOO PLAIN

If the top of a tall chest of drawers, a secretary desk, or a built-in appears to stop too abruptly, you can make it look more graceful by adding a simple crown molding (also called a cornice) or even a bonnet, as shown below. Crown molding is often applied to a plain, flat board, known as a frieze board, which is first attached to the front and sides of the cabinet.

A bonnet is usually made as a separate construction that is fixed to the top of the piece. It may be a simple low box shape, or it may consist of scrolled swan-neck shapes complete with carvings and finials. The purpose of crown molding and of a bonnet is the same: to balance the whole piece better by providing a hat or lid for the body of the cabinet.

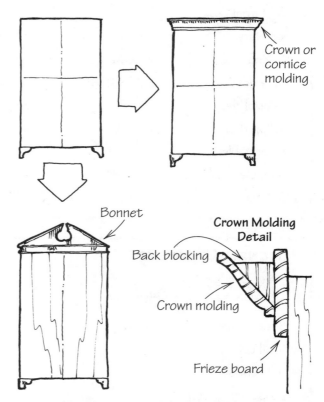

Crown or cornice molding

Bonnet

Crown Molding Detail

Back blocking

Crown molding

Frieze board

The top of a cabinet can be well-defined by a crown or cornice molding. A bonnet (bottom left) is a more elaborate crown.

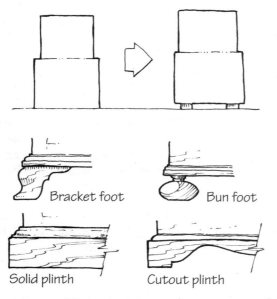

Bracket foot

Bun foot

Solid plinth

Cutout plinth

Most cabinets look better raised up off the floor, either on feet or a plinth.

CHEST LOOKS TOO NARROW

If a chest is too narrow or too high relative to its width, you can make it appear wider or shorter by emphasizing the horizontal lines. One way would be to make the base or plinth wider and let the top overhang the case more. Or you can try adding a "waist" in the form of a molded strip around the middle area of the piece, as shown below. Notice that locating the waist below the center of the cabinet has a distinctly different effect than locating it above the center. Other ways to emphasize the horizontal character of the piece are to divide it so that there are more dominant horizontal lines than vertical ones and to orient the grain horizontally.

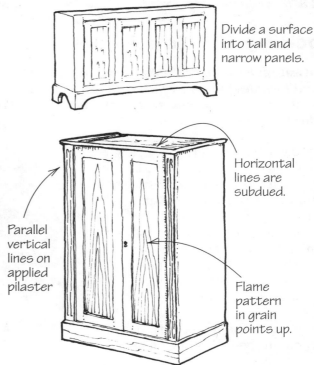

Divide a surface into tall and narrow panels.

Horizontal lines are subdued.

Parallel vertical lines on applied pilaster

Flame pattern in grain points up.

Emphasizing vertical lines helps balance a piece that is horizontal in form (top). The grain of the wood and applied moldings can also be used to bring out the vertical (bottom).

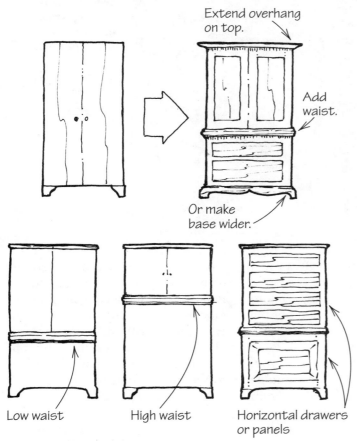

Extend overhang on top.

Add waist.

Or make base wider.

Low waist   High waist   Horizontal drawers or panels

Emphasizing horizontal lines helps balance a cabinet that is tall and narrow.

PIECE LOOKS TOO WIDE OR TOO SHORT

If a chest is too short or too wide relative to its height, you can increase the height by adding a base or crown. You can also make it appear taller or more narrow by emphasizing the vertical lines, as shown above. Divide any doors or panels vertically, and use strong-grained wood so that any pattern appears to point upward. Flat-sawn wood, for example, frequently has a flamelike pattern that should be oriented to take the eye upward.

Applied moldings are also very effective and relatively easy to use. Consider making long, narrow rectangles of moldings and applying them to vertical surfaces. You can also borrow vertical architectural elements, like columns or pilasters. Because parallel lines move the eye with great effect, they make the piece seem taller.

Mike Dunbar
Hampton, NH

Avoiding Structural Problems

Mocking Up Key Joints

PROBLEM: *I have designed a dining room table, but the look I have in mind includes joinery I've never made before. I'm concerned that the joinery won't be strong enough and look right with the design. Are there any precautions I can take?*

SOLUTION: I suggest that you take the time and effort to build a mock-up. Mock-ups can tell you about two things drawings can't—structural integrity and design integrity.

To start, look critically at your design and pick out the one or two places where you anticipate problems. Then mock up only those joints. Suppose you want to use a tusk tenon to join the stretcher of a trestle table to the leg boards, as shown on this page. Test the angle and thickness of the wedge to make sure that it tightens firmly without working loose.

On a traditional dining table, cut out and assemble one corner, where the two apron pieces fit into the leg. You need only 8 inches or so of each apron piece and the top 12 inches of a leg, as shown. That's enough to test the strength of your joint. If the leg has important details—an unusual taper or a funky foot—go ahead and make the entire leg as part of the mock-up. You can use less expensive wood as long as it is similar in strength. Mock up just enough of your project to answer your questions. Considering the number of hours you will spend building your design, the few hours it will take to do this can be invaluable. Plus if you want to sell your work, you can keep the mock-ups for future designs and as demonstration pieces when discussing design ideas with customers.

Full-scale joinery mock-ups like these show you exactly how the design will look and how strong the structure will be. Keep them on hand for future projects.

Making mock-ups also gives you a preview of the techniques required for making the real thing. This in turn will help you fine-tune the design so that it can be made efficiently with the tools and techniques that are available to you. This technique preview is valuable for every aspect of a design, from the joinery to the details.

If you are really unsure of your project's merit, you can mock up the entire piece and ask a couple of woodworker buddies to critique what they see. Then play with the design, the materials, and the joinery before building the real thing.

If you want to focus on questions of only design and not structure, make a scale model of your project. Models can be fun, they let you experiment with different materials, and they reveal things about a design that don't show up on a two-dimensional drawing.

David Page
Swarthmore, PA

RELATED INFO:
Making Scale Models,
page 3

Avoiding Sagging Shelves

PROBLEM: *I made a bookcase using ¾-inch-thick plywood shelves with a ¼-inch-thick strip of solid wood on the front edge. The shelves are sagging noticeably—and they're only half full. What should I have done differently?*

SOLUTION: How much a shelf will sag is dependent on several factors: the material, the length of the span, the thickness of the shelf, the load placed on the shelf, and how the ends of the shelf are attached to the cabinet. These factors are interrelated and, taken together, determine how well a shelf will resist deflection under load. Let's look at each one:

Material. The best material for shelves is solid wood or plywood. Steer clear of composite sheet goods, such as medium-density fiberboard (MDF), hardboard, and particleboard. They sag easily unless reinforced with solid wood. Solid wood resists sagging better than plywood because all of the grain runs along the length of the shelf. In fact, under the same conditions, solid wood will deflect about half as much as veneer-core plywood and a fifth as much as lumber-core plywood. You can strengthen plywood by gluing solid-wood edging on the front and back of the shelf, using biscuit joints or splines to align the parts.

The species of wood used can also make a difference. Generally, denser, harder woods are less likely to sag than lighter, softer woods. Most hard woods resist sagging quite well. See "Maximum Shelving Spans" on page 12 for a comparison of materials.

Length and Thickness. The distance the shelf will span is an important factor because as shelf length increases, sagging increases rapidly. If you double the length of a shelf, it will sag not twice as much but eight times as much, as shown. Similarly with thickness, a shelf that is twice as thick will be eight times as resistant to deflection. So a small decrease in length or increase in thickness can greatly reduce deflection.

Load. The amount of weight on the shelf and the placement of that weight contribute greatly to sagging. A shelf with twice the weight at the center will sag twice as much as a shelf that has no weight on it. But distributing that same weight evenly along the shelf will reduce deflection by a third.

Attachment. Finally how the shelf is attached to the cabinet makes a difference in how much it sags. An adjustable shelf that simply rests on shelf supports will sag as much as five times more than one that is firmly anchored to the cabinet sides.

One of my shop-tested rules is that if the ends aren't anchored, I won't make a ¾-inch veneer-core plywood shelf longer than 30 inches, and I won't make a ¾-inch lumber-core plywood or ¾-inch solid-wood shelf more than 36 inches long. If you increase the thickness of a solid-wood shelf to 1 inch, you can extend the length to 48 inches with minimal deflection if the load is not unusually great. When installing or assembling projects with shelves, be sure to position any natural bow in the shelves with the arch up; this will cause any deflection that occurs to straighten the shelves.

Ben Erickson
Eutaw, AL

RELATED INFO:
Choosing Manufactured Panels, page 44;

Retrofitting Sagging Shelves, page 286

Original board

Double the length = 8 times the deflection

Increasing a board's length increases its deflection dramatically, while increasing its thickness reduces deflection dramatically.

Double the thickness = ⅛ the deflection

Wood Movement as a Design Factor

PROBLEM: *How wide can a piece of wood be before I have to think about problems due to movement? Are there any guidelines for how much movement to expect from tabletops or panels?*

SOLUTION: Think of a board as a bundle of tiny straws running lengthwise through the wood. Due to this structure, wood absorbs and releases moisture from the air around it. It expands as it absorbs moisture and contracts as it dries out. The only relevant movement to be concerned with is movement across the grain, not along the length of the wood fibers. Still, movement across the grain is a factor that has to be respected and accounted for in most projects. Here are the questions you need to answer:

What is the moisture content of your wood? Knowing that, you can make reasonable projections about how the wood will behave as you work with it. If you are serious about woodworking, buy a moisture meter (hygrometer) and use it. See "Sources," beginning on page 298. It's the only practical and reliable way to determine the moisture content of wood.

Furniture-grade hardwood should be about 8 percent moisture content. Kiln-dried wood may come out of the kiln at 8 percent moisture content, but it will pick up moisture if it is stored outdoors and may have a higher moisture content than the retailer claims.

Always let wood acclimate to the moisture level in your shop for a week or two before you begin any project. If your wood has a moisture content of 12 to 15 percent or more, expect more shrinkage after you bring it into an environment that has lower humidity. Familiarize yourself with the average seasonal moisture levels of the area you live in when factoring for wood movement. In the southwestern region of the United States, which is very dry, wood will have less seasonal movement than in the humid extremes of the Northeast.

How were the boards you're using oriented in the tree? Are you using flat-sawn or quarter-sawn boards? Are there some of each in your batch? Tangential movement (tangent to the growth rings) in wood is considerably greater than radial movement shrinkage (across the growth rings, or along the radius), as shown at the top of the opposite page. This accounts for the greater stability in quarter-sawn boards and for the relative instability—cupping and twisting—of flat-sawn wood. If your wood is relatively wet or you are uncertain of the moisture content, mill your wood to final size in stages several days apart. Then you can deal with some of the unwanted movement before you reach the final dimensions.

What finish will you use? Finishes that more completely seal the wood surface (varnish, urethane, shellac, lacquer) will help control moisture loss and gain better than a penetrating finish (Watco Danish Oil, tung oil). Regardless of which finish you use, be sure to finish both sides of the wood equally. Otherwise, the wood will exchange moisture unevenly and cause boards to cup.

A rule of thumb: For any application where the parts are at least 4 inches wide, you should take into account the movement of the wood. Specifically, for a 12-inch-wide panel, assume that the wood will expand and contract as much as ¼ inch over the seasons. Gluing narrow boards into wide panels does not change the net expansion/contraction ratio one bit, unless you're able to glue narrow pieces of quarter-sawn stock.

David Page
Swarthmore, PA

RELATED INFO:
Avoiding Stepped Glue Lines, page 48

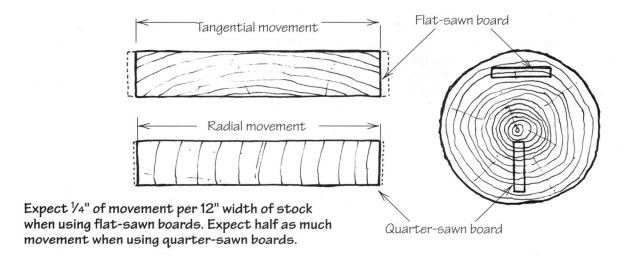

Expect ¼" of movement per 12" width of stock when using flat-sawn boards. Expect half as much movement when using quarter-sawn boards.

Avoiding Bad Miter Joints

PROBLEM: *When I make miter joints in wide stock, they tend to open up over time. How can I prevent this?*

SOLUTION: This is an inevitable consequence of changes in moisture content. Changes in air humidity cause changes in wood moisture content. When humidity and the moisture content of wood increase, the wood expands. When humidity and the moisture content of wood decrease, the wood shrinks. Unfortunately, the expansion and shrinkage don't occur uniformly. Dimensional changes in the direction of the grain are so small that they can be ignored. Across the grain, however, the expansion and shrinkage will be quite noticeable. The drawing at right shows how this difference in the amount of expansion or shrinkage changes the angles in a miter joint.

The only way to stop the wood from expanding and shrinking is to stop the moisture content from changing. Some surface coatings (finishes) will slow the change in moisture content in wood, but no finish will stop it. In a nutshell, if you can't hold the humidity to within a narrow range, you can't stop the miter joints from opening up. In well-designed furniture, the parts are arranged so the wood can expand and contract without causing problems.

Bob Moran
Emmaus, PA

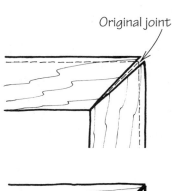

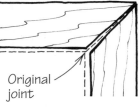

As moisture content increases, wood expands in width but not in length (top). As moisture content decreases, wood shrinks in width but not in length (bottom).

Designing Site-Built Projects

PROBLEM: *I'm making a large corner cabinet and don't know how I'll get it in place. First of all, the thing is quite big. Second, I don't think there's a square corner in the house, so the angles are all off. How should I approach this?*

SOLUTION: Most of your problems will evaporate if you stop thinking "furniture" and start thinking "carpentry." I'd build this thing right where it's going to stand. In many cases, large cabinets look better built into the house than free-standing.

Start by screwing cleats to the walls to support the shelves; then cut the shelves to fit by measuring them individually. Make sure everything is level as you go along. When the shelf layout is in place, plumb the fronts of the shelves and trim anything that doesn't line up; then plan a face frame to attach to the shelves. The type of face frame, and whatever moldings and details you want to add to it, will establish the design of the piece, and it will hide all the other work from view. If you ever have to move a shelf to accommodate new components, you can remove the face frame and easily move the cleats. You can finish the face frame before you install it.

To finish the interior, I'd remove the screws that hold the pieces to the wall and finish the pieces separately, reinstalling them afterward using the screw holes for positioning.

If you ever decide to move, the built-in cabinet will be a feature that will help sell the home, and you'll want something different in the new place anyway.

Jim Cummins
Woodstock, NY

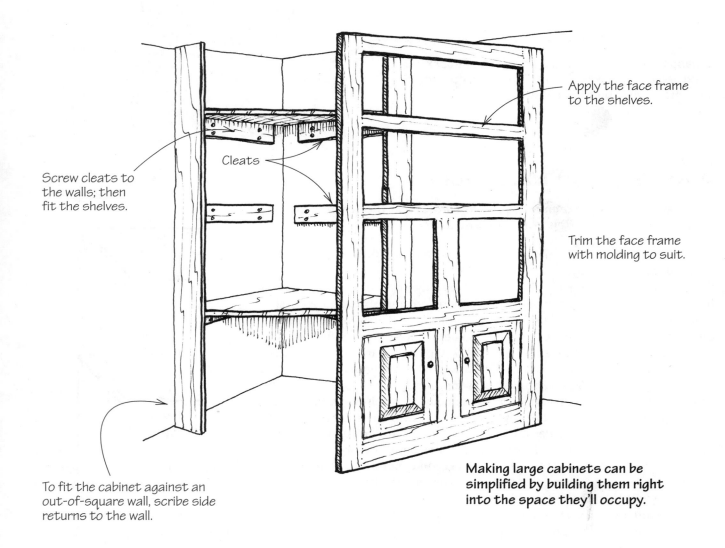

Apply the face frame to the shelves.

Cleats

Screw cleats to the walls; then fit the shelves.

Trim the face frame with molding to suit.

To fit the cabinet against an out-of-square wall, scribe side returns to the wall.

Making large cabinets can be simplified by building them right into the space they'll occupy.

Enhancing Design Details

Sketching Alternative Designs

PROBLEM: *I'd like to add more individuality to the pieces I build, but I bog down when it comes to planning design details. Got any advice for somebody who can follow plans but isn't much of an artist?*

SOLUTION: Effective designers are quick with a pencil, often throwing dozens of concepts onto paper before deciding on a path for a particular idea. You can use the same shortcut they use, and you don't need to be able to draw.

Many cabinets are just a basic box with details added. Make a sketch or tracing of a project, then photocopy this bare-bones outline a dozen times.

Start throwing variations on these copies, without going into too much detail at first. Try a variety of moldings around the top of a bookcase, for example, or vary the shapes and sizes of panels in a door. Consider even the wildest schemes—just get them all down on separate sheets. Some of your best ideas might come when you are least trying to think of them—seeing a piece of background furniture on a TV show, for example.

If you know the basic size and shape of a cabinet but are unsure of how to divide it into component parts, draw the basic "box," make several photocopies of it, and then pencil in various arrangements.

Have your copies handy so you can record items easily. When you discover the details that "make" the piece, take note of them and adapt them to your own projects. And the pile of drawings you reject might provide you with an idea for another project some time, so your creative energy won't be wasted.

Jim Cummins
Woodstock, NY

Locating Knobs and Hinges

PROBLEM: *Are there standard locations for hinges and pulls on cabinet doors?*

SOLUTION: The hinges on traditional frame-and-panel cabinet doors align with the horizontal rails. This is visually pleasing and separates the hinge screws from the mortise-and-tenon joint.

To locate the knobs on kitchen cabinets and other cabinets that have high top doors and low bottom doors, divide the door height into quarters or sixths. Position the knobs one-quarter to one-sixth of the door's total height, measuring from the top or bottom of the door. This will make the knobs easy to reach and visually interesting. It's best to center the knob on the width of the door stile; however, if the stile has a molded edge, either inside or out, discount the molded section when centering the knob. On large casework, like an entertainment center or armoire, locate the knobs and handles where they are most comfortable for the user to reach.

Ben Erickson
Eutaw, AL

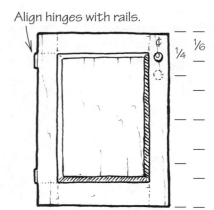

Align hinges with rails.

Locate knobs ¼ or ⅙ of the door's length from top or bottom.

Creating No-Show Hinges

PROBLEM: *I'm trying to mount cabinet doors so the hinges are not visible. I've used the invisible "barrel" hinges that mount in drilled mortises, but they allow too much play. European hinges won't work because they take up too much space on the inside of the cabinet. What other options do I have?*

SOLUTION: I've found two good solutions to this problem. The first is knife hinges, sometimes referred to simply as pivot hinges. These specialized hinges come in various sizes to fit the size and weight of the door. When a knife hinge is installed in a routed mortise on the top and bottom edges of the doors, only the small brass knuckle upon which the door pivots is visible. Although the brass arm of the hinge can be seen when the door is open, it's unobtrusive compared to other hinges.

The second no-show hinge solution involves a technique that was developed in China seven centuries ago. Integral pivot pins are formed on the ends of one door stile. The pivot pins slip into drilled holes in the top and bottom of the cabinet. This arrangement requires that the top overlap and extend beyond the door. This hinge works nicely on a plywood door because the pivot can be shaped onto an edge strip before it is applied to the door, as shown in *Top View* and *Front View*. On a frame-and-panel door, the pivot is formed by cutting a notch in the ends of the hinged stile, as shown in *Frame-and-Panel Door Detail.*

In either case, the hinge design must include a means of removing the door. One way to achieve this is to use screws to attach the section of wood that contains the top pivot

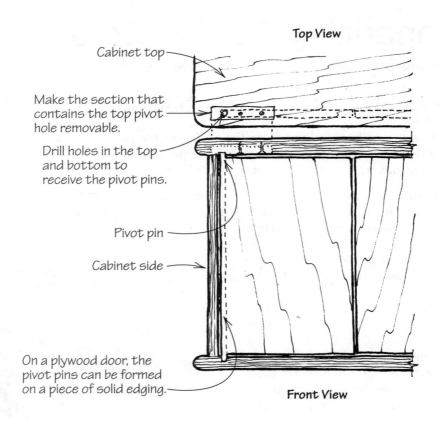

Top View

Cabinet top

Make the section that contains the top pivot hole removable.

Drill holes in the top and bottom to receive the pivot pins.

Pivot pin

Cabinet side

On a plywood door, the pivot pins can be formed on a piece of solid edging.

Front View

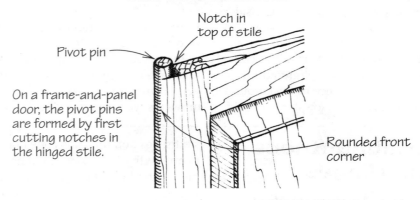

Frame-and-Panel Door Detail

Notch in top of stile

Pivot pin

On a frame-and-panel door, the pivot pins are formed by first cutting notches in the hinged stile.

Rounded front corner

Make your own no-show hinges by forming pivot pins on the door and putting them into holes in the cabinet top and bottom. The technique works just as well on a plywood door with solid edging (top) and a frame-and-panel door (bottom).

hole so that it is removable. On a small cabinet, the whole top could be removable. Or, on a banded plywood door, you can attach the pivot banding with screws. This edge of the door will always be hidden from view, so the screws won't be visible.

With the integral pivot pin hinge, it is always necessary to round-over the front corner of the door stile or banding to allow the door to pivot without binding against the cabinet side.

David Page
Swarthmore, PA

Alternative Drop-Leaf Table Edge

PROBLEM: *I'm looking for an alternative to the standard rule joint edge treatment for a contemporary drop-leaf table design. I don't want to just butt the edges either. Any suggestions?*

SOLUTION: This question is a little more complicated than it seems at first and requires a consideration of hinges. Any standard cabinet hinge can be screwed to a tabletop and a leaf to make a drop-leaf table. The edge detail in such a situation could be fairly wide-ranging, as shown below left. However, if you use a standard hinge, the edge of the leaf in the down position will always hang beyond the edge of the fixed top. Because of this, many edge details become unappealing. Also, the edge is more vulnerable to snagging clothing, as well as to breakage.

The special drop-leaf hinge has a short leaf and a long leaf to offset the pivot point. This allows the rule joint to mate neatly when it is closed and to sit safely under the fixed top when it is down. You can contrive other options using the drop-leaf hinge, but the difficulty then is to make certain that the leaf edge can clear the edge of the fixed top as you move it up or down. An attractive variation is shown below right. This solution requires that you cove the edge of the leaf, but the cove is basically invisible. You can rout it with a core-box bit on a router table.

David Page
Swarthmore, PA

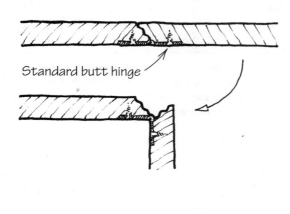

Standard butt hinge

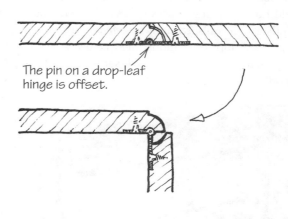

The pin on a drop-leaf hinge is offset.

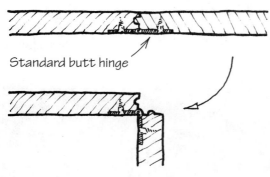

Standard butt hinge

You can make a variety of drop-leaf edge joints with standard butt hinges, but they won't be very appealing when the leaf is down.

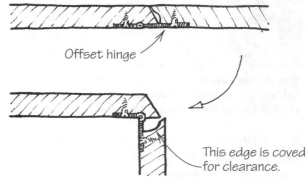

Offset hinge

This edge is coved for clearance.

With the standard rule joint edge (top) and this more contemporary looking alternative (bottom), the edge of the leaf swings under the top when opened.

USING REPETITION AND CONTRAST TO SPICE UP YOUR DESIGNS

Your joinery is perfect, and the dimensions of your furniture are pleasing, but your designs still don't hold attention. For lasting interest, think repetition and contrast.

Repetition is easy. You can use it by being aware of related dimensions, parallel lines, similar turnings, roundovers on all edges, dovetails in different locations, pegs in mortise-and-tenon joints, repeating grain in drawers, and book-matched tops.

Harmonious contrast is harder to achieve. For instance, all your lines don't have to be straight. Use a curved line as an interesting contrast. The top of a bed's headboard might be a convex curve. The rail on a table could have a gentle concave curve. Curved legs might set off straight rails, straight stretchers, and the straight lines of the top, as demonstrated below. A piece with mostly curved lines might have some straight lines in opposition.

The subtle curves at the bottom and top of these table legs contrast harmoniously with the dominant straight lines throughout the rest of the piece.

Negative spaces contrast with positive spaces. A cabinet with paneled doors might use glass in two doors to contrast with the wood panels in two others. The crest rail for a chair or bench might have an elliptical hole, as shown above right. A bench top might be divided into two seating areas with a space in between. Wide back slats for a chair might have holes with an interesting shape.

Use of both dark and light woods can add interesting contrast, as shown at right. Accent woods with wild grain will contrast with the plain wood in your furniture. You can also vary grain orientation.

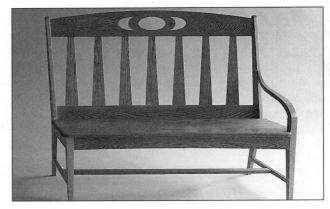

The shapes cut into the crest rail on this bench open up negative space in the rail, which creates stronger balance between the rail and the positive-negative spaces created by the slats below.

Detail adds contrast and interest; try including chamfered or coved edges, beading, exposed dowels, or string inlay. Another idea is to position important features off center; for instance, a drawer pull might be placed at one-third the distance from an edge rather than at the center, where you're used to seeing it.

W. Curtis Johnson
Corvallis, OR

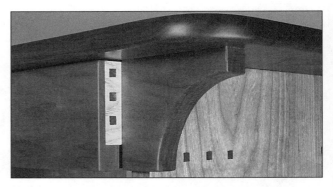

This corner detail of a desk shows the strong contrast created by using a dark wood as an accent on a lighter wood. It also demonstrates a repeating pattern that is, in this case, revealed only when the drawer is opened.

Adding Molding to Enhance Plain Projects

PROBLEM: *I just started building a large entertainment cabinet, and already I can see it's going to be too plain for its size. What can I do?*

SOLUTION: Large pieces of furniture and built-ins often seem too plain if they are composed of nothing but large, flat surfaces. Without some element that visually decreases their size, they can easily become overpowering boxes that dominate a room. A solution that has been understood for centuries is the application of moldings. Moldings have concave and convex surfaces that create an interplay of light and shadow, which the eye finds interesting and pleasing. These areas of light and shadow add depth to an otherwise large, flat surface. Moldings form lines that can be used to break up large surfaces into smaller areas. To make the flat sides of a cabinet appear smaller, try using moldings to create a smaller rectangle on the cabinet's side, as shown below left and right. Make a scale drawing to see the effect before you start cutting the moldings.

You can apply the same technique to a door. If it is a flat plywood door,

use moldings to mimic a frame-and-panel construction. Even on a large frame-and-panel door, you can apply moldings to the panel's raised field to make the door appear smaller.

Drawer fronts can also be made to look more interesting and less clunky with moldings. On drawers, the moldings are usually applied to the outer edges. Cock beading, a common treatment, is a strip of wood about ¼ inch thick or less, set into a shallow rabbet in the drawer's edge, as shown above right. The edge of the beading is rounded, and it projects beyond the surface of the drawer front. Cock beading was traditionally applied to drawers with veneered fronts to protect the fragile veneer edges. And because it projects above the drawer's surface, cock beading creates subtle bands of light and shadow. This gives a bank of drawers depth and helps break up a broad surface.

Mike Dunbar
Hampton, NH

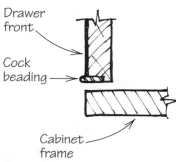

Cock beading applied to drawer fronts helps break up an otherwise flat surface and also protects fragile veneer edges.

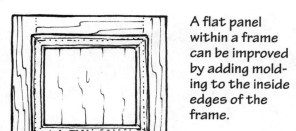

A flat panel within a frame can be improved by adding molding to the inside edges of the frame.

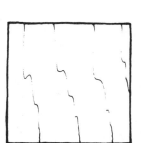

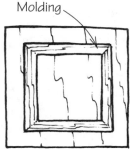

A broad, flat panel, like a cabinet side, will look smaller and more interesting with molding applied to mimic frame-and-panel construction.

Applying Molding to Conceal Simple Construction

PROBLEM: *I've built some cabinets using butt joints reinforced with screws, and I'm looking for a good design detail to conceal my down-and-dirty methods.*

SOLUTION: Screw holes and exposed plywood edges can be concealed with thoughtful design elements, and the one I use the most is applied molding. I cover my screw holes and butt joints with 1½ to 2 inches of wide, flat molding strips that are ⅜ to ½ inch thick, as shown below.

Covering the cabinet corners with applied molding allows me to overlap the case parts in either direction. I can also make smaller cabinets, assemble them into larger configurations, and cover the seams with the molding.

I generally plane my molding stock to ½ inch thick. I also will resaw 4/4 (four-quarter) stock and plane it to ⅜-inch finished thickness, which works just as well and saves some wood. You can choose to cut the mating edges of the molding at a 45-degree angle, but the overlapping edges look just fine. The trick is keeping the edges sharp so the butt joints are clean.

At the base, I use a rounded 3- to 4-inch base molding made with ¾-inch material. I gently round the top edge and butt the vertical molding strips against the top of the base molding. This gives a nice stepped transition from the thinner edge molding to the base molding. The finished effect looks very much like a frame-and-panel cabinet side.

Dennis Slabaugh
Naples, FL

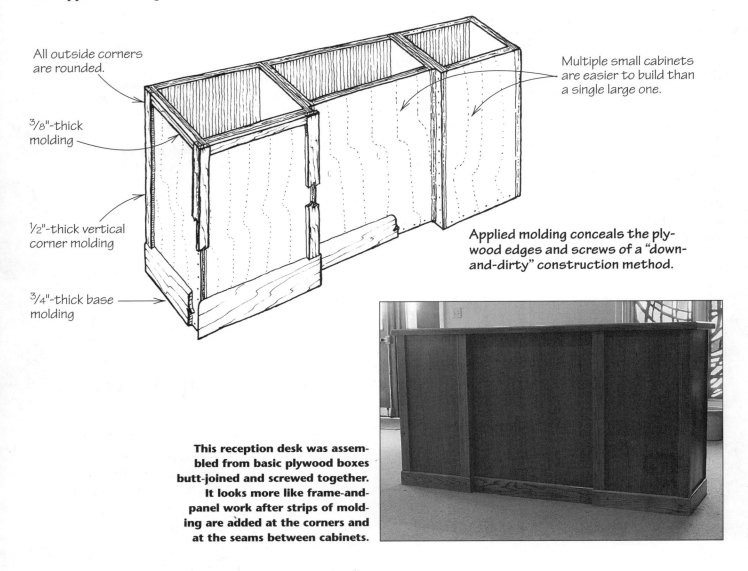

All outside corners are rounded.

⅜"-thick molding

½"-thick vertical corner molding

¾"-thick base molding

Multiple small cabinets are easier to build than a single large one.

Applied molding conceals the plywood edges and screws of a "down-and-dirty" construction method.

This reception desk was assembled from basic plywood boxes butt-joined and screwed together. It looks more like frame-and-panel work after strips of molding are added at the corners and at the seams between cabinets.

Drawing Plans and Laying Out Parts

Making Drawings from Photos

PROBLEM: *I'm often asked to make furniture from a photo in a catalog. Usually I just guess at the dimensions, with fair results. Is there a more precise way to develop drawings from photos?*

SOLUTION: Yes there is, but there still may be a little guesswork involved. Start by taping the photo (or a photocopy of it) to a sheet of paper. The paper should be big enough to give you 6 to 8 inches above and to the right of the photo in which to work. Extend both the vertical and horizontal lines of the piece of furniture out onto the paper, as shown on this page. If the piece is complex, you might want to begin with just a few basic lines, such as those that show the overall height and length, to avoid confusion. Extend the other lines, such as those showing the spacing and height of the drawer faces, as you need them.

Now take an architect's rule, and find a scale on it that allows you to measure the overall dimensions of the piece. Catalogs usually list these dimensions, giving you a place to start. If not, you'll have to estimate. Angle the rule across the extension lines that stick out to the side of the photo until the measurement equals the dimension you want. For example, if the piece you want to make is 30 inches tall, place the rule on the drawing with the 0 on the bottom extension line; then pivot the rule until the 30 aligns with the top line. Draw a line along the rule at this angle. You'll now be able to read the scaled dimensions between the other extension lines along this diagonal. Repeat the process across the lines extending above the photo

Both horizontal and vertical measurements can be taken from a photo using an architect's rule. Once you decide which scale is appropriate, be sure to use that scale for all the measurements.

to determine the overall side-to-side dimension of the piece.

If the photo shows enough of the side of the piece, you can use the same routine to develop the front-to-back measurements. Otherwise, you may have to do a little more estimating. Once you draw in the diagonal lines, take the dimensions from them to make shop drawings at whatever scale is most convenient.

Ken Burton
New Tripoli, PA

Avoiding Inaccurate Layout Lines

PROBLEM: *If I use a pencil—even a sharp one—for laying out mortises and tenons, my cuts are often inaccurate. Is there a special tool I should use?*

SOLUTION: When laying out actual cut lines for mortise-and-tenon work, I put away my pencils and go

for my pocket knife or marking knife. My pocket knife, with two beveled edges, is great for cross-grain marks, and it's always close at hand—in my pocket. But if I use it for marks that run with the grain, the pocket knife blade will sometimes follow the grain and move away from the straightedge. That's why I prefer marking knives: One side is flat and the other side beveled. The beveled edge pushes the flat side against the straightedge for a cut line as straight as the straightedge, as shown below left. I have two marking knives, one with a right-hand bevel and the other with a left-hand bevel, so that I can always keep the flat side against the straightedge no matter which side of the straightedge I'm working on.

A good straightedge is as necessary as a good marking knife when it comes to accurate marking and measuring. For short measurements, I have a 3-foot Starrett engraved ruler that allows me to put the knife edge in one of the etched markings and repeat measurements with a great deal of accuracy, as shown at left.

Unlike a pencil line, the incision left by a marking knife minimizes tear-out and makes it easier to set up a cut. A cut mark along the edge of a board will allow you to place one tooth of the saw right against the mark. When turning spindles, you can use a cut line to separate the turned part of a leg from the square portion; the effect is clean, with minimal tear-out. Using a cut line when marking mortise shoulders makes getting uniform mortises much easier by giving you a shoulder to place the chisel against. In fact, a cut line is superior to a pencil line for almost all purposes.

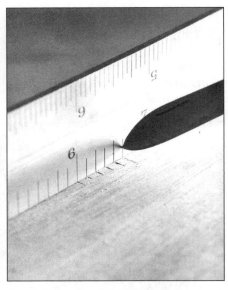

A marking knife with a single beveled edge leaves a crisp line to follow, even when cutting with the grain.

An engraved ruler allows you to tick off measurements very accurately by setting a knife right in the engraved line and striking a mark on the wood.

E. E. "Skip" Benson
Camden, ME

Scribing Accurate Lines with a Pencil

PROBLEM: *My marking gauge is great for laying out parts accurately, but it leaves shallow cuts in the wood. Is there any way around this?*

SOLUTION: Sure. Fit a pencil into your marking gauge. First bore a hole into the beam of the marking gauge at the end opposite the scribe. The hole should be slightly smaller than the pencil that will be used. Now shave, sand, or whittle down a pencil so that it fits into the hole. Sharpen the pencil lead to a knife edge (I rub the pencil across a piece of sandpaper), and you will have a fine, precise layout tool.

Robert Treanor
San Francisco, CA

This standard marking gauge serves double duty: One end leaves sharp cut lines; the other makes clearly visible pencil lines that can be erased.

Determining Odd Frame Angles

PROBLEM: *I was asked to make an odd-shaped trapezoidal frame for a painting. How do I figure and set the angles for something that's, say, 27 × 16 × 25 × 18 inches?*

SOLUTION: Solving this problem is easier than it may seem. The key is to make a full-scale pattern of the frame and use the mitered corners to set the saw cuts. Trace or draw the outside shape of the frame onto mat board, and then draw parallel lines representing the frame members, as shown. Draw the miter lines on the mat board, then cut out the sides using a knife and straightedge. Mark each side of each corner to distinguish the four corners. You'll have four pieces that can be used against the saw blade and the miter gauge to give you the exact cut angles and lengths for frame pieces, as shown. You can use this same trick for any panel or opening that isn't the traditional "square" shape.

Jim Cummins
Woodstock, NY

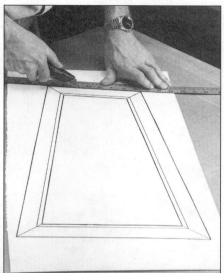

Draw an odd-angled frame on spare mat board, connect the corners to show the miter angles, then cut out the parts.

Hold the mat board pieces against the miter gauge to set the blade angle, and use the mat board pieces to transfer the actual length of each frame part to the stock.

Enlarging, Transferring, and Reversing Patterns

PROBLEM: *I know how to use a grid to transfer patterns from books. Is there a better way to copy a pattern?*

SOLUTION: There are a number of other strategies you can try to make laying out patterns easier. If you have access to a photocopier that enlarges, you can use it to blow up patterns to full scale. Take along a tape measure so that you can check the dimensions. You may have to experiment a little to get the exact size required.

Once you have a full-sized photocopy of the pattern, making a reverse image is a snap. Place the photocopy face down on another piece of paper and go over it with a very hot clothes iron (don't use steam). Enough of the toner will transfer from one sheet to the other to give you a readable pattern. See the photo on page 24.

If you don't have access to a photocopier, you're not out of luck yet. While you may have to use a grid to enlarge your pattern, you can still use a hot iron to make the reverse image. Simply draw out the original curve with an iron-on transfer pencil (available from most fabric and crafts stores). Then use the iron to transfer the pattern as described on the previous page.

An even lower-tech solution to transferring and reversing patterns once you have them drawn to full size is simply to trace them. To facilitate this, tape the original to a window with the image facing you for an exact copy, or away from you for a reverse. Then tape another sheet of paper on top of the first. The light coming through the window should make it easy to see the original pattern to make a tracing.

Ken Burton
New Tripoli, PA

Press a hot iron against a standard photocopy, and the image appears on the paper underneath.

SIGN-MAKING LAYOUT SIMPLIFIED

*I*f you ever set out to make a wooden sign, you may find that the hardest part is laying out the lettering. There's a tool that makes this job easier, and it may be closer than you think.

The almost limitless number of fonts and type sizes on today's personal computers make a PC the perfect tool for laying out sign lettering. Select the font and type size desired, and print out a sheet with the lettering laid out as it will appear on the sign. For large signs, use software designed to produce banners, or print out large letters on individual pages and tape them together. Use a thin layer of white glue or spray-mount adhesive to glue the sheet to the board you will carve. After the glue dries, carve directly through the paper and into the wood, following the outline of the lettering carefully. This approach works whether you're carving with hand tools or with a router bit. After you have finished, scrape or plane off the remaining paper. Using this method, there is no time-consuming layout of lettering, and your letter spacing and alignment are already calculated for you.

Ben Erickson
Eutaw, AL

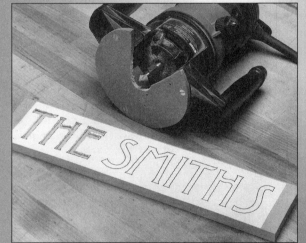

The paper layout for this sign was printed from a standard word processing program, eliminating the need to arrange individual letters.

Laying Out Curves

PROBLEM: *I'd like to make a kitchen island with a radiused end, but curves have always given me trouble. Can you give me an overview for making this type of cabinet?*

SOLUTION: Making curves, whether they are made by cutting solid stock or by bending wood or plywood around curved forms, is technically challenging in and of itself. When there are multiple curves that have to fit together, as in the cabinet you describe, the task becomes even more demanding. If you try to make curved parts independent of one another, there's a good chance that they won't all fit together perfectly.

The key to making projects with multiple curves is to make a template for each curved part. To do that, you must draw the whole structure full-scale, showing all of the components in their correct relationship to each other. Then you can make full-scale templates and verify each template as you make it against the full-scale plan. Once all of the templates have been made and labeled, you can be confident that all the parts of the project will fit together.

Tony O'Malley
Emmaus, PA

Drawing an Ellipse or Oval

PROBLEM: *I want to make an elliptical coffee table, but don't know how to draw the shape. What's the best technique?*

SOLUTION: I've used two different techniques for drawing ellipses, or ovals. The string-and-pins technique requires a deft hand because you have to keep consistent pressure on the pencil as it's guided around a string and two pins. While you can draw the entire ellipse in one continuous motion, it's easy to end up with a slightly lopsided ellipse, and you may or may not notice the slight irregularity until it's too late. Draw a few practice ellipses to get a feel for the tension on the string you're using. File a notch just above the pencil lead so the string won't slip off, and hold the pencil vertically as you draw. The string-and-pins technique is a good choice if precision is not necessary.

For larger ellipses, or when I want greater precision, I use a framing square to draw the shape one quadrant at a time, as shown in *Makeshift Trammel Method*. This technique produces the accuracy of using an ellipse trammel—a mechanical tool that draws (or routs) perfectly symmetrical ellipses—without the trouble of building such a device. It's a makeshift trammel, but it's the best way to draw accurate ellipses.

Bob Moran
Emmaus, PA

String-and-Pins Technique

Step 1. Draw 2 lines, A-B and C-D, that are perpendicular to each other and that cross at their midpoints, E. The 2 lines define the length and width of the desired ellipse.

Step 2. Adjust a compass to the distance A-E; then with the compass point at C, mark points F and G.

Step 3. Insert pins at F and G, place a pencil point at C, then tie a piece of string into a loop so that it is taut around both pins and the pencil point.

Step 4. Keeping the string taut, draw the ellipse.

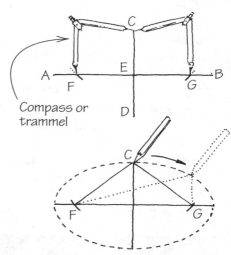

Makeshift Trammel Method

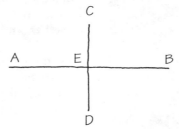

Step 1. Draw 2 perpendicular lines, A-B and C-D, crossing at their midpoints, E. A-B should be the length of the desired ellipse; C-D should be the width.

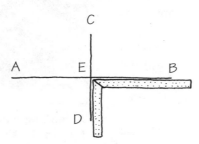

Step 2. Tack or stick straightedges along E-B and E-D. If your ellipse is small enough, you can stick a framing square to the stock using double-sided tape.

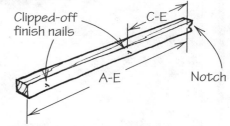

Step 3. In the end of a stick of wood that is an inch or so longer than A-E, cut a shallow notch. Drive fine finish nails through the stick at the positions shown. Clip off the tips of the nails so that they protrude slightly less than the thickness of the straightedges.

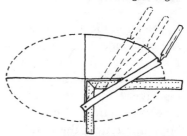

Step 4. Holding a pencil in the notch and the protruding nails against the straightedges, draw ¼ of the ellipse. Reposition the straightedges to draw each of the remaining 3 quadrants of the ellipse.

AVOIDING MEASUREMENT MISTAKES

Everyone's heard the old adage "Measure twice, cut once," but I think that the smartest woodworker is the one who can avoid measurements as often as possible.

Tape measures, rulers, calipers, even micrometers all introduce the opportunity for human error. When you want to make a cut that's dead-on, your best bet is to put away the rulers and rely on a few basic techniques for transferring measurements and making cuts.

STORY STICKS, BAR GAUGES, AND MARKING GAUGES

The most basic nonmeasurement measuring device is a story stick. In essence, a story stick is simply a board that displays key dimensions, either for a particular sequence of cuts or for an entire project. In use, all of the dimensions are transferred from the stick, eliminating repetitive measurements. See the photo below.

You don't need to measure diagonals to check for square; just make sure that the diagonals are equal. Slide the ends of a bar gauge into one set of diagonal corners, lock the sticks together, and then check the other diagonal.

Story sticks tell the same story every time. Measure and mark a set of dimensions (here, the mortise locations on stiles) on a straight stick, then use it to transfer the marks to each workpiece.

Next on the evolutionary ladder is the bar gauge. A bar gauge is an excellent tool for transferring dimensions, but because it is adjustable, it is good for only one dimension at a time. A bar gauge excels at jobs like squaring up frames or cabinets. To measure across diagonals, simply set the bar length so that both tips touch, then check the opposite diagonal. See the photo at top right.

The marking gauge is useful for all sorts of tasks, particularly laying out dovetails, mortises, and tenons. Like a bar gauge, a marking gauge can be set to a numerical measurement, but is best used when transferring dimensions, such as the exact thickness of a board for laying out pins and tails. Unlike a pencil line, which can sometimes get confusingly thick,

A marking gauge is the ideal tool for transferring the thickness dimension of one board to part of another board it will mate with, as when laying out dovetails.

the knife point on a marking gauge indicates exactly where to make the cut and even helps to guide the blade as you start the cut. See the photo at the bottom of the opposite page.

GANG CUTS, STOP BLOCKS, AND TEMPLATES

The other half of accurate woodworking is making the cut. The object is to make the fewest cuts and take the fewest measurements possible. The simplest way to do this is by cutting a number of pieces at once, or gang cutting, as shown below. I recall when I made a hall table several years ago. Because I cut the legs individually, they were slightly different in length, and the table wobbled. I wound up recutting all four legs to get rid of the wobble. Had I gang-cut the four legs, the table would have been rock solid.

When you cannot make all the cuts in a single pass, use a stop block. A stop block provides a reliable reference for making multiple cuts. Consider purchasing or making a few blocks to use on your table saw and chop saw. See the photo at bottom left.

You may think of templates as useful only for parts with curves. But parts with numerous odd angles can also be made more simply, and without repeated measurements and angled saw cuts, by using a template. To make your template, lay out the pattern carefully on a piece of ¼-inch hardboard. Trace the shape onto the hardboard and cut it with a band saw. Using this template, trace the shape of the part onto the workpieces, and cut them out on the band saw, just wide of the lines. Then use a clamp or double-sided tape to attach the template to each workpiece. Trim the workpiece against the template with a flush-trimming bit, as shown below. No matter how many parts you need to make, your last piece will be as precise as your first.

Joe Wajszczuk
Jersey City, NJ

Use a combination square to even the ends of a gang of parts; then hold them firmly while making the cut.

A good stop block should stay put when you butt workpieces against it repeatedly.

A complicated series of angled cuts could be used to produce parts like this, but making a single template and then routing the parts against it is much easier and ensures that all the parts will be identical.

LAYING OUT POLYGONS BY BOB MORAN

Squares and rectangles are the basic building blocks of woodworking design. These shapes are easy to work with because our tools and machines are designed to produce wood that is flat and square. But shapes like the triangle, pentagon, hexagon, and octagon break the monotony and open the door to more creative project designs.

You can draw these polygons with a straightedge and any tool that measures the necessary angles, like a protractor, bevel gauge, or draftsman's adjustable-angle gauge. But to draw polygons with perfectly equal angles and sides, the best tool to use is a compass or trammel.

Drawing a Pentagon or 5-Pointed Star

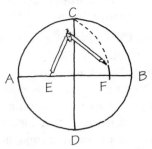

Step 1. Draw a circle with diameters A-B and C-D at right angles. Find the midpoint, E, of one radius.

Step 2. With a compass point at E and the compass set to distance E-C, mark point F.

Drawing a Triangle with Equal Sides

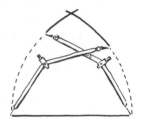

Step 1. Draw a line; then set a compass to the length of the line. With the compass point at the end of the line, draw 2 intersecting arcs.

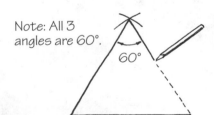

Note: All 3 angles are 60°.

60°

Step 2. Draw lines joining the ends of the original line with the intersection of the 2 arcs.

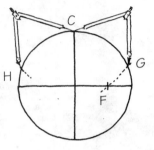

Step 3. With a compass point at C and the compass set to distance C-F, mark points G and H.

Step 4. With the compass set to the same distance, C-F, and the compass point at H and G, mark points I and J.

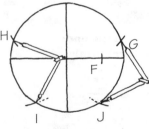

110°

Step 5. Connect the marked points to draw a pentagon or a 5-pointed star.

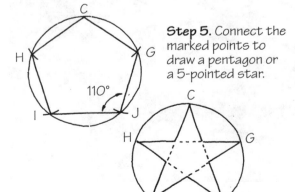

Drawing a Hexagon or 6-Pointed Star

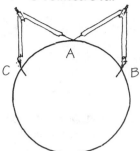

Step 1. Draw a circle and mark a point A on it. With the compass still set to the radius of the circle, and the point of the compass at A, mark points B and C.

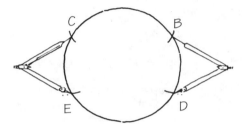

Step 2. With the compass at the same setting and the point of the compass at B, then C, mark points D, then E.

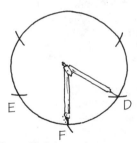

Step 3. Move the compass point to D or E and mark point F.

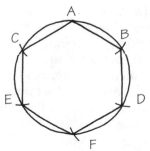

Step 4. Connect the marked points to draw a hexagon or a 6-pointed star.

Drawing an Octagon

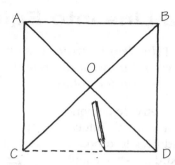

Step 1. Draw a square to define the size of the octagon; then draw diagonals A-D and B-C intersecting at O.

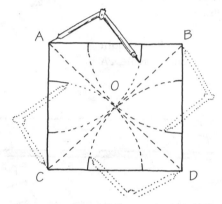

Step 2. Set a compass to the distance A-O, and with the point of the compass at each of the corners, draw arcs as shown.

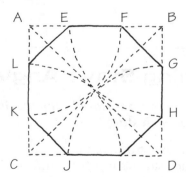

Step 3. Connect the ends of the arcs to draw an octagon.

Shop Math and Geometry

Dividing a Line into Equal Segments

PROBLEM: *When I divide a board or part into equal segments mathematically, I always end up with discrepancies. Is there a more accurate and reliable method for doing this?*

SOLUTION: Use geometry. To demonstrate, let's say you want to attach four equally spaced pegs to a board by dividing the board into five equal spaces. On a piece of scrap plywood or large mat board, draw a line that is the same length as the board you want to divide. Then follow the rest of the steps shown.

Rick Wright
Schnecksville, PA

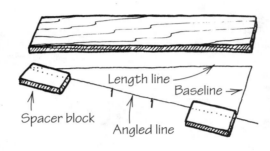

Length line

Baseline

Spacer block

Angled line

Step 1. Draw a line the same length as the workpiece (length line).

Step 2. Draw a slightly longer line at an angle to the length line and roughly divide the angled line into the number of spaces you want to create.

Step 3. Crosscut a spacer block to the approximate length of one of the spaces, and step off equal spaces along the angled line.

Step 4. Connect the end point of the last space with the end point of the length line to form the baseline of a triangle.

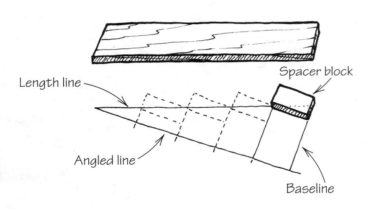

Length line

Spacer block

Angled line

Baseline

Step 5. Set the end of the spacer block on the baseline of the triangle, and mark where it crosses the original line. Then draw a line parallel with the baseline.

Step 6. Repeat the process to mark off the remaining spaces along the original length line.

Determining Stave Angles

PROBLEM: *I want to make a staved column. How do I figure out the bevel angle for each stave?*

SOLUTION: In stave construction, the angle at which each stave is beveled is determined by the number of staves, as expressed in the following formula:

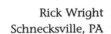

$$\frac{360°}{\#\ of\ staves} = stave\ angle$$

For example, to find the stave angle for a six-sided column, you would divide 360 by 6 to get 60 degrees.

This formula holds true regardless of the diameter of the column and will work for columns with any number of staves.

When cutting a beveled stave on the table saw, remember that the angle gauge on most table saws is referenced from a 90-degree square cut, not from the table. So, if you want a 60-degree bevel angle on the edge of a board, set the saw blade to 30 degrees (90 – 60 = 30).

Don't rely on the saw's gauge when it comes to setting blade angles. Instead, bevel a test piece of stock, cut it into the required number of pieces, and then check to see if the pieces can be assembled together into a closed form with all the joints tight. If the last piece fits perfectly, then you have the angle set properly. If there is a gap, then slightly increase the blade angle. If there is not enough room for the last piece, then slightly decrease the blade angle. Cut another piece of scrap into pieces and check the new setting.

Ben Erickson
Eutaw, AL

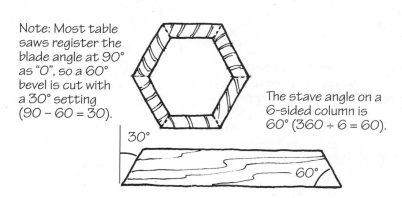

Note: Most table saws register the blade angle at 90° as "0", so a 60° bevel is cut with a 30° setting (90 − 60 = 30).

30°

The stave angle on a 6-sided column is 60° (360 ÷ 6 = 60).

60°

To determine the bevel angle in stave construction, divide 360 by the number of staves.

Crosscut a set of short pieces from a sample stave. If they fit together tightly, the angle is correct.

Dividing a Cylinder into Equal Segments

PROBLEM: *I'm building a three-legged turned-cylinder pedestal. How do I lay out the location of the legs on the pedestal so that the legs will be equally spaced?*

SOLUTION: It is easy to lay out the legs if you have a lathe with an indexed headstock. Otherwise, your best approach is to convert the circumference of the pedestal into a straight line and divide that line into equal lengths. A low-tech way to go about this requires a strip of paper, a pair of dividers or a compass, and a pencil. Wrap the strip of paper around the bottom edge of the pedestal, and strike a pencil mark where the strip overlaps itself. When you unwrap the strip, the distance between the end of the strip and the pencil mark is equal to the circumference of the pedestal.

Open a pair of dividers to approximately one-third of the length that represents the circumference—make a rough guess using a tape measure. Step off the one-third-length increments. If the tip of the dividers falls outside the overall length after the third step, close up the dividers by roughly one-third the error. Conversely, if the last step of the dividers falls short of the mark, open up the dividers by about one-third the error. Once the steps are equal, mark the paper strip, rewrap it around the pedestal, and transfer the marks to the cylinder. These marks are the centerlines of the legs.

Robert Treanor
San Francisco, CA

A strip of paper wrapped around a cylinder records the circumference as a line, which can then be divided into equal segments using dividers.

Finding a Center for Routing an Arc

PROBLEM: *I need to rout a large arc to make trim for an arched window frame. I made a pattern from the window opening and I know the radius, but how do I locate the centerpoint of the arc?*

SOLUTION: Finding the center of the arc requires using the same method as finding the radius. The radius is the distance between the router bit and the pivot point of the trammel. Since you have the arc already, you can find the radius, as shown at right. Secure the pattern to a bench or a set of sawhorses so that it won't move while you're laying out the lines.

Bob Moran
Emmaus, PA

Step 2. Draw lines perpendicular to A-B and B-C at their midpoints, then extend them to meet at O.

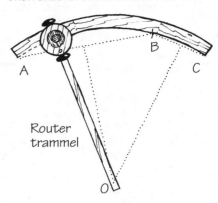

Router trammel

Arcs to be routed

To rout an arc with a router trammel, you need to find the center of the arc. Follow these 3 steps:

Step 1. Draw lines connecting any 3 points (A, B, and C) on the desired arc.

Step 3. Use O as the center for routing the arcs.

Finding the Radius of an Arc

PROBLEM: *I want to cut a perfect arc in a table apron. I know the length and height of the arc; how do I figure the radius?*

SOLUTION: You can approximate the radius by holding a flexible piece of scrap wood at the end points of the arc and then bending it so that it touches the high point of the arc. But in order to work this way, you'd need a third hand or an assistant to draw the arc. Plus the arc would not be perfectly symmetrical. Drawing an arc with a set of trammel points is a more accurate and repeatable technique, but you do need to find the radius. Here's a convenient formula:

$$R = \frac{(L \div 2)^2 + H^2}{2H}$$

Where L = the length of the arc, H = the height of the arc, and R = the radius of the arc

In the example shown at right, the length of the arc is 24 inches and the height is 2 inches. Applying the formula to the example looks like this:

$$R = \frac{(24 \div 2)^2 + 2^2}{2 \times 2} = \frac{144 + 4}{4} =$$

$$\frac{148}{4} = 37 \text{ (inches)}$$

To draw the arc, set your trammel points to the radius and clamp your workpiece to a bench. You can locate the centerpoint of the arc easily by trial and error, or use the technique shown above.

Robert Treanor
San Francisco, CA

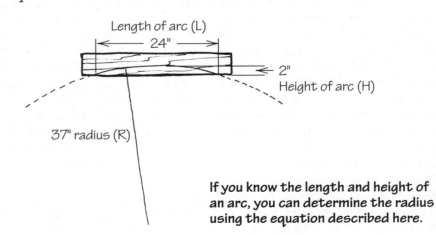

Length of arc (L)
24"
2"
Height of arc (H)
37" radius (R)

If you know the length and height of an arc, you can determine the radius using the equation described here.

Working with Figure and Grain

Grain Contrast in Book-Matched Panels

PROBLEM: *My book-matched panels turn distinctly different shades when finished. Can I prevent this?*

SOLUTION: This is the inevitable result of book matching. One board shows grain that faced the inside of the tree, while the other piece reveals grain that faced the outside. Light will always reflect differently between two book-matched boards. I find the result beautiful and think it enhances a fine piece of furniture. If you think about the effect when designing, you can use it to advantage.

If you prefer to minimize the contrast between light and dark, orient the growth rings the same way, as shown at far right.

You won't get the symmetry of grain that is possible with book matching, but light will be reflected more evenly. You'll minimize contrast most if you start with a

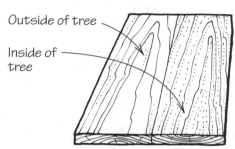
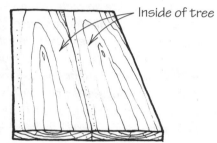

Light source

Outside of tree

Inside of tree

Inside of tree

A book-matched panel (left) displays one of the tree's outside faces and one inside face, creating sharp contrast. Reduce contrast by showing the tree's same faces (right).

board that has fairly flat and symmetrical grain.

In my work, I take great pains to display the inside of the tree on all the show faces if I do not book-match.

The inside has a richer-looking texture and a deeper reflection.

Frank Klausz
Pluckemin, NJ

Arranging Boards for Best Grain Match

PROBLEM: *I've built a handful of projects so far and on every one, the wood grain just doesn't look right when I'm done. What am I doing wrong?*

SOLUTION: I suspect that the problem is the way you're arranging the boards for glue-up. There's a lot for you to keep track of when you're deciding how to arrange your boards, including:

• The assembled grain patterns. You want patterns that are pleasing, drawing the viewer's attention to the piece rather than leading the eye off in some other direction.

• Final surfacing of the assembled panel. You want to arrange the boards so that the grain runs in the same direction. Otherwise you may get tear-out in some of the boards when you plane the glued-up panel.

• How your finish will affect the look. If the grain is running in varying directions, your adding finish could produce unpleasant changes in appearance.

To get the most pleasing appearance, first, don't leave the arrangement to chance. Arrange the boards in several different ways and note the one you like the best.

Second, try to achieve symmetry in the arrangement. If you are arranging a glue-up for two panels that will hang side by side, you might prefer symmetry in the two doors as a pair.

Third, arrange all of the glue-ups for a project so that you can see them all at once. If you take your time and test different arrangements, you'll be much more likely to produce a piece that's pleasing to your eye.

Bob Moran
Emmaus, PA

Inlaying Wood across the Grain

ONE OF THE CARDINAL RULES OF WOODWORKING *is that you can't glue cross-grain because wood expands and contracts across the grain in response to changes in the moisture content of the air around it. But few wood-working rules are absolute. All mortise-and-tenon joints, for example, are glued cross-grain. What's the deal?*

Part of the answer has to do with scale. The tenons on a typical kitchen cabinet door are 2 inches wide or less. The range of expansion/contraction in a piece this narrow is very negligible, perhaps less than 1/64 inch. The panel on the same door (and the amount of expansion/contraction) is likely to be at least five times that wide. The other part of the answer has to do with flexibility. Wood fibers are flexible enough to withstand the small amount of movement that a mortise-and-tenon joint will undergo.

Understanding the tendency of wood to expand and contract may make inlaying wood across the grain seem like a bad idea. But I've had success doing just that in a number of applications. For example, to dress up some flat solid-wood panels, I inlaid 1/4-inch-wide banding to form a rectangle within the panel, as shown on this page. I was concerned that the mitered

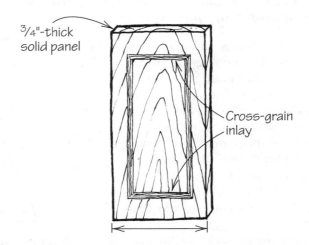

3/4"-thick solid panel

Cross-grain inlay

Before inlaying across the grain, consider the width of the panel, whether the wood is kiln dried, and even the finish that will be used.

corners of the inlay would open up when the panel expanded, or that the inlay would be forced up out of its groove when the panel contracted. But after several years, there's never been a sign of a problem.

I was similarly concerned when I wanted to add a small inlay of contrasting wood along the mitered

Laying Out Right on the Wood

PROBLEM: *I buy more than enough wood for my projects but still end up with parts that are badly matched in terms of figure and grain. How can I avoid this?*

SOLUTION: This happens when we rather blindly tear into our material, confident that the 20 board feet specified in the project plans will be enough, but not taking the trouble to determine exactly where each piece of the project is coming from. Another result of haste is coming up short one small but critical piece of stock, sending you scrounging

through the scrap bin or back to the lumberyard.

To avoid such unpleasant surprises, take the time to lay out and label all of your parts right on the wood itself before making a single cut. This simple practice does three things:

- Ensures you'll get the best yield from the wood you have

- Tells you the precise sequence of rips and crosscuts you'll need to follow when you cut each board
- Allows you to select adjacent parts for the best grain and color match in the finished project

On this last point, note that to get a good sense of the wood's grain and color, and to select the best face of each board, you may need to give the wood a light planing before laying out the parts. If you don't have a planer or the wood is not flat enough to take a skim cut, plane selected areas with a hand plane.

corners of a solid wood cabinet. See the drawing on this page. I was also worried that even a small amount of movement could break the glue bond, and that the inlaid wood might pop out of its rabbet. So I routed a groove into the corner at a 45-degree angle, as shown. This trapped the wood more securely, and also looked more symmetrical and interesting. The results have been equally satisfying—there has been no evidence that the cross-grain glue bond has been disturbed.

There are several reasons for success here: The solid wood that received the inlay was only 6 or 7 inches wide; the material was kiln dried to 8 percent moisture content; and the finished projects are not in a climate that undergoes radical changes in humidity. All of these factors combine to produce a situation in which the panels expand and contract very little, if at all.

In my case, I used inlay that was only ¼ inch wide × ⅛ inch thick. A larger piece of wood might make a difference and lead to problems. Also, in both cases I used epoxy, which doesn't allow the slight movement (known as cold creep) that would reveal small shifts at a glue line. I created a tight fit by tapping the inlay into the groove with a hammer and wood block. Finally, I finished both projects with an oil finish. Any movement around the inlay is less likely to be visible under a penetrating finish than a surface coating finish like varnish or lacquer.

Woodworking rules are not absolute. By experimenting with designs that test the limits of the material and question the established rules and conventions, you're sure to have occasional failures. But you'll also become a better woodworker and designer.

David Stern Lightner
Philadelphia, PA

RELATED INFO:
Wood Movement as a
Design Factor, page 12

To rout a groove in a corner, cut a 45° notch in a block of wood and attach it to the router base.

Position the boards where you can see them all at once. I often lay them across a few 2 × 4s on the floor and then crosscut them right there with a circular saw.

First mark any defects like knots and end checks. Then select the largest parts or those that will get the most visibility, and work your way down to the smaller and less important parts. Finally be sure to identify even the smallest components, or you might come up just one short.

Tony O'Malley
Emmaus, PA

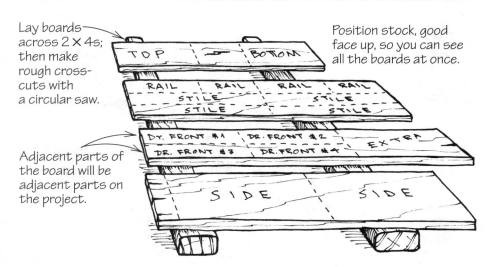

Lay boards across 2 × 4s; then make rough crosscuts with a circular saw.

Adjacent parts of the board will be adjacent parts on the project.

Position stock, good face up, so you can see all the boards at once.

TOP   BOTTOM

RAIL | RAIL | RAIL | RAIL
STILE | STILE
STILE | STILE

DR. FRONT #1 | DR. FRONT #2 | EXTRA
DR. FRONT #3 | DR. FRONT #4

SIDE   SIDE

To best match the grain of parts (and to get the best yield), lay out all the parts right on the wood before making any cuts.

MATERIALS
SOLUTIONS

CHOOSING MATERIALS

Detecting Curly Figure	37
Limiting Exposure to Formaldehyde	37
Making Strong and Stable Compound Curves	38
Judging Surface Checks	39
Making Lightweight Tabletops	39
Lumber Lingo	40
Choosing Wood for Speakers	40
Selecting Wood for Puzzles	41
Buried "Treasure"	42
Picking Wood for Utensils	42
Using Peel-and-Stick Veneer	43
Using Foam Panels in Woodworking	43
Choosing Manufactured Panels	44

WORKING WITH MATERIALS

Laminating Two Dissimilar Woods	46
Preserving Bark on Birch Logs	46
Creating a Four-Sided Quarter-Sawn Look	47
Avoiding Stepped Glue Lines	48
Plywood Panels Made from Cutoffs	48
Milling a Stump to Yield Figure	49
Handling Figured Veneer	49

DEALING WITH BLEMISHES AND DEFECTS

Removing Sticker Marks from Wood	50
Saving Wide Stock That Cracks or Splits	51
Salvaging Spalted Turning Blanks	52
Coping with Stained Pine	52
Removing Mold and Mildew Stains	52
Disposing of Sawdust and Wood Shavings	53
Straightening Warped Panels	53
Understanding Case Hardening	53
Taking Ripples out of Veneer	54
Restoring Warped Plywood	54

STORING AND DRYING LUMBER

Protecting Wood from Warping	55
Conditioning Wood to Stop Warping	55
Storing Lumber	56
Vertical Plywood Storage Rack	57
Storing Burled Turning Blanks	58
Drying Wood in a Microwave	58
Drying Stumps	58
Storing Veneer	59
Checking Moisture Content	59

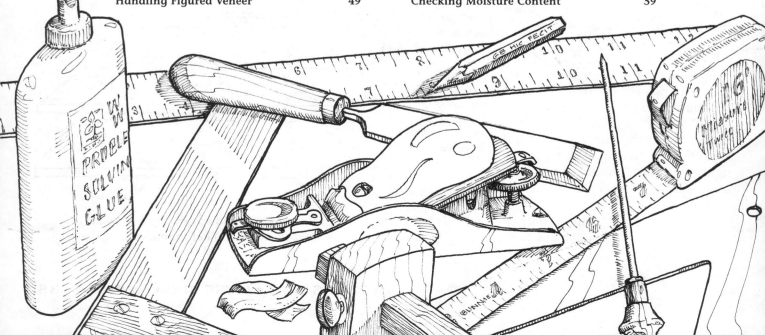

Choosing Materials

Detecting Curly Figure

PROBLEM: *How can I determine whether a log has curly figure before I cut into it?*

SOLUTION: It's almost impossible to detect curly figure by looking at the bark of a tree. You need to skin off the bark with a drawknife after the tree is felled in order to be able to look for the horizontal ridges that indicate curly figure. The spacing and depth of the ridges often tell how highly figured the wood is, but they won't tell you how far into the log the figure goes. Curly figure is often found in localized patches under branches or at the base of a tree; it doesn't always run the full length of the log. Only a log with ridges running its whole length will yield fully figured boards, so check about halfway up the log by stripping away a band of bark all the way around. The ridges might encircle the log, or they might run only along one face. This will tell you which side to slab for figured lumber. To determine how deep into the log the figure goes, you'll have to cut off a section from one end and split it.

Rick Hearne
Quarryville, PA

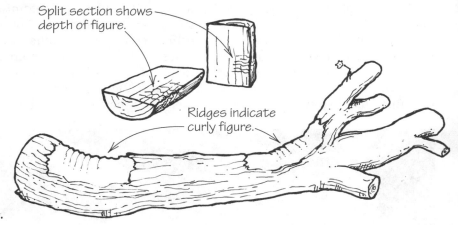

Split section shows depth of figure.

Ridges indicate curly figure.

To check for curly figure, remove the bark and look for horizontal ridges on the surface. Splitting a section of the log (top) will show how deeply the figure runs.

Limiting Exposure to Formaldehyde

PROBLEM: *I get a bad allergic reaction to plywood dust, apparently due to the formaldehyde content. Are there any plywood products that are free of this stuff?*

SOLUTION: Nearly every man-made wood product, including plywood, contains some formaldehyde, an ingredient in the glue that holds the plies together. Exterior-grade plywoods are made with a type of glue called phenol-formaldehyde. This emits much less formaldehyde than most interior-grade and hardwood plywoods, which are made with urea-formaldehyde glues. Hardwood wall paneling, particleboard, flakeboard, and chipboard are also made with urea-formaldehyde glues.

For some applications, you might try using exterior-grade plywood. To make sure that you're getting an exterior grade, look for the American

Plywood Association (APA) grade "EXT" stamped on each panel. If core voids are a problem, choose marine-grade exterior plywood, which is made to a specification that minimizes voids and edge gaps. A very small percentage of hardwood plywood is made with phenol-formaldehyde glues, but this special-order product may be hard to find.

There's also a paneling product called Medex. See "Sources," beginning on page 298. This is an exterior-grade, waterproof, medium-density fiberboard (MDF). It's made of pressed wood fibers with smooth face surfaces and does not contain formaldehyde. Medex is not quite as strong as plywood, but is a good choice for interior cabinetry, fixtures, and furniture. It comes in various thicknesses in 4- or 5-foot sheets up to 18 feet long. A ¾-inch-thick sheet of 4 × 8 costs about $50. It accepts paint and laminates, machines easily, and holds screws and nails.

Robert G. Flower
Alburtis, PA

Making Strong and Stable Compound Curves

PROBLEM: *I'm making a cabinet that has sides that bend in two planes. I know I can use bending plywood to curve in one plane. Is there any product that will bend in two planes?*

SOLUTION: When I want to make a compound curved form like yours, I make a sandwich with a layer of end-grain balsa between two sheets of ⅛-inch plywood. End-grain balsa is a boat-building material that has a fiberglass backing on one face. See "Sources," beginning on page 298. End-grain balsa will bend in two directions at the same time, and when you glue plywood or another stable material to each side, the compound bend will hold and take on structural integrity.

I use West System epoxy (see "Sources," beginning on page 298) to glue plywood to the end-grain balsa. This epoxy seems to hold tightly to the end grain—something standard woodworking glues don't do. If I don't want the surface of the plywood to show in the finished structure, I veneer the plywood using regular wood glue, which holds well on the long-grain surfaces of the plywood and the veneer. If the edges are exposed, I then cover them with edge banding.

The thickness of the banding will depend on the amount of wear it might get. The thicker the banding, the more difficult it will be to place in the plywood-balsa wood sandwich.

It is difficult to place veneer on a compound curved surface, but it can be accomplished with carefully cut veneer or with veneer that has been put in place with hot hide glue and a veneer hammer. If the veneer is stretched too much, it will crack as it dries. Only a bit of experience and trial and error will tell you how far you can go. If you need to use several pieces of veneer to cover your curve, overlap the edges and temporarily glue them to each other with the hot hide glue. You can then cut through both pieces with a sharp knife, veneer saw, or X-Acto blade, and remove the lower layer. To bond the top layer to the plywood, apply heat with an iron to reactivate the hide glue. This process produces a tight, nearly invisible fit.

E. E. "Skip" Benson
Camden, ME

Because it is lightweight and flexible, end-grain balsa is a useful building material for creating parts that have compound curves. Designed for boat-building, it works well for furniture, too.

Judging Surface Checks

PROBLEM: *I'm considering buying some lumber, but it has a lot of surface checks. How can I judge the depth of the checks and whether the wood is salvageable?*

SOLUTION: If you can, purchase a foot or two from the end of a board so that you can see a cross section of the plank. This will tell the whole story about the depth of the checking. If that's impractical, you can get a fairly good idea about how deep the checks are by using a stiff piece of paper, a strip of index card, or a piece of thin plastic. Probe into one of the larger cracks at several locations. You'll be able to tell how much planing will be required to remove the checking.

Also, you may want to consider whether it's even desirable to remove the checking. Even if a plank has fairly severe checking, there should be very little, if any, loss of structural strength. If an extremely large crack goes all the way through a plank and runs nearly full length, it would be smart not to use the plank in a load-bearing application.

Dick Boak
Nazareth, PA

To determine how deeply surface checks penetrate a piece of rough lumber, use an index card or a piece of stiff paper to probe the cracks.

Making Lightweight Tabletops

PROBLEM: *I'm building a long conference table that will have a span of more than 12 feet between the legs. What's the best way to make the tabletop so that it's light and stable but strong enough to span this distance?*

SOLUTION: I found an answer to this problem while working with boatbuilders, who use a variety of materials that are very useful for me as a furniture maker. One product is a plastic honeycomb material, as shown. This particular brand is called NIDA-CORE (see "Sources," beginning on page 298), and it's a plastic extrusion with a polyester facing on each side. This facing is compatible with wood glue, epoxy, and contact cement. NIDA-CORE is dimensionally stable, does not react to moisture, and does not have the seasonal movement that wood has. Also, if you cut through the polyester facing on one side, you can even bend the material to create curved shapes.

Not only can you use NIDA-CORE and similar products to laminate with fiberglass, as boatbuilders do, but you can also bond it to a wide range of prefabricated panel materials, like aluminum, wood, steel, marble, glass, and Formica.

To use NIDA-CORE for your tabletop, cut the material to shape and size, then cover it with plywood on both sides and edge-band it. You then can veneer both faces of this sandwich to create a tabletop that looks like solid wood but without the weight or the dimensional instability.

E. E. "Skip" Benson
Camden, ME

You can make a lightweight and incredibly strong structure by applying plastic laminate or veneered plywood to a honeycombed plastic material like these samples called NIDA-CORE.

LUMBER LINGO

To the uninitiated, the language of the lumberyard may seem like a mix of 1 part logic and 3 parts mysticism. But it's easy to decipher, once you understand the basic terms.

GRADE

Hardwood is graded according to the amount of clear wood in each board. Graders note the knots, checks, and splits; then they visually break down a board into defect-free rectangular cuttings. The higher the percentage of these clear cuttings, the higher the grade of the board. Wood that's suitable for furniture making fits into one of the four grades listed in "Hardwood Lumber Grades" on the opposite page. FAS, or firsts and seconds, is the closest thing to defect-free. It has more than 83 percent clear wood on both faces. Nearly as clean is Select grade. This lumber has more than 83 percent clear wood on its good face, and no worse than No. 1 Common wood on its second face. No. 1 Common lumber yields between 66 and 83 percent clear wood on both faces, while No. 2 Common is 50 to 66 percent clear.

SIZE

Hardwood is pricey. Anybody who has bought a couple hundred board feet of cherry or walnut knows that. But it might not be as clear that the high value of hardwood also affects how it's cut and sold. Softwood for general construction is cheap enough that the sawyer can concentrate on cutting standard widths and lengths, regardless of the waste. But with a valuable hardwood log, the sawyer has to focus on maximizing the amount of good lumber, regardless of the end product's width and length. So you end up with wood of random sizes with nothing but the thickness consistent.

Hardwood thickness is usually described in quarters of an inch, *before* stock is planed. That means that you have to order stock that is thicker than the job's specifications require. If you need 1½-inch-thick cherry for shelves, you must ask a sawmill for 8/4 (called eight-quarter) boards. The boards will be roughly 2 inches thick and must be planed smooth. Home centers usually sell hardwood stock already planed, but the boards are described (and priced) as if they were still in the full rough thickness.

PRICE

Since hardwood lumber doesn't come in standard sizes, it can't be sold by the "stick." Instead, you pay according to the volume of a piece of stock, which is expressed as board feet. To calculate the number of board feet in one piece, multiply the thickness and width in inches by the length in feet, then divide by 12. For example, a board 2 inches thick × 6 inches wide and 10 feet long would compute this way:

$$\frac{2 \times 6 \times 10}{12} = \frac{120}{12} = 10 \text{ board feet}$$

When buying lumber, keep in mind that the best grade of wood may not always be your best choice. For

Choosing Wood for Speakers

PROBLEM: *Is there a preferred species of wood to use for speaker cabinets?*

SOLUTION: The "tone woods" used in musical instrument construction are not appropriate for a speaker because an instrument radiates sound in a different way than a speaker does. In guitar making, for example, a light wood is chosen for the top piece (soundboard) to vibrate and amplify the sound made by the strings. Dense woods, such as maple, koa, and rosewood, are used for the back and sides because of their ability to reflect the vibrations out through the sound hole. In the case of a radio cabinet or speaker enclosure, the speaker amplifies the sound quite well without any help from the wood. A light-toned wood, like spruce, redwood, cedar, or pine, would produce a lot of unwanted vibrations.

Density and stability are the most important properties for the wood in a speaker cabinet. A high-grade lumber-core plywood or medium-density fiberboard (MDF) that is at least ¾ inch thick would be my choice. You can cover either of these materials with a decorative wood veneer, or you could buy plywood with a hardwood veneer example, clear wood may not have the attractive figure you'll find in lumber of a lower grade—as in people, defects provide character. Also, the cost difference between top grade and lower grade lumber is often great, and, depending on your use, the yield may not be that much better. In a pinch, I recently bought FAS white ash to make narrow edging and facings for a computer work station that I'm building. I paid nearly twice as much per board foot as I would have paid for No. 1 Common white ash. Yet, for my needs, a No. 1 Common board would have yielded nearly as much usable wood as the FAS did.

Kevin Ireland
Wescosville, PA

HARDWOOD LUMBER GRADES

	FAS (FIRST AND SECONDS)	SELECT	No. 1 COMMON	No. 2 COMMON
Minimum length (feet)	8 (6 for walnut)	6	4	4
Minimum width (inches)	6	4	3	3
Amount of clear wood in board (percentage)	83⅓ both sides	83⅓ one side	66⅔–83⅓	50–66⅔
Minimum size of clear cuttings (inches)	3 × 84 or 4 × 60	3 × 84 or 4 × 60	4 × 24 or 3 × 36	3 × 24
Number of clear cuttings	1–4	1–4	1–5	No limit

surface ready for finishing. You could also use a dense, solid hardwood. Rosewood lumber will be next to impossible to find, but solid, imported hardwoods like padauk, morado, shedua, purpleheart, and wenge should be available. Red or white oak or curly maple would work well as domestic choices.

Dick Boak
Nazareth, PA

Selecting Wood for Puzzles

PROBLEM: *What are the best woods for scroll saw puzzles?*

SOLUTION: For a quality scroll saw (jigsaw) puzzle, the base should be ⅛-, ³⁄₁₆-, or ¼-inch cabinet-grade plywood. Avoid the construction grades—these often have uneven surfaces and internal voids and tend not to cut cleanly. Plywood with a poplar facing is my favorite; birch and maple facings are also good. For 1- or 2-square-inch pieces, ³⁄₁₆-inch plywood is the best thickness.

Sand the plywood lightly before attaching a paper picture, if that's your plan. Wallpaper paste powder is a good adhesive. I buy my paste from a paint or wallpaper supplier and apply it with a brush. Because of the wide variety of papers, pastes, and sizing requirements, I would experiment before gluing down a valuable print. With tools and materials clean and dust-free, press the print down with a hard rubber roller. Some adhesives may cause the plywood to warp. This probably won't be a problem in the finished puzzle but may prove to be a nuisance when cutting out the pieces. To avoid this distortion, try gluing a sheet of similar, but plain, paper to the back side of the wood with the same paste.

Once the adhesive is thoroughly dry, protect the picture with several spray coats of artist's fixative. For added durability, follow by spraying a coat or two of urethane varnish to both front and back. When cutting out the parts, have a clear plan of each cut in your mind, but don't draw the pattern of cuts on the picture—it's difficult to saw right on the lines and even more difficult to completely remove any visible lines. Saw with a new thin blade, and use a backing board to minimize back-side whiskering. If the puzzle is for small children, be cautious about the chemical content of all selected products, and don't make the pieces small enough to fit in a mouth.

Allan J. Boardman
Woodland Hills, CA

RELATED INFO:
Choosing Manufactured Panels, page 44

k Tip Quick Tip Quick Tip Quick

BURIED "TREASURE"

No doubt about it, there's nothing quite so painful as the sound of planer knives or a new carbide saw blade meeting metal in the middle of a board. With recycled lumber in fashion these days, hidden metal is a problem now more than ever. Old barn wood and wood from shipping pallets is in vogue, and there's no telling what nails, screws, and other hardware the recyclers may have missed when they disassembled somebody else's handiwork.

I first encountered such dangers many years ago, when customers regularly asked me to cut down old picture frames. I'd pull any visible nails, but broken-off tips often lurked in the corners, waiting to take big bites out my expensive chopper blades. What saved me from considerable future grief was the purchase of a battery-powered electronic stud finder, the kind that lights up when near metal. So far, it's never let me down.

Today, there's an even broader range of metal detectors that would do the job—the treasure detectors that beachcombers use, for example, or even the high-tech wands that security guards use at airports to foil felons. Whichever type you choose, if you use recycled lumber, a detector will probably pay for itself faster than any other shop accessory. One thing's for sure: If there's metal in your wood, better to find it before it finds you!

An ironic note is that a lot of metal in sawed logs comes from hunters who have shot trees in frustration. Pieces of iron and steel in recycled wood can give the wood a chance to shoot back, so always observe safety precautions and wear appropriate safety gear.

Jim Cummins
Woodstock, NY

Picking Wood for Utensils

PROBLEM: *I'd like to carve some wooden serving spoons. What woods and finishes are best for food utensils?*

SOLUTION: Hard, close-grained woods are the best choice for food utensils. Hardwoods are not only stronger than softwoods; they also finish nicely and stay smoother in service. Close grain keeps food from lodging in open pores. Many domestic fruitwoods fit the bill nicely. I prefer cherry, apple, pear, apricot, and plum wood.

Unfortunately, these woods—with the exception of cherry—are not commonly available at lumberyards. For this reason, I use primarily cherry for producing quantities of utensils. Maple, birch, and beech are also good and are commercially available.

Although I don't use tropical woods, I recently called the U.S. Department of Agriculture (USDA) Forest Products Laboratory to inquire about their safety for use with food. See "Sources," beginning on page 298. I learned that any latent toxicity is negligible in the wood's finished form. Allergic reactions would more likely come from breathing dust when working the wood. I was advised that the color that leaches from the wood into cooking water is basically a natural food coloring and of concern only for people with extreme sensitivities.

I use mineral oil as a finish. It is odorless and won't turn rancid like many food oils. I avoid polymerized, hardening oils because I worry about their melting into hot cooking oil during stir-frying or other high-temperature cooking.

Jonathan S. Simons
Lenhartsville, PA

Using Peel-and-Stick Veneer

PROBLEM: *I recently applied peel-and-stick veneer over ¾-inch plywood to build a set of kitchen cabinets. I finished the cabinets with three coats of a wipe-on oil finish. Soon after, the veneer started bubbling and lifting from the plywood. What went wrong?*

SOLUTION: Your finish may have penetrated through the paper backing of the veneer and kept the adhesive from bonding properly to the substrate. Pressure-sensitive adhesive that's used for peel-and-stick veneers is susceptible to any type of penetrating finish. The veneer may show no signs of trouble initially, but once there's a change in humidity, it will expand and lift off the substrates.

I have run many tests with peel-and-stick veneer and have found that it works best on small pieces and on pieces that are not exposed to great changes in humidity. It's also best to use a topcoat finish, like varnish or polyurethane. Apply one light coat as a sealer, so that the finish will be less likely to penetrate.

When purchasing peel-and-stick veneer, inspect the protective backing sheet. Bubbles in the sheet may indicate dried-out or insufficient adhesive in that spot. The best thing to do is return the sheet for a new one. See "Sources," beginning on page 298.

Salvatore Marino
New York, NY

Peel-and-stick veneer is so thin that penetrating finishes can affect the bond. Always apply a light sealer coat before using a full coat of finish.

Using Foam Panels in Woodworking

PROBLEM: *I'm designing a display stand for selling my work at local craft shows, and I want to find a lightweight substitute for plywood. What else can I use?*

SOLUTION: I've used rigid insulation panels for light structural applications like this for years. They're made from one of a variety of foams—polyurethane and polystyrene being very common. The panels come in various sizes and thicknesses and are available at most home centers. They're also relatively inexpensive.

You can cut the material safely and cleanly on the band saw or table saw. Be extra careful when you cut it on the table saw because it has a tendency to lift off of the table due to its light weight.

To make a lightweight counter, I first glue on a wooden edge-banding using polyurethane glue. Then I laminate both faces of the panels with plastic laminate or hardboard, using water-based contact cement. Use only water-based contact cements because lacquer-based products will dissolve the foam.

I've used a specific material called Gatorfoam (see "Sources," beginning on page 298) that's even better than rigid insulation panels. It's a foam core already skinned with a hard layer of impregnated paper. I made a 12-foot counter that I've used at trade shows for years. It comes in 4 × 8-foot sheets, so in order to make a 12-foot piece, I contact cemented two layers of ½-inch-thick board and staggered the joint. I then banded the foam with 1 × 1-inch hardwood strips. After covering both top and bottom surfaces with plastic laminate, I chamfered the edges and coated the wood with clear polyurethane for abrasion resistance. The counter sits on either a couple of horses or a fanfold base that I made for it. I love the looks of envy I get from the other displayers when at the end of the show I easily pick up my counter and walk away with it.

I've also cut half-lap slots in the material to form shelflike assemblies for displaying small items. The structures are very lightweight and they knock down for easy transport.

Fred Matlack
Vera Cruz, PA

Rigid foam panels can serve as a core material for laminated counters and display fixtures when light weight and easy transport are important.

Choosing Manufactured Panels

For convenience, choosing man-made panels instead of solid stock is like buying instant coffee instead of coffee beans. As soon as the wood enters your shop, it's ready to use—no flattening, straightening, or smoothing required.

These sheet goods have another advantage: They're very stable. A typical sheet of hardwood plywood won't cup, twist, or swell the way solid wood will, so you won't have to consider wood movement when you design projects.

The most common sheet goods used in the wood shop are hardwood plywood, fiberboard, and particleboard. "Panel Characteristics" gives a quick overview of the man-made boards that are most often used for woodworking. Here is a more detailed description of each type:

Hardwood Plywood

Hardwood plywood consists of face veneers of hardwood sandwiched around a core of cheaper woods. They might be softwood or hardwood veneer plies, or a composite material such as particleboard or medium-density fiberboard (MDF). Each ply is glued cross-grain to the next, a process that gives plywood its stability. Panels come from the factory sanded, typically to 180-grit. Because the face plies are hardwood veneers, hardwood plywood is perfect where the look of solid wood is desired. The face veneers are thin—$1/40$ to $1/28$ inch—so you need to be careful to avoid damaging the faces when handling sheets and when finish sanding.

Hardwood plywood comes in nominal thicknesses of $1/4$ inch, $1/2$ inch, and $3/4$ inch, but actual thickness is slightly thinner than the stated size. For example, $3/4$-inch-thick plywood is typically $23/32$ inch thick, or $1/32$ inch under the nominal size. Panels are typically 4×8 feet. European panels, like those made of Baltic Birch, are sized to the metric system and come in odd sizes, typically about 5×5 feet.

Veneer-core (VC) plywood is made from veneer plies that are glued together in alternating directions, making it relatively lightweight. It provides good strength for holding screws or other fasteners. These qualities make VC plywood a good choice for casework.

A typical sheet of $3/4$-inch-thick VC plywood has 7 plies—5 core plies and 2 face veneers. Higher-grade VC plywood, like Baltic Birch, Finnish Birch, or Apple Ply, has more plies—usually 13 in a $3/4$-inch-thick panel—and the plies are void-free. The greater number of plies makes the panels stiffer and more stable. With these plywoods, you

can leave the edges of the multiple plies exposed and sand and polish them for decorative effect. That's not possible with lesser grades of VC plywoods, which are likely to have small voids in the core.

Solid-core plywood consists of hardwood face veneers glued to a medium-density fiberboard (MDF) or particleboard core. Solid-core costs less than VC plywood, and it's void-free. It's also flatter than VC plywood, making it a good choice for tabletops or free-hanging doors. However, solid-core is heavy, and it doesn't get high marks for stiffness or holding screws.

Lumber-core plywood has a core that is made from strips of solid wood that run in the same direction as the face veneers. Thin crossbanding plies are glued between the solid-wood core and the face veneers to stabilize the panel. With its core of edge-glued solid wood, lumber-core is the stiffest of all hardwood plywoods, making it a good choice for projects that require spanning long distances with minimum deflection. And lumber-core has excellent screw-holding power. Drawbacks are its tendency to twist or cup if not held down, and its relatively high cost.

Combination cores are a fairly recent innovation in the plywood industry and were developed to make the best use of wood waste and marginal timber. The cores of this type of plywood typically combine three plies of veneer in the center and a layer of MDF or particleboard on either side. Face plies of hardwood veneer fit around this sandwich.

Fiberboard

Medium-density fiberboard (MDF) is a common choice among professional woodworkers who need a smooth, flat substrate for veneer work. This type of panel is made from very fine waste wood fibers mixed with glue. The mixture is pressed flat under heat and tremendous pressure, then sawed to size and sanded.

Unlike plywood, MDF comes in very precise thicknesses. A $3/4$-inch-thick panel is right on the money. Suppliers stock sheets in $1/4$-inch, $1/2$-inch, and $3/4$-inch thicknesses, and the standard panel size is $1/2$ inch bigger than 4×8 feet to allow for later trimming.

MDF is an ideal material for jigs, fixtures, and templates. It's the perfect choice as a substrate for veneers, plastic laminates, or paint. Surfaces and edges can be routed to take a sharp, crisp profile.

Regular wood screws don't grab well in MDF; instead you need to use screws with deeper threads or design your projects with knock-down fasteners.

Hardboard, sometimes referred to as Masonite, is similar to MDF in that it is made from pulverized fibers. Because it's commonly available in only ⅛- and ¼-inch thicknesses, this type of panel is more suited to fixture work and jigs than to furniture making. Hardboard is slightly denser than MDF, and tempered hardboard is even denser than regular hardboard. But hardboard's edges have a tendency to fuzz, and the burnished surface needs roughing up with sandpaper before gluing. Hardboard is available with vinyl- or melamine-coated (plastic) surfaces.

PARTICLEBOARD

Often called flakeboard or chipboard, **particleboard** is similar to MDF, but instead of wood fibers it contains wood chips. The result is a panel with all the advantages of MDF—uniformity, stability, and flatness—but with a coarser texture. It's one of the least-expensive panels you can buy.

Particleboard is an ideal choice when your project requires a dense board, such as a substrate for plastic laminate. Don't use it for veneer work, since the rough surface will telegraph through the veneers. Cabinetmakers use particleboard for countertops and cabinets.

Particleboard is generally available in a wider selection of thicknesses than plywood or MDF. Suppliers stock all the standard thicknesses, from ¼ inch to ¾ inch, as well as panels that are as thick as 1 inch, 1¼ inches, and 1½ inches.

Sawed or routed edges in particleboard are rough, so you must band them with a solid material. You'll get the smoothest cuts in particleboard by using sharp carbide cutters. And, as with MDF, working with particleboard requires good dust collection.

Andy Rae
Lenhartsville, PA

PANEL CHARACTERISTICS

	VENEER-CORE HARDWOOD PLYWOOD	SOLID-CORE PLYWOOD	LUMBER-CORE PLYWOOD	MDF	PARTICLE-BOARD
Cost	Birch $50; Walnut $80	Birch $40; Walnut $60	Birch $100; Walnut $140	$35	$20
Weight (pounds)	55	100	60	105	95
Flatness	Fair	Good	Fair	Excellent	Good
Rigidity	Good	Fair	Excellent	Fair	Poor
Screw holding	Good	Fair	Excellent	Fair	Poor
Uses	Architectural work, cabinets, kitchens, shelving, paneling, and painted surfaces	Flat work like tabletops and free-hanging cabinet doors	Shelving and other work where rigidity is needed	Substrate for veneer, plastic laminate, and paint; jigs, fixtures, and templates	Countertops, substrate for plastic laminate, jigs

SOURCE: Data from the American Plywood Association, the Hardwood Plywood and Veneer Association, and the National Particleboard Association.

Working with Materials

Laminating Two Dissimilar Woods

PROBLEM: *I want to make a walnut chest with a cedar interior. Is it okay to laminate ½-inch-thick cedar to ¾-inch-thick walnut to make the sides, or will this create problems due to differences in the two woods?*

SOLUTION: To ensure that your chest will last for years, you should rethink the construction. Eastern red cedar's range of seasonal expansion and contraction is 60 percent that of walnut. This will cause a laminated panel to deform as the two woods expand and contract to different dimensions. If you try to constrain the panel from deforming, the stresses will simply relieve themselves by cracking or delaminating the wood.

I suggest this: If you're building a six-board chest—four sides, a bottom, and a top, all made of glued-up or single boards—let the walnut be the structural support. Install the cedar as a nonstructural liner, attaching it so that it can expand and contract independently of the walnut. For example, if the cedar is tongue-and-groove, blind-nail it to the walnut through the tongue. If it's square-edged, screw or tack it on, making sure the cross-grain dimension between fasteners is no more than 3 to 4 inches for any one board. If you're building a chest with frame-and-panel sides, glue up the cedar as a separate panel, and float it in the same groove as the walnut panel.

Ric Hanisch
Quakertown, PA

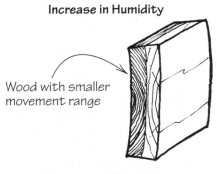

Increase in Humidity

Wood with smaller movement range

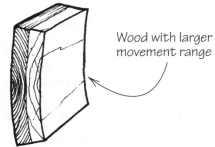

Decrease in Humidity

Wood with larger movement range

Woods having dissimilar ranges of expansion and contraction will cup when laminated.

Preserving Bark on Birch Logs

PROBLEM: *How can I keep the bark on the birch logs that I'm using for rustic furniture?*

SOLUTION: Birch bark, while beautiful, is very delicate. Proper handling and drying of the wood are essential for keeping the bark on. First be careful not to knock the bark while felling the trees or working the poles. A bruised spot will darken, and it may peel. My first choice is gray birch, sometimes called "old field birch," with yellow birch running a close second. Pick the healthiest specimen you can find, and harvest the tree in the dead of winter, or at least before the sap starts to rise. If your design permits, use poles that are under 3 inches in diameter. Larger stock will shrink more in the drying process, loosening the bark and causing excessive end checking.

Birch is prone to decay, so it's important to dry the felled poles properly. The easiest method is to stack and sticker the wood in a heated room in your house, using a small fan directed at the ends of the poles to blow air through the stack. If that method isn't convenient, a dehumidifier tent is the next best thing. You can make one from a sheet of plastic, a fan, and a small heat source, like an electric heater. Keep the ends of the tent partly open, stacking the poles and blowing air over them as already described. Don't let the temperature get over 100°F—you don't want to bake the wood. Either way, cut a few extra poles in case you lose a few to checking as they dry.

Don't put a finish on the completed work: It tends to muddy the clean appearance of the bark. As a final touch, use a stiff-bristled paintbrush to gently remove any loose bark.

Greg Harkins
Jackson, MS

Creating a Four-Sided Quarter-Sawn Look

PROBLEM: *I've seen a number of pieces of old oak Mission furniture that have legs with quarter-sawn figure on all four sides. How is this possible?*

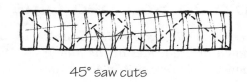

45° saw cuts

SOLUTION: There are two ways of accomplishing this effect. First you can glue up each leg from four pieces of quarter-sawn stock, mitering the pieces together at the corners. Rather than trying to glue the four pieces together at once, I prefer to glue them in pairs, as shown at right. After the glue dries, run each leg half over the jointer to clean up the second glue surfaces, and glue the halves together, as shown at the bottom.

To create quarter-sawn figure on all sides of a log, cut triangles, assemble in pairs, then into full squares.

Gluing the legs in two stages takes a little longer, but the frustration saved is worth the time spent. You would quickly realize that trying to keep four pieces aligned correctly as you clamp them together can be a real headache. Gluing in two stages means that because you can joint the second glue surfaces after the first glue-up, the miter angles on each leg half need to be just close, not perfect.

A second approach is to make the legs from solid quarter-sawn stock and then to dress up the nonquarter-sawn surfaces with veneer. You can either saw your own quarter-sawn veneer out of solid stock, or purchase the veneer from a veneer supplier.

Ken Burton
New Tripoli, PA

Notched glue blocks help keep the clamp pressure distributed evenly when you glue pairs of leg quarters (*left*). An alternative clamping method is to saw a 45-degree notch in a board and glue the halves together by clamping them down in the notch (*right*).

A different set of notched glue blocks is necessary when gluing the leg halves together. Holes at the apex of the notches protect the corners of the leg.

Avoiding Stepped Glue Lines

PROBLEM: *Awhile ago I made a table with a 2-inch-thick top, and now I notice ridges at the glue lines. What caused this, and how can I prevent it in the future?*

SOLUTION: More than likely, you ended up with ridges because the boards on each side of the glue line expanded and contracted at different rates. Movement in thickness depends on how a board was cut from the log. Flat-sawn boards move more than rift-sawn boards, and quarter-sawn boards are the most stable. If you glue a quarter-sawn edge to one that's flat-sawn, the flat-sawn one will move more, and you'll end up with steps or ridges. The fact that your boards are relatively thick compounds the difference.

Unfortunately, I can't think of any easy repair for this problem. Simply flattening the top at this point won't prevent the ridges from reappearing when changes in moisture content cause the wood to move again.

In the future, take care to join boards that have similar end-grain orientation. As an added benefit, you'll get a nicer grain match on the faces of your boards.

Paul Anthony
Hellertown, PA

Boards that are cut from different parts of a tree will differ in stability, and this can cause problems at glue lines.

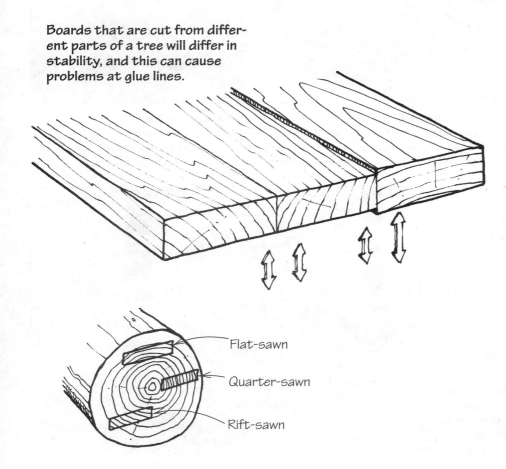

Flat-sawn

Quarter-sawn

Rift-sawn

PLYWOOD PANELS MADE FROM CUTOFFS

When you're completing a project made with expensive hardwood plywood and you're running out of material, the last thing you want to do is go to the home center to buy another full sheet. Instead, make the parts you need by edge-gluing your plywood cutoffs.

The process is much the same as creating large panels by edge-gluing solid wood. Gather your cut-off plywood pieces, and match them for grain direction. Then, using biscuits to aid in alignment and add strength, glue the pieces edge to edge. In many cases, proper grain matching results in a plywood panel that looks and works like a full piece of sheet material. This method lets you eliminate much of your scrap pile, avoid trips to the home center, and save money. In addition, you won't end up with large, nearly whole sheets of leftover plywood that you have to store and preserve once a project is done.

Dennis Slabaugh
Naples, FL

A good way to use up plywood cutoffs is to edge-glue them into larger panels. Use biscuits or a tongue-and-groove-type joint to keep the faces even.

Milling a Stump to Yield Figure

PROBLEM: *How should I mill a walnut stump to yield some burl figure?*

SOLUTION: First, stumps don't necessarily contain true burl—a conglomeration of dormant buds. Some people use the expression "root burl" as if it exists at the root of every tree. I wish it did, but all except one of the walnut stumps I've ever cut up contained mostly mild, swirling figure in the center (where the wood also tends to be pithy). In many stumps, the small area where the roots meet the trunk is extremely curly, but this area doesn't yield much wood—maybe enough for a gunstock.

True burl is usually found in protuberances on the tree trunk, often just above or below ground level. To mill a stump, first wash it off well with a hose to remove stones and dirt. Using an old chain on your chain saw, begin by ripping the stump in half along the axis of the trunk. If there is burl or appealing figure to be found, this cut should reveal it. If you're a turner, you might use one of the halves to make a bowl, or you might halve one of the pieces again to look for good turning or carving material. Your other option would be to slab the stump into whatever thicknesses suit your work by making a series of cuts parallel to the first.

Michael Mode
Champlain Valley, VT

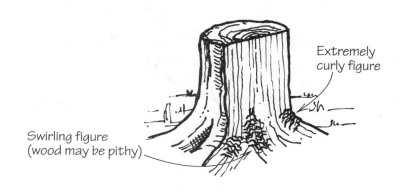

Swirling figure
(wood may be pithy)

Extremely
curly figure

Burls may be hidden
just below the
ground.

Potential
natural-
edged bowl

A plain stump (top) may contain curly or swirling figure, but only a burl stump (bottom) will yield the remarkable figure of burl.

Handling Figured Veneer

PROBLEM: *The veneer that I'm working with is so curly, I can't handle it to joint the edges. What can I do?*

SOLUTION: Wet it. A light coating of moisture to both faces with a spray mister will flatten it temporarily while you trim the edges for seaming.

Also, when you apply glue to one face of any veneer, it will curl toward the dry side. Getting it onto a panel or into a vacuum press becomes a nightmare. Spray a mist onto the dry side to counteract the curling. A small amount of moisture won't affect the glue bond on the opposite face.

Tony O'Malley
Emmaus, PA

A fine coat of water from a spray mister will usually flatten veneer enough to cut the edges. Spray both faces, or else the whole piece will curl into a tube.

Dealing with Blemishes and Defects

Removing Sticker Marks from Wood

PROBLEM: *I recently bought a load of green oak lumber and promptly stacked and stickered it so that it would dry. Now I see that the wood has developed black stains around the stickers. What caused this, and how can I prevent it from happening in the future?*

SOLUTION: The stains you describe could be from any number of things. First, because of its high content of tannic acid, oak will stain whenever it comes in contact with iron. Check that your pile is not in direct contact with any metal supports, nails, or other objects containing iron. Also, if the wood is stored outside, be sure the pile is safe from any runoff. Water running off sheet metal can pick up enough iron to stain.

If iron contamination doesn't seem to be the problem, check your drying methods. While air-dried stock should be covered from direct sun, it still needs plenty of good ventilation. If your stock is not getting enough air circulation, it may be home to molds or fungi. And if you used stickers made from green wood, the problem may be magnified at the spots of wood-to-wood contact. Consider repositioning your wood or installing a small fan to increase the air circulation. Also, make sure that the pile is sufficiently protected from ground moisture. See the drawing on this page. And consider using stickers made from dried wood.

I've heard some woodworkers swear that you should make stickers from the same type of wood you're drying. Personally, I think that it's silly to buy stock just to sacrifice several board feet for stickers, and ripping wet stock isn't my idea of a fun weekend project. My solution is to make a supply of "sticker stock"—3/4-inch-thick kiln-dried strips—from shop leftovers. I make my stickers from "neutral" stock, such as pine, cedar, even medium-density fiberboard (MDF). Avoid woods like oak and walnut that contain high levels of tannic acid. So far, I haven't run into any incompatibility problems.

As for removing the marks that are already on your wood, it shouldn't be a problem, assuming that you haven't yet dimensioned your stock. Minor stains from water or rust, or even ultraviolet radiation, are rarely deeper than 1/16 inch, and they should disappear after a pass or two through the planer.

Joe Wajszczuk
Jersey City, NJ

Corrugated roofing protects the stack from rain and direct sunlight.

Locate 3/4"-square stickers directly over 4 × 4s.

6-mil plastic sheeting covers 4 × 4s and protects the stack from ground moisture.

Space 4 × 4s 16" apart on well-drained ground.

Drying wood outdoors is a matter of carefully stacking and protecting the wood from the elements.

Saving Wide Stock That Cracks or Splits

PROBLEM: *I purchased a thick, wide walnut plank with the intent to build a tabletop. In the last few months, the plank has started splitting along one end. What can I do to save this piece of beautiful wood?*

SOLUTION: Gluing and clamping the ends to eliminate the cracking isn't a good idea; this would only conceal the stress within the plank, and the plank would probably open up again in the not-too-distant future.

To eliminate the crack, the first step is to relieve the internal stress within the wood. The best way to do this is to rip the plank into thinner sections,

joint the wood, and reglue. I recommend using a thin-kerf blade in your table saw in order to minimize wood loss and the resulting breaks in the grain lines.

If you don't mind leaving the crack as is, you might consider installing one or more butterfly keys made from contrasting wood. Besides stabilizing the crack, a butterfly key can make

for a bold visual element. There are a number of commercial inlay sets that make installing butterflies about as easy as cutting Christmas cookies, and they make sense when you have to make a large number of identical keys. For smaller jobs, I prefer to custom-size the keys and install them individually. Here is my three-step method:

Make the key. I try to make my keys to be about half the thickness of the plank I'm trying to save—anywhere from ⅜ to ⅝ inch thick. Lay out the key's shape on your material and cut to your lines using a band saw. Then clean up the edges of the key with a sharp chisel.

Cut the mortise. Center the key perpendicularly across the check, and trace around it with a sharp pencil or marking knife. Use a sharp chisel to form the shoulders of the mortise. Then remove the rest of the waste with a chisel or router. Don't make the cut too deep. When you install the key, you want it raised above the surface by about 1/32 inch. If you use a router to clean out the mortise, work the tool in a clockwise direction, moving from the center to the outside edges. After you've reached final depth, clean the corners and edges of the mortise with the chisel.

Glue in the key. Your key should be an exact fit in the mortise. If it seems too tight to install, you can chamfer the inside edges of the key a little. Then apply a small amount of glue, and tap the key in place with a mallet. After the glue has dried, you can make the butterfly flush with the tabletop. To avoid cross-grain sanding scratches, I use my block plane to remove most of the material, then follow up with a sharp cabinet scraper, and finally finish the entire surface with my random-orbit sander.

Step 1. To ensure a tight fit when using butterfly keys, use a band saw to cut the key to shape; then use a sharp chisel to clean up the edges.

Step 3. You can freehand rout the waste out of the mortise. Just stay well inside the layout lines and pare to the lines with your chisel.

Step 2. Use the key as your template, and lay out the mortise with a marking knife or razor-sharp pencil.

The finished result. Note: The key should sit just proud of the surface when you glue it in. After the glue dries, plane, scrape, or sand it flush.

Joe Wajszczuk
Jersey City, NJ

Salvaging Spalted Turning Blanks

PROBLEM: *I've got some spalted wood that I'd like to turn, but it seems so punky that I'm afraid it will fall apart as I work it. Is there any way to salvage the wood?*

SOLUTION: As you've discovered, the fungus that gives spalted wood its dramatic figure can also destroy the wood fibers, leaving you with a blank that's soft and unstable. But if you don't mind the cost of the cure, there's a simple way to firm up the wood for turning: Saturate the punky parts with cyanoacrylate glue (CA glue, also known as Super Glue).

CA glue is available in large, 2-ounce bottles from most mail-order woodworking suppliers. See "Sources," beginning on page 298. It comes in three thicknesses; you want the thinnest, which has the consistency of water. I assume that your wood is at least stable enough to let you partially rough out the blank; otherwise, it's probably not worth saving. So before you apply the glue, turn the blank to about 1 inch in thickness. Then shut off the lathe, and soak the interior and exterior of the blank with glue. It will flow right through the fibers, so spin the blank slowly by hand to distribute the glue evenly. Once you've soaked the entire blank, let it sit for a few minutes until the glue hardens. To speed curing, spray it with an accelerator, which is sold with CA glue by most mail-order woodworking suppliers.

When the glue is hard, start turning the blank as you normally would. Stop every few minutes to check for soft areas that the glue hasn't reached, and soak these with glue. When you've turned to the desired final thickness, you can sand as you normally would.

There are a couple of things to remember if you use this process. First, CA glue and accelerator give off strong fumes that at the very least will make your eyes burn, so always work in a well-ventilated area. Second, like all glues, CA glue seals the wood pores. This prevents the wood from absorbing stain or a penetrating finish as untreated wood normally would, so plan your finishing accordingly.

Kevin Ireland
Wescosville, PA

Coping with Stained Pine

PROBLEM: *Much of the pine available in my area has black and gray streaks. Is it possible to bleach the wood to make the color uniform?*

SOLUTION: No, the stain cannot be bleached. The staining and streaking in question is the result of a staining fungus that grows only in the sapwood—especially during warm weather—and causes a stain that varies from smoky gray to blue-black. The stain penetrates throughout the sapwood, so bleaching is ineffective, and you can't plane it out either. To get unstained pine, you must work only with the heartwood or find lumber that has been cut, sawn, and dried in the wintertime. Chemical treatment to discourage fungal growth is being phased out for environmental reasons, and discolored pine is becoming more common. Personally, I find the patterns of grain interesting, particularly at the junction of heartwood and sapwood.

Jim Sunderland
Pleasantville, Nova Scotia

Removing Mold and Mildew Stains

PROBLEM: *A bowl I'm turning from green wood developed mold or mildew stains when I left it overnight. How can I remove the stains?*

SOLUTION: The first step is to kill whatever is causing the stain, then move on to the stain that it left. Sodium hypochlorite, the main ingredient in commercial bathroom mildew removers, will kill the mold or mildew. As luck would have it, that is also an ingredient in household laundry bleach (Clorox and Purex are common brands).

Apply bleach full strength, and remember to use goggles and gloves. If a stain remains after you've treated the mold or mildew, try a 5 percent solution of oxalic acid in water. You'll find oxalic acid in powdered form at a paint or hardware store. Sponge it on, and let it dry overnight; then wash off the residue with fresh water. Wear a dust mask and goggles while mixing—oxalic acid powder is a toxic irritant.

Michael Dresdner
Puyallup, WA

DISPOSING OF SAWDUST AND WOOD SHAVINGS

When you find yourself knee-deep in sawdust and wood chips, it's time to look for new ways to get rid of the stuff.

- Sawdust makes great animal bedding. If you don't have animals, your friends and neighbors who do might take some off your hands. (Don't use walnut sawdust as animal bedding because it can be toxic.) After it has served its purpose as animal bedding, it can go into the compost pile. Sawdust needs nitrogen in order to break down so it probably wouldn't be good to add fresh sawdust to your compost pile unless you are also going to add nitrogen. Horse stables also use sawdust and shavings to keep down the mud in the stalls.
- Gardening is another area that can use up some of your sawdust pile. Blueberries and rhododendrons thrive in a mulch of sawdust because the sawdust helps keep the soil acidic. Putting sawdust on garden paths helps keep the weeds down and the mud out of the house. Walnut sawdust has growth and germination inhibitors, so keep it separate and put it only where you don't want anything to grow.
- If you are joining or turning hickory or cherry, you can package up these shavings to use in the barbecue or smoker for added flavoring. Just sprinkle some onto the briquettes or on the bottom of the gas grill and you will gain a reputation as a gourmet cook.

Bill and Joanne Storch
Corvallis, OR

Straightening Warped Panels

PROBLEM: *Awhile ago, I glued up and thicknessed some panels for some frame-and-panel doors. By the time I was ready to use them, the panels had warped. Is there some way I can salvage them?*

SOLUTION: You don't say whether the stock suffered cupping (warp across the grain), bowing (warp along the grain), or twist (propeller-shaped warp). Cup can be fairly easy to correct. Bow and twist present more difficult problems.

You can remove cup by moistening the concave side to expand the wood cells, while heating the convex side to shrink the wood cells. To do this, I lay the wood, concave side down, on a damp towel and suspend a floodlight above it for heat. I allow the wood to cup slightly in the opposite direction because it often moves back toward the original warp a bit as it cools.

Often, the only thing you can do to salvage bowed or twisted material is to cut it into shorter lengths. However, I have had some success with one method for straightening bow and twist. Recently some unattached drawer fronts I'd made bowed and twisted slightly when the relative humidity in my shop fell drastically. I placed them in a room with a humidifier, and within 24 hours they were flat again. A dehumidifier should yield similar results if your wood has bowed and twisted because of a rise in the relative humidity.

It's always a good idea to monitor the relative humidity in your shop so that you can estimate how it will affect your wood. I check relative humidity with an inexpensive moisture meter (hygrometer). See "Sources," beginning on page 298. If I'm going to be away from the shop for a couple of weeks or longer, I seal milled boards in a couple of layers of plastic wrap to prevent them from warping due to humidity changes.

Lonnie Bird
Gallipolis, OH

Understanding Case Hardening

PROBLEM: *I bought some kiln-dried cherry that seemed free of defects. When I ripped the boards, they immediately started to warp. What happened?*

SOLUTION: Your question indicates "immediate warp," so there's no doubt your lumber was case hardened. This is a drying defect that results in abnormal tension in the outer wood fibers of a board. Tension occurs when a board's outer fibers dry and begin to shrink while its inner fibers remain moist and full-size.

When case-hardened lumber is ripped, the cut imbalances the fiber tension, and the wood warps. In normal drying procedures, lumber is conditioned by brief steaming at the end of drying. This swells the outer fibers, canceling the tension. Properly done, conditioning creates stress-free lumber.

Gene Wengert
Madison, WI

Taking Ripples out of Veneer

PROBLEM: *My stack of veneer got wet, and now it's rippled and bubbled. It's unusable. Is there any way to salvage it?*

SOLUTION: You can flatten veneer easily by following these steps. First you need to wet it with a solution that will make the veneer flexible and strong. Thoroughly mix 1 part denatured alcohol, 1 part glycerin (available at most pharmacies), 2 parts white glue, and 4 parts water. Using a wide brush, apply the liquid to both sides of each piece of veneer. Let it soak in for five minutes.

Next compress the veneer using a system that will hold the veneer flat as it dries. In my system, I sandwich each piece of veneer between layers of fiberglass window screen and then sandwich each of these piles between layers of newspaper, as shown on this page. The newspaper absorbs the excess moisture from the veneer, while the window screen keeps the wet veneer from sticking to the newspaper. Once you've wrapped up all of the veneer, sandwich the entire mass between caul boards—I use scrap sheets of ½-inch particleboard—and clamp the caul boards together to hold everything flat.

The newspaper will become wet fairly quickly, so change the paper two or three times on the first day. Reclamp the pile each time, and leave the clamps in place overnight. On the second day, remove the screen from the package. Again, change the newspaper two or three times over the course of the day, but don't bother to reclamp the sandwich in between; just place a heavy weight on top to keep the pile flat.

On the third day, the veneer is ready to use. If you're not going to be using it right away, make sure you place a flat board or weight on top of the veneer to keep it flat. The newspaper isn't necessary at this stage.

Marc Adams
Franklin, IN

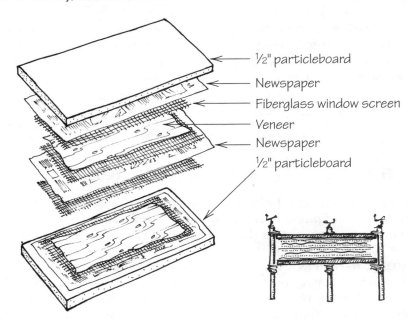

½" particleboard
Newspaper
Fiberglass window screen
Veneer
Newspaper
½" particleboard

To reflatten veneer, wet it with a solution of alcohol, glycerin, and glue. Sandwich the wood between layers of window screen and newspaper, then clamp the whole thing between sheets of particleboard.

Restoring Warped Plywood

PROBLEM: *It seems that plywood warps as soon as I bring it into my shop. What can I do to counteract the warpage?*

SOLUTION: Warped plywood is not uncommon. Fortunately it's fairly easy to fix. To unwarp large panels, first try to bend them back. To do this, I lay a panel so that it is convex, with each end resting on a 2 × 4. Stack weights onto the panel until it just starts to sag the other way. Generally, I've found that it takes about a week to correct ½-inch sheets.

Another way to correct the problem is to moisten the inside of the cupped face with a damp sponge or plant mister. Water should expand the wood on the inside face and help it bow outward. You can also combine both methods.

AVOIDING THE PROBLEM: Plywood problems stem from a combination of two situations: Moisture gets into the wood, and the plywood is improperly stored. If you are working in a basement shop that has a cement floor, be sure to keep the stock off of the cement. See "Vertical Plywood Storage Rack" on page 57. Plywood can wick moisture up from even a dry cement floor. Leaning sheets against the wall can also contribute to bowed panels, especially a masonry wall, which may wick moisture like a concrete floor. Panels should be stacked flat at least a few inches off the floor or kept as perpendicular as possible.

Joe Wajszczuk
Jersey City, NJ

Storing and Drying Lumber

Protecting Wood from Warping

PROBLEM: *I brought some new lumber into the shop and left it on my concrete floor overnight. The very next day, the boards were warped. What happened?*

SOLUTION: When you allow your wood to remain in contact with bare concrete, you'll always risk warping. That's because the wood quickly wicks moisture from the porous concrete. This is a problem particularly in humid weather, when a basement shop is likely to be wet. To protect your wood, separate it from the concrete. Ideally, this means putting it on a rack as soon as you get it, with stickers between each piece to promote air circulation. If it's not possible to store the wood immediately, at least place a sheet of plastic film, some scrap-wood stickers, or scrap plywood between your lumber and the concrete floor to protect it.

As for the wood that's warped, there's not much you can do to restore it. Your best bet is to crosscut the stock to yield the longest, straightest, thickest pieces possible, or plane out the warp and settle for thinner boards.

Kevin Ireland
Wescosville, PA

Conditioning Wood to Stop Warping

PROBLEM: *Even though I always buy first-rate lumber, it seems to warp a lot as I cut it into the smaller pieces. Why?*

SOLUTION: You are probably experiencing one of three problems. First, if the warping occurs only on a few pieces, it's likely that these boards contain reaction wood. This is wood that has internal stresses either due to the conditions under which the tree grew (such as an area of high winds or a sloping site) or because the wood grew near a branch or defect in the tree. Boards that contain reaction wood are going to behave poorly, no matter what you do to them, and should be avoided.

Second, if the warping occurs on most of your stock, then the conditions in your shop are probably different from those where the wood was stored before you bought it. When you bring the pieces inside, their outside surfaces adapt fairly quickly to the new environment, gaining or losing moisture depending on the conditions inside. The insides of the planks lag behind, however, creating a moisture imbalance within the wood itself. Pieces that are cut before the moisture content has a chance to reach an equilibrium may warp.

The third possibility is that the wood was not dried properly to begin with. Drying wood is a tricky business, and paying a premium for your stock doesn't guarantee that it was dried perfectly.

Now for some solutions. Assuming that you're working with well-seasoned lumber, you'll have fewer problems with warpage if you store the planks in your shop for one to three weeks. This will allow them to acclimate before you start to cut them up. Stack the pieces on stickers to allow even air circulation.

It also may be a good idea to cut the wood to size in stages. First rough-cut your pieces so that they are somewhat oversized in both width and thickness. Let them sit for a few days, then cut them to final size. This way,
if any warpage occurs, you can remove it when you dimension the parts. This is an especially good strategy if you're resawing thick pieces into thinner ones. Also, if you're planing a piece to significantly reduce its thickness (say, from 1 inch down to $\frac{1}{2}$ inch), remove an equal amount of wood from each side of the board to keep it in balance. You should also store the parts on stickers in between work sessions.

A final note: Occasionally, you may hear a woodworker advocate storing wood in the room where the project will eventually be placed. I don't think that this is a very good idea. With the exception of wood flooring (which should be allowed to adjust to the conditions in the room), storing wood outside your shop is impractical and may cause more problems than it solves. If the conditions in the room don't match those in your shop, then the wood is likely to move anyway once you bring it to the shop to work on it.

Ken Burton
New Tripoli, PA

Storing Lumber

PROBLEM: *I have a small shop that doesn't have much storage space for lumber. What are my options?*

SOLUTION: Lumber storage can be a problem, even in a large shop. Regardless of shop size, ideally you should have at least enough room to stack for a few weeks the pieces for your next project. This allows them to adjust to the local moisture level and reduces the chance that they'll warp once you machine them. See "Conditioning Wood to Stop Warping" on page 55. The best way to store this wood is horizontally, with ¾-inch-thick stickers spaced 16 to 24 inches apart between the pieces. Placing the wood on stickers allows air to circulate around the pieces so that they can adjust to changes in humidity.

The obvious place to create such a stack is on a lumber rack built against a wall. But if space is tight, you may have to seek more creative solutions. See the drawing on this page. Take a look above your benches and machinery. You could easily install metal shelf brackets high on a wall to hold a small stack of wood. In a pinch, you could also add some crosspieces between exposed ceiling joists and store your wood in the ceiling.

Another possibility is to stack the pieces on the floor under some of your equipment. I often use the space under my table saw's outfeed table to store pieces before I surface them. If your floor is concrete, however, be sure to put down stickers first, and add a piece of plywood for extra protection, to keep the wood away from the moisture in the floor.

If stacking your stock horizontally is out of the question, you can store wood vertically. The drawback is that pieces stored on end tend to bow under their own weight. One partial solution is to lean the boards so that only the tip of one edge is in contact with the floor, as shown on this page. While pieces leaning this way are somewhat precarious, they tend to stay flatter.

Ken Burton
New Tripoli, PA

To store lumber efficiently, use whatever combination of methods works best in your shop.

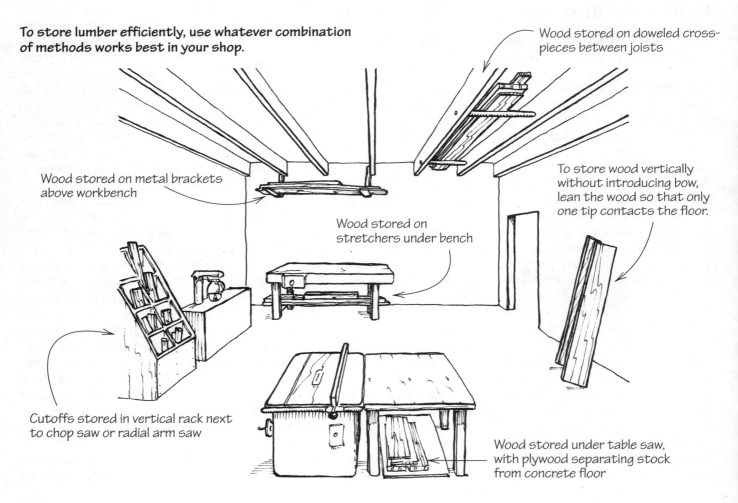

Wood stored on doweled crosspieces between joists

Wood stored on metal brackets above workbench

To store wood vertically without introducing bow, lean the wood so that only one tip contacts the floor.

Wood stored on stretchers under bench

Cutoffs stored in vertical rack next to chop saw or radial arm saw

Wood stored under table saw, with plywood separating stock from concrete floor

VERTICAL PLYWOOD STORAGE RACK BY JOE WAJSZCZUK

*F*inding the space to store bulky sheets of plywood and other man-made boards can be difficult, especially in a small shop. Here's a rack that I developed that takes up very little space while keeping the sheets from cupping and bowing.

The sheets are held securely in place by a 1 × 4 brace that has a slot on one end. The brace fits over hinged lock bolts that are mounted on the wall. When you flip up the brace, the lock bolts swing down and out of the way, providing easy access to the wood. Also with this system, the bolts are out of the way if the rack is empty, so there's nothing to poke into you as you walk by.

To attach the lock bolt assembly to the concrete wall in my basement, I used lag screws and lead shields. You could screw right into the studs if you're using this rack in a garage or shed. Note that if you use the rack in a basement, you'll need to separate your plywood from the concrete to keep it from warping. I nailed furring strips to the wall with masonry nails and fit a couple of scrap wood risers underneath the plywood.

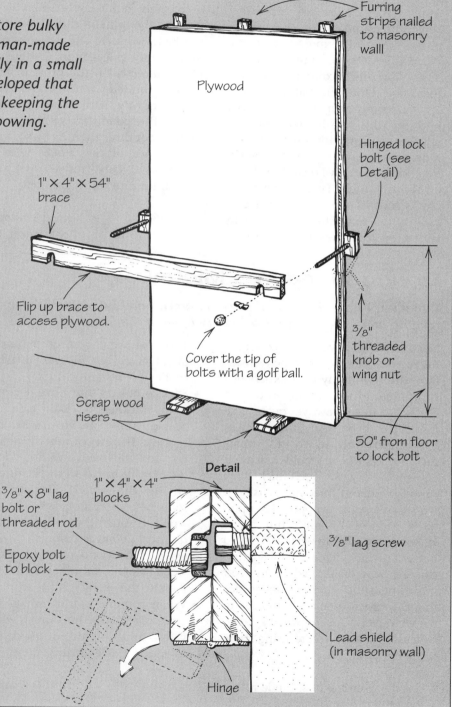

Furring strips nailed to masonry walll

Plywood

Hinged lock bolt (see Detail)

1" × 4" × 54" brace

Flip up brace to access plywood.

Cover the tip of bolts with a golf ball.

³⁄₈" threaded knob or wing nut

Scrap wood risers

50" from floor to lock bolt

Detail

³⁄₈" × 8" lag bolt or threaded rod

1" × 4" × 4" blocks

Epoxy bolt to block

³⁄₈" lag screw

Lead shield (in masonry wall)

Hinge

Storing Burled Turning Blanks

PROBLEM: *I have some burled wood that I'd like to use for turning. How can I store it so that it will dry without excessive checking?*

SOLUTION: To dry nonspalted areas of a burl, cut it into blocks that are about the size you want to turn. Apply Woodsealer (see "Sources," beginning on page 298) or a similar product to all exposed surfaces. Woodsealer lets moisture through at a very slow rate to control checking of the wood. Store the blocks indoors under a loosely wrapped plastic cover, and flip the plastic frequently to release condensation. After six to nine months, rough-turn the blocks into bowls that have a wall thickness of about 1 inch. Finish drying the blocks indoors, uncovered in a cool spot. If you can't store the blocks in your shop or house, store them in a ventilated shed so that they are off the ground and away from direct sun.

Spalted blocks can also be dried in a shed; don't cover them with plastic, though, or they'll get too punky to work. To encourage spalting, simply pile rough (unsealed) blocks directly on the ground in a moist, shaded area. Cover the blocks tightly with black plastic. Check the condition of the spalt after about three months by scoring the surface of the blocks with a chain saw. Look for the telltale spalt lines and color changes.

David Ellsworth
Quakertown, PA

Drying Wood in a Microwave

PROBLEM: *I have some small pieces of green wood I'd like to use for turning and carving. Can I safely dry them in a microwave oven?*

SOLUTION: Yes, if you work carefully. Microwave drying is much faster than air drying. My own experience is limited to drying green-turned bowls in a microwave oven. I've found that a bowl of 1/8-inch thickness can be dried in about 25 minutes; the same bowl would take a full day to air dry. An inch-thick bowl can dry in about three hours using a microwave oven, as opposed to up to three months by air. Thin green wood is very pliable when emerging hot from the microwave oven and can be bent or shaped easily. Not many guidelines have evolved yet for this new practice, so try it yourself to see what works for the wood species, shapes, and sizes you're using. Here are some tips:

- Use the oven's defrost mode rather than full power.

- Take the wood out of the oven about every ten minutes to let it cool before resuming drying.
- Stick to objects that have a maximum thickness of about an inch, though this can vary with the species. The maximum thickness you can microwave without danger of splits or cracks can be affected by the wood's density, its mineral composition, whether the wood is open-grained or tight-grained, and much more.
- Do a trial drying run with scrap wood before committing a valuable piece to the oven.
- When running a trial, weigh the piece often to see how much water is lost, to get an idea of the drying rate, and to tell when it's done.

Michael O'Donnell
Caithness, Scotland

Drying Stumps

PROBLEM: *How should I dry a stump log that I plan to cut into 2-inch slabs for tabletops?*

SOLUTION: Drying slabs of wood for tabletops is risky at best. Stump wood usually has interesting grain patterns, but its unpredictable shrinkage after drying encourages warps and cracks. Here's how you can try to dry the wood. First cut the log into slabs that are a little thicker than you want for the tabletop; this allows for warp and shrinkage. Seal the end grain and any area around knots to prevent fast drying. Asphalt roofing cement is a good sealing material, or try Anchorseal, a wax emulsion specially formulated for sealing wood during drying. See "Sources," beginning on page 298.

Dry the slabs very slowly. One way to do this is to put the slabs in a freezer or cold room for six months or longer. Another method is to put the wood outside in a cool, shady spot with high humidity and little wind. With this last approach, you risk the wood getting moldy and stained.

For a stable tabletop, you'll need to get the moisture content of the wood down to 6 or 7 percent. To do this, you'll have to monitor the moisture content with a moisture meter (hygrometer) until it drops to about 20 percent. After that, put the wood in a heated drying area like a solar kiln or a heated room until the wood's moisture content drops to the 6 to 7 percent range.

An alternate approach is to soak the wood in polyethylene glycol, also known as PEG. See "Sources," beginning on page 298. PEG reduces shrinkage, and the cracking and warping that result, by replacing the moisture in the wood.

Gene Wengert
Madison, WI

Storing Veneer

PROBLEM: *I need to store some expensive burl veneer for several months before I use it. What's the safest way to deal with this delicate stuff?*

SOLUTION: First of all, if you've bought sequence-type veneers, like book-matches or flitch cuts, you should number the pieces as soon as you open the veneer pack. This way, if you drop the pack during handling, you can return the pieces back to the proper sequence. Mark the veneer with chalk, not a felt-tip marker or a wax pencil—they're too difficult to remove later. Also, since the end grain of the veneer can tear and crack as you handle it, it's a good idea to tape each end with masking tape. See the drawing on this page.

As far as storing goes, you should always place your veneer in a flat, horizontal position, and it's a good idea to cover it with particleboard or plastic to keep dust from settling on it. It's important to keep your veneer away from wet areas and from direct sunlight, which can cause the color to fade. You might want to hang a moisture meter (hygrometer) in the same area as the veneer so that you can monitor moisture conditions. If the air gets too humid, the veneer could get moldy, or it could expand and later shrink unexpectedly after you've cut it to size. If the air is too dry, the veneer could become brittle and crack at the touch. You can prevent both of these conditions by moving the veneer to an area that has the proper moisture conditions and letting the wood acclimate before using it.

Marc Adams
Franklin, IN

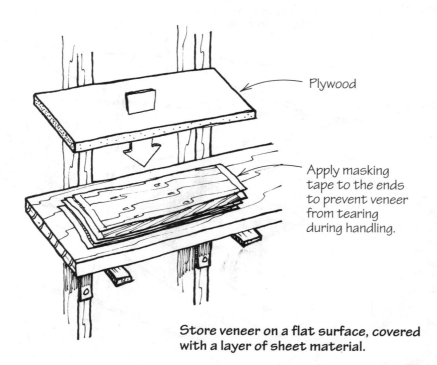

Store veneer on a flat surface, covered with a layer of sheet material.

Plywood

Apply masking tape to the ends to prevent veneer from tearing during handling.

Checking Moisture Content

PROBLEM: *I have a stack of walnut that's been air dried in a barn for 12 years. How do I know whether it's ready to use for furniture?*

SOLUTION: For furniture making, wood should be dried to a moisture content that places it in equilibrium with the environment in which it will be used. For most areas of the United States, 6 to 8 percent moisture content (MC) is ideal. Your air-dried lumber probably won't be dry enough for indoor use because it is in equilibrium with the outside air, which is usually much wetter than air indoors. Chances are that the wood is at 12 to 16 percent MC—too "wet" for furniture.

To assess your wood, you need to check it with a moisture meter (hygrometer.) If your moisture meter shows that the MC of your lumber is too high, you can have the stock dried at a local sawmill equipped with a kiln. It's also possible to air dry the wood indoors, as long as you have a space that can maintain a relative humidity of around 40 percent (typical of most homes). Sticker the boards to allow air to circulate, and stack the pile on a flat surface. Use your hygrometer to monitor the MC. A few weeks is all it should take to get the wood down to 7 percent.

When it comes to walnut, I prefer the air-dried variety for several reasons: It's usually less expensive, and the wood's rich color hasn't been muted by steaming (a common kiln process used to color the walnut sapwood). In addition, air-dried wood is free of drying stresses such as case hardening, which can cause wood to warp or split unexpectedly.

Lonnie Bird
Gallipolis, OH

Stock Preparation Solutions

JOINTING STOCK

Jointing End Grain	61
Avoiding Tear-Out When Jointing	62
Jointing Small Pieces	62
Getting Tight Edge Joints and Flat Panels	63
Face Jointing on the Planer	63
Jointing Edges on the Planer	64
Jointing on a Router Table	64
Jointing Edges with a Hand Plane	65
Jointing a Wide Board on a Narrow Jointer	66

PLANING WOOD

Reducing Planer Tear-Out	67
Avoiding Planer Snipe	68
Using Winding Sticks to Check Stock	68
Planing Short Stock	69

Planing Thin Stock	69
Preventing Warp after Planing	70
Reducing Hand Plane Tear-Out	70
Replacing a Spoiled Part	70
Surface Planing with a Hand Plane	71

RESAWING THICK STOCK

Resawing on Track	72
Keeping Resawed Boards Flat	73
Resawing on the Table Saw	73
Log-Milling Band Saw Setup	74

WORKING WITH VENEER

Preparing Veneer Joints	75
Registering Veneer	76
Routing Veneer Seams	76
Cutting Veneered Plywood without Tear-Out	77

Jointing Stock

Jointing End Grain

PROBLEM: *My saw often leaves noticeable blade marks on end grain, and sanding them out takes forever. Can I clean these off on the jointer? What's the best way?*

SOLUTION: Jointing the end grain is effective for removing saw marks, and it will reduce the time needed to sand the end grain. You may have discovered that saw marks and uneven sanding show up more dramatically in the end grain than on the face or edges of the wood.

You will find out quickly that if you pass the end grain completely across the jointer, the trailing edge will tear out. To eliminate this, I use a simple technique that involves passing the end grain across the jointer in two directions.

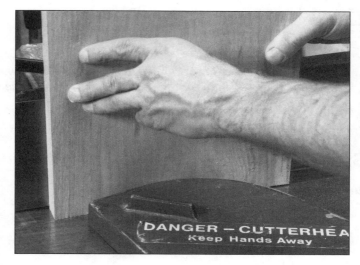

To avoid tear-out when jointing end grain, first joint about an inch or two in from one edge. Then flip the board, and joint the remainder from the other edge.

Clamping a scrap to the back edge of a narrow board makes jointing the end a more stable operation. Also, the edge of the scrap, not the edge of the workpiece, will splinter out.

First I joint one end about an inch or two and then turn the board around and joint from the other edge, going across the entire length, as shown above. You will not experience tear-out on the trailing edge now because that surface has already been cut from the other direction.

An alternative approach, better for narrow boards, is to attach a scrap block to the back edge of the board and let it splinter out, as shown at left. With either technique, be sure to take a very light cut. Finish up the edge by sanding it until it's smooth.

End grain that will show, as on a solid tabletop, should be as smooth as possible by the time you apply finish to the project, so that the finish looks the same for all edges.

Rick Wright
Schnecksville, PA

Avoiding Tear-Out When Jointing

PROBLEM: *How can I avoid tear-out when edge-jointing boards?*

SOLUTION: First make sure that your knives are installed flush with the outfeed table. Then set the infeed table for a light cut, and feed the board with the grain running downhill toward the infeed table, pushing the board slowly and steadily. If the board tears out, try reversing the board and jointing in the opposite direction. If you still get tear-out, your knives are probably dull.

There's a trick for keeping a section of the knives sharp just for edge jointing: Set the fence about an inch or so from the far end of the knives (away from you), and use this arrangement for face jointing. When you need a super-smooth edge, move the fence back that last inch to expose the reserved spot, and edge-joint on super-sharp knives.

Lonnie Bird
Gallipolis, OH

RELATED INFO:
Twenty-Minute Tune-Up: The Jointer, page 259

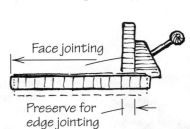

Face jointing

Preserve for edge jointing

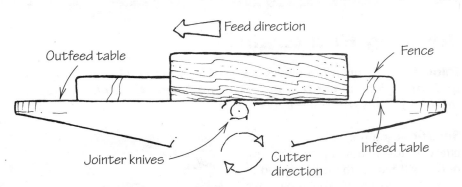

Feed direction

Outfeed table

Fence

Jointer knives

Cutter direction

Infeed table

When jointing, orient grain so it faces downhill toward the infeed table (right). When face jointing, position the fence to preserve the far end of the knives for edge jointing (left).

Jointing Small Pieces

PROBLEM: *How can I joint the edges of pieces that are too small for the jointer?*

SOLUTION: Use a router. Face the router's fence with a longer wooden fence, and then attach a strip of thinner material (such as a piece of plastic laminate) to the outfeed side of the fence. Secure the router upside down and use it like a miniature router table.

Graham Blackburn
Bearsville, NY

Jointing small pieces of stock is straightforward if you use a router equipped with a straight bit and a wooden fence. A strip of plastic laminate on the outfeed half of the fence creates the necessary offset.

Getting Tight Edge Joints and Flat Panels

PROBLEM: *No matter how carefully I joint the edges of boards, when I glue them together, I get either bad joints or a panel that's not flat. How can I correct this problem?*

SOLUTION: When jointing stock to be edge-glued, if the jointer's fence is not set at exactly 90 degrees, you'll end up with a panel that does not glue up flat. The solution is to run the boards across the jointer so that for each joint, one board's top face and the adjacent board's bottom face run against the jointer fence. This cancels out the effect of the fence being slightly off a true 90 degrees.

An easy way to do this is to lay out the panel as it will be glued up and draw a large triangle across it. Stack the boards up, keeping the same ends together, and carry them to the jointer. As long as all the same ends of the boards are fed through the jointer first, the glued up boards will be flat. A drawback is that this approach sometimes forces you to joint against the grain, which can cause tear-out.

Ben Erickson
Eutaw, AL

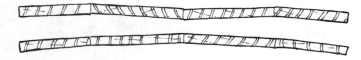

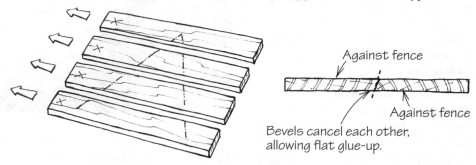

If your jointer fence is even a hair off 90° to the blade, your boards will join together like this (exaggerated for clarity).

Against fence

Against fence

Bevels cancel each other, allowing flat glue-up.

To cancel the effect of an out-of-square fence, alternate the face of the board that you hold against the fence as you joint the edges. To make sure that you alternate the faces, lay them out as they'll be glued together and mark an X at the same end of each board. Then joint the boards by feeding them all in the same direction.

Face Jointing on the Planer

PROBLEM: *I need to flatten some warped stock, but I don't have a jointer. Is there any way to "joint" a board on my planer?*

SOLUTION: Yes, you can joint on the planer, but you need to make a sled that will support the stock. Otherwise, the machine's rollers will temporarily flatten the warped lumber as it's fed through the planer, and it will come out just as twisted as it was when it went in.

Make a plywood or particleboard sled that is as wide as your planer bed and as long as the longest board you want to plane. Attach a stop to the back end of the sled to prevent the stock from moving on the sled. The stop needs to be lower in height than the final thickness of the board you want to plane. Now insert shims or wedges under the areas where the board does not lie flat on the sled. I find that cedar shingles make convenient wedges and that slips of cardboard make excellent shims. The shims and wedges will prevent the rollers from flattening the board as it passes through the machine.

Set the planer for a very light pass and feed the board through. The planer will remove the high spots first and then progressively flatten the top face of the board. When the top face is flat, or nearly so, plane the second face without using the sled.

W. Curtis Johnson
Corvallis, OR

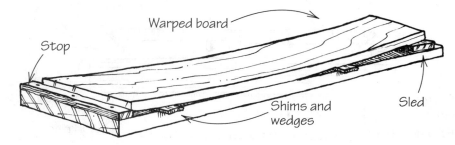

Warped board

Stop

Shims and wedges

Sled

To face plane a warped board, support it on a flat sled using shims and wedges. Note: The stop must be thinner than the final thickness of the board being planed.

Jointing Edges on the Planer

PROBLEM: *After jointing the edges of some boards, then ripping the stock to width, I cleaned off the sawed edges on the jointer. The boards were not all exactly the same width. What went wrong?*

SOLUTION: Most woodworkers are familiar with this fundamental sequence: Joint one face of a board, plane the second face, joint an edge, rip the board to width, and then joint the sawed edge clean. Sometimes, though, you'll often joint more off one piece than another, or more off one end of a board than another. The difference is sometimes inconsequential, but often it can throw off critical operations. To correct and avoid this problem, use your planer to take that last "jointing" cut.

Planing a stack of boards on edge cleans the saw marks and ensures that all the boards are exactly the same width.

Begin with rough stock that's a couple of inches longer than needed and slightly wider than called for. Joint a face of each piece and then an edge.

You now have two good, flat surfaces—a face and an edge. Rip the stock to width plus about 1/16 inch. Next plane the second face flat, the way you normally would. Then gather together all the pieces that are the same width, turn them on edge, and run them through the planer, as shown above. If necessary adjust the cut and run the boards through until you have the proper width.

To help keep a stack of thin boards vertical, use a clamp or double-sided tape to attach an L-block square to the infeed table.

Jeff Day
Perkasie, PA

Jointing on a Router Table

PROBLEM: *I can't afford a jointer, and I'm not patient with hand planes. How else can I get straight and square edges on boards after sawing them?*

SOLUTION: You can make perfect edge joints with a router table, a sharp straight bit, and an offset fence. You can create an offset on a router table fence either by using separate infeed and outfeed fences or by adding a shim to the outfeed half of a single-piece fence. With separate fences, set the outfeed fence so that it's exactly even with the tangent of the cutter, as shown. Then set the infeed half of the fence so that the router bit trims approximately 1/16 inch from the edge of the workpiece. With a single-piece fence, set the fence to make a 1/16-inch-deep cut, then glue or tape a shim to the outfeed half of the fence. A strip of plastic laminate makes a perfect shim.

Use a double-fluted carbide straight bit at least 1/2 inch in diameter. For superior results, use a bit with spiral flutes. Make two passes on each sawed edge. The first pass cleans up the saw marks and gets rid of any irregularities. The second pass gives you a clean, straight edge.

David Page
Swarthmore, PA

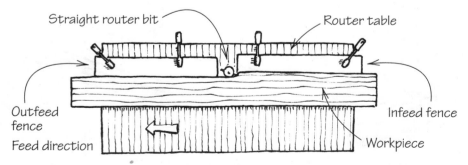

Straight router bit — Router table

Outfeed fence

Feed direction

Infeed fence

Workpiece

To joint a board on a router table, first set the outfeed fence so that it is even with the cutting edge of the bit. Then set the infeed to take a 1/16" cut. Make sure that the fences are parallel.

Jointing Edges with a Hand Plane

A SHORT JOINTER IS NOT A GOOD TOOL FOR PLANING LONG EDGES, especially if the edges will be glued together for a panel or tabletop. But if all you have is a short jointer, you may find yourself trying to do the impossible anyway.

Edge-jointing with a hand plane is often easier and faster than trying to manhandle a long board across the bed of a short jointer. All you need is a vise and a sharp plane or two.

If the boards' edges are rough-sawn or very crooked, start with a jack plane (about 18 inches long) with its blade set to take a relatively thick shaving. This will remove the rough saw marks and yield an approximately straight edge. Check the edge with your longest straightedge or snap a chalk line on one of the faces for this preliminary straightening.

Now use the longest plane available—a jointer plane is typically 20 to 24 inches long—to true the edge. The longer the plane, the more effectively it will bridge any dips and hollows and remove the high spots in the edge of the board. Use a straightedge repeatedly to check your progress. If, when held lengthwise on the edge being planed, the straightedge can be swiveled around any point along its length, that point needs to be planed off. When the edge is completely flat, all points of the straightedge will contact the edge equally and no swiveling will be possible.

As you are planing the edge straight, also check that the edge is square; use a small try square held every few inches along the board's edge. Where it is beveled, plane the edge square. Then take a light continuous shaving from the whole length of the edge with the plane centered over the edge.

If you are jointing two edges that are to be joined together, use the first edge, already planed straight and square, to gauge the progress on the second edge. When the edges are flat and square enough for the second to be rested securely on the first, position them edge to edge as they will be joined. With a light source directly behind the joint, check from the front for light showing through. These are the low spots. Mark the high spots, and continue planing until no light shows through the joint.

Graham Blackburn
Bearsville, NY

Step 1. Plane off the high spots. A long jointer plane bridges low spots better and makes straightening an edge easier.

Step 2. Use a try square along the edge of the board to check squareness.

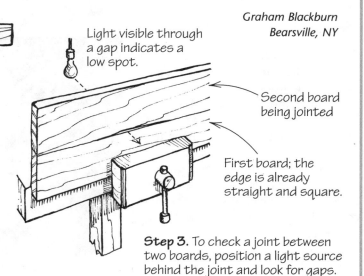

Light visible through a gap indicates a low spot.

Second board being jointed

First board; the edge is already straight and square.

Step 3. To check a joint between two boards, position a light source behind the joint and look for gaps.

Jointing a Wide Board on a Narrow Jointer

PROBLEM: *I want to face-joint some 11-inch-wide pine boards, but I have an 8-inch jointer. Is there any way to do the job?*

SOLUTION: There are several ways, but I'll mention just the best one, which works anytime you want to joint a board that's wider than your jointer.

Get a piece of laminate or posterboard—something that's about 1/16 inch thick and big enough to cover the rabbeting table on your jointer. Lay it on the rabbeting table, and adjust the jointer's depth of cut until the laminate is just flush with the outfeed table, as shown in *Step 1*. Remove the "shim" and take a cut off a little more than half of one face of a board, as shown in *Step 2*. Now tape the shim onto the rabbeting table. Flip the board end for end and cut the other half of the same face, riding the previously cut area on the shim, as shown in *Step 3*. The cuts should be nearly flush.

Fred Matlack
Vera Cruz, PA

ANOTHER VIEW: Set the jointer fence for the widest cut and run the board over it. Then adjust the fence to cut only the remaining portion of the board. It will be obvious that this approach requires a bit of freehand finesse. But the goal is to get the face flatter than it already is, not dead flat. If you then plane both faces of the board alternately in the planer with a couple light passes each, the board will be reasonably flat.

Tony O'Malley
Emmaus, PA

Step 1. Use a shim to set the rabbeting table for about a 1/16" cut. A layer or two of plastic laminate works well.

Step 2. Take a "rabbeting" cut into the face of the board. Set the fence so that you're cutting about half the width of the face.

Step 3. Tape the shim to the rabbeting table. Now plane the other half of the face with the previously cut portion riding on the shim.

Planing Wood

Reducing Planer Tear-Out

PROBLEM: *I often get tear-out when machine planing. How can I prevent this?*

SOLUTION: The first step is to read the grain of the wood and feed the board into the jointer or planer so that the cuts are made "with the grain." You can read the grain on the edge of a board, but a more reliable technique is to read the face and end grain, as shown at top right.

Another approach is to reduce the cutting angle by grinding a back bevel on the blades. The blades on most planers and jointers meet the wood at an angle between 50 and 60 degrees, as shown at bottom right. This cutting angle—designed more for cutting softwoods than hardwoods—produces an aggressive cut that tends to tear out the contrary grain on highly figured hardwoods.

Figured hardwoods cut much more cleanly with a scraping action, so I modify my planer and jointer blades to reduce their cutting angle. This involves back beveling the blades, as shown at bottom right. The back bevel results in a thicker cutting edge, which stays sharp longer. I send my blades and a drawing of the desired profile to a professional sharpening service for back beveling. When I get my blades back, I hone just the primary bevel (not the back bevel) with my 6,000-grit waterstone to remove the wire edge. The reduced cutting angle does limit the amount of wood you can take off in one pass, so take lighter cuts.

David J. Marks
Santa Rosa, CA

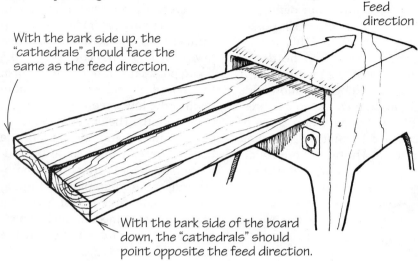

With the bark side up, the "cathedrals" should face the same as the feed direction.

Feed direction

With the bark side of the board down, the "cathedrals" should point opposite the feed direction.

To minimize tear-out when planing, you'll get better results if you read the end grain and face grain, rather than the edge grain.

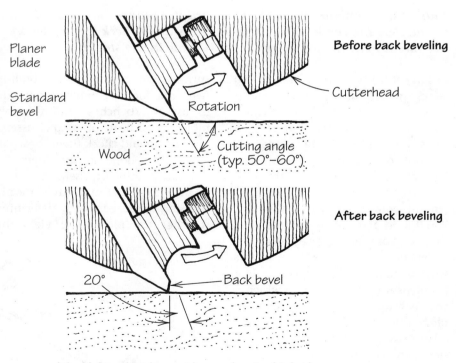

Planer blade

Standard bevel

Rotation

Wood

Cutting angle (typ. 50°–60°)

Before back beveling

Cutterhead

20°

Back bevel

After back beveling

A back bevel reduces the angle at which the wood fibers are cut, also reducing tear-out.

Avoiding Planer Snipe

PROBLEM: *My planer always leaves a "snipe" at the end of every board. What can I do?*

SOLUTION: First reduce the bed-roller height all the way to zero, and wax the bed. If you still get snipe, it's probably from deflection of the bed itself as the stock passes under the feed rollers. This can be minimized by reducing the downward pressure of the feed rollers. If your machine doesn't allow this adjustment, you can keep the pressure uniform by butting a piece of scrap before and after the stock you are surfacing. That way both rollers will exert pressure during the entire passage of the good piece.

Bob Moran
Emmaus, PA

ANOTHER VIEW: Planer snipe—a deeper cut across the end of a board—is caused by the pressure rollers. When you feed a board into the planer, only the infeed roller is in contact with the board for the first few inches of the cut. When the board passes under the outfeed roller, the board is pressed down more against the table, reducing the depth of cut slightly. The opposite sequence causes snipe at the back end of the board. You can limit snipe by supporting the board better and by properly adjusting your planer: Unplug the machine and adjust the feed rollers as explained in the owner's manual. If there are rollers on the bed of the planer, make sure that they are positioned properly, too.

These other techniques will also limit sniping:

- Always joint one face of a boards before planing so that there is no cup or twist; planing twisted boards is a sure way to force the rollers out of alignment.
- Use roller stands to support long boards.
- When planing more than one board, butt the boards end to end as you feed them through, so that the feed rollers are under constant pressure.
- As a final resort, rough-cut each piece long enough to allow for cutting off the snipe after planing.

Ben Erickson
Eutaw, AL

Using Winding Sticks to Check Stock

PROBLEM: *I sometimes find that a board I've planed flat has twisted by the time I'm ready to use it. Is there a way to check for this before I've already cut the joints and invested time in the stock?*

SOLUTION: Use a pair of winding sticks, which are simply straight sticks. The use of winding sticks is based on the principle that parallel lines lie in the same plane. To demonstrate, hold a straight stick horizontal at arm's length, and another one horizontal at half arm's length. Now sight across the two. You'll find it easy to tilt them so they're close to perfectly parallel. When laid across workpieces in this way, winding sticks are convenient for measuring the degree to which a case is torqued, a plank twists, or a plane sole is not dead flat.

For example, I learned early on to sight across the pair of sawhorses that I use for assembly supports. My barn floor can create nonparallel support surfaces, which could yield a built-in twist in a door or cabinet. If you plan to use workbenches and assembly tables for accurate planing or assembly, you should check them for winding if you hope to use them for accurate planing or assembly.

On a twisted rough-sawn plank, winding sticks can help determine whether the plank will yield the thickness you need once the twist is planed out. To find out, place your winding sticks across each end of the plank, step back, and sight across them. Shim up one end of either stick until both of the sticks are parallel.

I keep stable, 1/2-inch-square × 12-inch-long teak rippings handy for checking wooden plane soles and for planks or frames up to 12 inches wide and 5 feet long. For larger work, I turn the nearest long, straight scrap strips into instant winding sticks.

Ric Hanisch
Quakertown, PA

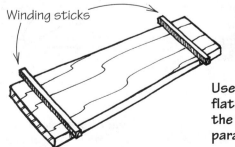

Winding sticks

Use winding sticks to gauge flatness. If the top edges of the winding sticks are not parallel, the board is twisted.

Planing Short Stock

PROBLEM: *I have some cutoffs that are too beautiful to discard but too short to feed through my planer. How can I safely thickness short boards?*

SOLUTION: A router can thickness short stock easily. All you need is a carriage to guide the router across the stock. I made my carriage by inserting the guide bars that came with my router through two lengths of hardwood, as shown at right. If necessary you can buy aluminum or steel rods that are the right length and diameter for your router.

To use the router as a thicknesser, first lock the fence guide bars into the router base and fit the bars to your hardwood guides. Then secure the stock to the bench with double-sided tape. It is important that the bench be perfectly flat; otherwise any twist in the bench can be transferred to the material. Lock a wide straight bit into the collet of the router, and take progressively deeper cuts while running the skids along the bench surface.

Robert Treanor
San Francisco, CA

With the router's guide bars inserted through holes in the blocks, and the stock attached to the bench with double-sided tape, rout the surface of a board until it's flat.

ANOTHER VIEW: There is a safe way to surface short pieces, although it does take a little time. Cut or hand plane the edges of the pieces to make a half-decent gluing surface. Then glue two runners to the edges. The runners should be slightly thicker than the pieces that you are surfacing and at least 12 to 14 inches long.

Try to keep the runners as close to parallel as possible during glue up. Once the glue dries, you can joint and plane the assembly just as you would a longer board, as shown at left.

If you have several short pieces to surface, you can glue them between a single pair of runners; just make sure that the pieces are all the same width.

Ken Burton
New Tripoli, PA

Given the high cost of wood, it can pay to make good use of scraps. Once this piece of walnut is planed to the right thickness, the runners will be cut away, leaving a usable piece that might otherwise have been tossed in the burn bin.

Planing Thin Stock

PROBLEM: *When I plane thin stock, it tears out severely. How can I stop this from happening?*

SOLUTION: There are two common obstacles to planing thin stock with a thickness planer. First, some machines have a stop that keeps the knives from getting very close to the table. Second, the feed rollers on some planers can obstruct thin stock or lift it off the bed, causing it to self-destruct.

A scrap of laminated particleboard with a cleat screwed to the back edge makes an excellent planer board. With it you can plane stock to ⅛" or less without tear-out.

The simple solution to both problems is to make a removable "planer board" that provides an elevated continuous table for the wood to ride on, as shown above. My own board is a piece of ¾-inch medium-density fiberboard (MDF) the width of the planer table, with a cleat underneath to keep it from feeding through the machine. I wax the MDF occasionally to reduce friction; a melamine or plastic laminate surface would probably work even better. In any case, avoid using rough-surfaced materials, like construction-grade plywood or raw particleboard.

The planer board should sit flat on the entire planer table. On a machine with table rollers, you can either lower the rollers beneath the table surface or cut shallow dadoes in the planer board to bridge them. A planer board has no side rails to keep stock from drifting off, but this isn't a problem as long as you feed the stock straight in.

Planing stock as thin as 1/8 inch with a planer board should be easy on a well-tuned machine with sharp knives. In fact, you should be able to plane material as thin as 1/16 inch, but use stock 6 inches longer than necessary because you can expect some snipe at the ends of the board.

Peter Korn
Rockport, ME

Preventing Warp after Planing

PROBLEM: *My wood warps after planing or resawing. How can I prevent this?*

SOLUTION: Two conditions cause wood to warp after planing or resawing. The first is uneven moisture content in the wood. This may reverse itself once the wood has reached equilibrium with the air in your shop. Stack the planed wood on stickers and check it after it has dried for a couple of weeks. A fan blowing air through the stack will aid in drying.

A second cause of wood warp is uneven internal stress. In this case, cutting up the wood into shorter parts is about all you can do.

AVOIDING THE PROBLEM: Resawing almost always yields some warping. To allow for this, resaw so that the wood is oversized; then sticker it and let it adjust to shop conditions before you begin the final planing.

Ben Erickson
Eutaw, AL

Reducing Hand Plane Tear-Out

PROBLEM: *I'm trying to hand plane an oak panel, but I'm getting a lot of tear-out. What can I do to reduce it?*

SOLUTION: Tear-out occurs as wood fibers split apart in front of the plane's cutting edge. It can have several causes. Assuming that the blade is sharp, the problem might be the flatness of the plane's sole or the size of the mouth opening. You can check flatness with a straightedge and correct it by rubbing the sole against silicon-carbide sandpaper.

More than anything else, a small mouth opening will help eliminate tear-out. Adjust the frog to move the blade forward, leaving a very small gap in front of the blade. That way, the section of the sole that is immediately in front of the blade will hold down the wood fibers so that they can't tear out. Set the blade for a very light cut, and make sure it is clamped securely by the lever cap.

Of course, not all boards can be hand planed without tear-out, no matter how well your plane is tuned. Planing at a diagonal to the grain can help. Your best bet, though, may be to use a scraper plane or cabinet scraper, either of which will surface contrary wood with no tear-out whatsoever.

Peter Korn
Rockport, ME

Surface Planing with a Hand Plane

PLANING A BOARD FLAT WITH HAND PLANES *may seem like an impossible chore. But if you have a board that's wider than your planer, your only other option may be to rip the board into narrower parts, plane them, and then glue the parts back together. That will take a lot of time and usually will make a beautiful board less attractive.*

When you plane by hand, it's not the planing itself that's so difficult. It's getting the board flat and to an even thickness that's a challenge. So the task is really about gauging what you're starting with and knowing what areas to plane to make the board flat. Is it bowed, cupped, or twisted; or is it simply thicker at one end or along one edge than the other? Planing a board flat is essentially the process of reducing the high spots. Start by determining which areas need to be planed, as shown below left.

Cupping or bowing produces high spots that can be marked with chalk or a broad carpenter's pencil. You can then plane the marked areas with a jack plane, working in any convenient direction. When a straightedge can be held in any direction across the board without showing gaps anywhere under its edge, then the surface should be smoothed with a finely set smoothing plane, worked with the grain. After flattening one face, mark the thickness around the edges and ends and plane the opposite face down to those lines.

You can determine twisting by using a pair of winding sticks. See "Using Winding Sticks to Check Stock" on page 68. Place one stick at the end of the board, and position the second progressively farther from it, sighting across the tops of the sticks. If the surface is flat, the top edges of the sticks will be parallel; if the surface is twisted, however, one stick will angle up, indicating where the surface needs to be planed down further.

If a board is flat but thicker at one end, cut a narrow rabbet in the thick end and place one winding stick on this shelf. Make the top edge of this winding stick parallel to the top of the other stick that is placed at the thin end of the board, as shown below right. Now you can plane down the remainder of the board to the level of the rabbet and the faces will be parallel.

Graham Blackburn
Bearsville, NY

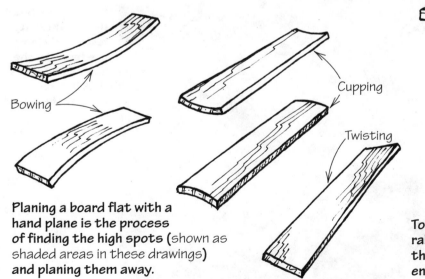

Bowing

Cupping

Twisting

Planing a board flat with a hand plane is the process of finding the high spots (shown as shaded areas in these drawings) **and planing them away.**

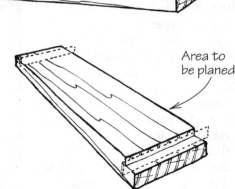

Area to be planed

To plane a board of uneven thickness, cut a rabbet in the thicker end, and plane down the area between the rabbet and the thin end. Use winding sticks to gauge flatness.

Resawing Thick Stock

Resawing on Track

PROBLEM: *I would like to resaw lumber on my band saw, but the blade wanders and sometimes bogs down in the cut. What's causing this, and how can I correct it?*

SOLUTION: Blade drift is a common problem on band saws. A band saw blade seeks its own cutting direction for a number of reasons, including the set and condition of the teeth. Whatever the reasons for drift, the way to compensate for it is by setting a fence parallel to the feed direction.

One way to do this is to make an L-shaped fence of plywood or solid wood. Make it about as high as the stock you want to resaw and about as long as your band saw table. The vertical part of the L will support your stock; the horizontal part gets clamped to the table, as shown at top right.

To determine the angle at which to clamp your fence, use a scrap about 18 inches long. Joint one edge of it, and then gauge a line on it to the width of your desired resaw cut. Saw freehand along the cut line, allowing the blade to dictate the feed direction, as shown at top right. Halfway through the cut, turn off the saw while firmly holding the scrap to the saw table. Without moving the scrap, place your fence against it, clamp the fence to the table, and complete the rest of the cut, as shown at bottom right. If the blade doesn't fight the direction of the cut, you've found the right approach. Now you can cut your workpiece with this same fence setup.

Paul Anthony
Hellertown, PA

To determine a band saw's direction of "drift," scribe a cut line along the edge of an extra piece of stock, then cut along the line freehand.

Stop the saw after cutting about 8", hold the board firmly where it rests, and clamp the fence to the band saw table so that it rests against the board.

Keeping Resawed Boards Flat

PROBLEM: *Whenever I resaw boards, the stock goes wild, cupping and twisting. Can this be prevented?*

SOLUTION: Resawed stock has a tendency to cup. That's because resawing exposes the center of the stock, and the center often has a higher moisture content than the outside surfaces. The resulting moisture imbalance often leads to a cupped board. To minimize the problem, immediately clamp the resawed boards so that they're flat, then allow them to dry for several days. To allow air circulation, place a few wood spacers (stickers) between the boards before adding the clamps, as shown.

Tom Begnal
Kent, CT

Clamping resawed stock flat with stickers between each piece will allow the newly exposed inner surfaces of the wood to dry to a moisture content that is similar to the outside faces. Leave them clamped as long as possible—several days at least.

Resawing on the Table Saw

PROBLEM: *I want to resaw some boards, but I don't have a band saw. Can I use my table saw?*

SOLUTION: Definitely, but with some limitations. If I have one or two narrow pieces to resaw in half, I always turn to the table saw even though I have a band saw too. The table saw cuts quickly, and it's a snap to set up since the fence is right there waiting.

But even with a thin-kerfed blade, the table saw wastes more wood with each cut than the band saw does. So it's not my tool of choice if I'm trying to squeeze as many pieces out of a board as possible.

The table saw's depth of cut limits the width of boards you can resaw. On most 10-inch saws, figure about 6 inches as the maximum—that's a 3-inch full-depth cut from each edge of the board.

There is clearly more opportunity for mishap when resawing on the table saw. Thin pieces that have been cut from wide boards can sometimes buckle or split, and the results can be unpredictable and dangerous. Very thin pieces, such as those used for bent laminations, can slip down through the slot in the saw's table insert and stall the motor or kick back at you. A zero-clearance plywood insert will prevent this mishap.

For safe table saw resawing, you must start with boards that have one flat face to ride against the fence and an edge that is square to that face to ride against the table. Use a push stick and hold the board firmly against the fence. If you need to make a cut from each edge, flip the board end for end so that the same face is against the fence, as shown below.

Bob Moran
Emmaus, PA

If you resaw a board in a single pass, always use a push stick (*left*). To resaw wider boards, make a series of passes into each edge with the same face against the fence (*right*).

SHOP-MADE SOLUTIONS

LOG-MILLING BAND SAW SETUP BY JEFFRY LOHR

So you've salvaged a nice 10-inch-diameter walnut tree that your neighbor was about to cut up for firewood. But resawing a log of this size into planks on a 14-inch band saw looks intimidating, even dangerous.

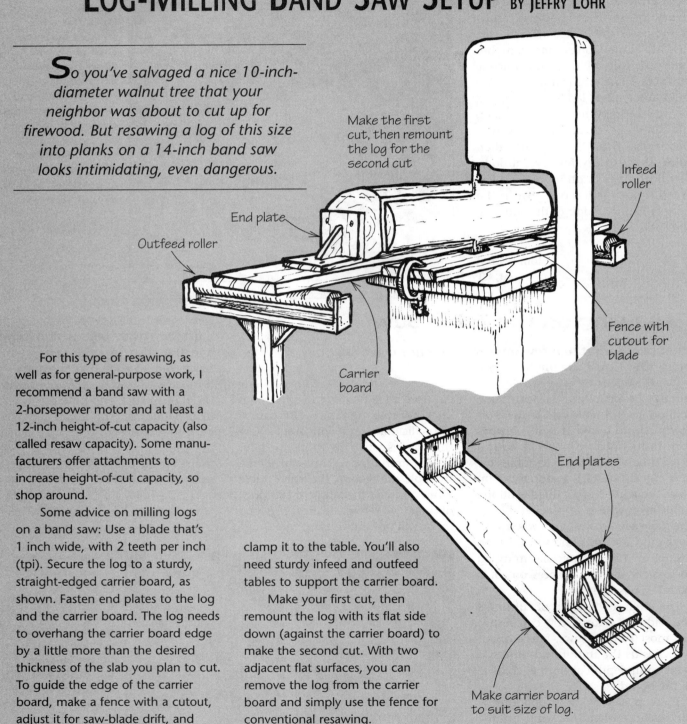

Make the first cut, then remount the log for the second cut

Infeed roller

End plate

Outfeed roller

Fence with cutout for blade

Carrier board

End plates

Make carrier board to suit size of log.

For this type of resawing, as well as for general-purpose work, I recommend a band saw with a 2-horsepower motor and at least a 12-inch height-of-cut capacity (also called resaw capacity). Some manufacturers offer attachments to increase height-of-cut capacity, so shop around.

Some advice on milling logs on a band saw: Use a blade that's 1 inch wide, with 2 teeth per inch (tpi). Secure the log to a sturdy, straight-edged carrier board, as shown. Fasten end plates to the log and the carrier board. The log needs to overhang the carrier board edge by a little more than the desired thickness of the slab you plan to cut. To guide the edge of the carrier board, make a fence with a cutout, adjust it for saw-blade drift, and clamp it to the table. You'll also need sturdy infeed and outfeed tables to support the carrier board.

Make your first cut, then remount the log with its flat side down (against the carrier board) to make the second cut. With two adjacent flat surfaces, you can remove the log from the carrier board and simply use the fence for conventional resawing.

Working with Veneer

Preparing Veneer Joints

PROBLEM: *I want to cut a batch of veneer to one size, then join the pieces in pairs. Is there any way to cut them in a batch instead of one at a time?*

SOLUTION: Thin sheets of veneer are difficult to deal with; but when preparing them for joining, a thick caul helps to guide and control very unwieldy pieces. Depending on the length and the width of the material, I will use 8/4 (eight-quarter) or 4/4 (four-quarter) construction-grade fir to hold the veneer together in a bundle while running it through the jointer or table saw. To apply pressure equally, I shape the caul so that the middle is thicker than either end, as shown. I make the cauls a bit longer than the veneer that I'm handling so that they can be screwed together with drywall screws to hold the veneer firmly. The sequence of drawings shows how I use the cauls to joint and saw a batch of veneer.

E. E. "Skip" Benson
Camden, ME

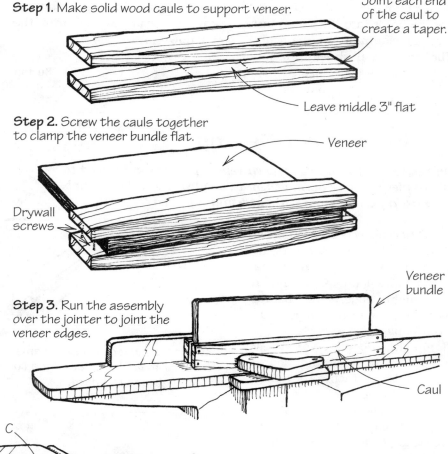

Step 1. Make solid wood cauls to support veneer.

Joint each end of the caul to create a taper.

Leave middle 3" flat

Step 2. Screw the cauls together to clamp the veneer bundle flat.

Veneer

Drywall screws

Step 3. Run the assembly over the jointer to joint the veneer edges.

Veneer bundle

Caul

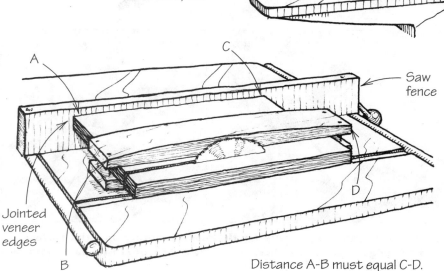

A

C

Saw fence

D

Jointed veneer edges

B

Distance A-B must equal C-D.

Step 4. Butt the jointed edge of the veneer against the saw fence, then move the cauls to the opposite edge of the veneer and position them so that they are parallel to the jointed edge of the veneer.

Step 5. Saw the veneer just wide of the caul, then joint the sawed edges as in Step 3.

Registering Veneer

PROBLEM: *I've had some trouble with veneer slipping out of position when I'm trying to glue up. How can I prevent this?*

SOLUTION: The best way to get veneer to stay where you want it is to tack it to the substrate with small brads before clamping. Cut both the veneer and the substrate so that they are slightly larger than the size you want for your finished piece. Drive the brads into the excess just before you clamp up. Set the heads so that they are flush with the surface. Two brads per veneered face are all that are required—one at each end of a centerline running with the grain. Don't tack down the corners, or you'll prevent the veneer from expanding as it picks up moisture from the glue; this can cause the veneer to buckle or split. After the glue dries, you can cut away the brads as you trim the piece down to size.

Ken Burton
New Tripoli, PA

Use small brads, one at each end, to keep veneer from sliding around at glue-up. Make sure the brads are in the waste area that will get cut off.

Routing Veneer Seams

PROBLEM: *I want to make my own veneer panels, and I need to join two pieces before gluing them to a substrate. What's the best way to get a perfect seam without using a jointer?*

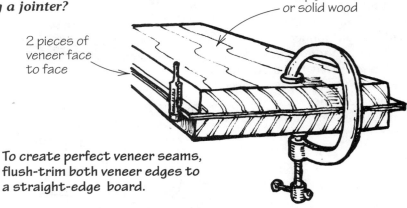

3/4" plywood
or solid wood

2 pieces of
veneer face
to face

To create perfect veneer seams, flush-trim both veneer edges to a straight-edge board.

SOLUTION: Find two boards, preferably hardwood, one with a perfectly straight edge. You can also use pieces of plywood as long as one has a dead-straight edge. The boards should be a few inches longer than the veneer pieces.

Clamp the two pieces of veneer face to face between the boards with about 1/16 inch protruding. Then trim the veneer with a flush-trimming router bit against the lower-board edge, as shown at left. I prefer to move the router in a climb-cutting direction to prevent chipping. By the way, you can also trim the veneer using a sharp plane. Once you start skimming the edges of the boards, stop.

To assemble veneer before pressing, I use clear packaging tape, as shown at right. It's always on hand, easier to apply, and far easier to remove than paper-and-glue veneer tapes.

Tony O'Malley
Emmaus, PA

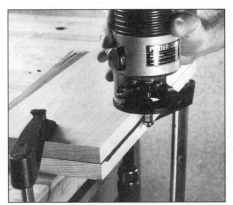

After you rout the edges (*left*), lay the seams together on a flat surface, butt the edges tightly together, and apply a strip of plastic packaging tape along the entire seam (*right*).

Cutting Veneered Plywood without Tear-Out

PROBLEM: *I get very frustrated when I cut plywood across the face grain on my table saw. Regardless of what I try, the veneer at the edge of the cut tears out. How can I get better cuts?*

SOLUTION: There are several things you can do to alleviate the problem. You may get good results by implementing one of them, or you may have to try them all.

Always cut with the good face up. Plywood nearly always has an A side and a B (or C) side. The saw blade cuts downward into the veneer facing upward and will tear out less than the veneer on the bottom side. Also, the higher you raise the blade, the less it will tend to tear the top veneer. Raising the blade, however, *increases* tear-out on the bottom veneer where the blade exits the cut and also makes it a more dangerous process with all that excess blade exposed.

Use a good blade. Most woodworkers are quick to blame their blades. True, a 60- or 80-tooth carbide blade with an alternate top bevel (ATB) grind is the first choice for cutting plywood, but a top-quality blade is quite expensive. Instead, you can buy a good-quality 36-tooth combination blade for less than half as much

that will serve you especially well if you use these tips.

Check the saw's arbor. If a new blade still produces tear-out, you may have excess vibration or wobble in the saw arbor. Woodworking supply houses sell inexpensive saw blade stabilizers, which are basically two large metal washers that fit on each side of the saw blade to reduce flexing. They may reduce your depth of cut, but that should not be a problem when you're cutting plywood.

Use a zero-clearance insert. The standard metal throat plate that comes with most table saws has an extra-wide opening to allow you to set the blade at any angle between 45 and 90 degrees. This wide slot leaves the wood on the bottom face unsupported and allows more tear-out. To get cleaner cuts on the bottom face, make or buy a zero-clearance insert, as shown on this page. They're easy to make from $1/2$-inch hardwood plywood. Trace the pattern of your existing insert onto the plywood

and cut it out on the band saw. Then file and sand it to fit. Once it fits well, you can make a whole batch by flush-trimming each one against the first one. If the plywood is slightly thick and sits proud of the saw table, sand the face until it is level. If it is too thin, drill and add small setscrews into the four corners and adjust the screws until the insert is flush with the table surface. Clamp across the insert with a piece of scrap wood to hold it securely while you start the saw and raise the saw blade up through the wood. Zero-clearance inserts also prevent small scraps from being sucked down between the blade and the throat plate.

Score and tape the cut line. This technique is really two tips that work well together. After marking your measurements, wrap the cut line in masking tape. Next, use a marking knife or utility knife to scribe the line through the tape. Scoring the cut precuts the surface veneer. The tape helps hold down any wood splinters that might otherwise get lifted by the blade. When making the cut, keep the blade to the waste side of the line.

Make the cut in two passes. Some professional cabinet shops employ table saws equipped with a small blade in front of the primary blade. The smaller blade scores the surface veneer before the larger blade makes the cut. You can produce the same effect with any saw simply by making the cut in two steps. For the first pass, raise the blade so that the teeth just score the wood—about $1/32$ inch. Then, without moving the fence, adjust the blade height to finish the cut.

A zero-clearance insert reduces tear-out when you cut veneered plywood.

David Page
Swarthmore, PA
and
Joe Wajszczuk
Jersey City, NJ

CUTTING AND SIZING
SOLUTIONS

RIPPING LUMBER

Ripping Thin Stock	79
Safe Ripping on the Table Saw	80
Ripping Thick Stock	80
Repeat Fence-Setting Jig	82
Ripping Beveled Stock	83
Using Angle Iron for Straight Rips	83

CROSSCUTTING LUMBER

Crosscutting Long Pieces	84
Crosscutting with a Miter Saw	85
Making Miters on Small Parts	85
Wider Cuts on a Miter Saw	85
Crosscutting Delicate Stock	86
Working with a Balky Miter Gauge	86
Squaring Off Unwieldy Stock	87
Setting Up Compound Miter Cuts	88

Crosscutting Small Stock on the Table Saw	88
Making Accurate Picture Frames	90
Setting Up Narrow Crosscuts	92
Crosscutting Acute Angles	92
Squaring Off an Odd-Shaped Workpiece	93
Crosscutting Wide Pieces	93

CUTTING SHEET GOODS

Cutting Plywood for Best Yield	94
Sawing Odd-Shaped Panels	94
Cutting Large Panels on the Table Saw	95

OTHER SIZING PROBLEMS

Cutting Polygons on the Table Saw	96
Cutting to Fit As You Go	96
"Stretching" Special Boards	97
Band-Sawing Delicate Material	97

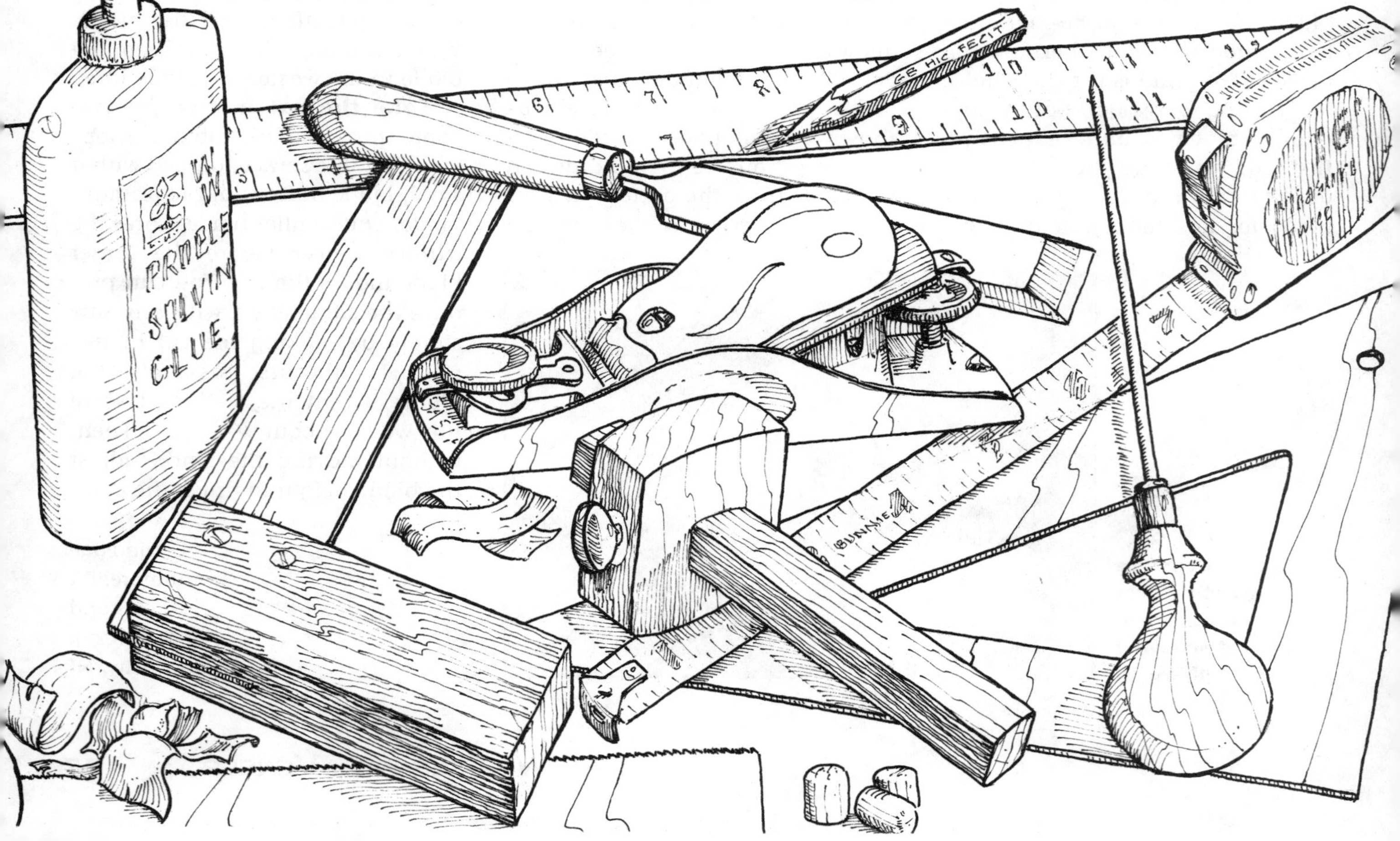

Ripping Lumber

Ripping Thin Stock

PROBLEM: *When I rip thin stock, the wood sometimes vibrates and self-destructs. Can I do anything to prevent this?*

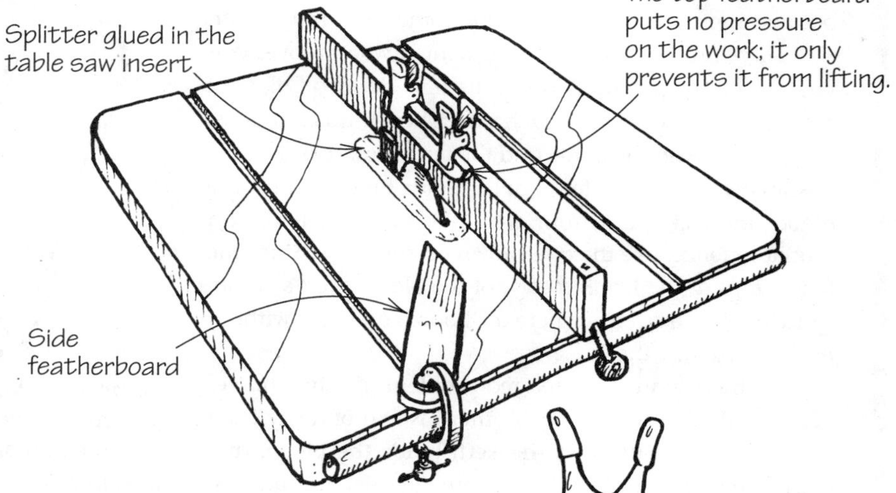

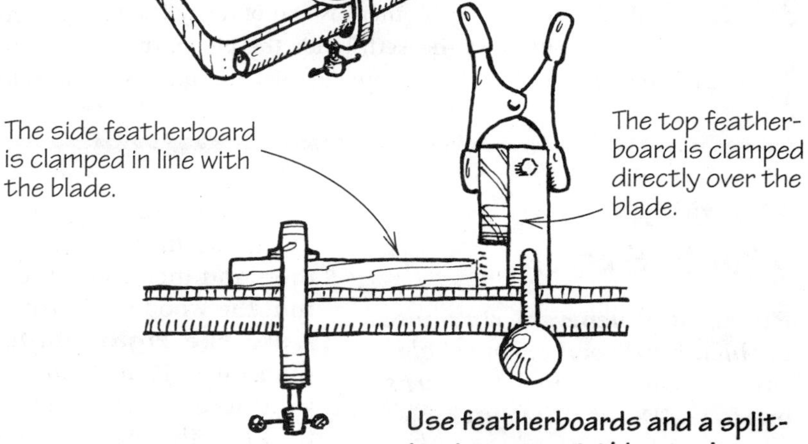

SOLUTION: I often make picture frame molding as small as ½ inch square, and pieces like these tend to vibrate as your stock does. One solution I've found to reduce the movement is to add a small splitter and provide a track or tunnel that the work can ride through as you make the cut.

First extend the slot in a zero-clearance table insert back beyond the blade, as shown. You can glue in a wooden splitter that will keep the kerf open and guide both the work and the offcut safely beyond the table. Then to add even more control, clamp a featherboard directly ahead of the blade to press the wood against the fence and dampen vibration.

Also, such thin work has a tendency to ride up on the back of the blade. To prevent this, I usually add another featherboard directly over the cut to hold the work to the table the whole distance it's in contact with the blade.

With such a setup, the entire run of the molding is uniform; there are no blade tracks, which can result from work moving around; and feeding the saw becomes straightforward, so that you're in control rather than tense and anxious—a real safety bonus. When I'm ripping multiples,

each stick pushes the previous one through the tunnel. The last stick can be pulled through at the outfeed side, which would be extremely dangerous without the featherboards.

Jim Cummins
Woodstock, NY

Splitter glued in the table saw insert

Side featherboard

The top featherboard puts no pressure on the work; it only prevents it from lifting.

The side featherboard is clamped in line with the blade.

The top featherboard is clamped directly over the blade.

Use featherboards and a splitter to support thin stock so that it doesn't vibrate during the cut. Run the stock through the "tunnel" created by the featherboards.

SAFE RIPPING ON THE TABLE SAW

Ripping on a table saw is quite straightforward, as long as your stock has a flat surface, a straight edge, and no internal stresses that will make it change shape as you saw it. The catch is that boards that have moved from the lumberyard to your shop may no longer be flat and straight, and you seldom know whether a board has internal stresses until you're partway through ripping it.

Internal stresses occur when one portion of a board has a tendency to bend in one direction while an adjacent portion has a tendency to bend in a different direction. The halves of a board with internal stresses will bend in opposite directions if you saw the two halves apart. When they do, they can bind against the blade, or one part can become wedged between the blade and the rip fence. While these stresses are not common, they cause accidents because most woodworkers tend to forget they may occur.

There are two types of stress-related wood movement you need to be prepared for. In the first, the two halves of a board bend away from each other. When this happens, the part between the blade and the fence assumes a curve, pushes away from the fence at its center, binds against the blade, and kicks back. Your defense is to routinely use an auxiliary fence, like the one shown on this page. Since the fence stops at the leading edge of the blade, there's empty space beyond the fence where the board can curve without pushing against the fence.

In the second stress-related problem, the two halves of a board bend toward each other instead of away from each other. This narrows the kerf, binds the blade, and causes the wood to kick back. Your first defense against

this is to routinely use the splitter that table saws come equipped with. This is not a total defense, however, because the board may bind on the splitter itself, making it difficult to feed the board. So your second defense

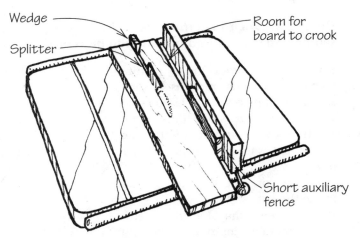

Wedge

Splitter

Room for board to crook

Short auxiliary fence

To prevent boards that crook from kicking back, install a short auxiliary fence. To stop boards that pinch the blade from kicking back, use a splitter and jam a wedge into the kerf.

Ripping Thick Stock

PROBLEM: *Whenever I rip a piece of thick hardwood on my table saw, the edge of the stock burns or glazes. What's the cure?*

SOLUTION: There are a number of things that can cause the wood to burn—and there are a number of possible remedies. I'd suggest you try the following steps:

Check your fence. Your fence should be dead parallel with your blade. If it's even slightly toed in,

your stock will be pinched between the blade and the fence, creating drag and increasing the likelihood that the wood will burn.

Use the right blade. For ripping on a 10-inch table saw, you want to use a sharp blade with 24 to 40 teeth and an alternate top bevel (ATB) configuration. Blades with more teeth tend to bog down because they don't have enough gullet space to efficiently remove the long-grain chips that result from ripping. If you've got the right blade mounted on your saw, check to see that it's sharp and free

of pitch. Dull or dirty blades can also cause burning and glazing.

Switch to a thinner or smaller blade. Obviously, with a more powerful motor, your saw will be less likely to bog down in a cut and burn the wood. But if you'd rather not spring for a new motor, you can improve power less expensively by investing in a thin-kerf blade or a blade with a smaller diameter—say an 8-inch blade for a 10-inch saw. Thin-kerf blades improve performance because there's less metal hammering into the wood, and therefore less resistance. With a is to keep a wedge, like a shim shingle or a stubby screwdriver, handy. As soon as you notice the kerf closing against the splitter, turn off the saw and insert the wedge into the kerf behind the splitter, as shown on the opposite page. Push it in far enough to relieve pressure on the splitter, then turn on the saw and continue.

You also may run into ripping problems if the edge of a board following the rip fence isn't straight. In this case, the board feeds along a crooked line, causing the blade to bind in the kerf and kick back. Check for straightness by sighting down the edge or by holding a straightedge against it. (The straightedge should be at least as long as your table saw's rip fence; the rip fence itself can be the straightedge.) If you find humps or hollows, remove them on the jointer or with a hand plane. If both edges of the board are so wildly irregular that

straightening one of them will be a major undertaking, you can attach a straightedge to the stock and run it against the fence to rip the opposite edge.

The remaining difficulty is ripping a board that isn't flat. If a board rocks on the saw table or twists as you feed it, it will bind on the blade even though you're feeding it in a straight line. The best defense against this possibility is to flatten the board on the jointer or with a hand plane before ripping it. You will need to flatten it before using it in your project anyway. However, if a board is too wide for your jointer or if flattening it across its full width will make it too thin, then you need to look for other solutions. The best alternative is to rip the board with a band saw or portable circular saw. Or, if the board is no more than 3 or 4 feet long and has a modest amount of cup, you can usually prevent binding on the table saw by using an auxiliary rip fence, sawing with the convex side down, and maintaining downward pressure just on the fence side of the cut line, as shown on this page.

Bob Moran
Emmaus, PA

Press down here.

Auxiliary rip fence

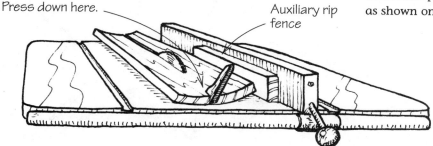

To rip cupped boards safely, saw with the cupped side up and apply downward pressure in the center.

smaller-diameter blade, you're reducing tip speed while increasing torque. This reduces the likelihood that the saw will bog down.

Check your power. You're not going to get full power out of a 20-amp motor if you're using a 15-amp extension cord. Also, if your saw is on the same circuit as a major power drain, like your dust collector, you may not be getting all of the electricity you need. For best performance, your saw should be on a separate 20-amp circuit.

Study your feed rate. I've listed this last, but it may be something you

want to consider early on. If you're feeding the wood too slowly, your blade can heat up in the cut and distort slightly, causing it to bind in the cut and burn or glaze the wood.

Of course, none of these cures may help if you're working a species like cherry, which is notoriously prone to burning. In this case, your best bet may be to rip your stock $1/32$ inch wider than you need and then clean up the edge with a sharp hand plane.

Kevin Ireland
Wescosville, PA

Ripping thick stock is not intimidating if you've got the right blade and ample power.

REPEAT FENCE-SETTING JIG BY ROB YODER

You know the situation: You've got your saw's rip fence set for a specific cut when you realize you're one part short on another operation and you need to move the fence to cut that part. How do you get your fence back to the original setting without a lot of fussing and fudging? Use this little device. It's especially useful for alternating between two fence settings, and it works on the table saw or a router table with miter gauge slots.

To make the jig, cut the parts according to the dimensions provided in the "Materials List." You can make the fence-setting bars longer to expand the jig's capacity. The miter gauge bar should fit perfectly, yet slide smoothly, in your miter gauge slot. Cut the dado for the miter gauge bar and glue the bar in. Then cut the dadoes for the fence-setting bars. Cut the rabbets in the ends of the locking plate. Drill the hole through the locking plate and the base, and assemble the jig.

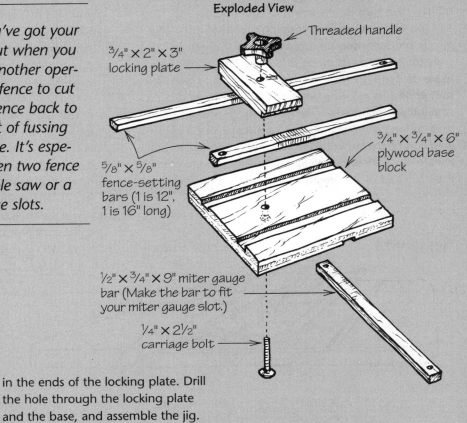

Exploded View

Threaded handle

3/4" × 2" × 3" locking plate

3/4" × 3/4" × 6" plywood base block

5/8" × 5/8" fence-setting bars (1 is 12", 1 is 16" long)

1/2" × 3/4" × 9" miter gauge bar (Make the bar to fit your miter gauge slot.)

1/4" × 2 1/2" carriage bolt

MATERIALS LIST		
Part	**Quantity**	**Dimensions**
Base	1	3/4" × 3/4" × 6"
Miter gauge bar*	1	1/2" × 3/4" × 9"
Fence-setting bar	1	5/8" × 5/8" × 12"
Fence-setting bar	1	5/8" × 5/8" × 16"
Locking plate	1	3/4" × 2" × 3"
HARDWARE		
Carriage bolt	1	1/4" × 2 1/2"
Threaded handle	1	1/4"

*Make to fit the miter gauge slot on your saw

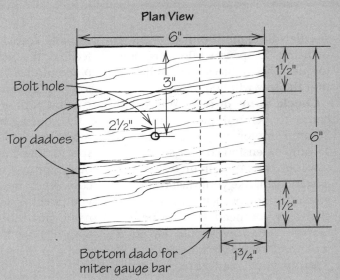

Plan View

6"

Bolt hole

Top dadoes

3"

2 1/2"

1 1/2"

6"

1 1/2"

Bottom dado for miter gauge bar

1 3/4"

Ripping Beveled Stock

PROBLEM: *I tried to rip some stock that has a beveled edge, and I really botched the cut when the beveled edge slipped under the bottom of my fence. How can I make this kind of cut accurately?*

SOLUTION: This problem has caught everybody at least once. The best solution is to plan the sequence of cuts so you can rip the piece with the point of the bevel riding up on the fence rather than down below, where it will invariably slip under the fence. Sometimes you can just flip the work over to reorient the bevel; at other times you have to make the bevel cut last.

Another solution to the problem is to make an auxiliary fence that's faced with aluminum flashing, bent out at the bottom to form a lip that covers the gap. This raises the edge of the board just slightly, affecting the angle of the cut without creating a noticeable difference, for most work. My decided preference would be to plan ahead rather than make a jig to "catch up."

Jim Cummins
Woodstock, NY

When you rip with a beveled edge against the fence, have the point of the bevel up so that it can't slip under the fence.

To register a fence setting so you can return to it, place the jig in the miter gauge slot, slide one of the bars against the fence, and lock the handle. To register a second fence setting, reverse the jig and repeat the process. Be sure to hold the first bar still while setting the second.

Quick Tip Quick Tip Quick Tip Quick

USING ANGLE IRON FOR STRAIGHT RIPS

Here's a trick I use for straightening crooked or wavy-edged stock. Simply tape a piece of angle iron to the concave edge of the board to serve as a straightedge. For thin stock, block up the angle iron so that it doesn't drag on the table. Pass the board through the saw with the flat edge of the angle iron against the rip fence. Remove the angle iron, flip the board, and pass it through the saw again for a straight board with parallel sides.

Mark Torpey
Madison, NJ

A length of angle iron taped to a rough-edged board allows a straight rip cut to be made.

Crosscutting Lumber

Crosscutting Long Pieces

PROBLEM: *I use my table saw for making crosscuts, but when I need to crosscut a long piece of stock, I have trouble supporting the off end. This makes getting true 90-degree cuts difficult. What can I do?*

SOLUTION: The tendency in crosscutting long pieces on the table saw is for the off end to "trail" behind as the piece passes through the blade, throwing the cut out-of-square. A radial arm saw or sliding compound miter saw solves the problem by moving the saw blade, not the heavy wood. But if you don't have those options, try the simple combination shown below. The crosscut sled is made from plywood and scrap hardwood and has hardwood runners that ride in the table saw's miter gauge slots to keep the sled parallel to the blade. The modified sawhorse sits to the left of your saw to support the long end of your stock as you run it past the blade. You can make the horse quickly from 2 × 4 lumber or scrap, but make sure that the top bearing piece is hardwood—the harder the better. Blunt the point of the bearing piece slightly by taking a couple of passes with a hand plane, then sand it and wax it to diminish friction. Or, to take it a step further, table saw a kerf down the center of the point on the bearing piece and epoxy in a strip of thin metal. File and sand it smooth, then wax it. Your stock will run smoothly across this surface.

To further support your stock, you can clamp it to the sled. Then one hand can support and help push the board while the other pushes the sled.

David Page
Swarthmore, PA

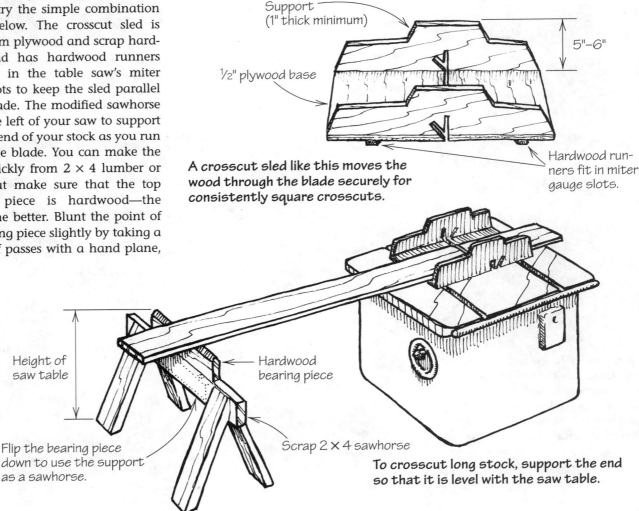

Support
(1" thick minimum)

½" plywood base

5"–6"

Hardwood runners fit in miter gauge slots.

A crosscut sled like this moves the wood through the blade securely for consistently square crosscuts.

Height of saw table

Hardwood bearing piece

Flip the bearing piece down to use the support as a sawhorse.

Scrap 2 × 4 sawhorse

To crosscut long stock, support the end so that it is level with the saw table.

Crosscutting with a Miter Saw

PROBLEM: *I need to crosscut some rough lumber to shorter lengths on my electric miter saw, but it's an awkward and scary operation. How can I make these cuts safely?*

SOLUTION: Rough-cutting unplaned boards creates tension in the wood, often causing the saw kerf to close like the "jaws of death" on your saw blade. This can happen with any type of saw, including handsaws. Also, since unplaned boards are rarely straight or flat, they tend to move when you cut them, often forcing the blade to bind in the cut. You might find that the safest way to make these cuts is by using a portable circular saw; but a miter saw can do the job, too, if you follow a few simple guidelines:

Support the stock. To keep the wood from binding, you need to keep it level and square to the blade. We've built outriggers and fences on both sides of our miter saw that hold the wood level with the saw table and in line with saw fence. If you don't want to go to this trouble, you could just set up the miter saw on a counter or even the shop floor and install scrap-wood blocking to the left and right of the blade to support your work.

Orient your stock. If a board is obviously cupped or bowed, position it so that the concave face is up and the crowned edge is against the fence.

Cut wide stock with two plunges. Cut halfway through the width of the wood with the first stroke, then flip the wood over and complete the cut.

Bill and Joanne Storch
Corvallis, OR

Making Miters on Small Parts

PROBLEM: *How can I make repetitive angled cuts in pieces that are too small to be safely run through the table saw?*

SOLUTION: You can make accurate angled cuts using a modified bench hook, as shown on this page, which works as a one-sided miter box. The base and the front hook are pretty much like those on any other bench hook. What's different is the back hook, which is wide and tall. (I make mine no less than 2 × 2 inches.) Use a protractor or square on the back hook to lay out the angles you want to cut. Then carefully saw them with a dovetail saw or a backsaw. You can now align your workpiece with one of these custom miter slots and precisely and safely cut your work.

Graham Blackburn
Bearsville, NY

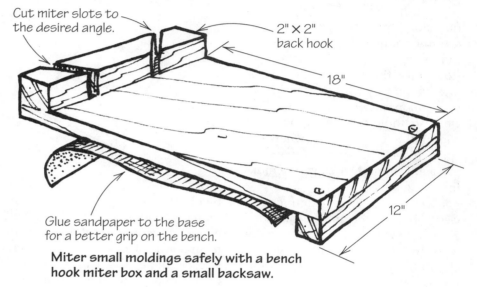

Cut miter slots to the desired angle.

2" × 2" back hook

18"

12"

Glue sandpaper to the base for a better grip on the bench.

Miter small moldings safely with a bench hook miter box and a small backsaw.

Quick Tip

WIDER CUTS ON A MITER SAW

If you've done any amount of work on a miter saw, you've probably come up against a board that was just a hair too wide for your saw. The obvious solution is to make the most of the cut and then flip the board to finish it. But chances are if you do that, the last section of solid wood will break off as you turn the board, damaging your finished piece. Here's a better idea: Insert a piece of flat scrap under the workpiece to raise it. Since a chop saw cuts in an arc, raising the work will put it higher on the arc and increase the effective width of cut.

Kevin Ireland
Wescosville, PA

Crosscutting Delicate Stock

PROBLEM: *I need to square the ends of a batch of narrow, thin pieces. How can I support the wood so that it won't vibrate and blow up when it passes the blade on my table saw?*

SOLUTION: You can accurately and safely cut small pieces by running a piece of flat scrap through your saw to create a carrier, like the one shown at right. This carrier, with its edge flush with the saw blade, can ride along the fence, or it can have a runner attached to the bottom so that it will track in the miter gauge slot. Since the edge of the carrier lines up directly with the saw blade, you can position and clamp your work so that it's directly over the edge of the carrier—that's where the cut will be. This gives your workpiece full support when you're making a cut.

A De-Sta-Co lever-action clamp (see "Sources," beginning on page 298) often will work fine to hold the work, or you can make a simple clamp by tapping some brads into the carrier and snipping off the heads. When you press the work onto the brads, they'll hold it tightly enough to make the cut. If you plan to make a lot of cuts of the same size or angle, you can hot-glue a back support to the carrier and glue on stops to position the work without relying on the simple line-of-sight setup.

Jim Cummins
Woodstock, NY

Step 1. Run the scrap sheet stock by the blade to create a carrier that's flush with the edge of the saw blade.

Step 2. Align the layout mark on the workpiece with the edge of the carrier, clamp the workpiece to the carrier, then make the cut.

Step 3. For repeat cuts or angled cuts, hot-glue a back support and stop block to the carrier.

Working with a Balky Miter Gauge

PROBLEM: *When I crosscut with my miter gauge, the cuts are never consistent. Some end up square, some are more than 90 degrees, and some are less. What's the cause, and how can I fix this?*

SOLUTION: If your miter gauge doesn't fit tightly in the table slot, you can end up with the problems you've described. Also, if the gauge head isn't tight on the bar, you'll get errors. You can minimize the effect of play in the table slot by applying side pressure on the gauge so that the bar is always pressed against the side of the miter gauge slot when you cut. A better course of action, however, may be to ditch the miter gauge and instead use a crosscut sled for these cuts.

Bob Moran
Emmaus, PA

RELATED INFO:
Crosscutting Long Pieces, page 84

A modest size cross-cut sled is a good alternative to a miter gauge for most 90° cuts.

Squaring Off Unwieldy Stock

PROBLEM: *I need to square the end of a tabletop that's way too large to support with the miter gauge on my table saw. Any suggestions?*

SOLUTION: There are three methods you can use, all of which rely on clamping a straightedge to your stock. First you can let the edge of the saw table guide your work. Lay out your cutline, then measure back from this line and make a mark that is equal to the distance from the edge of the saw table to the outside edge of the saw blade. Clamp a straightedge *under* the board at this second mark, as shown in *Option 1*. Now you can run the board across the table using the straightedge as a fence that bears against the edge of the table saw.

If your workpiece is too big to handle on the table saw, clamp a straightedge across the top of the stock and make the cut with your circular saw, as shown in *Option 2*. For the best cut, use a fine-toothed saw blade.

Finally, you can rough out the cut on your band saw, then clamp the straightedge flush to the line and make a finishing cut with a router and flush-trimming bit, as shown in *Option 3*. With the last two options, you can reduce tearout by first scoring the cutline with a sharp razor or knife.

Tom Begnal
Kent, CT

> **RELATED INFO:**
> **Crosscutting Long Pieces,
> page 84**

Option 1: The Table Saw Edge. Lay out a line on the underside of the panel. Clamp a straightedge to the underside of the work and guide the straightedge against the edge of the saw table.

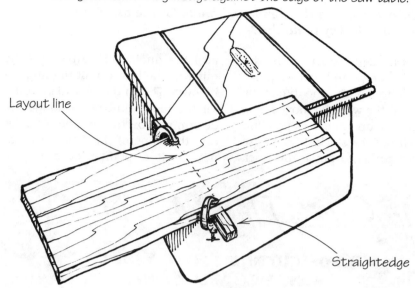

Layout line

Straightedge

Option 2: A Circular Saw. Clamp a straightedge to the top of the work and make a cut with the circular saw.

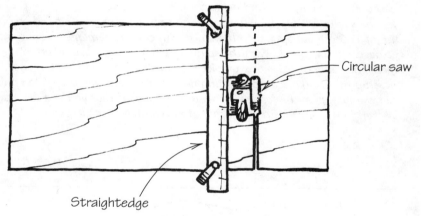

Circular saw

Straightedge

Option 3: A Router and Flush-Trimming Bit. Rough out the cut on the band saw, then clamp a straightedge to the underside of the work and rout to the line.

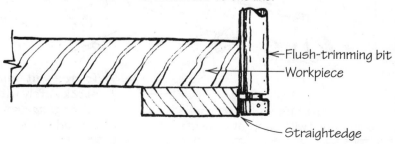

Flush-trimming bit
Workpiece

Straightedge

Setting Up Compound Miter Cuts

PROBLEM: *I want to make a set of planters, but I'm having a devil of a time determining the compound angle for the tapered sides. Is there a simple way to do this?*

SOLUTION: Let's start with the basics. A compound cut requires that simultaneously the blade be angled and the work be moved past the blade at an angle. Depending on the size of the stock, I try to use the miter gauge to guide the stock past the angled blade because the miter gauge has a built-in gauge of its own. The angle at which you'll set the blade and miter gauge are determined by the number of sides and the slope of the finished product, be it a planter or a picture frame. You can find the correct angle combinations listed in a compound miter angle chart, but you'll still be stuck with some trial and error. That's because the angles frequently are between degrees—29½ degrees, for example.

I learned of this solution from F. B. Woestemeyer, a New Jersey woodworker who figured a way to develop a template to find and set the angles with little measurement. His method lets you take the information you know (the number of sides and the slope angle) and use it to make a template block that will give you the information you want to know (the blade angle and the miter gauge angle). It's an ingenious example of pure applied geometry.

First plane a piece of scrap stock to about 1½ × 2½ × 16 inches. A piece of 2 × 3 will work, as long as all the sides are square. Rip this piece on edge with the blade tilted to the known slope angle that you want the assembled planter to have, as shown in *Step 1* on the opposite page. Let's say that the angle is 10 degrees; the blade will be set at 80 degrees to the table, or 10 degrees subtracted from 90.

Next reset the saw blade to whatever bevel angle you'd use on the edges of the pieces if the work were straight-sided (45 degrees for four sides, 30 degrees for six sides, for example). With the miter gauge set at 90 degrees, and the sawed face of the setup block facing up, crosscut the setup block, as shown in *Step 2*.

Now flip the setup block to the other side of the blade so that the sawed face is down and the beveled end is up, as shown in *Step 3*. With the beveled end snug up against the blade so that the entire leading edge is touching the blade, adjust the blade angle so that the blade lies flat against the beveled end.

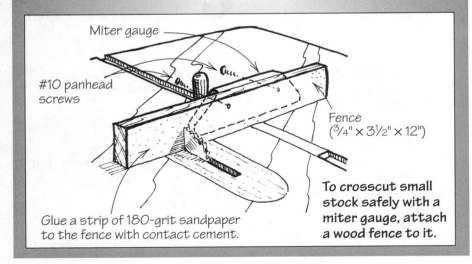

(Note: For a six-sided planter with a 10-degree slope, this will amount to only a ½-degree adjustment. The greater the slope and the fewer the number of sides, the larger this adjustment will be.) Finally, without moving the end of the setup block from the blade, slide the miter gauge up against the edge of the setup block and lock the miter gauge at the correct angle.

Now you're ready to make all the compound cuts. To make a container like a planter, crosscut all the parts to length first. Then cut one edge of each side first, as shown in the top photo. To cut the second edge, set a stop on an auxiliary fence and make all the cuts, as shown in the bottom photo.

Jim Cummins
Woodstock, NY

After using the set-up procedure shown in the drawings, cut one edge of all the sides first.

Step 1. Set the saw blade to the slope angle of the finished work, and rip a setup block on edge.

Blade angle = slope angle

2" × 3" setup block

Fence

Slope angle

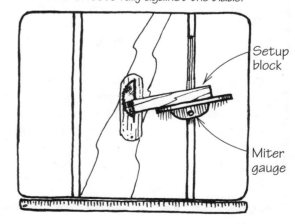

Then set a stop on an auxiliary fence to cut all the second edges with the pieces on the other side of the blade.

Step 2. Crosscut the end of the setup block with the sawed face up.

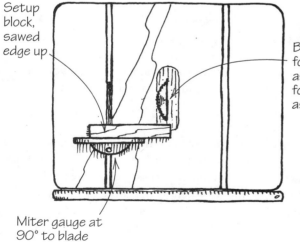

Setup block, sawed edge up

Blade at 30° for 6-sided assembly, 45° for 4-sided assembly, etc.

Miter gauge at 90° to blade

Step 3. Move the miter gauge to the opposite side of the blade. Flip the setup block so that the sawed face is down and the beveled end is against the blade. Adjust the blade angle and the miter gauge angle so the beveled end rests fully against the blade.

Setup block

Miter gauge

MAKING ACCURATE PICTURE FRAMES

You can test your skill on the table saw—and test the saw's accuracy—by making mitered picture frames. Even a slight gap in the miters shows that something's gone wrong. But with a good setup and a few basic techniques, you can get tight joints in even the trickiest of frames.

Getting accurate miters depends, first, on having your table saw set up properly, with the blade at a true 90 degrees to the table (or 45 degrees for some cuts) and the disc of the blade set parallel to the miter slots. See "Twenty-Minute Tune-Up: The Table Saw" on page 252 for information on these setups. Then you can use a 45-45-90-degree artist's triangle to set both the blade and miter gauge. Some shops use dedicated sliding crosscut sleds, but I abandoned one early design I built myself because it was just too big and clumsy to have around. Instead, I rely on two miter gauges, one for each side of the blade. Having two miter gauges is handy anyway, even if you're not expecting to cut zillions of miters, because you can leave various jigs and fences attached to one gauge while keeping the other one plain.

Once you have the saw set up correctly, you can get into the actual cuts. Here are some of the common problems you're likely to encounter and the solutions you can use:

CUTTING COMPOUND MITERS

The tilted moldings for picture frames, crown moldings, and tray edges require compound miter cuts. But many of these moldings have hollow backs and inadequate bottom support, which means that you can't stand them up to cut them on the saw table. Yet you can almost always support these moldings in a way that allows them to be cut as if they were square.

The solution is to use a shaped block behind the work to hold it at the correct angle during the cut. Just make the block to fit the angle of the back, as shown on this page.

CUTTING WIDE MOLDINGS

Crown moldings and pieces with flared sides are often too wide for the table saw to cut upright. To make these moldings, first mount the work on a support base, as shown at left on the opposite page, and make the deepest cut you can make. Then saw away the waste that's holding the two pieces together.

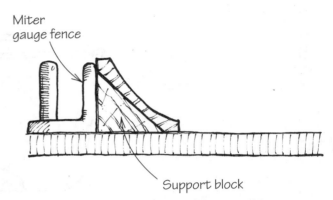

Miter gauge fence

Support block

To cut compound miters on the table saw, use the miter gauge and a support block to stabilize the molding.

Don't worry about the accuracy of this second cut; your goal at this stage is just to keep the miter edge clean. Next lay the work flat on the saw table and tilt the blade so that it butts flat against the miter cut. Now set the miter gauge so that it matches the angle of the work to the blade, and finish the cut. See the drawings on the opposite page. In effect, the first partial cut you made has determined the angles required for a compound miter, and by setting both the miter gauge and the blade tilt from the wood itself, you've removed the chance of math error and gauge-adjustment error.

MAKING ODD-SHAPED FRAMES

Occasionally I'm asked to make a frame for an irregularly shaped painting, with varying lengths for the sides and a different angle at each corner. The same problem applies when one or more of the frame parts is a different width. Unless you're making covers for out-of-square boat hatches or similarly unusual work, you won't often have a need for this solution. But if you do, it's a lifesaver.

To make an odd-shaped frame, trace or draw the shape full-sized on cardboard. Then add lines that represent the edges of the molding. Using a mat knife and straightedge, cut out this "frame" and bisect each miter from inside to outside corner. Use these four templates to set the miter gauge for each cut. Determine the length of each side from the template as well. See "Determining Odd Frame Angles" on page 23 for more details.

MITERING TWISTED STOCK

If you have twisted frame parts or stock that is basically straight but that won't lie perfectly flat on the saw table, you can still cut good miters if you use this technique:

Miter the four sides about 1 inch too long. Don't worry about the twist at this stage; just make your cuts. Next glue together the opposite corners to form Ls, and recut the remaining miters to the correct length. Keep the L-joints flat on the table, even if it means that one or the other of the points of the miters you're cutting isn't flat as it passes the blade. The angle you're cutting will compensate for any twist. Now when you assemble the frame, it will lie flat, with tight miters. You may still need to sand, plane, or carve the face of the molding to get the joints to match perfectly.

All of these methods involve complicated mathematical and geometrical problems in three dimensions. But by reducing the problems to the simplest cuts and using those cuts to set the machines, you can get the problems back into the two dimensions you are most comfortable with.

Jim Cummins
Woodstock, NY

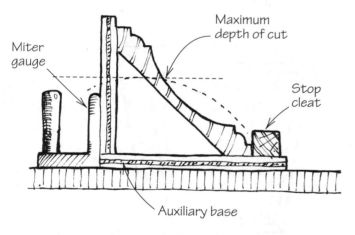

To cut moldings that are beyond the height capacity of your saw, first support the molding on an auxliary base and cut as deeply as you can (above). Then cut the molding free with a handsaw or band saw, and use the cut end to set the blade tilt and miter gauge angle (right).

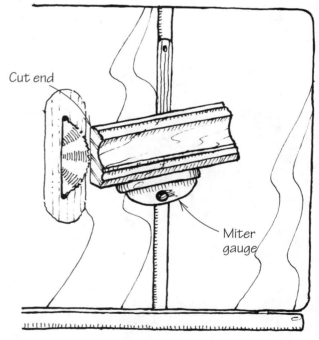

Setting Up Narrow Crosscuts

PROBLEM: *For crosscutting, I'd like to use the fence on my table saw to set the cut. I'm afraid, though, that when I'm sawing narrow pieces, the end will bind against the fence as I pass over the blade, causing kickback. How can I avoid this?*

SOLUTION: Make a small bridge that will fit over the table saw fence; then clamp it to the fence in front of the saw blade, as shown below. Back up the workpiece with your miter gauge, and register the end of the work against the bridge rather than against your saw fence. This way you can accurately gauge the length of your workpiece while still preventing your stock from binding.

Graham Blackburn
Bearsville, NY

To keep your stock from binding when making crosscuts, gauge your workpiece off a stop clamped to the fence. A carriage bolt and wing nut apply enough pressure to clamp the stop to the fence.

Crosscutting Acute Angles

PROBLEM: *I need to miter across the ends of cabinet parts, but because the cabinet is a trapezoidal shape, the angle on two of the corners is beyond the 45-degree capacity of both my table saw and my sliding miter saw. How can I make the cuts?*

SOLUTION: You could stand the parts on end on the table saw to cut the miters, as you would to saw the bevels on a raised panel. But that works only for relatively short and wide pieces.

For longer and narrower pieces, you need to work with the stock lying flat. Jack up the end of the workpiece opposite the cut end to increase the angle of cut beyond 45 degrees.

Start by drawing the angle of cut on the edges of the stock. Use scrap pieces to verify the angles before cutting the real parts. Then set a bevel gauge to the angle you want to cut.

A compound miter saw is ideal for this situation because you don't have to move the workpiece—simply prop up the end and make test cuts until you hit the angle. Moving the support block toward or away from the blade fine-tunes the angle. A sliding compound miter works the same way and can cut much wider pieces.

On the table saw, the process is similar, but you have to move the workpiece across the blade. I use a shop-made crosscut sled because it supports the stock better than a miter gauge and because both the workpiece and the block move as a unit.

Tony O'Malley
Emmaus, PA

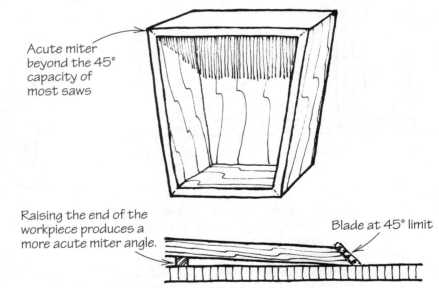

Acute miter beyond the 45° capacity of most saws

Raising the end of the workpiece produces a more acute miter angle.

Blade at 45° limit

To cut miters greater than 45° on the table saw, lay out the cut on the stock, set the blade to 45°, and raise the opposite end of the stock on spacers. Move the spacers in or out from the blade to fine-tune the angle.

Squaring Off an Odd-Shaped Workpiece

PROBLEM: *I've built a wall cabinet with an irregular opening that resembles a D. I've made the door, and the curved edge fits the opening exactly. Now I have to make a straight cut for the hinged edge, but I don't have any reference for making this rip cut. What can I do?*

SOLUTION: I once saw a boatbuilder solve an even trickier problem with an "instant" saw fixture, like the one shown below.

First locate the straight cutline on the door or part by holding the curved portion against the opening it fits into. Next rip a piece of plywood that is a few inches larger than your door, and place the door on the plywood with your intended cutline directly above the edge, as shown. Clamp the door to the plywood with tabs and stop blocks, and make the cut. You could also clamp the door to the plywood with toggle clamps, or simply lay a few long scraps over the door and screw them to the plywood.

Another approach that will work is to mark the cutline as previously described, cut wide of the line on the band saw, and trim to the line using the jointer or a router and flush-trimming bit.

You could even use a circular saw and straightedge guide. Whichever method you choose, expect to do some hand work to get a good fit.

Jim Cummins
Woodstock, NY

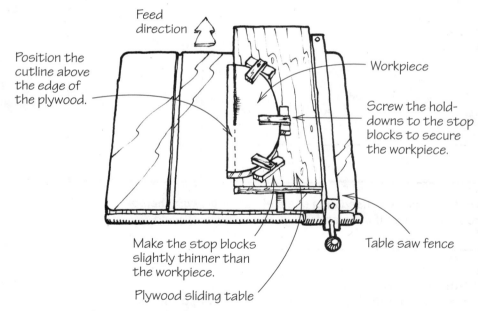

Feed direction

Position the cutline above the edge of the plywood.

Workpiece

Screw the hold-downs to the stop blocks to secure the workpiece.

Make the stop blocks slightly thinner than the workpiece.

Table saw fence

Plywood sliding table

To make a straight cut on an irregular workpiece, clamp it to a piece of plywood with the cutline directly over the edge of the plywood.

Cutting Sheet Goods

Cutting Plywood for Best Yield

PROBLEM: *I always seem to end up with a large amount of wasted material when I cut plywood. How can I work more efficiently?*

SOLUTION: As always, "the devil's in the details," and in this case, "details" means careful planning. When I work with plywood, I make a scale drawing using a blank 4 × 8 sheet of paper, and I draw hash marks showing 6-inch divisions. I then make photocopies of the sheet and use these diagrams to sketch out components. This takes a bit of trial and error, but after I've maximized my material, I list the parts on each sheet and number the sheets. This then becomes my cutting list for laying out parts on the plywood.

If you have a personal computer, you can automate this process using any of a number of inexpensive shareware programs. See "Sources," beginning on page 298.

Dennis Slabaugh
Naples, FL

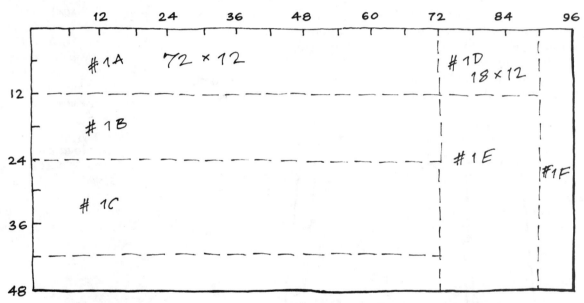

Laying out all of the parts you need on a scale sheet of plywood helps you plan the best sequence of cuts and will give you the best yield.

Sawing Odd-Shaped Panels

PROBLEM: *I need to cut the triangular plywood parts for a corner cupboard, but they're too big to support with just the miter gauge on my table saw. How should I handle this?*

SOLUTION: Here's a trick that will work for cutting your triangular shelf as well as for making other difficult cuts, like sawing the ends of a wide butcher block tabletop or squaring up a large piece of sheet material: Make a long guide strip that will fit in your saw's miter slot and attach it to the back of the workpiece, as shown at the top of the opposite page.

The guide strip can be made from a close-grained hardwood, like maple, or from a length of ⅛-inch aluminum flat bar stock that's the same width as your miter gauge slot. The aluminum is stiffer, and it won't get mistaken for scrap and thrown away. I like to drill and countersink ⅛-inch holes every 6 inches along the guide strip so that I can use it with any width stock.

Fasten the strip to the workpiece with screws so that it's exactly parallel to your cutline. It is helpful to have the strip extend a few inches beyond each edge of your work so that you can complete the cut with full control.

Bill and Joanne Storch
Corvallis, OR

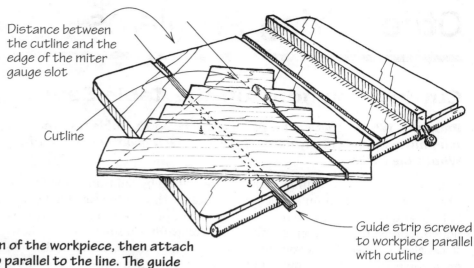

Distance between the cutline and the edge of the miter gauge slot

Cutline

Guide strip screwed to workpiece parallel with cutline

Lay out a cutline on the bottom of the workpiece, then attach a wood or aluminum guide strip parallel to the line. The guide strip rides in the miter gauge slot while making the cut.

Cutting Large Panels on the Table Saw

PROBLEM: *What is the best way to set up my table saw for cutting 4 × 8 plywood panels and other large sheet goods?*

SOLUTION: With the right setup, a table saw can make cutting panels easier and more precise. Without it, you're in for a dangerous and difficult job. Start with an extension table on the outfeed side of the saw that's large enough to support at least half the 4 × 8 panel after you push it through the blade. See the drawing below right. If you want to make wide cuts, you'll also need an extension table to the left or right of the blade. For a "roving" support, buy or make a portable, height-adjustable roller stand. Sometimes you'll use this as a side extension; at other times you'll want it on the outfeed side. It depends on the panel size and where you're making the cut.

Since heavy panels can easily knock a light-duty rip fence out of alignment, it's best to equip your table saw with a high-quality rip fence if you plan on cutting panels regularly. Aftermarket rip fences are readily adaptable to side table

extensions, and most of these fences are longer than standard models. This means you'll have more of a guiding edge to work against.

Even if you have extension tables and a premium rip fence, it's still a good idea to precut a full-sized panel with a circular saw—especially if you're working solo. Cut your "good" piece to be oversized by ⅛ inch or so, and you'll have a lot less weight and size to pass through the table saw blade.

When you're guiding a panel against the rip fence to make a cut, direct your feed pressure diagonally at a point on the rip fence that's just an inch or so ahead of the spot where the saw blade enters the wood.

Tim Snyder
Nazareth, PA

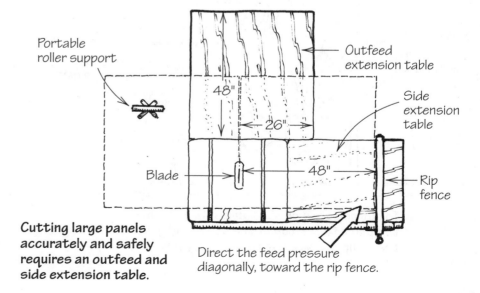

Portable roller support

48"

26"

Blade

Outfeed extension table

Side extension table

48"

Rip fence

Cutting large panels accurately and safely requires an outfeed and side extension table.

Direct the feed pressure diagonally, toward the rip fence.

Other Sizing Problems

Cutting Polygons on the Table Saw

PROBLEM: *When I try to cut a polygon shape on the table saw, the sides always come out unequal. There must be a good way to do this. What's the trick?*

SOLUTION: The key to cutting even-sided polygons is not a miter gauge, but rather a good pattern. To make a pattern, draw the polygon on the stock. Next cut near the layout lines on a table saw or band saw. Sand carefully to the lines on a disc sander to get the polygon sides even.

If you're making several polygons, I recommend a technique called pattern-sawing. Make a small pattern of the desired polygon shape, and then use it as a template to run against an auxiliary table saw fence to cut the actual polygons, as shown. With this setup, you can change the size of the polygons you are cutting by adjusting how far the fence overhangs the saw blade, and you can produce as many polygons as you want. For safety, screw a handle to the pattern, stand at the side of the saw when cutting, and allow enough room for cutoff waste to pass between the saw blade and the regular fence.

B. William Bigelow
Surry, NH

RELATED INFO:
Laying Out Polygons, page 28;
Making Multiple Parts,
page 105

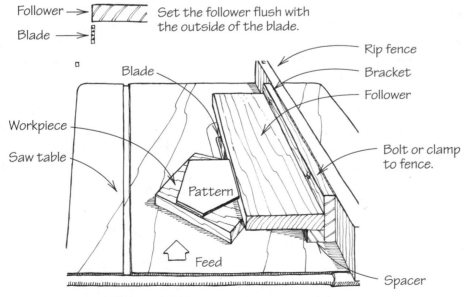

Follower — Set the follower flush with the outside of the blade.
Blade —

Blade
Rip fence
Bracket
Follower
Workpiece
Saw table
Pattern
Bolt or clamp to fence.
Feed
Spacer

To cut polygons on the table saw, attach a template to the top of the stock and guide the template against the auxiliary fence.

QUICK TIP

CUTTING TO FIT AS YOU GO

If you cut all the pieces for a project at the outset, chances are good that something won't fit together as perfectly as planned.

Instead, when building from a plan, I begin by cutting only those parts that do not rely on another part or assembly for fit. For example, rather than cutting a drawer front to the dimension specified in the plan, I build the assembly that forms the drawer opening. Then I can measure the opening to get the real size of the drawer front. I use a similar system when cutting rails and stiles for a cabinet face frame. After cutting the stiles to length, I clamp them to the cabinet edges. I can then measure the distance between the stiles to determine the location of the shoulder cuts for the rails.

Another way to fit your part is to first cut the part from scrap wood and then use this dummy piece as a "ruler" to measure for the real piece. I use this method for cutting shelves to the proper width. This way, if you do cut a piece too short, you have lost nothing more than a little time and a piece of scrap wood.

Dennis Slabaugh
Naples, FL

"Stretching" Special Boards

PROBLEM: *I know this is going to sound silly, but I have a beautiful piece of walnut that's just a little too small to fit as a drawer front on my cherry hall table. Is there anything I can do to "stretch" the wood?*

SOLUTION: You didn't say whether your stock was too short for the opening or if it was too narrow. Regardless, you have a few options depending on how figured the wood is and how the options will affect your design.

First and easiest, you could border the walnut with cherry to match the table or with a second contrasting wood like ebony or holly. Second, if the wood is too small in width only, you could rip it in half and glue a piece of contrasting wood in the center. Again you could use an offcut of the cherry from the table or work in another contrasting wood.

There's also a third, and slicker, option, and that's to cut the walnut on a diagonal, shift the halves to increase the size, and reglue them, as shown. If you shift the boards in one direction, you'll make the piece wider. Shift it in the other and it will become longer.

Obviously, this trick won't work with highly figured stock like crotch walnut; you'd never be able to align the figure well enough to disguise the shift. In a case like that, though, you could add a strip of contrasting wood as an intentionally bold design feature. But if your wood has relatively consistent figure, the shift should be almost invisible.

Kevin Ireland
Wescosville, PA

You can extend or widen a special piece of wood by cutting it on the diagonal and then gluing the halves together. Shifting the diagonals in one direction makes the wood longer (*top*). Moving them in the other direction makes the wood wider (*bottom*).

Quick Tip Quick Tip Quick Tip Quick

BAND-SAWING DELICATE MATERIAL

I once salvaged some ivory key tops from a dead piano at the town dump. When I wanted to cut one to size for use as an inlay, I figured the band saw would tear it up. After scratching my head for a few minutes, I used double-faced tape to attach the ivory to a larger piece of pine, which served as both backup and carrier. The border of the pine allowed me plenty of room to grab and guide the work without getting my fingers too close to the blade, and because the pine support resisted vibration, the cut went without a hitch.

Jim Cummins
Woodstock, NY

BENDING AND SHAPING
SOLUTIONS

ROUTING AND CUTTING PROFILES

Cleaning Scorched Routed Edges	99
Matching Molding Profiles	100
Matching Moldings with Table Saw Cuts	100
Dealing with Cupped Panels	101
Dust Chute for Freehand Routing	101
Routing Narrow Moldings	101
Preventing Tear-Out on Stopped Router Cuts	102
Routing Raised Panels	103
Routing Small Workpieces	104
Climb-Cut Routing to Reduce Tear-Out	104
Routing Profiles along Curved Edges	104

CREATING SHAPES

Making Multiple Parts	105
Pattern Routing Thick Stock	106
Making Tighter Turns on the Band Saw	106

Matching Curved Trim to Irregular Openings	107
Boring Spheres	108
Re-turning a Spindle on the Lathe	108
Turning Chair Rungs the Same Length	109
Drilling Tight Curves	109
Shaping Shelf Support Pins	109
Turning Long Posts on a Short Lathe	110
Turning a Perfect Cylinder	110
One-Shot Tapering Jig	111
Cutting Coves on the Table Saw	112

BENDING WOOD

Making Quick Bending Forms	114
Determining the Spacing for Kerf Bending	114
Planing Jig for Tapered Laminations	115
Inexpensive Bending Steamer	116
Multi-Purpose Bending Table	118
Avoiding Steam Bending Breaks	119

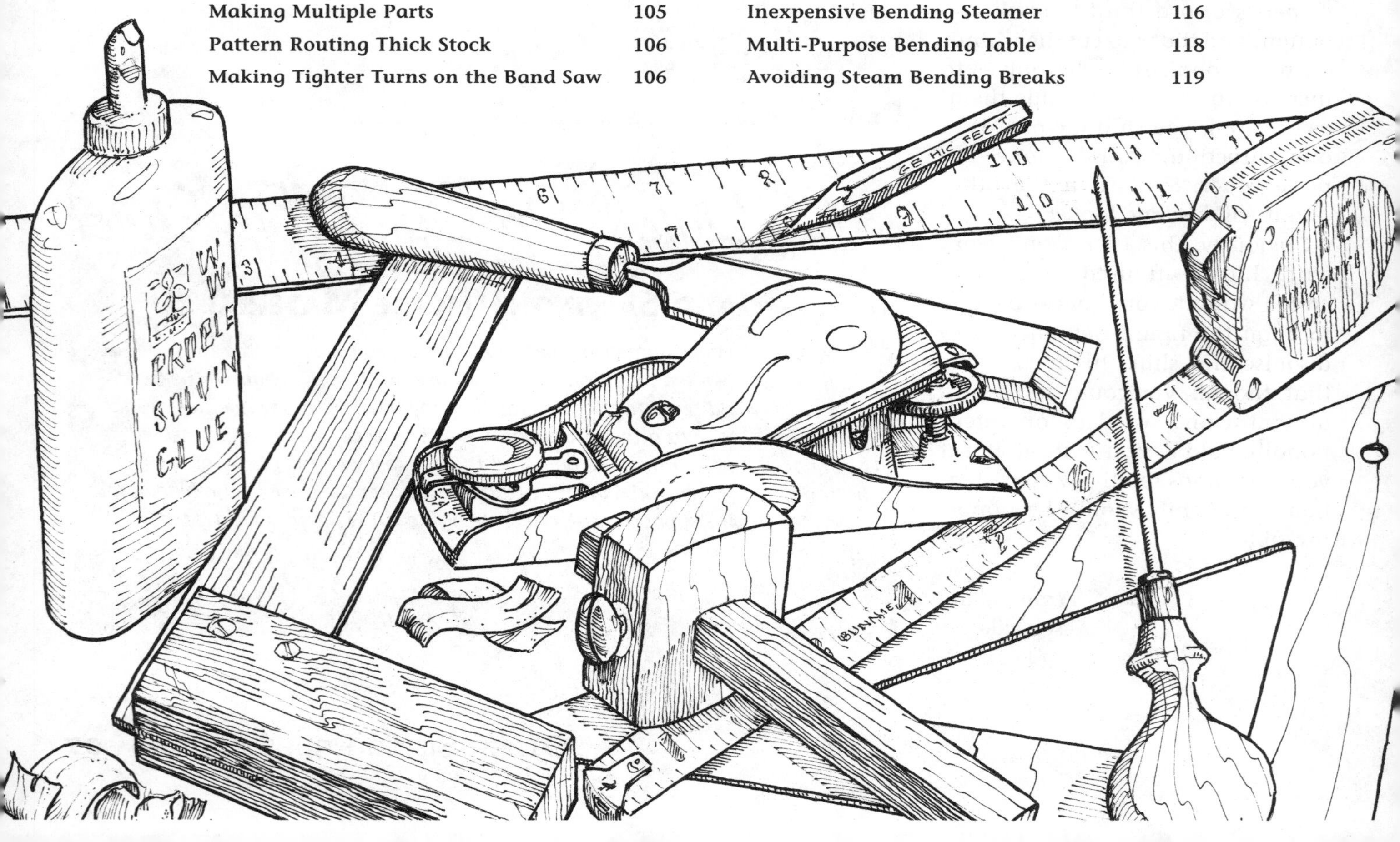

Routing and Cutting Profiles

Cleaning Scorched Routed Edges

PROBLEM: *I routed the edge of a cherry tabletop and ended up with some sections of the profile that were so badly burned, they looked more like ebony. How can I clean up the edges without sanding my fingers raw or ruining the crispness of the profile?*

SOLUTION: I recommend scraping the edge with a scraper that is shaped to the exact profile of the wood. Using a felt-tip marker, carefully draw the profile you want on one corner of a standard cabinet scraper. Then grind and file that shape into the metal. Hold it against the actual wooden edge from time to time to check the accuracy. To make guiding the scraper easier, I make a fence for it, as shown. On the band saw, I split a scrap of wood and then I clamp the scraper in the kerf with a small C-clamp. Running the scraper along the edge of the wood removes the scorch marks in no time. After that, you can proceed with regular sanding.

AVOIDING THE PROBLEM: Your burn marks were probably caused by a dirty or dull cutter, or improper feed speed. If you're using high speed steel bits, switch to carbide. They hold a sharp edge much longer. If you're already using a carbide bit and are still having trouble with scorching, try cleaning it with a little oven cleaner. If this doesn't help, you may need to have the bit sharpened. Even carbide bits get dull eventually.

With regard to feed speed, you should move the router or the workpiece at a moderate pace. Your hands, eyes, ears, and nose will tell you how quickly or slowly to rout the profile without burning or splintering the wood. Take particular care at the beginning and end of each pass. Taking light passes will help as well. It is also helpful if you can make each cut in a single motion, without stopping to change your grip, or hand position. Rehearsing each cut before turning on the router may show you how to move so you can complete the cut smoothly.

David Page
Swarthmore, PA

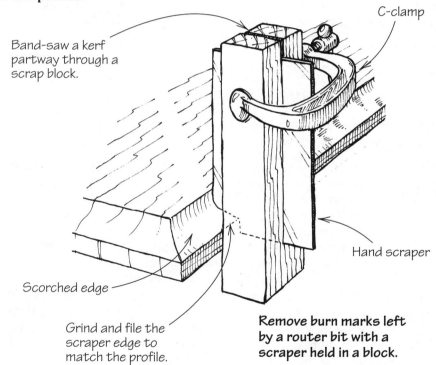

Band-saw a kerf partway through a scrap block.

C-clamp

Scorched edge

Hand scraper

Grind and file the scraper edge to match the profile.

Remove burn marks left by a router bit with a scraper held in a block.

Matching Molding Profiles

PROBLEM: *I want to make an exact replica of a small cabinet I saw in a museum, but I can't find any router bits that will match the profile of the moldings. Any suggestions?*

SOLUTION: Moldings are divided into two categories—simple and complex. The simple shapes include forms you probably are familiar with, such as beads and ogees. Complex moldings are composed of two or more simple shapes. These complex moldings are the ones for which you usually have trouble finding the right bit. Or, on the rare occasions when the perfect bit exists, you'll think that it must be machined from solid gold, judging from the price tag it carries. Fortunately, you can often accomplish the same result by stacking the molding profiles, as shown. Before you start cutting wood, it is a good idea to sketch out the finished profile you want to accomplish. Experimenting without having a general idea of what you want is a waste of both time and wood. Once you've planned your profile, start with strips of wood that are thick enough and wide enough for the simple molding profiles you are going to be using. Run the profiles on the edges. Tack the first layer in place.

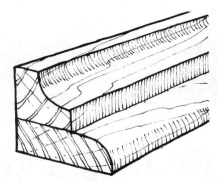

2 or more simple moldings can be stacked to form any number of more complex shapes.

Continue to add the additional layers and tack them in place until you have accomplished the final profile.

Mike Dunbar
Hampton, NH

Matching Moldings with Table Saw Cuts

PROBLEM: *How do I match a small section of molding missing from an antique I am restoring?*

SOLUTION: The most efficient method of reproducing molding depends on how much you have to make. You can always have a router bit made, or grind a scraper blade to the appropriate shape, but for a small piece of molding, it usually isn't worth the time or expense. I usually find that I can duplicate almost any profile with a handful of carving chisels without spending a lot of time, effort, or money.

If it's a very small section, say a piece 3 inches long or less, I will usually carve it freehand with gouges or flat chisels. Start by laying out the profile on the end of an appropriate piece of stock. I do this by either tracing around a piece of the actual molding or by using a contour gauge.

Draw guidelines down the entire length of the workpiece (always make the piece a little longer than the size you actually need) to aid in keeping the profile straight. Rough out the general shape with a flat chisel. Then carve the profile to its final shape with chisels and gouges of the appropriate shape. Smooth away any tool marks with sandpaper to finish up.

For longer sections of moldings, I use the table saw to rough out the profile before moving on to my chisels. Again, lay out the profile on the end of your stock. You may want to start with a piece that is somewhat wider than the width you need so that it is safer to feed through the saw. Adjust the blade height so that the saw cuts just shy of the layout line, as shown. Position the rip fence to guide the stock through the cut. Readjust the fence and the blade height as needed to cut away the waste across the entire profile. When all the waste is cut away, refine and finish the profile with chisels, gouges, scrapers, and sandpaper.

Rick Wright
Schnecksville, PA

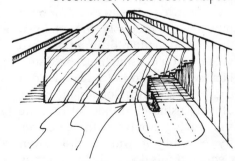

Rip the molding from wider stock after it has been shaped.

Outline of desired molding

You can duplicate a molding profile on the table saw by making a series of cuts with the blade at varying heights. Plane, scrape, carve, and sand away the remaining waste afterward.

Dealing with Cupped Panels

PROBLEM: *Even though I carefully surfaced and glued up my stock, the panels I made for a set of raised panel doors cupped a little bit. Now I'm afraid that when I make the angled cuts across the ends of the panels, the bevels won't be even. Is there any way to deal with this problem, short of resurfacing the panels?*

SOLUTION: As long as the cupping isn't severe, the way to deal with it is to keep the panels clamped flat as you cut them. Sandwich the panel between two stout cleats before making the cross-grain bevel cuts, as shown below. The cuts parallel to the grain won't require cleats, unless the panel also has some bow.

Tom Begnal
Kent, CT

With a couple of clamps and two straight cleats, you can flatten an unruly panel so that your bevel cuts will be even across its width.

k Tip Quick Tip Quick Tip Quick

DUST CHUTE FOR FREEHAND ROUTING

When routing without a fence on the router table, such as when you're cutting with a piloted router bit, dust and chips are a problem. To catch wayward dust, make the box shown and hook it up to the hose of your shop vacuum. Clamp it to the table so that the opening is close to the bit. When necessary, use the edge of the dowel as a guide pin to start your work.

Andy Rae
Lenhartsville, PA

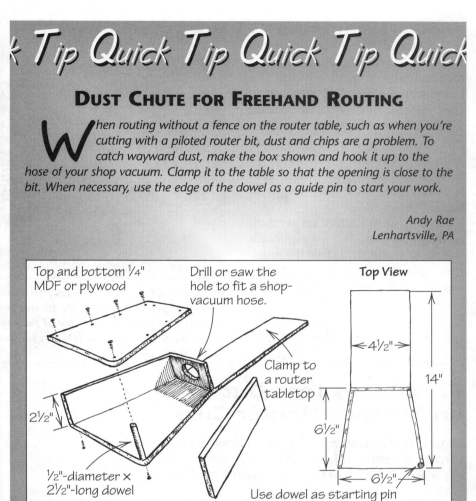

Top and bottom ¼" MDF or plywood

Drill or saw the hole to fit a shop-vacuum hose.

Clamp to a router tabletop

2½"

½"-diameter × 2½"-long dowel

Use dowel as starting pin

Top View

4½"

14"

6½"

6½"

Routing Narrow Moldings

PROBLEM: *I want to make a display cabinet with glazed doors, but routing the narrow mullions for the glass panes scares me. How can I safely rout these narrow pieces?*

SOLUTION: The best way to rout most narrow moldings is to avoid the issue. Prepare a wide piece of stock that is as long as you need. Rout the profile along one edge, then rip the narrow piece off on the table saw. Repeat as necessary until you have all the pieces you need. This won't work as well for moldings such as mullions, however, because the pieces have a profile that has been cut on both sides.

For such moldings that require multiple cuts, you have to take a

different approach. Start by making three featherboards to attach to your router table, as shown at the top of page 102. Position one on the fence, directly above the bit, to hold the molding down on the table. Position the other two flat on the table (one on the infeed side of the bit, the other on the outfeed side) to hold the molding against the fence. Now turn your attention to the fence itself. The problem with routing both sides of a narrow molding is that the cuts often remove so much stock that the molding can tip. To stabilize the molding as you're cutting it, make an auxiliary fence that fills in the cut you're making and attach it to the outfeed side of your regular fence, as shown at right. For example, when rabbeting a narrow mullion, the auxiliary fence should be a small rectangular strip that matches the width and depth of the rabbet.

You may want to enlist an assistant to help you rout. The featherboards will make it difficult to feed the moldings smoothly, and any hesitation may cause the stock to burn.

Ken Burton
New Tripoli, PA

Narrow mullions can be tricky to rout safely. But with featherboards to keep the pieces held tightly to the fence and table, and an auxiliary fence (*shown along the outfeed side of the regular fence and in the inset*) to keep them from tipping, the job can be handled with a minimum of hassle.

Preventing Tear-Out on Stopped Router Cuts

PROBLEM: *I'm routing a stopped chamfer on the four corners of some table legs. Where I stop the chamfers, the wood always tears out. How can I prevent this?*

SOLUTION: The solution is to start the cut at the stopped end first. It's easiest to do this operation on a router table because you can set up stops that keep the cuts consistent. Clamp a stop block on the router table fence to locate the stopped end of the cut, as shown. You may need to add a longer extension fence for this job. Position the end of the workpiece against the stop and pivot the work into the cut, creating the stopped end of the chamfer. Then rout the remainder of the edge.

If the chamfer is stopped an equal distance from both ends, repeat the process from the second end. If the chamfer stops a different distance from each end, you'll need to set two stops, one on either side of the bit.

Bill and Joanne Storch
Corvallis, OR

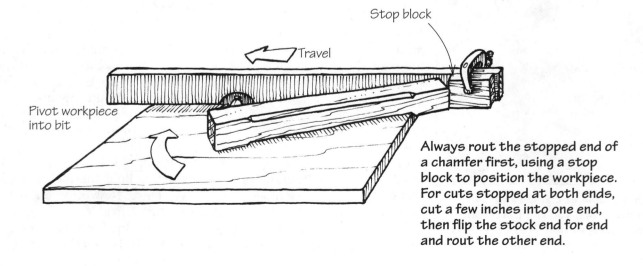

Stop block

Travel

Pivot workpiece into bit

Always rout the stopped end of a chamfer first, using a stop block to position the workpiece. For cuts stopped at both ends, cut a few inches into one end, then flip the stock end for end and rout the other end.

ROUTING RAISED PANELS

The router table is a good tool for raising panels, but you have two rather different styles of router bits to choose from. With one, the panel is oriented vertically against a tall fence; with the other, the panel lies flat on the router table.

Whichever you choose, there are some guidelines to keep in mind whenever you raise panels with router bits:

- Take a series of light cuts, making the final cut no more than 1/8 inch deep.
- On each pass, rout the ends of the panels first, then the edges. This eliminates the cross-grain tear-out at the corners.
- Use panel raising bits only in a router table.
- To prevent a kickback and to keep your hands at a safe distance from the cutter, use hold-downs and featherboards whenever possible.

HORIZONTAL PANEL RAISERS

Because of their large size (see the photo below), horizontal panel raising bits should be used with special caution. And before you spend a bunch of money on one, consider the following:

- You need a powerful router (2 horsepower or more) to swing these big bits.
- You'll need to limit the depth of cut on each pass to no more than 1/16 inch.
- Your router must have adjustable speed to keep these large-diameter bits within the safe tip speeds recommended by the manufacturer, typically 10,000 to 12,000 rpm.

Raising a panel with a vertical bit requires a tall, sturdy fence, and a fingerboard to hold the panel tight against the fence.

If you observe this list of cautions, you can make beautiful raised panels with these router bits. They typically have a ball-bearing guide, which means that you can easily raise curved panels. And because the panel lies flat on the router table, the setup and routing process are straightforward.

VERTICAL PANEL RAISERS

A good alternative to the horizontal panel raisers is the vertical-style bits, like the one shown above. Their biggest advantage is that they can be used in a standard-speed router. They'll even give decent results when used with a 1-horsepower router, as long as you take a series of light passes. The drawbacks to these bits are that they are available in fewer profiles than horizontal bits and are more prone to leaving cutter marks on the wood. The vertical fence takes a little more time to set up and may limit the size of the panels you can work with practically. Before starting, make sure that the fence stands square to the table.

Bob Moran
Emmaus, PA

Due to their large size, horizontal panel raisers look more like hell-raisers, but if you follow a few basic cautions, you can produce perfect results safely.

Routing Small Workpieces

PROBLEM: *I need to rout the edges of very small blocks of wood and don't want an ogee manicure. How can I accomplish this?*

SOLUTION: Routing small pieces of wood on a router table is just plain dangerous. We do as much of the routing as possible while the stock is large enough to hold onto, even if this means starting with an oversized piece, then cutting it down to size later. Eventually, however, you'll come upon a cut that can be made only with the piece cut to its final dimensions.

We have two methods for this situation. The first is to use double-sided tape to attach the small piece to a larger, safer piece. You can even cut the larger piece to accommodate your workpiece or to give it a straight edge to run along a fence.

The second method is our favorite: Grab the piece between the jaws of an adjustable hand screw clamp. Not only does this effectively move your hands away from the cutter, but the wooden jaws increase the surface area of the router table. The clamp also adds to the mass, decreasing the chance of a dangerous kickback.

Bill and Joanne Storch
Corvallis, OR

Routing a small piece doesn't have to be terrifying. Simply grab it with a hand screw clamp and you'll have plenty of mass to hold onto.

Climb-Cut Routing to Reduce Tear-Out

PROBLEM: *I sometimes get a lot of tear-out when routing profiles and rabbets. How can I prevent or reduce this problem?*

SOLUTION: Using sharp bits and a steady, moderate feed rate are two routing basics. But sometimes you'll get tear-out even when you follow these rules. If you're encountering the problem consistently with a particular wood, "climb cut" it. Climb cutting is simply moving the router in the direction opposite the way that you normally would. Climb cutting all but eliminates tear-out, but it tends to push the router away from the edge of the work. The cutter can even run suddenly along the edge of the workpiece because it's being pulled into the wood. When you climb cut, remove material in several passes and keep an extra-firm grip on your router.

Paul Anthony
Hellertown, PA

Creating Shapes

Making Multiple Parts

PROBLEM: *I want to make a batch of toys for a local group that collects them to distribute during the Christmas season. What's the best way to cut out all the identical parts I'll be needing?*

SOLUTION: There is no single answer to this question because each piece you want to reproduce is likely to present its own set of challenges. However, here are a few strategies that you can use, adapt, and combine to manufacture almost anything.

The key to all of these strategies is to start with an accurate template. It's worth putting a little extra time into making sure your template is the exact shape of the part you're after, as any mistake here will be transferred directly to the finished product. Make your templates from ¼-inch Masonite or hardwood plywood. Paper and cardboard just won't hold up. Once you have your template, you can use it in various ways to help shape your workpieces.

Perhaps the most basic method is to use the template as a layout device to trace the shape you're after onto your workpieces. But rather than trace and cut each piece individually, stack and cut as many pieces at one time as possible. If the pieces are thin, you may be able to stack six to ten and cut them all at once on the band saw. This means that you have to trace the template shape only once—on the top piece. Hold the stack together with double-sided carpet tape and stay about ¹⁄₁₆ inch outside the layout lines as you cut. As an alternative to carpet tape, try several dabs of hot glue.

Then, with the pieces still stacked, you can work them down to their final shape with a hand plane, a

One good way to make identical curved parts is to use a flush-trimming bit, a template, and a table-mounted router.

scraper, or a power sander—whatever it takes to get the job done. If you have the material, make a couple of extra parts. It's very little additional effort and could save time if one of the pieces gets lost or rejected. Pry the pieces apart and clean up any residual tape adhesive with mineral spirits and a light sanding.

If the band saw doesn't yield the precision you need, you can use either a router or the table saw to cut your pieces to match the template exactly. The router excels when it comes to curved work, while the table saw is my choice for straight cuts.

To rout a piece to match your template, attach the template to your workpiece with double-sided tape or hot glue. Mount a flush-trimming bit in your router and guide it

around the workpiece with the bit's bearing following the template. If the workpiece is large, you can use a hand-held router; for a smaller piece, it may be better to work on a router table, as shown. Regardless of which way you hold the router, start by cutting your pieces to within about ¹⁄₁₆ inch of final size on the band saw first. Routers aren't made for removing large amounts of waste material.

To cut pieces on the table saw to match a template, you need to make a follower that attaches to the saw's fence. This technique is described fully in "Cutting Polygons on the Table Saw" on page 96.

David Page
Swarthmore, PA

Pattern Routing Thick Stock

PROBLEM: *I need to pattern rout a piece of 1½-inch-thick stock, but my longest router bit is only 1 inch long. Can I still do the job?*

SOLUTION: The solution here is to use two different router techniques. First cut your shape on the band saw to within about ¹⁄₁₆ inch of the layout line. Then pattern rout partway through the thickness of the stock using a template and guide bushing, as shown in *Step 1*.

When you use a template guide, remember that the template must be offset a specific distance from the finished edge; that distance depends on the diameter of the guide bushing *and* the diameter of the bit you use. To calculate the offset distance,

subtract the bit diameter from the bushing diameter and divide the answer by two.

To finish the job, install a flush-trimming bit in your router table or router. Rout from the other side of the workpiece with the bit's bearing following the surface that's been template routed, as shown in *Step 2*. You'll end up with a finished edge that's perfectly even and square to the face of the workpiece.

Paul Anthony
Hellertown, PA

Step 1. Attach the template to the workpiece and rout partway through the edge with a 1" straight bit.

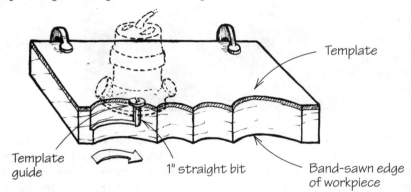

Template

Template guide

1" straight bit

Band-sawn edge of workpiece

Step 2. Use a flush-trimming bit to rout the remainder of the edge.

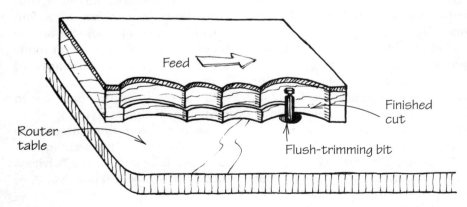

Feed

Router table

Finished cut

Flush-trimming bit

Making Tighter Turns on the Band Saw

PROBLEM: *I keep a ⅜-inch-wide blade on my 14-inch band saw. Often the blade binds when I try to cut tight turns. Is there a way to cut tighter curves without installing a narrower blade?*

SOLUTION: Using the widest blade you have is a good way to prevent overheating and binding during average use; however, it also means that you may run into turns that are too tight to negotiate. For example, a ⅜-inch-wide blade can cut curves no tighter than about a 1-inch radius. You can, however, make a wide blade turn on a dime by simply making a few relief cuts, as shown. Removing wood from behind the blade prevents binding. To tweak your blade for even tighter turns, try rounding over the back edge of your blade. With the saw running, hold an oilstone against the back corners of the blade.

Joe Wajszczuk
Jersey City, NJ

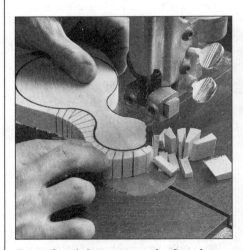

To make tight cuts on the band saw, first make a series of relief cuts. When you cut the actual shape, there will be less wood for the blade to bind against.

Matching Curved Trim to Irregular Openings

PROBLEM: *I want to make casing (trim) for an interior archway. I tried to cut the casing using a router trammel, but the curves didn't match because the arch wasn't a true radius. What can I do?*

SOLUTION: Your best bet is to make a template for the molding directly from the opening itself. Even if the arch were truly circular, it may still be easier to make a template, rather than trying to determine the exact radius.

First find the end points of the curve or arch and mark lines on the wall to show where the ends of your straight pieces of molding will meet the curved pieces, as shown in *Step 1*. Hold a square piece of scrap plywood against the wall so that the edges align with the lay-out lines you just marked, and scribe the curve onto the back side of the plywood. Find the center point of the opening along the bot-tom edge of the template and strike a perpendicular center line across the template. Later, use the center-line on the template to locate the

seam between two pieces of mold-ing at dead center of the opening. Band-saw close to the curved lay-out line and sand down to the line using a drum sander or a curved sanding block.

To draw the outside curve on the template, set a compass to match the width of the trim you want to have. Swing a series of arcs with the compass, placing the center points every inch or so along the inside curve, as shown in *Step 2*. Band-saw close to this new line and sand the curve smooth. Test fit the template against the opening.

If your trim will be flush with the inside edge of the doorway, you can now use the template to produce the curved trim. First cut the ends of the curved trim blank to fit against the straight trim. Next trace the curves from the template onto the trim

blank, using the end cuts to help position the template. Cut the curves on the band saw, staying just outside the lines. Then attach the template to your workpiece with double-sided tape. Rout the trim to match the template with a flush-trimming bit.

More likely, however, you'll want to make your trim so that it is set back a little bit from the edge of the wall, creating a little step, or reveal, between the two materials. To make this reveal, the curve of the trim has to be slightly looser than that of the arch. The easiest approach here is to make the inside curve of the template match the arch as described. Then draw a second inside curve, offset from the first by a distance equal to the reveal you want. Saw and sand this new curve smooth before cutting the outside curve.

Bill and Joanne Storch
Corvallis, OR

RELATED INFO:
Laying Out Curves, page 24

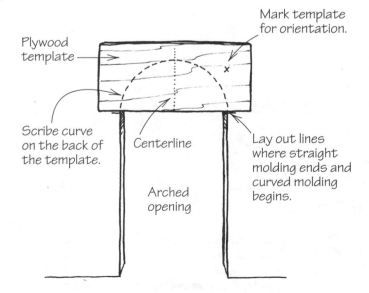

Step 1. Make a template by tracing the opening onto a piece of thin plywood.

Plywood template

Mark template for orientation.

Scribe curve on the back of the template.

Centerline

Lay out lines where straight molding ends and curved molding begins.

Arched opening

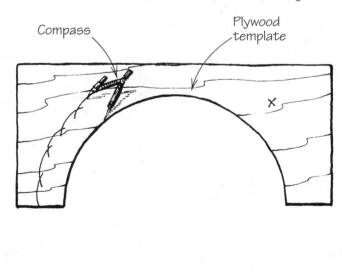

Step 2. Cut out the template, then use a compass to mark off the outside curve of the intended molding.

Compass

Plywood template

Boring Spheres

PROBLEM: *I need to bore a hole straight through a sphere. I tried clamping it in a drill press vise, but found it quite difficult to drill through the exact center of the sphere. Any suggestions?*

SOLUTION: It's easy to create a simple holding jig for the sphere. Select a flat piece of scrap stock that is thicker than the diameter of the sphere. Clamp this to the drill press table and use a Forstner bit that is somewhat smaller than the diameter of the sphere to bore a blind hole through the scrap. (For example, I use a ¾-inch bit for a 1-inch sphere.) Now chuck a brad point bit of the appropriate diameter into the drill press and cradle the sphere in the blind hole. The brad point will cut without any risk of the bit slipping off of the sphere and the blind hole will create just enough friction to hold the sphere in place. And, because the scrap stock has not been moved, the brad point bit will be centered over the sphere and your hole will be accurately centered.

Robert Treanor
San Francisco, CA

The 1" sphere being drilled rests in a shallow hole which was drilled with the ¾" Forstner bit (foreground).

Re-turning a Spindle on the Lathe

PROBLEM: *I tried putting a spindle back on the lathe to finish turning it several days after I had started turning it. The wood moved and the spindle no longer swings true. I still have to touch up a couple of spots. What can I do?*

SOLUTION: Place the piece back on the lathe and turn on the machine. As the spindle spins, hold a pencil against the tool rest and ease it up against the spinning wood. When you turn off the machine, you will find that the pencil has marked only the high side. Loosen the tail stock and place the lathe centers slightly off the original hole locations in the direction of the pencil marks, as shown. When you turn on the machine again, you will see that the wood spins much closer to true.

AVOIDING THE PROBLEM: Turn wood that is completely dry. Otherwise, it will continue to move as it seasons. Store the pieces in a place where the humidity is stable. Also, try to complete each spindle in a single session.

Mike Dunbar
Hampton, NH

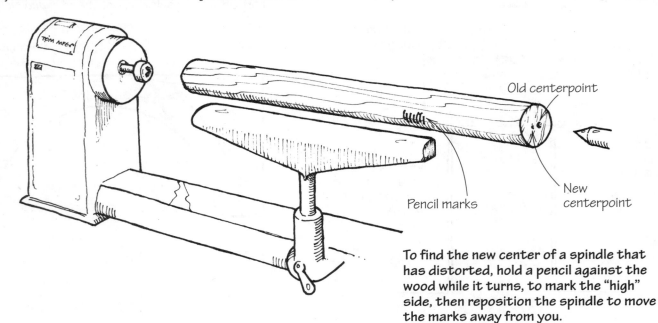

Old centerpoint

Pencil marks

New centerpoint

To find the new center of a spindle that has distorted, hold a pencil against the wood while it turns, to mark the "high" side, then reposition the spindle to move the marks away from you.

Turning Chair Rungs the Same Length

PROBLEM: *When turning chair rungs, such as those found on Shaker chairs, I have trouble getting all the rungs exactly the same length. What can I do?*

SOLUTION: The simple layout jig shown here can be manufactured from a narrow stick of wood and some screws. The stick you select should be about ¾-inch square and needs to be a few inches longer than the rungs you are turning. Mark the finished length of the rung as well as the tenon shoulders on the layout stick. Carefully drill pilot holes for #6 screws through the four layout lines. Drive the screws through the layout stick at the four locations so that the points of the screws protrude the same amount. After turning a rung to the desired diameter, hold the stick against the rung as it spins. The screw points will scratch the surface, laying out both the tenon shoulders and the overall length perfectly. For more complex turnings, add screws to the stick to lay out each individual cove and bead. Whenever you need to make duplicate turnings, the few minutes it takes to make a layout stick is time well spent.

Robert Treanor
San Francisco, CA

A scratch gauge will make short work of laying out a bunch of chair rungs, plus the shoulder-to-shoulder dimension will remain constant without your even having to think about measuring.

Drilling Tight Curves

PROBLEM: *Trestle table feet often have a long undercut that effectively creates four contact points on the floor. However, the tight radius at each end of the undercut can be difficult to cut. Is there an easy way around this?*

SOLUTION: Here's a quick-and-easy, three-step procedure that ensures a tight radius every time. First clamp the feet together so that the bottom edges butt together. Then chuck a drill bit of the appropriate diameter into your drill press. (For example, if you want a ¼-inch undercut radius, use a ½-inch diameter drill bit.) Bore a through hole at each end of the undercut. The holes should be centered on the line between the feet. After boring the holes, remove the clamps and band-saw the undercut on each foot.

Tom Begnal
Kent, CT

To simplify cutting these tight inside curves:

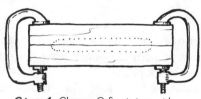

Step 1. Clamp 2 feet together.

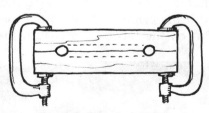

Step 2. Bore holes at the ends of cutouts.

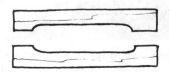

Step 3. Band-saw out the remaining waste.

Shaping Shelf Support Pins

PROBLEM: *How can I nicely round-over the ends of dowels or brass pins for use as shelf supports?*

SOLUTION: Chuck them into an electric hand drill and shape them against a disc sander. Make sure that the rotation of the drill opposes the rotation of the sander.

Paul Anthony
Hellertown, PA

Round the ends of a wood or brass pin by chucking it in a drill and spinning it against a disc sander.

Turning Long Posts on a Short Lathe

PROBLEM: *I need to make some 68-inch-tall solid porch posts, but my lathe bed has only a 36-inch capacity. What can I do?*

SOLUTION: The easiest solution is to turn each post in two or more sections. Then you can connect the pieces with a hanger bolt. First decide where you are going to make the break or breaks in the post. Locating a break adjacent to a bead will conceal the joint well.

After you have turned the separate pieces, drill a hole for the hanger bolt in the center of the ends that will be joined. Screw one end of the bolt into the first section of the post using vise grip pliers, as shown in the left photo. Then screw the other end of the post onto the protruding end of the bolt. For thicker posts, or columns, a band clamp can be used like an oil filter wrench to crank one half onto the other. A little glue spread on the post ends will help solidify the joint and seal it against moisture.

If the joint occurs on a straight section of the post, rather than in the valley under a bead, and the post will be painted, you can add biscuits across the joint for reinforcement. Screw the two sections together, and cut a series of biscuit slots across the joint. Glue biscuits into the slots and cut off the protruding halves. Fill any gaps with auto body putty, then sand the joint area smooth.

Bill and Joanne Storch
Corvallis, OR

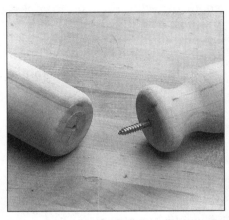 

A porch post turned in 2 parts is ready to be assembled (*left*). By locating the seam in the valley between 2 half-beads, the joint is practically invisible in the assembled post.

Turning a Perfect Cylinder

PROBLEM: *I'm trying to turn a straight cylinder, but I can't get a consistent diameter along the whole length of the turning. Is there a technique I can use to achieve this?*

SOLUTION: Try a block plane. First turn the stock more or less round. Then set a pair of calipers to the desired diameter, plus a scant 1/16 inch. Cut a clean groove in the cylinder with a parting tool and test it with the calipers, as shown in the left photo. When the calipers just slip over the cylinder, stop cutting. Cut a series of similar grooves about every 2 or 3 inches along the length of the cylinder to mark the diameter of the finished cylinder. Next roughly remove the stock between the grooves with a gouge. Now get out your block plane.

Remove the tool rest from the lathe. With the lathe turning, hold the plane on top of the cylinder so that the sole of the plane is parallel with the cylinder. Keeping the sole flat on the turning stock, turn the plane slightly clockwise so that it's at an angle to the stock, as shown below right. The more you turn it, the more it will cut. Move the plane evenly along the length of the cylinder until it is straight.

Jeff Day
Perkasie, PA

To turn a cylinder to a consistent diameter, rough out the shape and use a parting tool and calipers to mark the final thickness. Then use a block plane to shear the wood until you reach the bottom of the grooves formed by the parting tool.

AGAINST THE GRAIN

One-Shot Tapering Jig

THERE ARE SEVERAL GOOD TAPERING JIGS ON THE MARKET. *Each can be set to an infinite variety of tapers, and with a good deal of fussing you can get the precise taper you want. You can save a lot of time and money, however, by building a simple jig in your shop. This type of jig cuts only one taper, but it cuts that taper exactly, without fail, again and again.*

Start with a piece of plywood that is about 3 inches wider than the widest part of the tapered piece, and about 3 inches longer than the final tapered piece. Lay out the taper directly on the plywood, as shown below

left. Note that the edge of the plywood corresponds to the line the saw will follow. Cut along the layout lines on the band saw to make the jig.

If you've done your layout and cutting carefully, you can use the jig to set the rip fence. Place the widest part of the jig between the rip fence and the saw blade, and lock the fence in place. To make the cut, cradle your workpiece in the jig, as shown below right.

Jeff Day
Perkasie, PA

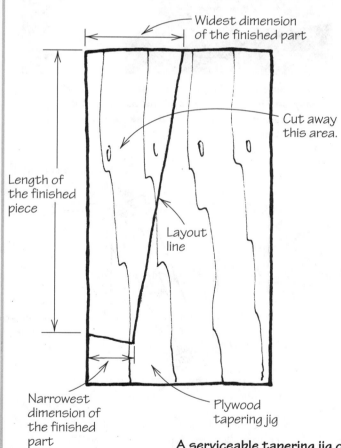

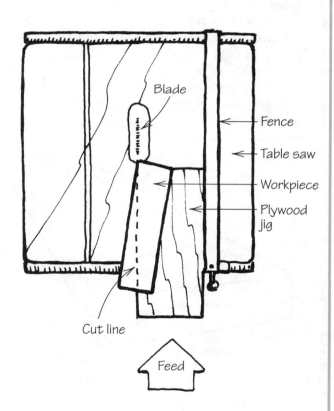

A serviceable tapering jig can be made from a piece of scrap plywood. Lay out the shape (above left). **Position the workpiece in the jig, set the fence, and make the cut** (above right).

CUTTING COVES ON THE TABLE SAW

Large cove moldings, like the cornice on a hutch or the crown molding for an entire room, are beyond the capacity of standard router bits. When you need a large cove, you can go to a professional shop that has a shaper and have what you want made. Or you can make it yourself on the table saw.

That's right, the table saw. Making cove moldings on the table saw is nothing new. But until you try it yourself, it will remain one of those elusive techniques that is easy to be skeptical about. Once you try it, you'll be skeptical no more.

To cut a cove, you simply run a board across the blade at an angle, as shown at right. A shallow angle—close to parallel with the fence—produces a narrow cove, while a steep angle—approaching perpendicular to the fence—produces a wide cove. You control the depth of the cove by adjusting the blade height. The most important aspect of this technique is to make very light cuts: Start with the blade only $\frac{1}{16}$ inch high, and raise it that small amount after each pass until you reach the final depth.

You can use any sharp blade to cut coves. Blades with more teeth will leave fewer ridges that have to be sanded out. You might also consider using a molding head cutter with a coving blade—this will leave a smoother surface still.

Cutting even very large coves for crown molding is easy on the table saw, as long as you take your time with the setup and make a series of very light cuts.

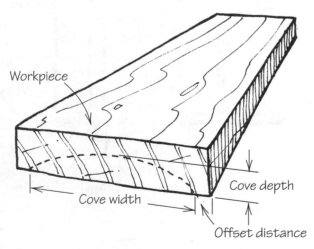

Step 1. Lay out the cove on the end of the stock.

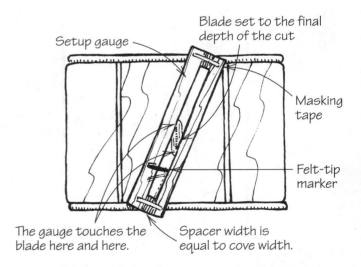

Step 2. With the blade height set to equal the cove depth, position a setup gauge at an angle so that both inside edges touch the saw blade.

To figure the angle and location of the fence relative to the blade, start by laying out the cove you want on the end of a piece of stock, as shown in *Step 1*. Set the saw blade to the final depth of cut for now.

Next make a setup gauge, like the one shown in *Step 2*. It could be an adjustable gauge, bolted together at the corners. But it's easier to cut strips of ¼-inch plywood and simply tape them together with spacers at the ends. The spacers should be equal to the width of the cove. Place the assembled gauge over the blade and shift it until one inside edge of the gauge touches the rear of the saw blade and the other inside edge touches the front of the blade. Draw a reference line along the inside edge of the right strip with a felt-tip marker, as shown in *Step 2*.

Now clamp an auxiliary fence (any 4- to 6-inch-wide board with a straight edge) parallel and to the

right of the angled line, as shown in *Step 3*. The distance between the line and the fence should be the same as the distance between the edge of the stock and the edge of the cove (the offset distance, as shown in *Step 1*).

Finally lower the blade so that it's barely above the table surface, and make the first cut, as shown in *Step 4*. Raise the blade slightly after each cut until you reach the final depth of cut. Make the last cut as light as possible to minimize the amount of sanding needed to clean up the saw marks.

Mark Duginske
Merrill, WI

RELATED INFO:
Sanding Coves, page 212

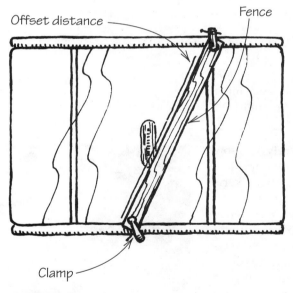

Step 3. Clamp an auxiliary fence to the saw table. The fence should be parallel to the pencil line but set away from the line by the offset distance laid out on the workpiece.

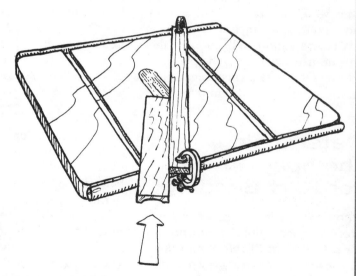

Step 4. Set the blade to a height of about ¹/₁₆". Guide the workpiece along the fence to make the first cut. Raise the blade ¹/₁₆" at a time until the cove is full depth.

Bending Wood

Making Quick Bending Forms

PROBLEM: *I was "volunteered" to fix a broken rocker on the rocking chair of a friend-of-a-friend. Is there a way to make a bent lamination quickly, without investing a lot in building the form?*

SOLUTION: For a quick, one-of-a-kind bend, as is required for replacing a rocking chair rocker, we've developed a reusable bending form that is made primarily from scraps. It works best for shallow curves made with narrow pieces (up to about 2 inches wide). Start by laying out the curve you need on a piece of scrap ¾-inch plywood, as shown. Then screw blocks of wood to the plywood along the inside of the curve. Make these blocks from pieces of a stout wood like oak or maple and place them 6 to 8 inches apart.

Wax everything well, to keep the glue-up from sticking to the plywood base and the blocks. Then spread glue on the laminates and clamp them to

Clamps

Wooden blocks

Plywood base

Bent lamination

To make a simple bending form, lay out the curve on a piece of ¾" plywood and screw evenly spaced blocks to the plywood along the curve.

the blocks to make the bend. We often will include an extra layer or two of ⅛-inch hardboard on the outside of the curve to protect the good stock from the clamps.

Bill and Joanne Storch
Corvallis, OR

Determining the Spacing for Kerf Bending

PROBLEM: *I want to kerf-bend a piece of wood to make an apron for a half-round table I'm making. How do I figure out how far apart the kerfs should be?*

SOLUTION: There are at least two ways of calculating exactly how far apart to space the kerfs. Both work, but seem to me to be more trouble than they're worth. What I've found is that if you space the kerfs more than 1 inch apart, the curve looks lumpy. The curve will also look lumpy if you space the kerfs

irregularly. So for a fairly shallow curve, like that for a table apron, I start by cutting a scrap with kerfs between ¾ and 1 inch apart (I pretty much eyeball the measurement). Then I test the piece to see if it will match the curve I'm after. Ninety-nine percent of the time, it does. Then I cut my workpiece using the same setup. For tighter curves, I start by spacing the kerfs about ½ inch apart. Regardless of the spacing, the set up for the cuts is the same: Screw an extension to your miter gauge and drive into it a small nail that is the necessary distance from the blade, as shown at right.

Ken Burton
New Tripoli, PA

Indexing the kerfs to keep the spacing equal is a simple matter of driving a small brad into a miter gauge extension fence.

PLANING JIG FOR TAPERED LAMINATIONS BY DAVID PAGE

Bent laminating is an efficient way to make curvacious parts that are strong and stable. However, if you want to make a bent lamination even more interesting by tapering it on the band saw, you'll end up with harsh glue lines across the face of the piece where you cut across the laminations.

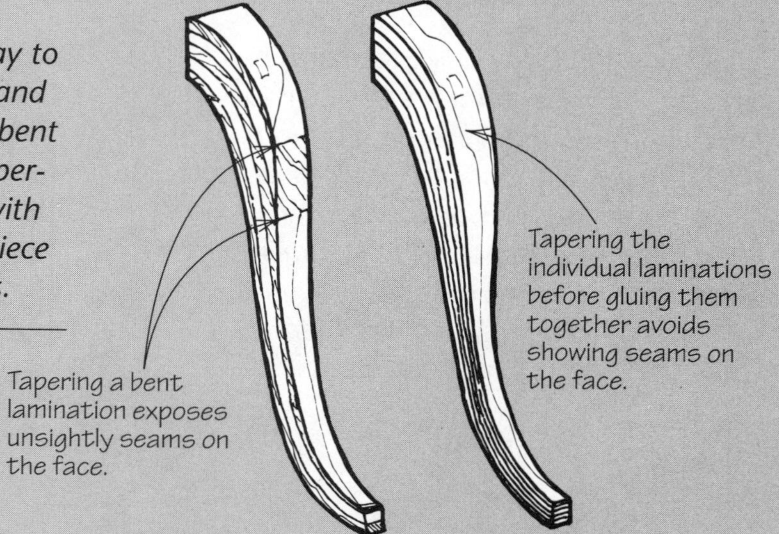

Tapering a bent lamination exposes unsightly seams on the face.

Tapering the individual laminations before gluing them together avoids showing seams on the face.

To avoid spoiling a project with these unsightly glue lines, you need to taper the individual strips of wood that make up the bent lamination. See the drawing above right. The planer is the machine for the job, and the simple jig shown below right will give you uniform results.

Make the jig quickly and cheaply from ¾-inch plywood and drywall screws. Build it just long enough to accept the stock to be tapered. With a straightedge, lay out the pitch of the floor on each jig side. Align the floor with the layout lines and glue it between the sides. Then glue and screw on the end pieces. If you make a wide jig, reinforce the floor with stiffening ribs that run between the sides. To determine the slope of the floor, you need to figure the amount of taper for each laminate. For example, if your finished lamination is 2 inches at the thickest part and 1 inch at the thinnest, and you are gluing up eight laminates, each one will be ¼ inch thick at its widest end and will taper to ⅛ inch. Therefore, the floor of the jig must slope ⅛ inch over its length. At the same time, the

Length of stock

Feed direction

Front lip must be smaller than the final thickness of the laminate's thin end.

Back lip

Front lip

Slope of jig's floor (exaggerated here for clarity) equals the amount of taper in each laminate.

Back

Front

Side

Reinforcing ribs

Drywall screws

lip at the high end of the jig needs to be smaller than the final thickness of the thin end of the laminate so that the planer won't cut into the jig. In this example, the jig would have a ¹⁄₁₆-inch lip at the high end and a ³⁄₁₆-inch lip at the low end.

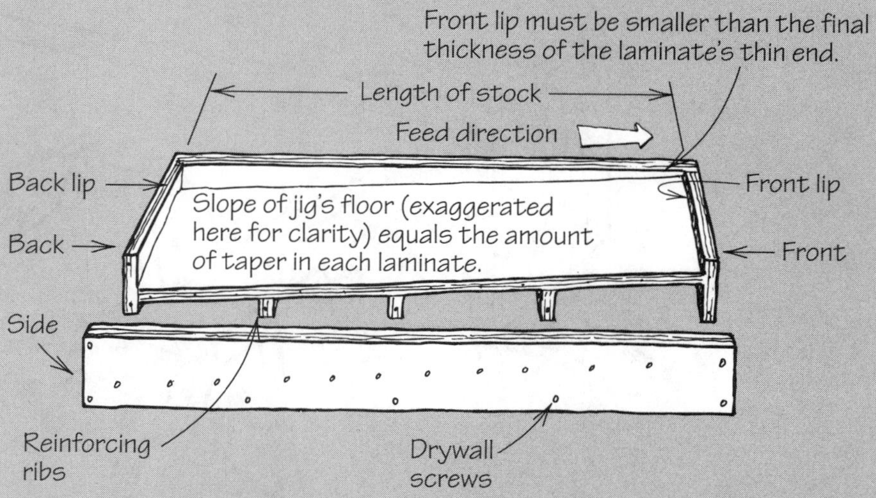

When preparing stock for tapered laminations, make the pieces

slightly thicker than the final thickness of the thick end to start with. That way the entire face will be completely planed on the final pass through the planer. Always feed the jig high end first through the machine. Once you have the laminations in hand, you can bend them as you would a regular bent lamination.

SHOP-MADE SOLUTIONS

INEXPENSIVE BENDING STEAMER BY DAVID PAGE

*I*f you think you'd like to steam bend the curved pieces on a project, but you don't anticipate many bending projects in the future, you can make a serviceable yet inexpensive steam box from common home center materials. This steamer is simple to make, yet durable enough to reuse if you later find a need for it.

End Cap Detail

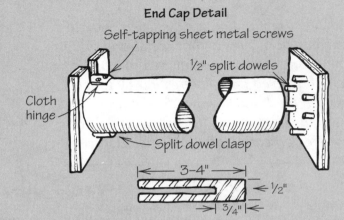

Self-tapping sheet metal screws

½" split dowels

Cloth hinge

Split dowel clasp

3–4"

½"

¾"

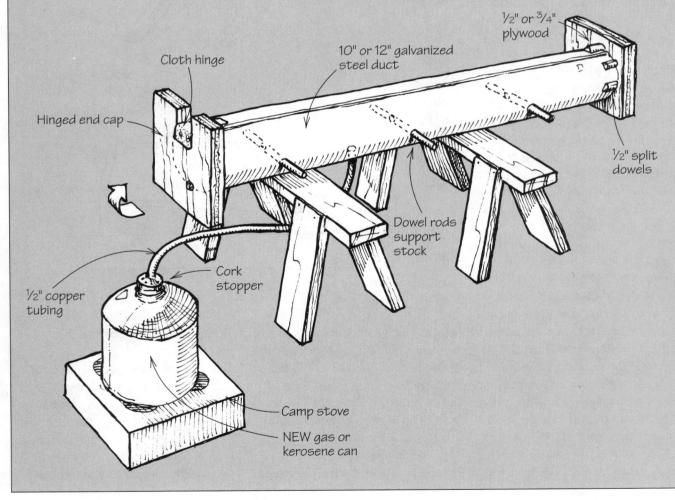

Cloth hinge

10" or 12" galvanized steel duct

½" or ¾" plywood

Hinged end cap

½" split dowels

½" copper tubing

Cork stopper

Dowel rods support stock

Camp stove

NEW gas or kerosene can

Start with a suitable length of galvanized steel duct. Orient the duct's seam so that it faces upward. This will keep the condensed steam from leaking out. Drill a hole into the bottom side of the duct. The hole should be the same diameter as the outside diameter of the copper tube. Also drill the same sized hole into the top of the metal can for the other end of the tube. Drill a second hole into the top of the can for the cork stopper. This will serve as a pressure-relief valve in case too much pressure builds up inside of the can.

Drill two series of holes along either side of the bottom of the duct, as shown at the bottom of the opposite page. Slide dowels through these holes, leaving an inch or so protruding from either side. The dowels form a shelf for your workpieces to rest on, keeping them off the floor of the steamer.

The ends of the duct must be capped to capture the steam. One cap can be more or less permanently fixed in place. The other is hinged to allow you to load and unload your workpieces. Make the caps from ½- or ¾-inch plywood. Hold the duct on end and trace around it to lay out the shape of the caps. On the end that will be permanently attached, drill six to eight evenly spaced ½-inch holes centered on this layout line. The exact spacing is not critical. Cut a 3- to 4-inch length of ½-inch dowel for each hole. Split each dowel along its length on the band saw, leaving the last inch uncut. Glue these dowels into the plywood holes, positioning the dowels so that the splits will grab the edges of the duct when the plywood is pressed against the duct, as shown in *End Cap Detail* on the opposite page.

For the hinged end cap, drill one ½-inch hole on the layout line at what will be its bottom-most point. Split a length of dowel and insert it into the hole to serve as a handle. At the top-most point, cut a notch into the plywood to create an opening for a hinge. Then make a cloth hinge from a piece of doubled up denim or canvas and attach it to both the duct and the plywood cap with self-tapping sheet metal screws. Wax the inside surfaces of both end caps to provide them with a little protection from the steam.

Set up the steam box on two sawhorses, with the hinged end slightly lower than the fixed end. Fill your gas can to about two-thirds of the way with water and insert the cork and one end of the copper tube into the holes in its top. Plug the other end of the copper tube into the steam box so that its end extends into the box about 1 or 2 inches. Light both burners if you have a two-burner stove. You should steam your wooden blanks one hour for each inch of thickness. You will be surprised at how much steam this steamer produces.

Note: Wear gloves when handling hot wood, and work quickly, as your bending "window" is only about a minute once the wood is removed from the steamer. Bending forms and clamps must be ready to go. Make extra wood blanks to compensate for pieces that fail.

MATERIALS LIST

Part	Quantity	Dimensions
Galvanized steel duct	1	10" or 12" wide
End caps	2	½" or ¾" × 14" × 14"
Heavy-gauge metal can*	1	2- to 5-gallon
Length of copper tubing	1	½" × 24"
Cork stopper (or a wad of aluminum foil)	1	To fit lid of can
2-burner camp stove	1	
Split dowel clasps	8–10	½" × 3"–4"
Self-tapping sheet metal screws	4	#8 × ½"
Scrap piece of sturdy cloth	1	6" × 6"

*A gasoline can or kerosene can is fine, but it must be new. The can should never have been used to hold fuel.

MULTI-PURPOSE BENDING TABLE BY E. E. "SKIP" BENSON

*B*ending wood can add a new
dimension to your furniture designs, but
building forms for *each individual curve*
can be an expensive proposition, especially
if you use a form only once or twice.

Instead of building a lot of
individual forms, consider building
a bending table, like the one
shown on this page. It can be
reconfigured easily to serve as a
form for almost any bend you're
likely to make. You can make
just the top, and support it on
sawhorses, then stow it out of the
way when you're done.

MATERIALS LIST

Part	Quantity	Dimensions
Sides	2	2" × 6" × 96"
Ends	2	2" × 6" × 45"
Legs	4	2" × 2" × 36"
Ledges	2	¾" × 1½" × 90" (or smaller to suit)
Crosspieces	30	¾" × 4" × 45"

HARDWARE

Drywall screws	As needed	3"
Drywall screws	As needed	1⅝"
Angle iron	30	2" × 3" × ¼"
Machine bolts with fender washers and nuts	30	¼" × 5"

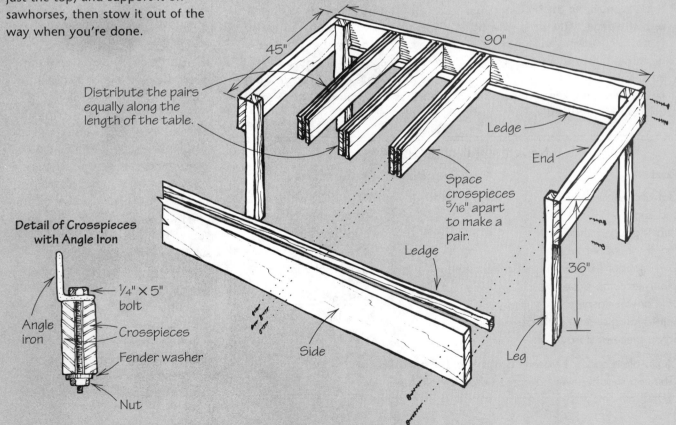

Distribute the pairs
equally along the
length of the table.

45"

90"

Ledge

End

Space
crosspieces
5/16" apart
to make a
pair.

Ledge

36"

**Detail of Crosspieces
with Angle Iron**

¼" × 5"
bolt

Angle
iron

Crosspieces

Fender washer

Nut

Side

Leg

Or you can add legs and use it as a general assembly table by adding a sheet of plywood over the top. You could even integrate the bending table into a workbench design.

The table's construction may seem to be on the heavy side, but it needs to be stout enough to support the weight of the many clamps you're likely to use in a complex bent lamination. The curves themselves are formed by positioning a series of angle irons along the crosspieces and bolting them into place. Exactly how many angle irons you'll need depends on the length of the pieces you're bending. I have about 30, which allows me to set up 2 bends on the table at the same time. Being able to make multiple bends at one time can save a lot of time (and fuel, if you're steam bending).

Pieces of angle iron bolted to crosspieces on this bending table allow for making a wide range of bends without making a different form for each one.

Avoiding Steam Bending Breaks

PROBLEM: *I steamed a piece of knot-free riven oak ($\frac{5}{8} \times \frac{7}{8}$ inch) for an hour, but it fractured when I tried to bend it to a 12-inch radius. What went wrong?*

SOLUTION: Bending wood is more art than science. I can tell you what you did right, but it's difficult to diagnose specific problems without inspecting the wood and observing your bending process.

Air-dried oak is a good choice of material for bending, and riving (splitting) the piece from the log was wise because it results in annular layers that run the full length of the piece. This reduces the chance of the wood splitting between rings that might otherwise run off the edge of a sawn piece. A good steam box will heat the wood to the necessary 180°F very quickly. I seldom steam a piece more than 15 minutes, so an hour should have been more than enough. As for technique, you need to work quickly before the wood begins to cool. As you bend the wood, pull it steadily, but don't yank it. A motion that's too quick won't give the fibers time to stretch.

It's possible that your log had begun to decay. Fungus often grows in wet wood—especially if bark was left on. Look for the blue or brown speckling that marks early stages of decay.

Mike Dunbar
Hampton, NH

ANOTHER VIEW: In order to prevent the wood from failing when steam bending, I always use a metal backstrap with end blocks, as shown below. To make the strap, cut a piece of galvanized sheet metal (18 gauge works well, as do the black banding straps that are used to hold shipping crates together) that is several inches longer than the piece that will be bent. Use sheet metal screws to attach wood blocks to each end of the strap. The distance between the blocks should be exactly equal to the length of the part you want to bend; any extra space defeats the purpose of the strap. To this end, you can attach one block to the strap through slotted holes, so that the strap can be adjusted to fit the bending blank perfectly. When the wood is removed from the steamer, place the backstrap against the outside surface of the bending blank with the end blocks against the ends of the blank. As you bend the wood, the ends of the blank will be forced against the blocks, and the strap will compress the outside surface, which should keep it from breaking.

Robert Treanor
San Francisco, CA

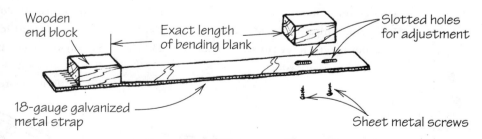

Wooden end block

Exact length of bending blank

Slotted holes for adjustment

18-gauge galvanized metal strap

Sheet metal screws

To minimize breakage when steam bending, support the stock in a metal backstrap.

JOINERY SOLUTIONS

IMPROVING CORNER JOINTS

Fitting Too-Tight Dovetails   121
Curing Loose Dovetails   122
Cutting Clean Dovetails   123
Filling Gaps at the Base of Dovetails   123
Routing Sliding Dovetail Slots   124
Combining Sliding Dovetail and
Dado Joints   125
Routing Sliding Dovetails   126
Removing Waste
for Half-Blind Dovetails   127
Making Mock Dovetails   127
Simplifying a Drawer Lock Joint   128

MAKING BETTER MITERS

Creating Gap-Free Case Joint Miters   130
Curing Gaps in Frame Miters   130
Getting Clean Miters
in Veneer Edge Banding   132
Mitering Crown Molding   133
Matching Mitered Profiles   133
Routing Spline Miter Grooves   134
Adding Splines to Picture Frames   134

FRAME JOINERY SOLUTIONS

Making Simple Cope-and-Stick Frames   135
Setting Up Cope-and-Stick Router Bits   136

MORTISE AND TENON SOLUTIONS

Dealing with Offset Joints   138
Fine Tuning Tenons   138
Removing Chips from a Mortise   138
Laminating Stock for Large Mortises   139
Cutting Tapered Wedges   139

Joining Three Sticks at One Point   140
Trimming Mortises Square   140
Mortising Round Stock   142
Routing Tenons on Round Stock   142
Mortise-and-Tenon Basics   143
Tightening Through-Tenons   144
Correcting Ill-Fitting Tenons   144
Concealing Uneven Frame Joints   145
Table Saw Tenons in a Single Pass   145
Mortising Jig for Separate
Tenon Joints   146

DOWELING AND DRILLING SOLUTIONS

Grooving Dowels for Better Joints   148
Sizing Tenons on the Lathe   148
Drilling Perpendicular Holes
without a Drill Press   149
Joining Short Spindles
to Make a Longer One   150
Doweling Difficulties Eliminated   150

HANDLING CASE JOINERY

Making Perfect Dadoes   151
Cutting Back-to-Back Dadoes   151
Concealing Dado Joints   152
Two Dado Routing Jigs   153
Making Accurate Half-Lapped Dividers   154
Setting Up Half-Laps   154

MAKING EDGE JOINTS

Cutting Biscuit Slots in Beveled Edges   155
Stacking Biscuit Joints   155
Fixing Misplaced Biscuit Slots   156
Rabbeting Edges without Tear-Out   157
Biscuit Joint Depression   157

Improving Corner Joints

Fitting Too-Tight Dovetails

PROBLEM: *No matter how carefully I cut my dovetails, a few of the pins are usually too tight. What's the best way to make them fit?*

SOLUTION: You can make fitting tight dovetails easier by undercutting the pins and tails in areas that won't be seen. Just be careful not to undercut too much of the mating surfaces or your joints won't be very strong. As a general rule, I try to leave at least 75 percent of the glue surfaces in contact with each other.

First undercut the bottom of the sockets on both the pin and tail boards. Leave a flat shoulder of about 1/16 inch on each side, and then angle your chisel to cut out a V. This removes the end-grain surfaces that might be slightly high and that might be keeping the boards from seating against each other. Because end grain doesn't provide much of a glue surface, you don't have to worry about weakening the joint by undercutting these areas. You can create a straight, flat shoulder during lay out: When you mark the line at the base of the pins and sockets, do so with a sharp knife. Make several passes until the line is deep enough to create the shoulder.

After you've undercut the end grain, stand the pin board upright in your vise. Carve out the interior of the pin with a 1/4-inch chisel.

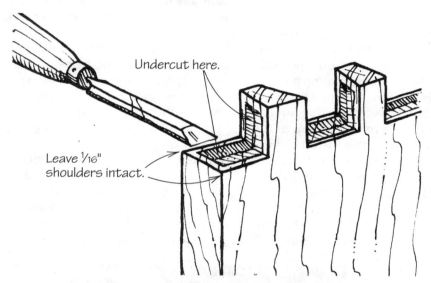

To make assembling dovetails easier, pare back all but the outer 1/16" of the contact surfaces.

This removes surfaces that might not be perfectly flat and which could interfere with assembly. Do the same on the tails.

Now test fit the joint. You've already removed most of the problem areas, but ease the sides gently together in case there are more. When you take the joint apart, any area that was binding will be shiny. Trim these areas back slightly with a wide, sharp chisel. The joint will only get tighter when there's glue in it, so keep testing and trimming until the joint slides smoothly home. Note that dovetail joints that are made with softer woods like pine and poplar can be forced together more easily than can those made with harder woods like maple and cherry. The harder the wood, the more thorough the fitting process should be.

Jeff Day
Perkasie, PA

121

Curing Loose Dovetails

PROBLEM: *What can I do if part of a dovetail joint that I have cut is too loose and leaves an unsightly gap?*

SOLUTION: Glue up the joint as usual. After the glue dries, saw along the loose joint line at a 45-degree angle with a fine saw to make the gap a consistent width. Then cut a strip of wood from material that is the same as the pieces you're joining together. The thickness of the strip should match the width of the saw kerf. Glue the strip in the kerf at a 45-degree angle and trim the ends flush. The strip will show end grain on both sides of the joint, blending in nearly perfectly with the ends of the mating pin and tail. For an extra tight patch, cut the strips slightly oversized, then squash them in a vise to make them fit the kerf. When you glue them in place, the strips will swell with the moisture from the wet glue and really wedge themselves in place.

Ben Erickson
Eutaw, AL

Hiding gaps in dovetails is a simple matter of cutting along the joint line to create an even gap (*left*), then filling in the saw kerf with a strip of matching wood (*right*).

ANOTHER VIEW: If your dovetails are too loose, you're not alone: Loose dovetails have been a problem ever since dovetails were invented. Likewise, there is a fix that dates back to medieval times: Wedge the pins.

If you get a chance to look at old furniture, look for a wooden shim that runs through the length of the dovetail pins. Look closely and you'll see it on old Pennsylvania painted dower chests, on the back of drawers, and on more complicated dovetail joints, like beveled and double-beveled joints.

So, if you find your dovetails aren't quite up to snuff, cut a slot down the middle of the pins with your dovetail saw. Japanese dozukis, which are great for cutting pins and tails, are a bit too fine for this. Use a regular dovetail saw or backsaw instead. Cut a slot in each pin, whether or not there's a gap. It will make it look like you *meant* to do this.

Make the wedge from the same wood as the pins. Begin by cutting a $1/16$-inch-thick slice of veneer from the edge of a board on the table saw. Guide the wood against the fence and let the veneer peel off on the other side of the blade. Cut the veneer into pieces about $1/2$ inch longer than the pins. Chamfer the end of each wedge to make it easier to drive. Assemble the joint the same way you assemble any other dovetail. While the glue is still wet, drive the wedge into the slot you've cut, forcing the pins to expand and close any gaps.

Jeff Day
Perkasie, PA

To make the slots for a wedged dovetail joint, cut down the center of each pin with a dovetail saw before assembling the joint. Insert wedges at assembly.

Cutting Clean Dovetails

PROBLEM: *Every time I try to cut a set of dovetails, my saw cuts start out fine, but then veer off my layout lines. What am I doing wrong?*

SOLUTION: First make sure your saw is sharp. A dull saw makes trying to cut a straight line a truly frustrating experience. Many hardware stores have a sharpening service that will sharpen a dovetail saw (or you can learn to sharpen your saw yourself—it's not that difficult).

Once you know your saw is sharp, take a look at your sawing stance. As your arm pistons back and forth with the saw, the motion should feel fluid, not forced. Try moving to one side or the other until you align yourself with the cut and your arm's natural swing. Also make sure your workpiece is held as low as possible in the vise. This will cut down on vibration and make sawing easier.

Also consider how much it matters if your first cuts don't follow the lines exactly. Regardless of whether you cut the pins or the tails first, you're going to make the second piece match the first. So if the angle varies a little on the first piece, who cares? As long as the cuts are square (on the pin board, they should be perpendicular to the end of the board; on the tail board, they should be perpendicular to the face) the joint will go together.

If your cuts on the first pieces are out of square, clean them up before cutting the second half of the joint. Check all the cuts with a small square and pare them into compliance with a sharp chisel, as shown, before scribing the mating piece.

Ken Burton
New Tripoli, PA

Before scribing the second half of a dovetail joint from the first, take a few minutes and double check to make sure that the cuts on the first piece are straight and square.

Filling Gaps at the Base of Dovetails

PROBLEM: *I cut a series of dovetails for a blanket chest and nearly every one has a gap where the base of the tail meets the pin. What can I do?*

SOLUTION: If you catch the problem before you glue the piece together, you have several options. First double check to make sure the sockets are clean and there aren't any chips or high spots to keep the tails from seating. If there are still gaps, you can cut the sockets slightly deeper to create a new shoulder. Use a straightedge to maintain a crisp shoulder, as shown in the photo on page 124. As you clamp the joint together, make sure that the clamps are bearing directly on the tails and not on the ends of the pins. You may need to make some special clamping blocks that bridge the pin ends, as shown at right.

If you discover the gaps after glue-up, you are pretty much limited to some kind of filler. You'll

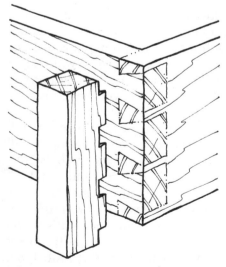

A dovetail clamp block isolates the clamp pressure on the tails.

get the best grain and color match if you use real wood. Slightly taper slips of a matching veneer (or a thinly cut piece of solid stock). Rub some glue into the gaps and tap the slips into place. Trim them flush after the glue dries.

If you'd rather use a commercial filler, I recommend the type you apply after finishing the piece. There are fillers on the market (Color Putty is one brand) that are made for this kind of application. Find (or mix) a good color match and wipe the putty into the gaps. Allow it to dry for a few minutes; then wipe away any excess with a clean rag.

AVOIDING THE PROBLEM: Establishing a consistent shoulder line is not at all difficult if you use a guide block. Mill up a piece of hardwood—

something tough, like maple—with faces and edges square. This guide block must be at least as long as the joint is wide.

After making all the angled saw cuts, and before chiseling out the waste, carefully clamp the square guide block precisely along the shoulder line, as shown in the photo at right. Now hold the flat of the chisel against the guide block. With a single mallet blow, cut the shoulder line. Then remove a chip of waste. by cutting at an angle through the waste down to the shoulder. I work half-way down from one face, flip the board, and repeat the process on the second face.

Robert Treanor
San Francisco, CA

To establish and maintain a straight, crisp shoulder line, clamp a straightedge on top of your workpiece to help guide the chisel.

Routing Sliding Dovetail Slots

PROBLEM: *The first time I tried to cut a sliding dovetail, I thought I was going to fry my router. The wood was smoking, the router was screaming, and the whole time I thought the bit was just going to snap right off. Now I have another project that calls for sliding dovetails. Isn't there a better way?*

SOLUTION: Sliding dovetails are definitely a challenge. Routing a dovetail slot simply flies in the face of Routing Rule No. 1, which stipulates that the full depth of a large cut has to be achieved by making a series of light passes. Because of the bit's profile, you have to make the cut in a single pass.

As a practical matter, most sliding dovetails don't need to be all that deep—¼ inch or so is adequate in ¾-inch material. So don't make them unnecessarily deep. But sometimes you'll want a ⅜- or ½-inch-deep cut and that's where the going gets rough. It makes matters worse if you're limited to a bit with a ¼-inch shank. What to do then?

Make a pass or two with a straight bit first. This will clean out the bulk of the waste material, leaving only the angled walls of the cut to be formed by the dovetail bit.

Use a straight bit that has a diameter that matches (or is slightly smaller than) that of the dovetail bit's waist, which is usually about three-quarters of the overall diameter. Set the bit to cut just shy of the groove's bottom, so that when you do make the dovetail cut, you'll get a clean finish cut on all three surfaces.

Bill Hylton
Kempton, PA

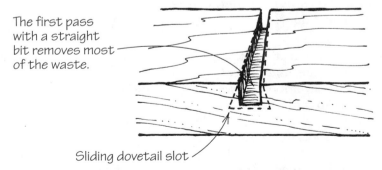

The first pass with a straight bit removes most of the waste.

Sliding dovetail slot

When routing sliding dovetail slots, always make a preliminary cut with a straight bit or your table saw.

Combining Sliding Dovetail and Dado Joints

PROBLEM: *On a chest of drawers that I'm trying to reproduce, the drawer rails are attached to the case sides with sliding dovetails. Then the drawer runners fit into shallow dadoes that have been cut across the case sides immediately behind the sliding dovetail sockets. [See the drawing below left]. What is the best way to get the sliding dovetail sockets and the dadoes to align?*

SOLUTION: There are two approaches to this problem. First, you could try to make the two cuts using the same setup. Start by clamping a straightedge to the case side and rout the dado, guiding the edge of the router along the straightedge. Then swap a dovetail bit for the dado bit and rout the sliding dovetail, using the same straightedge as a guide. The trouble with this approach is that you are continually resetting the router. Also, setting the depth of cut so that it is just right can be a pain, especially if you have to do it more than once.

Here's a better solution: Make all the dadoes first, either with a router or on the table saw. With this approach, the dadoes can run all the way out through the edges of the sides, so you don't have to stop them, as shown below left. (This was a standard practice in 18th-century furniture.) However, because the drawer rails will fit into both the dado and the sliding dovetail, the drawer rail and the runner must be the same thickness. Next build the simple jig shown below right. It features a runner that uses the dado itself to guide the sliding dovetail cut. Attach the jig to your router's base. Mount a dovetail bit in the router and set it to the appropriate depth of cut. Rout the dovetails by sliding the jig's runner along the dado. You can screw a stop to the jig to ensure that the dovetails all stop the same distance in from the edge of the case side.

Robert Treanor
San Francisco, CA

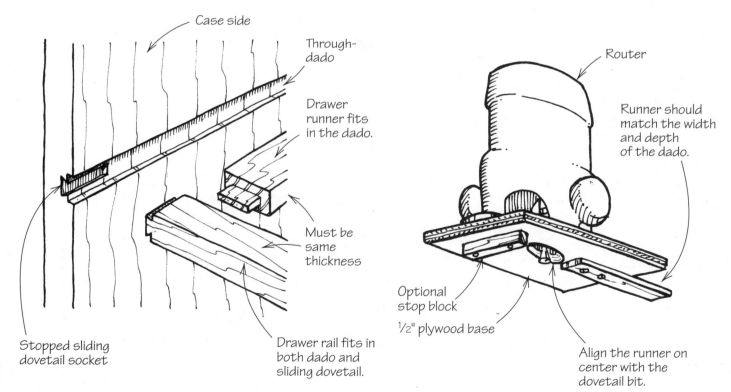

This jig (above right) is designed for routing a stopped sliding dovetail inside a dado (above left). Cut the dado first, then use it to guide the runner on the jig while you cut the dovetail slot.

Routing Sliding Dovetails

PROBLEM: *I just finished cutting a bunch of sliding dovetails on my router table. I used the same setup for all the cuts, but when I put the pieces together, some of them fit well and some didn't. What did I do wrong?*

SOLUTION: The trick to routing consistent sliding dovetails is to use two setups to cut the male part of the joint—one setup for each side. I suspect that you used just a single setup to cut both sides. That is, you cut one side of the joint, then you turned the piece around and cut the second side without moving the router table fence. This will work most of the time. But if your stock varies at all in thickness, that variation will show up in the dovetail. Even a small planer snipe is enough to cause trouble.

Instead, set up the router table to cut one side of the joint with the bit partially buried in the fence, as shown in *Step 1*. For all pieces, cut one side by running the stock along the fence from right to left. Then reset the fence so that there is space between it and the bit, as shown in *Step 2*. The exact space will depend on the size of the dovetail you want. Make some test pieces to set the spacing just right. When you have the fence set the way you want it, cut the second side of all the pieces by running them along the fence from left to right.

By cutting your dovetails with two setups, you can run the same side of the stock against the fence for both cuts. This means that the resulting dovetails will be a consistent thickness no matter how much the thickness of your workpieces varies.

You can use this practice for other operations as well. Whenever possible, use the same side and/or edge of a piece as a reference point. This will minimize problems if your wood has been cut inconsistently.

Ken Burton
New Tripoli, PA

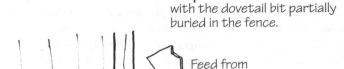

Step 1. Cut the first side with the dovetail bit partially buried in the fence.

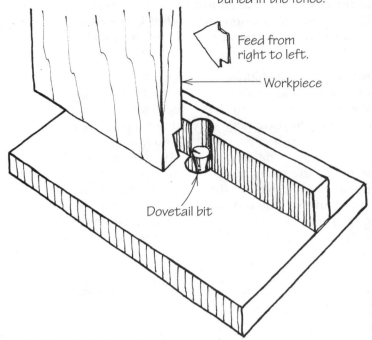

Feed from right to left.

Workpiece

Dovetail bit

Step 2. Adjust the fence to cut the second side, and feed the workpiece in the opposite direction.

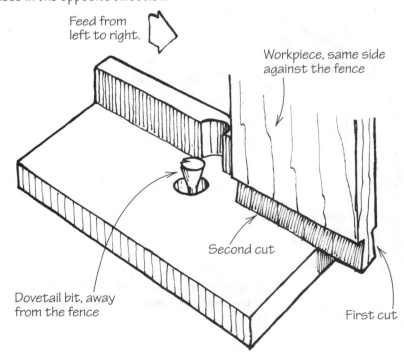

Feed from left to right.

Workpiece, same side against the fence

Second cut

Dovetail bit, away from the fence

First cut

Removing Waste for Half-Blind Dovetails

PROBLEM: *I use the old mallet-and-chisel routine to remove the waste from between the pins of half-blind dovetails. This method takes forever; is there a faster way?*

SOLUTION: You can speed up this task by drilling away most of the waste. After laying out the joint, I saw to the line in the usual manner. Then I make a quick trip to the drill press. Select a Forstner bit with a diameter that is slightly greater than the thickness of the tail board, and mount it in the chuck. Set the depth stop so that the bit stops just shy of the total socket depth. Drill out as much of the waste as possible, keeping the edge of the bit slightly away from the shoulder line. After you've finished drilling, chisel out the rest of the waste to finish the job.

Robert Treanor
San Francisco, CA

ANOTHER VIEW: My tool of choice for this time-eater is the router (besides, it appeals to my sense of irony to use a router to make hand-cut dovetails). After laying out the joints and making the required saw cuts, clamp a straight length of wood right along the shoulder line of the pin board, as shown at right. Chuck a pattern cutting bit (this is basically a flush-trimming bit with the bearing mounted on the shank, rather than at the end of the bit) in your router. Set the depth of cut to match the socket depth and rout away as much of the waste as possible. Finish cleaning the sockets with chisels. The beauty of this system is that, in addition to saving a lot of time, the router leaves the shoulder cut and the socket bottom perfectly flat and smooth.

Ken Burton
New Tripoli, PA

A Forstner bit can make short work of removing the waste from half-blind dovetail sockets.

Even if you rout away most of the waste, you've still made the cuts by hand, and you still have bragging rights for having made "hand-cut" dovetails.

MAKING MOCK DOVETAILS

Y ou can get the classy look of dovetail joints in small boxes and drawers without all the work that hand-cut dovetails require. I call it a mock dovetail; it's really a miter joint with dovetail keys added after assembly.

Once you've assembled the box, set up a dovetail bit in a router table. Make a cradle to hold the assembled box at a 45-degree angle to the table by screwing two strips of wood to a piece of plywood. Set a fence to locate the first dovetail and make the cut in all four corners. Adjust the fence for subsequent cuts.

With the same dovetail bit, shape a dovetail key onto a length of stock, carefully checking the fit. Then rip the key from the wider stock. Crosscut the individual keys to length and glue them into the slots.

Tony O'Malley
Emmaus, PA

To cut dovetail slots in a mitered corner, use a simple cradle jig to hold the box at a 45° angle to the table.

SIMPLIFYING A DRAWER LOCK JOINT

Let's say that you want to make a strong and good looking joint for a bank of drawers but don't want to spend the time to cut dovetails. Here's an alternative that's strong and attractive but far easier to make.

I recommend what's generally called a drawer lock joint, as shown. It's a strong joint because the two parts interlock. The drawer front is given a rabbet with a little tongue that fits into a slot in the drawer side. Unlike a plain rabbet joint, the parts are hooked together mechanically, so the joint doesn't require reinforcement with brads or nails.

Made on the table saw, the joint always looked overly tedious to me and required a lot of setups. But then I found a way to make all the cuts with a single router table setup. It does require a ⅛-inch slot cutting router bit (available from most mail-order woodworking suppliers), but once you've made this joint, you'll be using the slot cutting bit every time you want a strong and clean drawer or small box.

There are two limitations to the all-in-one setup: You have to use ½-inch-thick stock for the sides; and the front (which can be greater than ½ inch thick) overlaps and is flush with the sides. However, these are small concessions for a lot of efficiency. On the plus side, because it's so easy to make, you'll want to use this joint on all four corners of a drawer, not just the front. Also, it works as well with plywood as with solid wood drawer parts.

Start by setting the fence flush with the bearing so that the cutter can take a full cut. Position the top edge of the cutter so that it is ⅜ inch above the table, as shown in *Step 1* on the opposite page. Also add a ¼-inch plywood auxiliary fence to the main fence. The auxiliary fence must be high enough off the table to allow the drawer front to slide under the fence with about ¼ inch of space to spare. Attach the auxiliary fence with countersunk screws or clamps. (The clamps must be far enough apart not to interfere with the cut that is made on the drawer side in *Step 4*.) Then make the first cut on all the drawer fronts.

The second cut is identical to the first, except that for this cut you slip an ⅛-inch shim piece under the drawer front, as shown in *Step 2* (⅛-inch hardboard is ideal for this purpose, but any material will work).

The drawer lock is a solid mechanical joint. It can be made with a single router table setup as shown in the drawings (*opposite page*).

This cut simply widens the groove to ¼ inch without changing the setup.

Next stand the drawer front on end with its inside face against the fence and rout away part of the slender tongue, as shown in *Step 3*. This completes the drawer front part of the joint.

Finally, cut a slot in the inside faces of the drawer sides, as shown in *Step 4*. You'll be surprised at how perfectly this joint fits together—and how quick it is to make with a single setup.

Bill Hylton
Kempton, PA

Step 1. Make the first cut with the drawer front flat on the router table. The workpiece is against the fence, passing below the auxiliary fence.

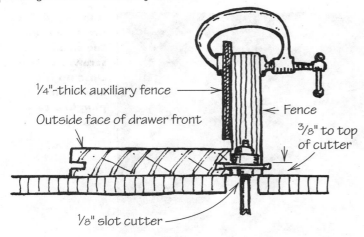

¼"-thick auxiliary fence

Outside face of drawer front

Fence

³⁄₈" to top of cutter

⅛" slot cutter

Step 3. Stand the drawer front on end and slide it along the auxiliary fence.

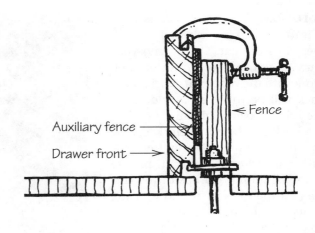

Fence

Auxiliary fence

Drawer front

Step 2. Place the drawer front on top of the shim piece, with the same face up as on the first cut, and make the second cut.

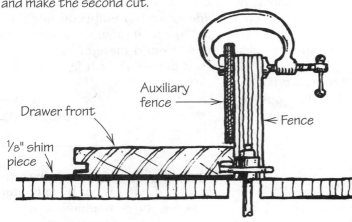

Auxiliary fence

Fence

Drawer front

⅛" shim piece

Step 4. Slot the drawer sides with the workpiece on end and against the auxiliary fence.

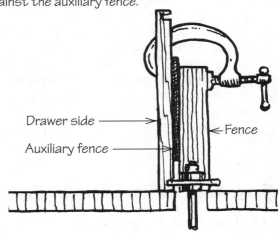

Drawer side

Fence

Auxiliary fence

Making Better Miters

Creating Gap-Free Case Joint Miters

PROBLEM: *Every time I try to build a cabinet case with mitered corners, the joints tend to gap. How can I fix these gaps, and is there any way to banish them from my work?*

SOLUTION: A mitered case is difficult to glue up, no matter how well the joints are cut. Organizing your glue-up can save you a lot of grief. Work with the case on its back. If the back will be rabbeted in place, cut the rabbets before glue-up, and slip the back in place to help keep the assembly square. Clamp the case with band clamps, and put picture frame or similar clamps at the corners on the front of the case. If the joints are accurate, you should be able to clamp the miters tight.

If, despite your best efforts, the miters still don't close perfectly, strike while the glue is wet. Hold a screwdriver at a slight angle to the miter. Slide the screwdriver along the miter, applying enough pressure to push the point of the miter into the gap. Repeat with the screwdriver on the adjacent side. The corner becomes slightly rounded as a result—even the best miters are intentionally rounded when they are sanded—and the gap is now closed.

Sometimes you end up with gaps on the inside of the case instead of

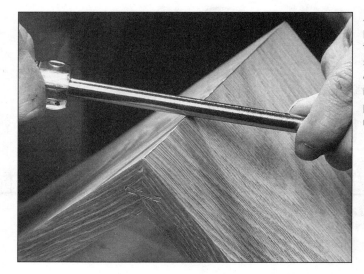

A little judicious pressure from the shank of a screwdriver can close up the inevitable gapping in a case miter joint.

on the case's outside. If you're patient and a bit on the compulsive side, you can fill these gaps with a commercial filler. I generally just leave them alone. A cabinet is designed to hold things—drawers, clothes, stereo equipment. Whatever it holds will hide the interior gaps from sight.

AVOIDING THE PROBLEM: If you frequently end up with gaps in your miters, the problem may be

caused by the way you're cutting the joint. One of the simplest ways to get an accurate miter joint is to rout it with a 45-degree chamfer bit in a hand-held router. Get a carbide bit with a ball-bearing guide, and guide it against a template made from a piece of ¼-inch plywood that you've cut for the job.

Jeff Day
Perkasie, PA

Curing Gaps in Frame Miters

PROBLEM: *I can't make a gap-free mitered frame to save my life. I must be doing something fundamentally wrong, no?*

SOLUTION: Whether they're in a face frame or a picture frame, miters tend to have gaps in them; it happens to all of us. The problem

can be either in the length of the individual parts or in the angle of the miter. But the root of the problem is miters in general: If one piece

is only slightly longer than the others, or if a miter is out by only half a degree, there is almost nothing you can do to correct things.

Almost. A picture framer's vise (see "Sources," beginning on page 298) has a small slot right at the corner which helps solve the problem. This slot is designed to let you trim a miter joint right on the vise without damaging your saw. Here's what you do: Put adjacent sides of the frame in the vise, and clamp them so that the miters are as tight as you can get them. Then cut right down through the joint with a fine-toothed backsaw, as shown on this page. The cut trims the long ends of the miter, allowing you to close the gap in the joint. Cut all the way through, remove the parts, and repeat on the remaining corners. Trimming has changed the length of the sides, and what you do to one corner you'll need to do to the others. Once you've trimmed all four corners, test the fit. The frame should now assemble perfectly. If it doesn't, repeat the process.

AVOIDING THE PROBLEM: If you're consistently trimming corners two or three times, you'll be better off if you invest some time perfecting the way you cut miters. If you're working on a table saw, begin by screwing a long, straight fence to your miter gauge. This supports the cut and keeps the wood from flexing and changing its angle slightly as the blade pushes against it. A strip of sandpaper glued along the length of this fence will help, too. The abrasive will help prevent the wood from inadvertently sliding out of position.

Once you've set your miter gauge, double-check the angle. The markers on the miter gauge are far too large for accuracy, so don't even look at them. Instead, check the angle by placing one face of a drafting triangle or speed square against the blade and the other against the miter gauge. When the angle's right, make a test cut on a piece that's at least twice as wide as the one in the frame. The extra width compounds any small discrepancies that might not be visible in a narrower test piece. Test fit your sample joint against a square to make sure you have a true

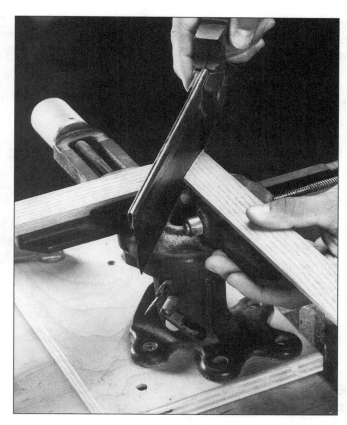

A picture framer's vise is the answer to cutting tight frame miters. A slot built into the vise allows you to trim an ill-fitting joint just before assembly.

90 degrees; then look for gaps. If the miter gaps at the outside, the angle you are cutting is too small. If it gaps at the inside, the angle is too large. Adjust the gauge accordingly.

In order for miters to fit perfectly in a frame, the length of the opposite sides must be exactly the same. To make sure that they are, clamp a stop block to the wooden extension on your fence. Position it so that you can butt one end of the frame against it, and use the saw to cut it to the desired length.

If you're working on a chop saw, the 45-degree stop tends to be accurate. You should still work with a fence and a stop block to ensure that each piece is the proper length. If the joint is consistently off, try putting a shim between the fence and the stock to adjust the angle slightly. Paper, masking tape, and playing cards all work well.

If you're working on a radial arm saw, minor variances are normal.

Your only recourse is to trim by hand on the picture frame clamps.

Jeff Day
Perkasie, PA

RELATED INFO:
Avoiding Bad Miter Joints,
page 13

ANOTHER VIEW: I've found that most often the culprit in a poorly cut miter joint is just a bad miter gauge setting. Here is a straightforward method for setting your saw so that it's dead-on before you cut the first miter. Set your miter gauge to 45 degrees according to the gauge. On two scrap pieces of wood, cut a sample miter. Lay them on a flat surface, put them together, and use any square that you are confident is truly 90 degrees to check that they form a true 90-degree corner, as shown at the top of page 132. It is a very good bet that in order to make the corner square, you will have to open the miter at either the inside or the outside of the corner. If the joint is open at the inside of the corner, angle the miter gauge more toward the fence. If it's open at the outside, pivot the miter gauge away from the blade. Keep making test cuts until your joint is perfect. If you can't get dead-on cuts despite your adjustments, then the problem may be a poorly fitting miter gauge, a bent or wobbly blade, or even a dull blade.

David Page
Swarthmore, PA

RELATED INFO:
Twenty-Minute Tune-Up:
The Table Saw, page 252

Instead of checking a miter cut at 45°, cut two miters on pieces of stock, hold them together, and check the corner with a reliable square.

Getting Clean Miters in Veneer Edge Banding

PROBLEM: *I use veneer tape to cover the plywood edges in cabinets that I build, but I often have trouble getting the miters on the tape to meet exactly at the corners. I think that I cut them accurately beforehand, but once I get them to the cabinets, I'm often disappointed. What am I doing wrong?*

SOLUTION: I suggest that you use a method adapted from a wallpaper hanging joint called a double-cut.

First cut the veneer tape to overlap at the corners and spread contact cement along both the tape and the plywood edge. Before placing the tape down on the box edge, lay a piece of waxed paper along each edge extending out a few inches from the corner. If you're using veneer tape with a heat-sensitive glue backing, skip the waxed paper and just iron down all but the last few inches of the tape.

Now use a sharp chisel or razor knife guided against a straightedge to cut through both pieces of overlapping veneer at the same time, thus trimming the miter to a perfect 45 degrees. When you're done, lift the veneer, remove the waxed paper, and press the perfectly fit veneer in place.

Robert Treanor
San Francisco, CA

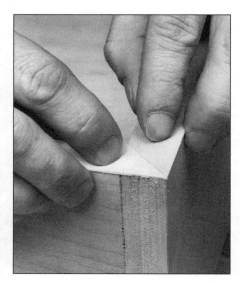

Cut the miter using a sharp razor knife. Both pieces of veneer tape overlap the corner, while the wax paper prevents them from sticking until after the miter is cut.

Mitering Crown Molding

PROBLEM: *I've tried mitering some crown molding to use as a cornice on a cabinet, but I keep getting it wrong. What's the trick?*

SOLUTION: If there's a trick involved, it's that you cut the molding upside down—but more on that in a moment. First, realize that crown molding requires compound miters. This is equally true for cornice molding attached to a cabinet and crown molding where the walls meet the ceiling. If you're trying to cut the molding flat against your saw table or fence, you'll have a devil of a time. You could determine the correct combination of blade angle and fence angle that would allow you to make the cuts with the stock laying flat, but there's a much easier method.

First hold the molding in position against your cabinet. Mark the base of the miter where the molding meets the side of the cabinet, and lay a mark across the face of the molding to indicate the direction of the miter cut—outward from bottom to top. Now the trick: Flip the molding upside down and position it on your saw, as shown. The edge that was against the cabinet should be against the vertical fence of the miter box or miter gauge. Attach a stop block to hold the molding at the correct angle. An L-shaped auxiliary fence works well on either the table saw or an electric miter saw. Using this arrangement, you can cut all of your miters with the blade square to the table or base of the saw, but at a 45-degree angle to the fence.

Tony O'Malley
Emmaus, PA

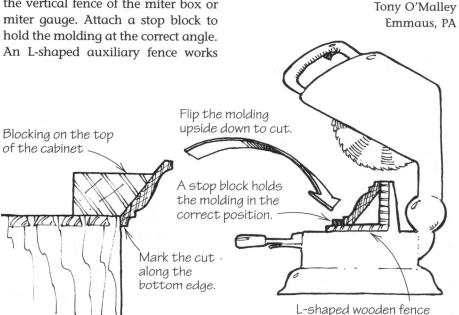

Blocking on the top of the cabinet

Flip the molding upside down to cut.

A stop block holds the molding in the correct position.

Mark the cut along the bottom edge.

L-shaped wooden fence added to the saw

The trick to cutting crown molding is to hold the stock in its correct wall-to-ceiling position—only upside down.

Matching Mitered Profiles

PROBLEM: *I am applying a molding using mitered joints. Unfortunately, the pieces of molding are not exactly the same. As a result, the two mitered surfaces will not line up as perfectly as I would like. Any suggestions?*

SOLUTION: You can usually blend the moldings together by slightly altering the shape of the one that overhangs. Use a file or even a wooden strip with a piece of sandpaper adhered to it. Gently abrade away the overhang. Be careful to do this blending over several inches. That way it will not be noticeable and will not show up as a repair.

AVOIDING THE PROBLEM: Even moldings bought at a lumberyard are not always exactly the same from length to length. However, some jobs are so large that you have to buy several lengths of molding. When you need to make miters, try to use the same length of stock for adjacent sides of the joint. You can also cut your own moldings on a shaper or router table. If they are all cut with the same setup, they will have the exact same profiles.

Mike Dunbar
Hampton, NH

When the profile on mitered moldings doesn't line up or match, blend in the overhang over a few inches using a plane, chisel, and sandpaper.

Routing Spline Miter Grooves

PROBLEM: *I'm trying to rout grooves in the mitered edge of a board for a splined miter joint. How the heck can I stabilize the router on such a narrow edge?*

SOLUTION: When routing grooves for spline miters, I clamp all four case sides together, as shown below. This creates a square shoulder for the router fence and at the same time provides a sufficient bearing surface for the router base. It also references the grooves from the outside of the miters, so that the case corners will line up, even if there is a discrepancy in the thickness of the boards.

When you're clamping, make sure that you line up the ends of the two center boards carefully. Any misalignment here will affect the placement of the groove.

Place your clamps as close as possible to the ends of the boards without obstructing the router's path. With the boards clamped, secure the assembly vertically in a vise or clamp it vertically to the edge of your workbench.

To make the joint as strong as possible, adjust your router fence to position the bit closer to the inside of the miter than to the outside. Then cut the first two grooves, unclamp the assembly, and line up the opposite ends of the same boards in the same manner. Clamp them and cut the next two grooves. Next switch the sandwich, placing the ungrooved boards between the ones you just routed, and repeat the procedure.

A variation of this approach is to use a slot cutting bit instead of a straight bit in your router. The bit's bearing guide eliminates the need for a fence to be clamped to the base of the router. Note that you may need to change the bearing to a smaller diameter to get the right depth groove.

Paul Anthony
Hellertown, PA

Step 1. Line up boards and rout grooves on both ends of the inner boards.

Step 2. Switch the outer boards to the inside and repeat Step 1.

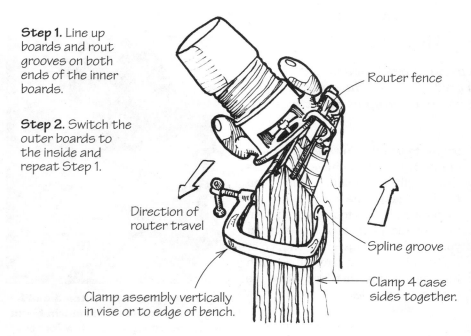

Router fence

Direction of router travel

Spline groove

Clamp 4 case sides together.

Clamp assembly vertically in vise or to edge of bench.

Adding Splines to Picture Frames

PROBLEM: *I want to reinforce some frames without using nails. How do I go about adding splines to a mitered picture frame?*

SOLUTION: The table saw provides the easiest method for cutting the spline slots. First glue up the mitered frames. After the glue is fully dried, clean off any glue squeeze-out.

Next make a cradle to hold the frame at a 45-degree angle to the table saw: Screw two strips of wood to a piece of plywood, as shown. Adjust the saw blade height to cut as deeply as possible without breaking through the inside corner of the joint. Set the fence to locate the spline and make the cut.

Now plane spline stock to fit snugly into the slots. Glue the splines in place, making sure that the edges of the splines contact the ends of the slots. Use a band saw to remove most of the excess spline material, and then clean up the corners with a belt sander.

Tony O'Malley
Emmaus, PA

When you cut spline slots in a mitered frame, make a plywood cradle to hold the frame. You may find it more comfortable to clamp large frames to the cradle.

Frame Joinery Solutions

Making Simple Cope-and-Stick Frames

PROBLEM: *I want to make a frame-and-panel door that has a molding profile that is along the inside edge of the frame, but I don't want to invest in the specialized router bits that make this type of cut. Is there another way to achieve the same result?*

SOLUTION: Yes there is. The traditional approach is to cut the profile, sometimes called sticking, along the edges of the frame parts. Then cut away the sticking from the areas that surround the mortises (usually on the frame stiles) and from the areas that have been mitered at the inside corners of the frame, as shown at top right.

After cutting the sticking, lay out the areas that need to be cut away from around the mortises on the face of each stile. Cut away the bulk of the waste on the band saw, staying about 1/16 inch away from your layout lines. Be sure to leave enough stock at the corners for the miters. Then set up a straight bit that's slightly wider than your frame pieces in a table-mounted router. Set the depth of cut so that the bit trims the pieces right to the shoulder of the sticking cut. Guide the stiles on edge along the fence to make the cuts, as shown at bottom right.

Cut the miters on both the stiles and the rails with a sharp chisel and a guide block. The guide block helps you maintain a perfect 45-degree angle, as shown in the photo at the top of page 136. If you're making

Mortise **Cut away sticking at mortise.**

Rail

Tenon

Stile

Sticking

Get the look of cope-and-stick frames without the fuss. After cutting the joints and routing a profile on the inside edges of all the parts, trim off the excess material around the mortise (below), then miter the ends of the profiles.

After you band-saw away most of the sticking profile around the mortise, trim off the remainder on the router table.

more than one frame of a given size, you may want to make up guide blocks that are mitered at each end, sizing them precisely to fit the various frame pieces. These specially cut guide blocks will save you from having to lay out each piece individually and will help you to make each piece the same size.

Robert Treanor
San Francisco, CA

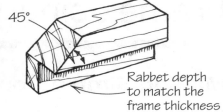

45°

Rabbet depth to match the frame thickness

The miters at the corners are best cut with a sharp chisel and a mitering guide block that fits against the frame edge.

SETTING UP COPE-AND-STICK ROUTER BITS

To get really clean-looking door frames, nothing beats a cope-and-stick joint. It's designed to give the look of a mitered profile along the inside edge of the frame—without having to cut and fit any miters.

There are several types of cope-and-stick router bit sets, but they all work essentially the same way. First you rout a profile, including the groove for the panel, around the edges of all of the parts. This is called the sticking cut. Then you cut the counterprofile, or the cope cut, into the ends of the rails. See below. The cope cut produces a short "stub" tenon on the ends of the rails that fits into the groove on the stile. For small

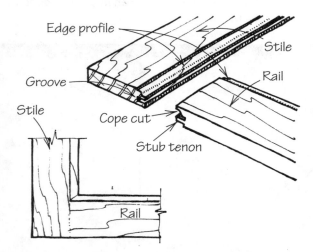

Edge profile

Stile

Groove

Rail

Stile

Cope cut

Stub tenon

Rail

The sticking cut is made on the inside edge of both rails and stiles, producing the edge profile and groove in a single pass. The cope cut is made on only the ends of the rails.

cabinet doors, this is a perfectly adequate joint. For larger doors, you can start with the cope-and-stick joint and add longer dowels or a separate tenon to reinforce the joint.

To set up the cut, start with stock that's perfectly uniform in thickness; small discrepancies will wreak havoc and frustration on the process. If possible use stock that's $13/16$ inch thick instead of $3/4$ inch thick. The added thickness creates a beefier lip of wood at the back of the groove. Also cut two or three extra pieces of stock for the setups. You may even want to go to the trouble of making both cuts on a couple of extra pieces before working on the real stock so that you can preview the entire process.

First make the sticking cut on the inside edge of all the rails and stiles, as shown in *Step 1* on the opposite page. Then cut all the parts to their final length.

Next adjust the cutter to make the cope cut in the rails. Test the fit carefully by holding the two parts on a flat surface like a machine table. The faces should be exactly flush when the parts are assembled.

Making the cope cut requires a square backer board to help push the rails past the cutter, as shown in *Step 2*. The backer board does two things: It helps keep the narrow ends of the rails square to the fence, and it prevents the back edge of the rails from chipping out at the end of the cut. Make the cope cut on

ANOTHER VIEW: To create a frame with a molded inside edge, add the molding after the frame has been assembled. This makes the task of constructing a frame-and-panel door easier from two aspects. First, the joinery is very straightforward. Just mortise and tenon the pieces together. No miters, grooves, or coping to worry about. Second, glue-up is a breeze because the panel is added later.

Make the frames, and glue them together. Then run a thin strip of wood around the inside of each frame to form the back of the panel groove. Glue and nail the pieces in place with small brads. Rout your face molding, then miter the pieces to fit inside the frames. Drop in the panel, then glue and nail the molding in place.

Ken Burton
New Tripoli, PA

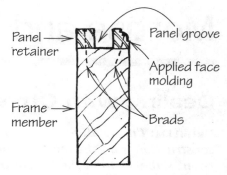

Dress up a simple frame by adding strips of molding after assembly.

---

one end of all the rails first, with the profiled edge of the rails facing forward, as shown in *Step 2*.

To make the cope cut in the other end of the rails, the profiled edge will face the backer board. Coping one edge of the backer board and flipping it over will engage the profiled edge of the rails snugly, as shown in *Step 3* and *Side View*.

Mark Duginske
Merrill, WI

Step 1. Cut the sticking profile on the inside edge of all the rails and stiles.

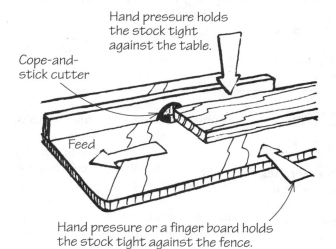

Step 2. After cutting the rails to length, make the cope cut on one end of all the rails.

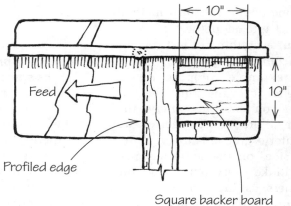

Step 3. Cope one edge of the backer board; then flip the backer board so that it mates with the profiled edges of the rails, and cope the second end of the rails.

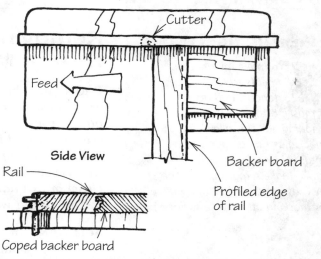

Mortise and Tenon Solutions

Dealing with Offset Joints

PROBLEM: *I'm building a chest of drawers using frame-and-panel construction, and the mortises and tenons are offset with several different setbacks from the face of the stock, which is driving me batty. Tell me there's a better way!*

SOLUTION: It can get pretty confusing when mortises, tenons, and grooves are offset. Traditional marking systems in the old days could tell a cabinetmaker the orientation of any piece of wood in a project. The machine age has its own methods. The trick is to adapt the plans so you can cut everything at just a couple of machine settings.

For example, prepare all the frame wood to the same thickness before you cut the joinery, then center all grooves. The easiest way to center a groove is to cut it from both sides on the same fence setting. Make every tenon the same thickness as the grooves so that you can cut a groove just deeper—

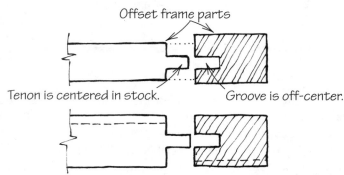

When a project plan calls for offset frame assembly, make parts the same thickness, cut joinery in the center of the stock, then plane the parts that are set back to create the offset.

not wider—to accept the tenon that fits there. Use the same plan when you make the tenons. Depending on your machine setup, cut tenons from both faces, which will center them, and whenever possible cut the top and bottom shoulders at the same settings as the cheeks, which will center these as well. You now have a piece that lets everything line up flush on both the face and back sides. If the design calls for offset faces, produce them by planing the stock after the joinery has been cut.

Jim Cummins
Woodstock, NY

Removing Chips from a Mortise

PROBLEM: *When I chop mortises, or even when I cut them with a plunge router, I find it a pain to evacuate the chips from the joint. Removing the work from the vise or digging around with a chisel or awl hardly seems satisfactory. What works better?*

SOLUTION: In this world of increasingly sophisticated technology, simple, low-tech solutions to problems sometimes are refreshing. To remove chips from mortises, I keep a length of plastic tubing at the bench. When it comes time to remove the chips from the joint, I simply blow through the tubing into the joint. The force of the air removes the chips, and I avoid getting chips in my eyes. Thin, flexible tubing can be found at most pet stores that sell supplies for aquariums.

Robert Treanor
San Francisco, CA

Laminating Stock for Large Mortises

PROBLEM: *I need to make a large mortise in a trestle foot to receive the upright part of the leg for a trestle table, but my plunge router can't cut deeply enough, and my chisels aren't up to the job. What's the solution?*

SOLUTION: You can make large mortises quickly and accurately by laminating two sides to a central piece that is the same thickness as the tenon you intend to use.

When making any kind of shaped foot, you should start with a rectangular workpiece, cut the joinery (in this case, the mortise is formed as part of the lamination), and then shape the completed glue-up as a solid piece. Start with the rectangular stock needed for the laminated workpiece, as shown. Draw the shape of the finished part on the outside face of one of the outside pieces. Carefully cut out the mortise on the center laminate. If the mortise will go all the way through, mark the mortise ends on the inside face of one of the outside pieces and align the middle pieces on the lines at glue-up. Plane the central laminate to the thickness of the desired tenon. Plane the tenoned piece at the same time and to the same thickness for a flawless fit. Glue the mortised part together, keeping the top edges aligned.

After the glue has dried, joint the top edge of the workpiece if necessary to provide a square shoulder for the tenon. Then cut out the final shape of the workpiece.

This technique is also an efficient way of creating a thicker workpiece than you have stock for. Use three layers of ¾-inch stock, for example, to build up a 2¼-inch-thick leg.

Graham Blackburn
Bearsville, NY

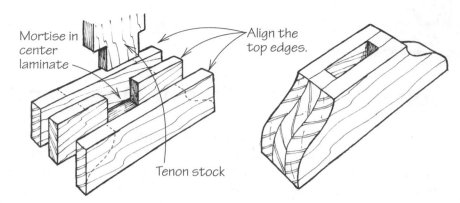

Beefy mortise-and-tenon joints are made easily by laminating the stock. First plane the center laminate in the mortise stock to the same thickness as the tenon stock (*above left*). **Then glue up the mortise assembly and cut to shape** (*above right*).

Quick Tip

CUTTING TAPERED WEDGES

Wedged tenon joints are strong and good-looking, but cutting all those wedges can be a nuisance. Here's a system I hit upon for cutting wedges on the band saw that makes the task a snap. Start with a blank that is as thick as you want the width of the wedges to be. The blank's length should match that of the wedges, and the blank should be at least 6 inches wide—basically a short offcut from a fairly wide board.

Angle the miter gauge on your saw about 2 degrees off-square. Hold the scrap against the miter gauge and make a cut off one end, then discard the scrap. Turn the blank over and cut off your first wedge, gauging its thickness either by eye or by making a mark on the saw table. Repeat the process until you have enough wedges. The actual angle of the resulting wedges will be about 4 degrees.

W. Curtis Johnson
Corvallis, OR

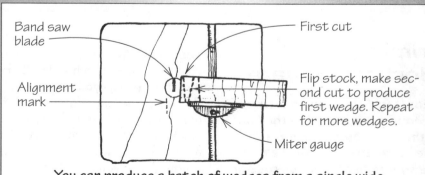

You can produce a batch of wedges from a single wide offcut by making repetitive angled crosscuts on the band saw, flipping the stock after each cut.

Joining Three Sticks at One Point

FOR A CHINESE-STYLE LAMP I WAS DESIGNING, I needed to come up with a way of joining three thin frame pieces at a single point to form the corners. My solution—an interlocking joint made up of four pieces: the lock rail, two identical slide rails, and a key—is shown. For my project, I used ¾-inch-square stock. Your design will dictate the length of the parts you will use, but remember to allow for a 2-inch overhang beyond the corner.

This joint is far easier to make than to describe, so I'll use photos to explain the process. Go ahead and make a practice joint as follows: Cut three strips of wood ¾ × ¾ × 12 inches. Mark two of the pieces "SR" for slide rail, and mark the remaining one "LR" for lock rail. Then follow the steps shown on the opposite page.

While this joint was new to me, it probably has been used for years. My inspiration came from the wooden puzzles I played with as a boy—they were made with pieces that slid together and were secured by a single wooden key.

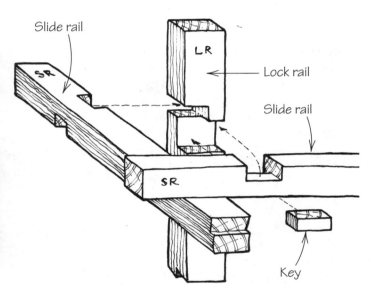

Two slide rails with identical notches fit around a lock rail. After you slip the 3 parts into alignment, use a small key to lock the joints securely.

Trimming Mortises Square

PROBLEM: *I finish my mortises by hand after removing the bulk of the waste on the drill press. I never get the walls of the mortise square to the face or edge of the stock. Is there a way to avoid the excessive trial and error of trimming and fitting?*

SOLUTION: Whether you drill out your mortises with a hand drill or on the drill press, you still have to chisel out the material between the holes. This is where it's easy to trim too little or too much and end up with mortise walls that are not square. Once you go off just a little, you'll end up widening the mortise, and then you're stuck with a sloppy fit. Instead, clamp a square block to the edge of the mortise and hold the back of the chisel tightly against it as you clean out the mortise, as shown in the photo. For mortises in the edge of a board, glue a spacer to a thin block of wood that can be clamped to the face of the board, as shown in the drawing.

Tom Begnal
Kent, CT

To assemble the joint, first slip the enclosed corner tenon of one of the slide rails into the ⅜-inch dado in the lock rail. If the fit is too tight, trim the edges of the rails slightly with a hand plane or stationary belt sander.

Push the remaining slide rail against the installed slide rail; then slide its tenon down into the exposed dado in the lock rail.

Finally, make a little key to fit into the notch that was left in the locking rail. Try to match the grain. You can taper the edge of the key with a piece of sandpaper to make it easier to slip in, but it should be a good tight fit.

Rob Yoder
Quakertown, PA

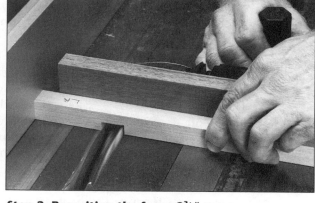

Step 2. Reposition the fence 2⅜" away from the blade, and cut a ¾" dado in one side of the lock rail.

Step 1. Put a ¾" wide dado set in your table saw, and set the depth of cut to exactly ⅜". Set the rip fence 2" from the blade. Dado the 2 slide rails on 2 sides to create a ⅜" × ⅜" "enclosed corner tenon." Guide the pieces with the miter gauge as you cut the dadoes, and use the fence as a stop for accurate positioning.

Step 3. Reset the width of the dado blade to ⅜", and double-check to be sure that the depth of cut is still ⅜". Reposition the fence so that it is 2" away from the blade. Hold the lock rail against the miter gauge. Dado the lock rail to hold the enclosed corner tenons that have been cut in the slide rails.

Holding the back of a chisel against a block that is clamped to the edge of a mortise helps you cut the sides of the mortise square to the face. For mortises on the edge of stock, make an L-shaped guide block (*right*).

Guide block

Workpiece

Mortising Round Stock

PROBLEM: *I need to cut mortises in large dowel stock, but it's tough to make them centered and straight. Is there an easy way?*

SOLUTION: Make a pair of matching V-blocks to hold your stock. Hold both blocks and stock in your woodworking vise with the edges of the blocks proud of the workbench surface. These edges form a surface that is parallel to the stock for the base of the router to run on, as shown.

The gap between the V-blocks will be centered on the stock so that, with a little careful planning, it can serve as a template for a guide collar. If necessary you can trim or add a slice of veneer to the V-block to adjust the width of the mortise.

Fred Matlack
Vera Cruz, PA

Squeezing a round workpiece between two matched V-blocks automatically provides accurate reference surfaces from which to cut centered mortises quickly and easily.

Routing Tenons on Round Stock

PROBLEM: *I want to rout tenons on the ends of dowels. How do I hold the round stock?*

SOLUTION: This is a job for the router table. If you're cutting round tenons, the setup is really easy. Use a relatively large straight bit and set the height to the difference in radius between the dowel and the tenon. For example, to get a ½-inch tenon on a 1-inch dowel, set the bit ¼ inch high.

Set a fence on the router table so that it determines the length of the tenon—I call this the end-stop fence. Then set another fence or guide block perpendicular to the first so that the fence or guide block positions the dowel over the center of the bit. Now all you have to do is rotate the dowel by hand as you slowly advance it over the bit until it reaches the end stop fence. Make sure to rotate it one full turn after you contact the end stop fence.

Rectangular tenons require a little different setup. Make two V-blocks and clamp the dowel between them. Make the blocks wide enough so that you can screw them together on either side of the dowel. Now set a fence to establish the length of the tenon and use a 90-degree pushblock to hold the block-and-dowel assembly perpendicular to the fence.

Fred Matlack
Vera Cruz, PA

To rout round tenons on round stock, set perpendicular fences to position the workpiece, then rotate it over the bit.

To rout rectangular tenons on round stock, set a fence to determine the tenon's length, hold the stock between V-blocks, and guide it over the bit using a miter gauge or push block.

MORTISE-AND-TENON BASICS

In theory, the mortise-and-tenon is a wonderful joint. It is strong, self-aligning, and relatively easy to cut. But in fact, it can be one of the most frustrating joints to make: The tenon is either too tight or too loose, and if you work by hand, part is often out of square.

The good news is that if you have a router and a table saw, you have all you need in your shop to machine perfect mortise-and-tenon joints. You just need to know how to go about it.

Cut mortises on the router table with a bit that is roughly half the thickness of the stock. Spiral upcut bits work best, cutting cleanly and easily, but a regular straight bit will do in a pinch. You can control the length of the mortise by marking the router table to show the bit location and the face of the workpiece to show the mortise location. See the photo below left. Make the mortise using a series of passes to keep the router from straining and to keep the cut smooth. You can clamp a stop block to the fence so that all mortises will end at exactly the same place.

Before you start routing, choose a face that will run against the fence and mark it. Make sure that the same face is always against the fence as you rout. This way, if the mortises are off-center, the variation will at least be consistent from piece to piece. You can compensate for the variation when you cut the tenon.

Cut tenons on the table saw with a sharp rip blade and a tenoning jig, as shown below right. The tenoning jig holds the stock on end and allows the rip blade to cut smooth tenon cheeks. You can buy a tenoning jig or make one from a few scraps of plywood. Cut a sample tenon and test fit it in the mortise. Make sure that the faces of the two pieces are flush with one another. If not, adjust the setting on the tenoning gauge to reposition the tenon. Cut all the tenons on both ends of a piece with the same face against the tenoning jig.

To cut the short faces of the tenons, turn the stock 90 degrees in the jig. Turn the piece to cut the second short face. Cut the tenon shoulders using the miter gauge, with the end of the tenon against the rip fence.

Jeff Day
Perkasie, PA

Rout the mortise by holding the workpiece against the fence above the spinning bit and pivoting it down onto the table. Marks on the table and on the piece show where to start and stop cutting.

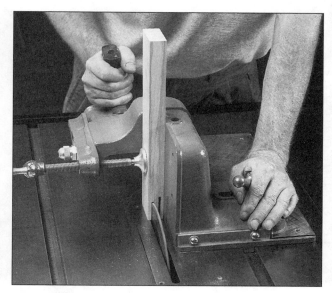

To get the best results from a tenoning jig, cut one side of all the tenons, then reposition the jig to cut the second side, leaving the same face of the workpiece against the jig.

Tightening Through-Tenons

PROBLEM: *The through-tenons on the stretcher on my dining table are too loose for their mortises. How can I tighten them?*

SOLUTION: You can wedge a tenon tight, but how you do so depends on where the slop is in the joint. If the tenons are loose top to bottom *or* side to side, you can install two wedges spaced an equal distance apart on the tenon to spread the wood and lock the joint tight, as shown below. If the slop is top to bottom *and* side to side, install a single wedge diagonally, as shown. This will spread the tenon in all directions. Note that the long edges of diagonal wedges need to be chamfered to fit tightly into the corners of the mortise. You can do this with a block plane or by rubbing the wedges against a sandpaper block.

The slots in the tenons should be about 1/16 inch wide and cut nearly to the end of the tenon. Make sure to drill a 1/8-inch hole at the end of the slot to prevent the rail from splitting when the wedge is inserted. The wedges should be a little longer than the slots into which they'll fit. This way if you mash the ends of the wedges when you install them, you can cut off the damaged part and end up with a crisp, clean look.

Glue the through-tenons into their mortises in the normal way, then put some glue on each wedge and drive it into the slot. If you are working with round tenons, you can reduce the chances of their splitting by positioning the wedge perpendicular to the grain of the mortised piece and driving it firmly but gently home. After the glue is dry, cut off the excess tenon with a flush cutting saw and smooth it to the mortise with a hand plane.

W. Curtis Johnson
Corvallis, OR

CORRECTING ILL-FITTING TENONS

To tighten up a loose tenon joint, glue a strip of veneer to the side (or both sides if needed) of the tenon, as shown in the top photo below. Then pare down the veneer for a perfect fit.

If a tenon is too tight for its mortise, take a light pass or two with a rabbet plane across the grain or use a hand scraper with the grain to make the tenon smaller. If more than a few shavings need to be removed, take the piece back to your tenoning setup and recut the tenon rather than fussing with the fit.

Ben Erickson
Eutaw, AL

To fatten up a loose tenon, glue veneer to the face or faces.

To fit a tenon that's tight, take light passes with a rabbeting plane, testing the fit after every few swipes.

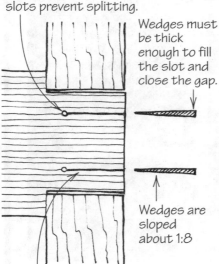

1/8" holes at the base of slots prevent splitting.

Wedges must be thick enough to fill the slot and close the gap.

Wedges are sloped about 1:8

Cut slots in the tenon on the band saw or with a handsaw.

Wedging through-tenons produces both a tight fit and a neat look.

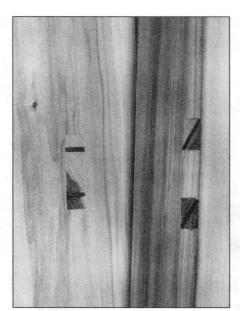

Tighten tenons that are loose in one direction with vertical or horizontal wedges (*left*). Use diagonal wedges (*right*) for tenons that are loose in both directions.

Concealing Uneven Frame Joints

PROBLEM: *When I finished some cabinets with frame-and-panel doors a few months ago, I sanded the doors perfectly flush. Now I can feel a sharp ridge at the joint line. What happened and how can I prevent it from happening again?*

SOLUTION: If the affected joints are accessible, you can rout a small V-groove along the joint lines; this will disguise the slight ridge. Or you can sand the pieces again and hope that the problem doesn't recur. A third option is to just accept the slight ridge as an inevitable part of working with a natural material.

AVOIDING THE PROBLEM: The problem was created when your wood moved slightly, as it's bound to do over the life of a piece. I suggest that in the future you detail the areas where stiles and rails meet by chamfering each piece. The resulting small V-groove detail adds visual interest, and, more importantly, it hides any wood movement.

I make the chamfer with a razor-sharp block plane, holding it at a 45-degree angle to the face of the workpiece. To make the end-grain cuts on the rails, I skew the plane slightly in the direction of travel to get a cleaner cut. Be sure to cut all the chamfers before gluing up the frame. I find that a chamfer that's about 1/32 inch wide is about right. One that's wider than that will display a V-groove that's too deep after the parts have been assembled. To get an even chamfer all around, make the same number of passes with the plane on all the parts.

Andy Rae
Lenhartsville, PA

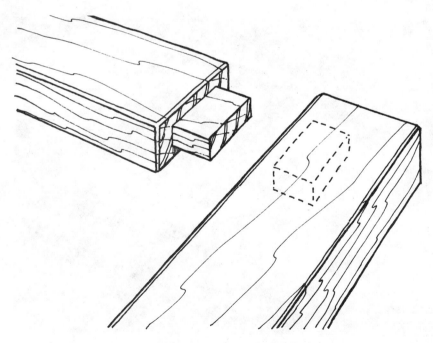

Chamfer the mating edges of frame parts to disguise wood movement.

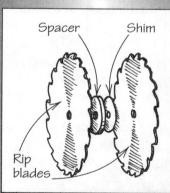

MORTISING JIG FOR SEPARATE TENON JOINTS BY KEN BURTON

If cutting tenons gives you a headache, don't bother cutting them. Instead cut mortises into both parts and make a separate tenon piece to fit.

A good method for making mortise-and-tenon joints is to cut mortises into both the stiles and the rails, and then fit a separate tenon piece into the mortises. It altogether eliminates the process of cutting tenons without reducing the strength of the joint. The separate tenon is then shaped to fit the rounded mortise shoulders.

Most mortising jigs are designed for routing mortises into the edges of the stiles. If you want to join your frames using separate tenons, you have to come up with another jig or setup for routing mortises into the ends of the rails. This jig is designed so you can mortise both parts with the same jig and the same setup. It can be made from a few square feet of plywood scraps and a little hardware. Pieces of threaded rod epoxied into lengths of 1-inch diameter dowel hold the stock in place.

Rout the rails first with the outside edge butted against one of the dividers, as shown in the photo at right. The router's edge guide locates the cut. Then mortise the stiles. To use the same stop setup for both cuts, position the ends of the stiles (or end marks if you leave

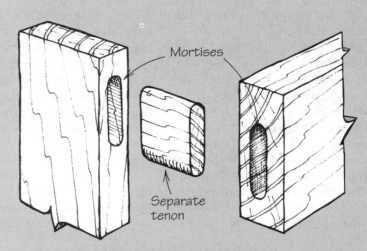

Mortises

Separate tenon

You can make a separate tenon joint by mortising both parts and adding a separate piece as the tenon.

Routing mortises into end grain is no different than mortising into edge grain. With this jig you can rout both parts using the same setup.

your stiles long until after assembly)
on a vertical line extended up from
the end of the divider.

When routing mortises, you'll get
the best results if you use a spiral
upcut bit, which more efficiently pulls
the chips out of the mortise. Also, use
bits with a ½-inch-diameter shank
because they'll flex less than bits with
¼-inch shanks.

Plane a length of separate tenon
stock to fit snugly in the mortises;
you should be able to slip a tenon in
and pull it out with firm hand pressure. Round the edges of the tenon
stock with a hand plane or router
before you crosscut the individual
tenons to length.

MATERIALS LIST

Part	Quantity	Dimensions
Front	1	¾" × 6¾" × 18"
Back	1	¾" × 10¾" × 18"
Dividers	2	¾" × 3½" × 6"
Braces	4	¾" × 2" × 3½"
Glue blocks	4	¾" × 1½" × 3"
Stops	2	¾" × 3" × 5"

HARDWARE

Threaded rods	4	⅜" dia. × 6"
Handles	4	1" dia. × 4"
Rubber feet	4	⅜" I.D.
T-nuts	4	⅜" dia.
Screws	As needed	1¼" or 1⅝"

Exploded View

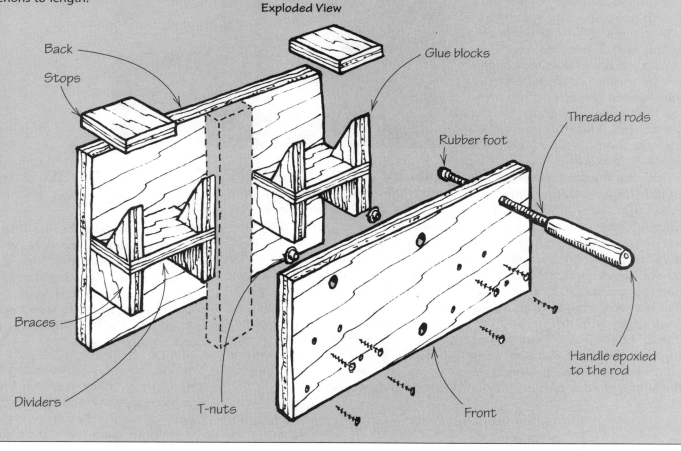

Back

Stops

Glue blocks

Threaded rods

Rubber foot

Braces

Dividers

T-nuts

Front

Handle epoxied
to the rod

Doweling and Drilling Solutions

Grooving Dowels for Better Joints

PROBLEM: *I recently made up a set of face frames, and I joined the corners with dowels that fit perfectly in a dry assembly. As I clamped the frames together during glue up, several of the joints split apart. What went wrong?*

SOLUTION: My guess is that you were using dowels that weren't grooved. Ungrooved dowels will act like pistons, forcing any excess glue to the bottom of the holes. Here's where the problem is: Glue, like water, cannot be compressed. So the resulting buildup of pressure must be relieved. With strong wood, you may find that you simply can't squeeze the joints together. With weaker wood, or if the dowels are too close to the edge of the board, your frame pieces may split apart.

To prevent this from happening again, use grooved dowels. These can be purchased from most suppliers. Or, for the occasional doweling job, you can groove your own dowels with a jig similar to the one shown. This simple device requires no more than a scrap of hardwood and two wood screws.

Drill into the scrap a hole that is slightly larger than the diameter of dowel that you will be using. Then drive into the scrap two screws that are perpendicular to the axis of the hole, as shown. After you drive the screws home, back them out and file the points to a knife edge. Reinsert the screws, aligning the filed edges with the axis of the dowel hole. Drive your dowels through the hole and the screw points will cut clean grooves along the length of your dowels.

Robert Treanor
San Francisco, CA

Two screws driven into a block of scrap wood make a simple dowel groover. The screws should be long enough so that their points protrude slightly into the dowel hole.

ANOTHER VIEW: While I generally don't like dowel joints, every once in a while I have to use one. Rather than stocking any of the pre-grooved dowels, I make my own. I start with a piece of dowel of the appropriate diameter that is long enough to cut into all the pieces I need. Then I cut a flat along one side by taking two or three passes with a block plane. This flat provides a good conduit into which excess glue can escape so that the joint can close.

Ken Burton
New Tripoli, PA

Sizing Tenons on the Lathe

PROBLEM: *I've been having trouble turning round tenons to an accurate final diameter. I use a pair of calipers, but they don't seem to give me more than a rough idea of where to stop turning. What's the best way to turn these tenons?*

SOLUTION: You can make a snug fitting tenon by drilling a sample hole in a piece of plywood and testing the tenon—*as you turn it.* It helps if you rough out the diameter of the tenon first. Set a pair of calipers to about $\frac{1}{32}$ inch more than the desired diameter, and cut the stock with a parting tool. Turn the tenon until the calipers just slip over it.

Now make a plywood gauge to test fit the tenon. In a piece of scrap $\frac{3}{4}$-inch plywood, drill a hole that is the same size as the one the tenon will fit into. Then cut the plywood into a rough circle. It's going to be on the lathe and could start spinning when you least expect it, so smooth the edges a little. Release your spindle and slip the hole over the lathe's center, as shown; then remount your piece.

Continue turning the tenon, testing its diameter by slipping the plywood over it. Because the gauge is thicker than calipers, and because it is made from the drill you'll use to create the mortise, it is more accurate than calipers. When the plywood slips over the tenon with a slight drag, the tenon is the right diameter.

Jeff Day
Perkasie, PA

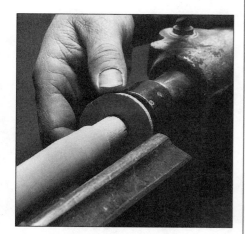

Once the tenons are turned roughly to diameter, slip the gauge onto the center, allowing it to bounce around there as you cut the tenon to final size. If your centers are larger than the gauge, turn down the very end of the spindle to a smaller diameter and allow the gauge to ride there.

Drilling Perpendicular Holes without a Drill Press

PROBLEM: *I don't have a drill press, and I don't intend to buy one, but I occasionally need to drill truly perpendicular holes. I bought a guide attachment for my hand drill, but it often hindered rather than helped. Is there is good way to drill perfect holes?*

SOLUTION: It isn't hard to get holes very, very close to perpendicular, which is probably sufficient 99 percent of the time. For the 1 percent when you need an absolutely perfect 90-degree-to-the-surface hole, go visit a buddy who has a drill press. And while you're there, make a series of guides on your friend's drill press that you can use in your shop. Start with a couple of hardwood blanks, $1 \times 1 \times 12$ inches and $1 \times 2 \times 12$ inches, with square sides. Use your best set of drill bits to drill a series of holes along the two blanks, beginning perhaps with a hole that's $\frac{1}{8}$ inch and progressing up to one that's $\frac{1}{2}$ inch. Write the diameter next to each hole, as shown below.

You may actually find it more functional to have three 4-inch blanks, or even a series of small blanks, each with a single hole. Be sure to leave room on each blank for a clamp that will hold the blank in place. For the smaller holes, the blanks will be thinner because the bits are not very long. However you work it out, keep these "jigs" in a particular place in your shop and pull them out when you need them. These blocks will come in handy, even to those who own a drill press, on occasions when the hole you need to drill can't be made on the drill press.

Another simple method for making vertical holes is to cut a couple of 90-degree guide blocks that you can clamp in position at the point where the hole will be drilled. (Use a trusty square to check that the guide blocks are indeed crosscut at 90 degrees.) Set these guides 90 degrees to each other so that you can control the x axis and the y axis. If you have a lot of identical holes to drill, such as when you make adjustable shelves in a cabinet, you can make a simple template or guide block, like the one shown in "Correcting Shelf Support Holes" on page 285, and let it also serve as your depth stop.

You may also want to try one of the bubble level attachments that are now available for hand drills; these show you when your drill is perfectly level or plumb.

David Page
Swarthmore, PA

The holes in these blocks were drilled on a drill press. The blocks can be used for drilling holes square to the face of the stock with a portable drill.

Joining Short Spindles to Make a Longer One

PROBLEM: *I want to make a long bed post by joining two short spindles with a dowel. How can I drill a hole in each piece to make a straight joint?*

SOLUTION: When you turn each piece, start so that the end to be joined is held by the tailstock center and don't leave any waste at that end. This way you'll have an accurately centered starter hole in the splice end from which you can locate your dowel hole.

Once your turnings are finished, drive a brad or screw through a piece of scrap wood to form a centering pin and place it on your drill press table, as shown at right. Lower the drill press table, carefully locate the centering pin so that it is the same distance from the drill press column as the drill bit is. Set the spindle in place on the centering pin. Now step back and check visually that the turning is parallel with the column. Then clamp the centering pin board to the drill press table. Turn on the machine and align the tailstock center mark with the center of the spinning bit as you advance the bit.

Fred Matlack
Vera Cruz, PA

To drill an accurate hole along the axis of a spindle use the center marks on the spindle for alignment. A center pin locates the bottom end (*bottom photo*), while the drill bit centers the top (*top photo*).

Doweling Difficulties Eliminated

PROBLEM: *I rely on dowel joints frequently and use a decent doweling jig, but I still routinely have alignment problems. How can I get better results?*

SOLUTION: If you find it a pain to accurately align dowel holes in two parts of a joint, don't bother. Instead, install the dowels *after* assembling the joint and let the exposed dowels act as decorations. Simply glue the joint together first. Even a plain, basic, end-grain butt joint will hold together well enough to allow you to add dowels after the fact. Once the glue is dry, drill the holes for the dowels and glue them in to strengthen the joint. Let the dowels stand proud, so that they can be sawed off later with a flush cutting saw and then hand planed even with the surface.

Small boxes, wall cabinets, even cabinet doors can be put together this way. If you don't like the look of round dowels, square off the top of the hole with a small chisel, and then make your own square-topped dowels. To do this, first drill a hole the same diameter as the dowel through a piece of 1/4-inch-thick steel. Then cut square stock sized to the diameter of the dowel hole, and drive the stock through the steel. Leave a square head on the dowel and cut it to length for your hole. Drive it home while holding the head in the proper orientation with a pair of pliers, until it's most of the way in.

W. Curtis Johnson
Corvallis, OR

Inserting dowels after assembly takes the tedium out of doweled butt joints and presents an opportunity for adding a design detail. You can make dowels from square stock, leave the ends square, and chop the top 1/4" of the holes square to match.

Handling Case Joinery

Making Perfect Dadoes

PROBLEM: *No matter how I cut them, my dadoes are always too loose. What's the secret to getting them just right?*

SOLUTION: One of the most common reasons that dadoes are too loose is that sheet material of a nominal size, say ¾ inch, is rarely that exact thickness—usually it is somewhat smaller. You can purchase router bits that are a shade undersize to match the actual thickness of the material, but with so many different plywood products, it's a hit or miss deal.

Instead, I cut my dadoes with a series of three cuts that result in a perfect fit, no matter what the thickness of the material. The secret is to use a combination of two spacers to help position the cuts. The first I call the dado spacer. It is made from a piece of the actual material I want to fit in the dado. The other is the "kerf spacer." This one exactly matches the kerf of the saw blade (or router bit) that I intend to use. I make the kerf spacer by sanding or planing a thin board or by adding masking tape to a piece of ⅛-inch hardboard so that it fits snugly in a saw kerf cut in a piece of scrap wood.

Lay out the dado cuts on your workpiece. Then hold the dado spacer against the fence and butt your

workpiece up against it, as shown in *Step 1*. Set the fence to cut the near side of the dado. Make the cut by sliding both the dado spacer and the workpiece along the fence. Then remove the dado spacer and make a second cut with the kerf spacer in place. See *Step 2*. With these two cuts perfectly defining the outside walls

Step 1. Make the first cut using a piece of shelf material as a spacer.

Step 2. Make a second cut using a "kerf spacer."

Step 3. Remove the waste with multiple cuts.

of the dado, you can then remove the waste from the interior with another pass or two. See *Step 3*. This system also works on the radial arm saw and when routing dadoes on a router table.

L. Jerry Hess
Tacoma, WA

Cutting Back-to-Back Dadoes

PROBLEM: *I want to make a set of shelves and need to cut back-to-back dadoes in the middle uprights. Since they're over 6 feet tall, I'm not comfortable using the table saw fence to register them. What are my options?*

SOLUTION: This is one of those rare times that the radial arm saw has it all over the table saw. Simply clamp an extension to the back of the fence, and clamp a stop block to the extension to locate each pair of cuts. Cut one side, then flip the board to cut the second.

But since the ol' radial isn't too popular right now, let's talk hand-held

router. It's a bit more fussy to set up, but it'll still do a great job.

Start by chucking up a straight bit that'll cut the width of dado that you want. Measure carefully from the bit's cutting circle to the edge of the router base. Call this measurement the offset distance. Now lay out the dadoes on one side of your workpiece. (Don't bother laying out the opposite side—you'll be cutting it to match.) Lay out a second line for each dado, placing the line the offset distance to one side or the other of the original layout lines.

Make a two-bladed T-square, as shown. The base of the T-square should be the same thickness as the material being dadoed, and the blades should be parallel to one another and square to the base.

Clamp the T-square onto the workpiece so that one blade aligns with the offset layout line. Rout the dado in one face, then flip the board over and rout the other face.

Fred Matlack
Vera Cruz, PA

Using a T-square with two parallel blades, you can rout pairs of back-to-back dadoes with a single setup.

Concealing Dado Joints

PROBLEM: *The outside blades on my dado set left deep score marks that show on the front edge of a bookcase. How can I hide them now and avoid them in the future?*

SOLUTION: When we don't want to see dado joints (good or bad) at the front edge of a case, we add solid edge-banding to the parts. If we're using plywood, we band the shelves and the case. With solid wood, you could band only the part that gets the dadoes and then notch the ends of the shelves to fit. However, we find it easier to band solid wood shelves and notch the banding than to cut a clean notch in the end of the shelf itself.

The key to getting clean results is the sequence: First cut the dadoes; then apply the banding and sand it flush with the case parts. Next cut back the edging on the shelf components; then assemble the case. The banding should be cut back the same distance as the depth of the dadoes. Make this cut on the table saw with the shelf up on its front edge and use the saw fence as a stop.

AVOIDING THE PROBLEM: Use a router bit to cut the dadoes. It won't

leave score marks showing at the front edge of your cabinet. A router also gives you the option of cutting stopped dadoes.

You can clean up table-sawed dadoes with a router bit that is specially designed to produce a perfectly flat bottom on an uneven or ragged dado, as shown at right.

Bill and Joanne Storch
Corvallis, OR

Dado cleanup bits will flatten out a ragged-bottomed dado. A ball bearing rides against the sides of the dado to guide the cutter.

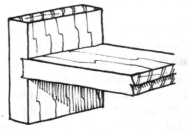 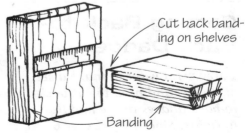

Outside blades on some dado cutters leave score marks (above left). **To conceal dado joints, add banding to the exposed edges of the parts** (above right).

TWO DADO ROUTING JIGS BY ROBERT TREANOR

Using a table saw to cut a dado in a long board or a stopped dado in any board is, at best, a risky business. My preference is to use a router for these cuts. But how best to guide the beast? One of these two jigs will do the job.

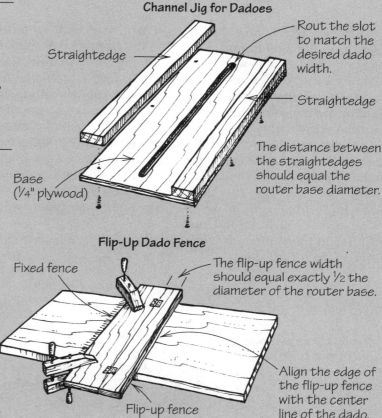

Channel Jig for Dadoes

Straightedge

Rout the slot to match the desired dado width.

Straightedge

Base (¼" plywood)

The distance between the straightedges should equal the router base diameter.

Flip-Up Dado Fence

Fixed fence

The flip-up fence width should equal exactly ½ the diameter of the router base.

Flip-up fence

Align the edge of the flip-up fence with the center line of the dado.

The first is a channel jig, where the router is guided by two straightedges, one on each side of the router's base. I use it mostly when I rout stopped dadoes, as it is quite easy to attach stop blocks to end the cuts precisely where I want them. Start making the jig by screwing one of the straightedges along one side of the plywood base. Then position the second straightedge, using the router base as a guide. The two straightedges should be parallel and the router should be able to travel the length of the jig without binding between or drifting away from the two straightedges. Once the straightedges are screwed in place, clamp the jig to a piece of scrap and rout a slot through the plywood base with a router bit of the appropriate diameter. The slot should start and stop a few inches from the jig's ends.

To use the jig, lay out both the length and the width of the dado on the work. Then simply align the jig with the layout lines. Clamp the jig and rout the dado. I've made several of these jigs, one for each size dado that I use frequently.

I call my second jig a flip-up fence. It is made from two straight pieces of plywood. I made mine as long as the longest dadoes I'm likely to cut—about 60 inches. The wider piece is the actual fence. The narrower fence serves as an alignment device. You'll need to make only one of this jig regardless of the width of the dado you want to cut because it uses the center of the dado, not the edge, as its reference point.

To build the fence, cut the pieces to the necessary sizes (be fussy when you cut the narrow fence to exactly half the diameter of your router base). Then clamp the pieces together edge to edge and screw the hinges across the seam. It's critical that when the two pieces are open flat, they butt to each other perfectly.

To use the jig, lay out the centerline of each dado you want to cut. Hold the jig open on your workpiece and align the edge of the narrow flip-up fence with the layout line. Clamp the jig in place, then flip the narrow fence back out of the way and guide your router along the wide fixed fence to rout the dado.

Making Accurate Half-Lapped Dividers

PROBLEM: *I made a set of half-lapped dividers for a shallow display box, and the dadoes don't line up perfectly. I cut each dado carefully on the table saw, using stops on the miter gauge fence. What more can I do to ensure accuracy?*

SOLUTION: We often make drawer dividers using the half-lap method. The keys to success are to work with stock that's exactly the same thickness and to cut the dadoes in all parts that are the same size at the same time. First decide how thick each divider will be—we usually make ours 3/8 inch thick. Next set up your dado blade and cut a dado that matches the thickness of your dividers in a scrap piece of wood. Take all of your dividers and run them through the planer until they just fit into the sample dado.

Then wrap each set of like pieces tightly together with masking tape, keeping the edges flush. Crosscut the bundled parts to length and lay out the dado cuts. By cutting the dadoes in the entire set of parts at the same time, you'll be done more quickly and all the dadoes will align perfectly. To save more time, apply glue to the all dadoes at the same time; do this before you remove the tape and separate the parts at assembly time.

Bill and Joanne Storch
Corvallis, OR

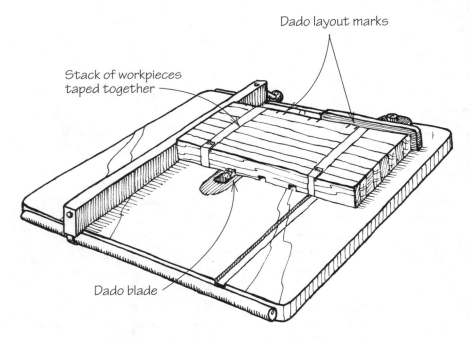

Dado layout marks

Stack of workpieces taped together

Dado blade

When cutting dados in a set of half-lapped dividers, tape them together and cut the whole bundle as if it were a single board.

SETTING UP HALF-LAPS

Half-laps look deceptively easy—until you cut one slightly too deep. Then either the surfaces you want to glue together don't quite touch or the faces of the joint are offset. For clean and strong half-laps, neither is acceptable.

To get the critical depth-of-cut setting just right, make a test cut on a piece of extra stock. The procedure is the same whether you're routing or sawing the half-laps and you don't have to cut the whole joint. Just nick off a little from the end of the stock, as shown below. Then flip over the stock and take a little off of the opposite face so that the two cuts overlap. If the depth of cut is too shallow, there will be a strip of wood between the cuts; a cut that's too deep will be obvious as well. You want to start with a cut that is too shallow and increase the depth until the two cuts meet perfectly.

*Bill Hylton
Kempton, PA*

The depth of cut on the piece at left is too shallow; in the middle, it's too deep; and at the right the cut is perfect.

Making Edge Joints

Cutting Biscuit Slots in Beveled Edges

PROBLEM: *I want to use biscuit joints to build a six-sided column, but I find it difficult to hold the biscuit joiner in position against the beveled edges of the stock. How can I make the joints I want?*

SOLUTION: Biscuit joinery is an excellent choice for the assembly of multi-sided columns because the biscuits help hold the pieces in alignment during glue-up, provided the slots were cut accurately. To begin with, you need a biscuit joiner with a fully adjustable, pivoting fence. If your joiner fence is limited to settings of 45 and 90 degrees, using it for columns with more than four sides is probably not worth the bother. Aside from that, the following will work for columns of four or more sides.

Start by beveling the edges of all of the column staves. The bevel angle can be calculated by dividing the number of sides into 180. For example: A six-sided column needs 30-degree bevels, an eight-sided column uses 22½-degree bevels, and a five-sided column has 36-degree bevels.

With two beveled staves clamped back to back, one bevel gives the fence a surface to register against while you cut the slots in the other bevel. Note that the slots are not centered, but are closer to the base of the bevel.

Clamp two adjoining staves together face to face in a vise with the bevels to be joined facing up. Mark the center lines for the biscuit locations along the edge of each stave. Hold the biscuit joiner in place on one bevel and adjust the fence so that it bears on the adjoining bevel, as shown on this page.

Make sure that the slots are positioned close to the base of the bevel for maximum depth. Try the setting on an extra piece of stock to make sure that it won't cut all the way through the stave.

C. E. "Chuck" Ring
Edgewood, NM

Stacking Biscuit Joints

PROBLEM: *I'm using thick stock and want to place two or three biscuits at each joint. One of the slots always ends up misaligned, preventing the joint from closing. What is the best way to accurately cut a stack of biscuit slots?*

SOLUTION: By stacking biscuits, you can double or triple a joint's strength, but there are practical limits to how

many biscuits you can fit in a joint. As a rule of thumb, you can stack two biscuits in stock that is at least 1 inch thick, and you can add another biscuit for every additional ½ inch of thickness. Allow at least 3/16 inch between biscuits and ¼ inch between a biscuit and the outside face of the material. The problem with multiple biscuits is that you have more chances to miscut one of the slots, and it doesn't take much of a miscut to prevent a stacked-biscuit joint from closing during glue-up.

The best solution for accurate slots is one that I apply whenever conditions allow: Use the base of the biscuit joiner, not the fence, as the reference for cutting each slot. The base of the machine provides a broader bearing surface as each cut is made. Plus, the relationship between the base of the machine and the cutter is fixed permanently, while the relationship between the fence and the cutter is adjustable and may move.

To cut the slots for a joint with two stacked biscuits, start with all the stock planed to the same thickness. Cut one set of slots with one face down against the bench. Then turn the pieces over and cut the second pair of slots with the opposite face down.

To add a third biscuit, use a flat piece of wood or plywood as a shim to raise the machine to the correct height for cutting the center slot, as shown at right.

C. E. "Chuck" Ring
Edgewood, NM

When stacking multiple biscuits in a joint, you'll have fewer problems with alignment if you use the machine's base rather than the fence to reference the cuts. A flat shim under the joiner raises it for the center slot.

Fixing Misplaced Biscuit Slots

PROBLEM: *One of the biscuit slots in a corner joint doesn't line up with its mate. Is there a quick method to fix this?*

SOLUTION: For misplaced or mismatched biscuit slots, the quickest remedy is to glue a biscuit in the slot, trim off the excess after the glue has dried, and recut the slot in the correct location, as shown.

Assuming that the new slot overlaps the old one, it's especially important that the glue be fully cured. Otherwise the remaining portion of the biscuit may come loose when you cut the new slot. If the slot has been cut on the wrong face and the patch will be on an exposed surface, you'll want to make a patch using the same wood.

First plane a piece of wood to the thickness of the slot ($5/32$ inch, typically); then trace the biscuit shape onto it. Cut out the biscuit-shaped patch on the band saw or scroll saw, leaving it a little oversized so that it will completely fill the slot.

Then block-plane a flat on both curves, as shown at the top of the opposite page. One flat ensures that the patch won't bottom out in the slot, while the other flat gives you a place to apply a clamp if necessary.

The goal is to make the ends of the patch fit very tightly. If the fit is good and the wood has similar grain and color, the finished patch will be barely detectable.

AVOIDING THE PROBLEM: Careful planning and layout and selecting material which is true and uniform along its dimensions will help you prevent many problems. A stable, level, and otherwise true work surface will add to the accuracy of slot placement. One such surface is the table saw top. You should ensure that the fence on the biscuit joiner, if used, is flat against the workpiece. If the fence is not used, the base of the biscuit jointer should be

If you misplace a slot, glue in a biscuit, then trim it back flush with the surface (*above left*). This gives you a clean starting point for recutting a new slot in the right place (*above right*).

flat against the work surface and the bottom of the workpiece should be held tightly against the bench or work surface.

When you plunge the cutter into the wood, make sure that there is no up or down movement when the plunge is made or when the machine is retracted; such movement will cause an enlarged slot, especially at the outer perimeter of the slot.

C. E. "Chuck" Ring
Edgewood, NM

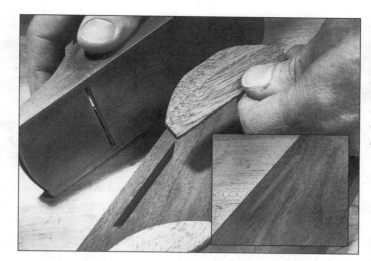

The patch is slightly oversized in length to ensure the ends fit tightly, while the flat ensures that the patch won't bottom out in the slot.

Rabbeting Edges without Tear-Out

PROBLEM: *Whenever I rout rabbets in the edge of a board, the wood splinters out unexpectedly—even if I take a couple of lighter cuts. Is there a better method?*

SOLUTION: Routing rabbets, especially large ones in hardwood, will strain your router and frequently result in severe tear-out or burning of the wood. Make life easier for yourself and your router bit by first cutting a 45-degree chamfer to remove much of the wood.

The chamfer can be made with a chamfering router bit or, if the rabbet continues along the entire edge of the board, it can be cut on the table saw with the blade tilted to 45 degrees. In either case, make the edges of the chamfer slightly inside the targeted edges of the rabbet, as shown below.

An alternative is to cut an undersized rabbet by taking two passes on the table saw. This rabbet can then easily be cleaned up and enlarged to the right size with little strain on the router or danger of tear-out.

Graham Blackburn
Bearsville, NY

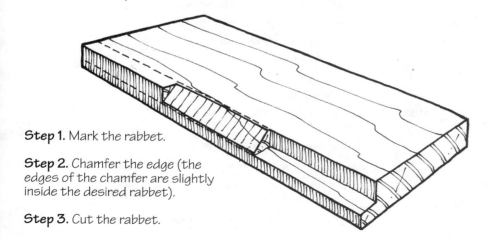

Step 1. Mark the rabbet.

Step 2. Chamfer the edge (the edges of the chamfer are slightly inside the desired rabbet).

Step 3. Cut the rabbet.

Biscuit Joint Depression

PROBLEM: *After carefully sanding and finishing a tabletop, I noticed a row of slight depressions along an edge joint that I had aligned with biscuits. What happened?*

SOLUTION: What you've experienced is biscuit "telegraphing." When you apply glue to a biscuit joint, it causes the adjacent wood to swell in roughly the form of the biscuit. If the joint is allowed to dry for a couple of days, the moisture will equalize and the wood surface will reflatten. If, however, you sand or plane the surface while it's still swollen, the result will be a depression in the wood when the moisture does equalize. Unfortunately, there isn't much you can do to fix your tabletop except resurface it and refinish it.

Bob Jardinico
Kingston, MA

RELATED INFO:
Wood Movement as a Design Factor, page 12

GLUING AND ASSEMBLY

SOLUTIONS

GLUING AND GLUES

Avoiding Chalky Glue	159
Reading Glue Labels	159
Gluing Oily Woods	160
Rescuing Sloppy Joints with Epoxy	160
Avoiding Glue Creep	160
Preventing Glue-Line Depression	161
Warm Box for Cold Shop Glue-Ups	161
Choosing the Right Glue	162

GLUING UP SOLID WOODEN PANELS

Controlling Slippery Glue Joints	164
Clamping Thin Panel Stock	164
A Lightweight, Adjustable Sawhorse	165
Gluing Up Wide Panels	166
Panel Wedge Clamps	167
Aligning Pipe and Bar Clamps	168
Remaking Edge Joints	168
Easier Glue Squeeze-Out Clean Up	168

ASSEMBLING CABINETS AND FURNITURE

Wrestling with Large Cabinets	169
Sawing Box Lids Safely	170
Strengthening Bracket Feet	170
Gluing Long Edge Miters	171
Building As You Go	171
Biscuit Joiner for Tabletop Fasteners	172
Attaching a Tabletop Invisibly	172
Aligning Edge Material with Countertops	174
Shop-Made Squaring Sticks	174

ASSEMBLING DOORS, DRAWERS, AND FRAMES

Making a That Door Fits	175
Assembling Flat Door Frames	175
Clamping Mitered Boxes	176
Clamping Through-Tenons	177
Squaring Doors and Frames	177
Assembling Shutters	178
No-Mar Clamping	178

INSTALLING DOORS, DRAWERS, AND HARDWARE

Perfect Spacing on Flush Doors and Drawers	179
Mounting Metal Drawer Slides	180
Aligning Drawer Fronts	181
Drawer-Mounting Inserts	182
Making Drawer Stops	182
Mounting a Crooked Drawer	183
Using European Hinges	184
Hanging Cabinet Doors	186

CLAMPING DIFFICULT ASSEMBLIES

Gluing Up a Staved Column	187
Clamping with Super Glue	187
Fire Hose Column Clamp	188
Deep Reach Clamping	188
"Rubber Bands" for Hard-to-Clamp Glue-Ups	189
Attaching Crown Molding without Clamps	189
Clamping Odd Shapes	190
Clamping with Wedges and Pegs	192
"Stretching" Your Clamps	192

USING FASTENERS

Improving a Screw's Hold in End Grain	193
Dealing with Broken-Off Screws	193
Removing Screws with Stripped Heads	194
Driving Brads and Small Nails	195
Gluing Wood Screws	195
Using Drywall Screws	195
Tighter Shaker Pegs	196
Using an Air Nailer without a Compressor	196
Avoiding Pneumatic Nailer Marks	196

INSTALLATION SOLUTIONS

Hanging Cabinets on a Bowed Wall	197
Fitting a Counter into an Alcove	198
Wall Cabinet Installation Support	199
Hanging Wall Cabinets	199

Gluing and Glues

Avoiding Chalky Glue

PROBLEM: *In cooler temperatures, my yellow glue appears chalky on the wood. Does this affect the strength of the joint?*

SOLUTION: Chalking indicates that the temperature is too cold for a good bond to form. When any white or yellow glue dries chalky, instead of clear, the glue hasn't cured properly and the glue bond will be weak. You should never use white or yellow glue in cold weather, just as you shouldn't use latex paint or water-based finish in chilly conditions. The exact temperature cutoff is difficult to pinpoint, and brands of glue vary. Chalking usually occurs in white glue when the temperature is in the middle to upper 40°s (F). For yellow glues, you can expect chalking when the temperature is in the upper 40°s or lower 50°s. An exception is Titebond II, which requires a minimum working temperature in the lower 50°s.

When glue bonds properly, the wood will split apart around the joint (*left*). When the temperature is too low, the bond will be weak and the joint may fail (*right*).

Don't be fooled by appearances: While chalking is visual evidence that the glue hasn't cured properly, there is always a risk of a weaker glue bond if the temperature is below 60°F, even if chalking does not show up.

Bob Flexner
Norman, OK

Reading Glue Labels

PROBLEM: *I glued a scarf joint on a canoe gunwale using resorcinol glue, but the next morning when I took the clamps off, the joint fell right apart. What happened?*

SOLUTION: Some glues are very sensitive to temperature. Resorcinol won't cure at all in temperatures that are colder than about 60°F. There's always a note to this effect on the back of the can.

Wash and dry that joint, make up a fresh batch of glue, and keep the repair warm somehow while the glue cures. If you can't bring the canoe into a warm room, you might be able to rig up a reflector lamp to shine on it all night. If neither option is possible, wait until summer.

Warnings and caution labels on products often seem inspired by lawyers or the government, and some of them are so obvious that it's easy to disregard them all. However, when the technicians and engineers at the factory persuade the manufacturer to give a technical note, it's usually worth considering.

Jim Cummins
Woodstock, NY

Gluing Oily Woods

PROBLEM: *I glued up some teak boards for a tabletop and when I ran the top through the planer, most of the joints failed. What went wrong?*

SOLUTION: Many woodworkers discover this problem only after they get a call from a disgruntled client or an irritated relative, so you're lucky it happened right after glue-up. The problem is that a number of exotic woods, including rosewood and teak, contain oily resins that if present on the surface of the wood will inhibit gluing. While you can usually get a seemingly sound joint initially, over time the glue joint fails.

To insure the best chance for a successful glue-up, you can do several things:

- Aim for perfection. Minor flaws in the joint that would have yielded a tolerable glue-up in non-oily woods will cause the same joint in an oily wood to fail.
- Use sharp tools to prepare surfaces that will be joined. Edge joints, for example, should be prepared with a razor sharp hand plane or on a section of the jointer where the knives are sharp and nick-free.
- Assemble the joint as soon as possible after milling. Freshly cut wood fibers have little oily resin at first, but oil in the wood will rise to the surface the longer the surface is exposed.
- Wipe the wood with acetone just prior to gluing. Acetone dissolves oil on the surface of the wood and dries quickly without leaving a residue of its own.
- For insurance, add biscuits or splines along an edge joints.

David Page
Swarthmore, PA

Avoiding Glue Creep

PROBLEM: *I have had trouble with glue creep on the seams of several tabletops. Why does it happen and how can I avoid it?*

SOLUTION: Glue creep is the tendency of a glue to flex or allow slight movement over time. It is the result of pressure on the joint. The pressure may come from outside—caused by, for example, the weight of sitting in a chair seat—or from within the joint, such as pressure that results when two boards expand and contract unequally. The evidence of glue creep is typically a fine ridge of hard glue that protrudes slightly at joint lines and seams. The seams on a tabletop are a classic place to find it, but any glued joint is susceptible.

To remove the resulting ridge, you can sand lightly with fine sandpaper and a sanding block, or scrape lightly with a well sharpened scraper. This is likely to necessitate refinishing the piece, and even after refinishing, there's no reason to believe that the glue creep won't recur in the future. Since this solution isn't ideal, your best bet is to keep glue creep from occurring in the first place.

AVOIDING THE PROBLEM: The main culprit in glue creep is—surprise—the glue. Some glues are more flexible and creep prone than others. See "Choosing the Right Glue" on page 162. But there are other factors. In a successful glue joint, the moisture in the glue penetrates both pieces of the wood that are being joined and creates the chemical bond that does the holding. If the wood is too wet, the glue penetration may be inadequate. With less glue absorbed, the glueline may therefore be thicker and more likely to creep.

So to prevent glue creep, make sure that your wood is sufficiently dry and properly milled so that the pieces mate well. Some woodworkers say that inserting a spline along the length of a long edge joint prevents glue creep. It may, since it interrupts the glue line, but it won't make your joint any stronger, and it's extra work.

It's also my perception (not backed by any scientific study) that glue creep is more prevalent on furniture that has been finished with penetrating oil finishes rather than surface finishes like lacquer or urethane. The oil finishes don't control the gain and loss of moisture from the wood as well, and would not hide the glue creep as well if it occurs.

David Page
Swarthmore, PA

Preventing Glue-Line Depression

PROBLEM: *A solid wooden top has developed depressions at the glue lines. What went wrong, and can I fix this?*

SOLUTION: You probably didn't allow enough drying time after gluing and before sanding. When you glue up with water-based glue, the water in the glue causes the boards to swell in thickness on either side of the glue line. This is most pronounced with soft woods, like pine. As this water evaporates, the boards shrink back to their original thickness. If you sand the surface before this shrinkage occurs, you will inadvertently remove too much material, and the areas around the glue lines will end up being thinner than the rest of the piece. Even though these depressions, or "sink marks," are just barely perceptible on the unfinished wood, they are easy to see in the reflection off the finished surface. Unfortunately, your only solution is to resand and refinish the surface.

Walt Morrison
Northport, NY

RELATED INFO:
Wood Movement as a Design Factor, page 12

Warm Box for Cold Shop Glue-Ups

PROBLEM: *My shop is hard to heat, and I've found that glues don't dry well in the cold. How can I glue up projects during the winter?*

SOLUTION: An easy fix for this problem is to place your work in a "warm box" that has been constructed of rigid foam insulation and heated with lightbulbs or a portable electric heater. The insulation panels can easily be stowed away flat when not in use.

Rigid foam insulation, available at building supply outlets, comes in very lightweight 4 × 8-foot sheets that you can easily tape together to make even a large box. You can make smaller boxes by simply scoring one side of this foil-faced material, then snapping it over to create one or more sides of a box. Place a bank of high-watt lightbulbs or a small, electric heater inside the box, away from the walls and the work. Hang a cheap thermometer inside the box to monitor the temperature until the glue-up is dry. Keep the temperature between 60° and 80°F, shutting off the heat source when necessary.

Paul Anthony
Hellertown, PA

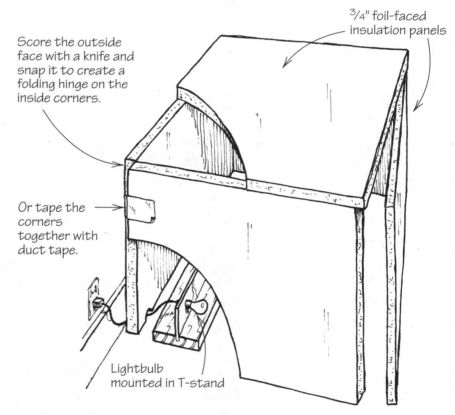

Score the outside face with a knife and snap it to create a folding hinge on the inside corners.

Or tape the corners together with duct tape.

¾" foil-faced insulation panels

Lightbulb mounted in T-stand

Most wood glues are more likely to fail when used in temperatures below 50°F. Lightbulbs provide the heat in this portable box used for gluing up when the shop is too cold.

CHOOSING THE RIGHT GLUE BY BOB MORAN

GENERAL-PURPOSE GLUES

	WHITE	YELLOW	CROSS-LINKING
Preparation required	Ready to use	Ready to use	Ready to use
Open working time	5 minutes	5 minutes	5 minutes
Clamp time/full cure	1 hour/12 hours	30 minutes/12 hours	30 minutes/12 hours
Minimum application temperature	50°F	50°F	55°F
Gap-filling ability	Poor	Poor	Poor
Moisture resistance	Poor	Fair	Good
Solvent resistance	Fair	Fair	Fair
Creep resistance	Poor	Fair	Fair
Open shelf life	1 year	1 year	1 year
Cost	Very inexpensive	Inexpensive	Inexpensive
Notes	Gums up abrasives	Good general-purpose glue	Moderate moisture resistance

	HOT HIDE GLUE	LIQUID HIDE GLUE	POLYURETHANE
Preparation required	Mix with water; use hot	Ready to use	Ready to use
Open working time	1–3 minutes	10 minutes	20–40 minutes
Clamp time/full cure	2 hours/24 hours	2 hours/24 hours	4 hours/24 hours
Minimum application temperature	65°F	70°F	68°F
Gap-filling ability	Poor	Poor	Poor
Moisture resistance	Poor	Poor	Excellent
Solvent resistance	Good	Good	Excellent
Creep resistance	Good	Good	Excellent
Open shelf life	3-week pot life	1 year	6–12 months
Cost	Inexpensive	Moderate	High
Notes	Good general-purpose glue	Good for occasional repairs of hide-glue joints	New; health hazards not fully tested; foams as it cures

WATER-RESISTANT GLUES

	PLASTIC RESIN (UREA-FORMALDEHYDE)	RESORCINOL	EPOXY
Preparation required	Mix powder with water	Mix powder with liquid resin	Mix 2 liquids
Open working time	20–30 minutes	10–30 minutes	5–60 minutes
Clamp time/full cure	12 hours/24 hours	12 hours/24 hours	None/varies
Minimum application temperature	70°F	70°F	40–65°F
Gap-filling ability	Fair	Good	Excellent
Moisture resistance	Very good	Excellent	Excellent
Solvent resistance	Excellent	Excellent	Excellent
Creep resistance	Excellent	Excellent	Excellent
Open pot life	2–4 hours	2–4 hours	10–60 minutes
Cost	High	High	High
Notes	Good water resistance	Excellent waterproof structural strength	Extremely versatile; lacks high heat resistance

SPECIAL-PURPOSE GLUES

	CYANOACRYLATE (SUPER GLUE)	HOT-MELT GLUE	CONTACT CEMENT
Preparation required	Ready to use	Heat in glue gun	Ready to use
Open working time	2–100 seconds	10–40 seconds	1–2 hours
Clamp time/full cure	N/A	N/A	Momentary pressure plus dry time
Minimum application temperature	40°F	N/A	60°F
Gap-filling ability	Not structural	Not structural	Poor
Moisture resistance	Excellent	Excellent	Excellent
Solvent resistance	Excellent	Poor	Poor
Creep resistance	Excellent	Poor	Poor
Open shelf life	6 months	Unlimited	6–12 months
Cost	Very high	Inexpensive	Moderately high
Notes	Versatile, durable instant bonding	Quick for temporary or lightly loaded joints	Suitable for bonding laminates and veneer

Gluing Up Solid Wooden Panels

Controlling Slippery Glue Joints

PROBLEM: *When I apply clamp pressure to a glue joint, the two mating parts often slide out of alignment. What can I do to prevent this?*

SOLUTION: To stop unwanted slippage, drive a couple of short brads into one of the parts, then snip the heads off so that about ¹⁄₁₆ inch is exposed. When the parts are assembled and clamped, the brads will grab and hold the parts in position. Caution: If the parts are to be cut, drilled or turned after glue-up, be sure to place the brads where they won't come in contact with a cutting tool.

Tom Begnal
Kent, CT

Clipped off brads will keep an edge joint from slipping out of alignment.

Clamping Thin Panel Stock

PROBLEM: *How can I keep thin boards flat when gluing them on edge? Even light pressure causes them to bow or buckle.*

SOLUTION: Make a pair of grooved stiffeners to fit over the ends of the thin boards. Make the groove slightly wider than the thickness of the boards to hold them securely without any wobble but not so narrow as to make removal difficult. And make the grooves as deep as possible without weakening the stock. Be sure to use stock that is beefy enough to withstand the clamping pressure. Wax the grooves so that the stiffeners don't stick to the work.

An extra pair of stiffeners that fits over the long sides of the glued-up panel will provide a better bearing edge for the clamps and help distribute the pressure more evenly.

Graham Blackburn
Bearsville, NY

Grooved stiffeners

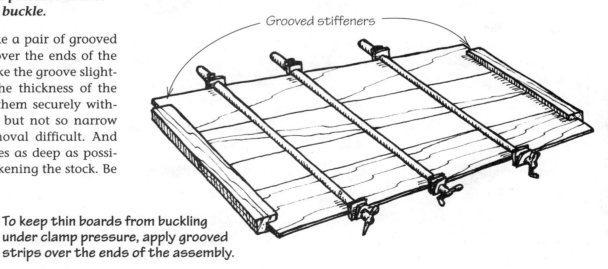

To keep thin boards from buckling under clamp pressure, apply grooved strips over the ends of the assembly.

A LIGHTWEIGHT, ADJUSTABLE SAWHORSE BY FRED MATLACK

A pair of sturdy sawhorses is a must for any shop, but different assembly jobs require sawhorses of varying heights. Making numerous sets is impractical, and they'd take up too much space.

These adjustable sawhorses are the solution. You can use just one set for most jobs around the shop, from catching stock as it comes off of the table saw to supporting large cabinets during assembly. These sawhorses are ideal for finishing also. I find myself using them as a convenient step-up for reaching the top shelves around the shop. And while they don't really stack, they do nestle together nicely.

You'll probably want to make a pair of these, so double the quantities in the "Materials List" right off the bat. Use a strong, tough wood like oak, ash, or hickory for these horses because those woods can take a beating.

Mill up the pieces as specified in the "Materials List," then lay out and cut the mortise-and-tenon joints. Each horse is made up of two sub-assemblies (the leg and stretcher assembly and the adjustable post and beam assembly). Dry assemble the horses completely to ensure that the tongue-and-groove joints align properly. Mark any corners you want to chamfer. Disassemble the horses and chamfer the edges you've marked. Now lay out and drill the

holes in the adjustable posts. Cut the tongues on the posts. Cut the matching grooves in the legs, making sure that they fit the tongues on the posts. Glue up the horses.

After the assemblies are dry, set the beam at a desirable height and

drill through each leg using one of the holes in the post as a guide. You can drill several holes in the post to correspond to often used heights. Bolt the posts and legs together and, if you wish, apply a light coat of oil to the finished horses.

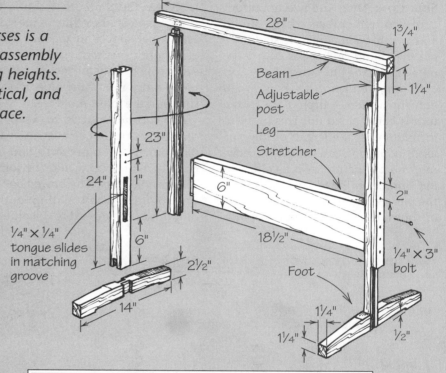

Part	Quantity	Dimensions
MATERIALS LIST		
Feet	2	1¼" × 2½" × 14"
Legs	2	1¼" × 1¼" × 24"
Adjustable posts	2	1¼" × 1¼" × 24"
Stretcher	1	1¼" × 6" × 20"
Beam	1	1¼" × 1¾" × 28"
HARDWARE		
Carriage bolts	2	¼"-20 × 3" with wing nuts & flat washers

Gluing Up Wide Panels

PROBLEM: *Something always goes wrong whenever I glue together boards to create wide panels. Typically, the edges of the boards are all uneven, or the glued up panel is twisted. What am I doing wrong?*

SOLUTION: There are two important goals to remember when gluing boards into wide panels. First, distribute the clamp pressure evenly. I use pipe clamps, but they have an annoying tendency to bow when tightened, often warping the panel that is being glued up. This problem increases with the length of the pipe used. While you can't eliminate bowing, you can neutralize it by alternating clamps on the top and bottom of the piece, canceling out any bowing, as shown below. Additionally, be sure to center the screw that drives the clamp head on the center of the stock. The panel should fit together easily and tightly without excessive pressure, which only increases bowing. Make a dry run of the glue-up to be sure that the joints mate well.

The second goal is to keep the assembly flat. Even with well-distributed clamp pressure, you can end up with badly aligned joints. This can be caused by bowed boards and by the wood sliding out of alignment at one end of the glue-up due to pressure at the other end. Two methods will help. Start the center clamp first and work outward toward the ends. If one of the boards is slightly bowed, you can force it into alignment with the adjacent boards by lifting or pressing down at the ends and applying the next clamp when it's just right.

A second method is more effective, especially if more than one of the boards are bowed. Make several pairs of battens and clamp them to the faces of the assembly. Shaping a slight bow onto the contact edges of the battens, as shown, forces the panels into perfect alignment.

Ben Erickson
Eutaw, AL

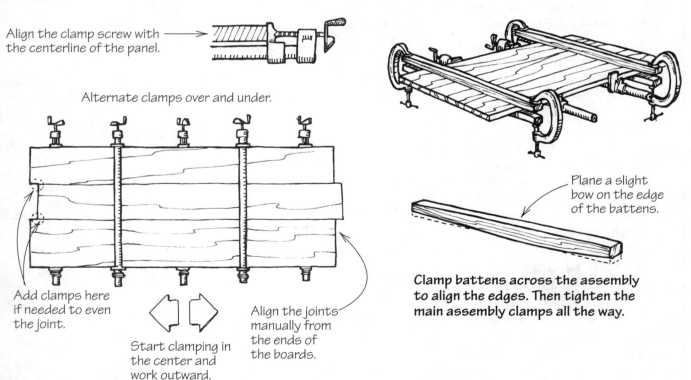

Align the clamp screw with the centerline of the panel.

Alternate clamps over and under.

Add clamps here if needed to even the joint.

Start clamping in the center and work outward.

Align the joints manually from the ends of the boards.

To distribute clamp pressure evenly, use as many of these techniques as possible.

Plane a slight bow on the edge of the battens.

Clamp battens across the assembly to align the edges. Then tighten the main assembly clamps all the way.

PANEL WEDGE CLAMPS BY ROB YODER

The main problem I have had with assembly is that I never have enough clamps, especially for jobs where I want to glue up a lot of panels. I'd buy more clamps, but they're too expensive.

MATERIALS LIST

Part	Quantity	Dimensions
Upper bar	1 per clamp	$1\frac{1}{2}"\times 1\frac{1}{2}"\times 42"$
Lower bar	1 per clamp	$1\frac{1}{2}"\times 1\frac{1}{2}"\times 42"$
Wedge	1 per clamp	$\frac{5}{8}"\times 1\frac{1}{4}"\times 8"$

HARDWARE

Bolts	2 per clamp	$\frac{5}{16}"\times 5"$
Wing nuts	2 per clamp	$\frac{5}{16}"$

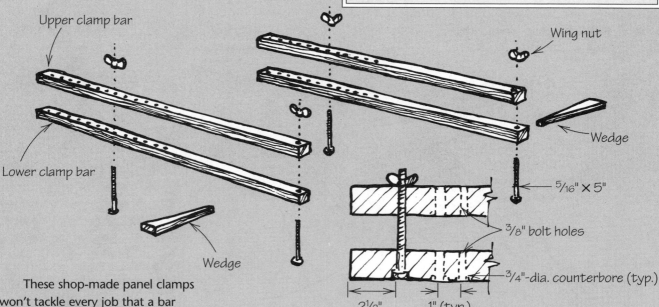

Upper clamp bar

Wing nut

Lower clamp bar

Wedge

Wedge

$\frac{5}{16}"\times 5"$

$\frac{3}{8}"$ bolt holes

$\frac{3}{4}"$-dia. counterbore (typ.)

$2\frac{1}{2}"$ 1" (typ.)

These shop-made panel clamps won't tackle every job that a bar clamp will because you have to enclose the glue-up within them. But unlike bar clamps, they keep the assembly flat while they make tight joints between the boards.

I made my clamps 42 inches long to accommodate a 36-inch-wide tabletop. The length of bolts determines the thickness of the boards you can glue.

Making the bars is simply a matter of drilling the equally spaced holes along the bars and cutting a pair of wedges. To use the clamps, slip your panel stock between the bars and between the two carriage bolts. Tighten the wing nuts; then drive a wedge between one of the bolts and the edge of the stock to squeeze the boards together. When the glue is dry, tap out the wedges and loosen the wing nuts to release the bars. Finish the bars with a couple of coats of urethane, or wax to prevent glue from sticking to them.

Aligning Pipe and Bar Clamps

PROBLEM: *I alternate my clamps above and below when gluing panels. How can I keep the clamps aligned?*

SOLUTION: The key to trouble-free panel glue-ups is applying even clamp pressure. Often you're forced to stumble through the job with clamps going every which way. Then you realize that one or another clamp is forcing the assembly to twist or the joints to be out of alignment.

These wooden holders fit ¾-inch pipe clamps and keep your clamps parallel to each other when edge-gluing panels, ensuring that the clamps are square to the boards to prevent slippage. (Note: The same system can be used for flat bar clamps by cutting the appropriately shaped notches instead of drilling holes.) It's important to make the holders wide enough to raise the clamp handles above the glue-up surface, so that you can tighten them without interference. Also, they should be thick enough to stand stable on edge. I face-glue ¾-inch stock to get 1½-inch thickness, but a straight 2 × 6 would also work.

Place the holders on a flat surface, such as your workbench or a level pair of sawhorses, to ensure that your panels glue up flat.

Andy Rae
Lenhartsville, PA

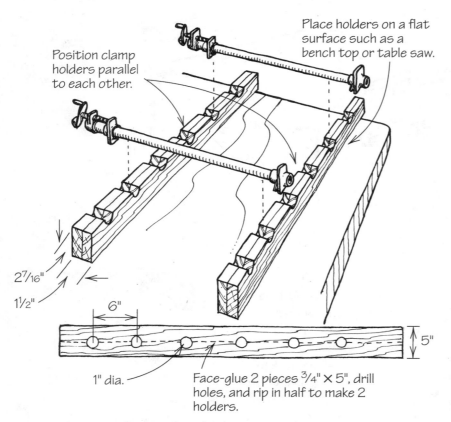

Position clamp holders parallel to each other.

Place holders on a flat surface such as a bench top or table saw.

2⁷⁄₁₆"

1½"

6"

1" dia.

5"

Face-glue 2 pieces ¾" × 5", drill holes, and rip in half to make 2 holders.

A set of clamp holders simplifies panel glue-ups by keeping all of the clamps parallel and in the same plane.

REMAKING EDGE JOINTS

It's a pain to notice after assembly that two boards did not glue together evenly or discover gaps in the joint. If you have extra width in the panel, rip the boards apart on the glue joint, rejoint the edges, and glue them back together. It seems obvious, but I often resist doing it anyway since it involves admitting that I messed up. However, remaking the joint usually ends up being quicker than trying to flatten it out by sanding or planing.

Ben Erickson
Eutaw, AL

EASIER GLUE SQUEEZE-OUT CLEAN UP

Cleaning up glue squeeze-out is always a nuisance, especially in a tight spot. For example, removing glue from the bottom of a small, deep box takes a lot of time and patience and some deft work with a sharp chisel.

The job can be made considerably easier by applying a thin coat of paste wax to the area of expected squeeze-out. Since glue won't stick to wax, the glue can be removed with little effort. Remove the wax residue thoroughly using a cloth dampened with acetone.

Tom Begnal
Kent, CT

Assembling Cabinets and Furniture

Wrestling with Large Cabinets

PROBLEM: *After gluing up a large cabinet, I realized that the thing was out of square and slightly twisted. How can I remedy this now that the glue is dry?*

SOLUTION: Large cabinets tend to have some flex in them, allowing you to make some adjustments without destroying your work or breaking the glue joints apart. But success is much more likely if you have a cabinet with a screwed-on back.

Remove the back if you've already attached it. Then find a large flat surface to work on—one that's bigger than the face of the case. If you don't have a flat bench or if the cabinet is larger than your bench, use the flattest floor area in your shop. Put the case face down and use winding sticks to make sure that the case is flat. Shim under the low corners to counteract any twist.

Measure the diagonals of the cabinet to check it for square. If the case is out of square, one diagonal will be longer than the other. Apply pressure across this long diagonal, as shown. This will require some monkeying. You can sometimes correct the problem with hand pressure alone. If you must clamp, work slowly and apply the least amount of pressure possible.

Once the diagonals are equal, attach the back. Screw down three corners, and double-check the diagonals. Make any necessary corrections, and proceed to screw the rest of the back in place.

AVOIDING THE PROBLEM: To avoid out-of-square glue-ups, test assemble the cabinet without glue before clamping, and check the diagonals. Slight changes in the position of the clamps can solve big problems.

Step 1. Position a large cabinet face down on a flat surface.

Step 2. Shim low corners and check for flatness with winding sticks.

Step 3. Clamp across a longer diagonal to square.

Step 4. Attach the back, double-checking for square as you go.

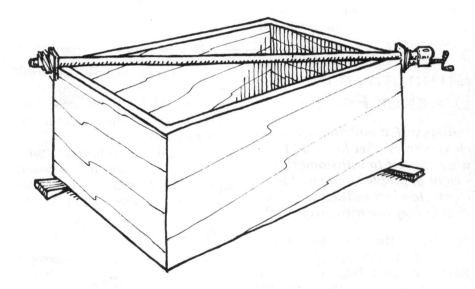

Align the center of the clamp screws with the center of the joint. Keep the distance between the cabinet and the clamp bar or pipe constant.

A cabinet can also go out of square once it's been placed in location for use. For example, placing a tall cabinet, such as a wardrobe, on an uneven floor can cause one side to drop, which will pull the cabinet out of square. Always level a cabinet before mounting the doors or drawers. If you expect that the cabinet will not sit level in it's intended location, include commercially made leveling feet in your design.

Jeff Day
Perkasie, PA

RELATED INFO:
Using Winding Sticks to Check Stock, page 68;
Squaring Doors and Frames, page 177

Sawing Box Lids Safely

PROBLEM: *When I cut the last side of a box lid free from the box, the lid invariably falls into the saw blade and damages the edges. How can I hold the parts securely but so that they can still be sawn apart?*

SOLUTION: After you have assembled the box sides, but before you attach the top or bottom, use a hot glue gun to tack small scraps inside the box where it will be separated into box and lid. Set the saw blade to cut through the box walls, and the scraps will hold both parts in alignment while the cut is being completed.

Graham Blackburn
Bearsville, NY

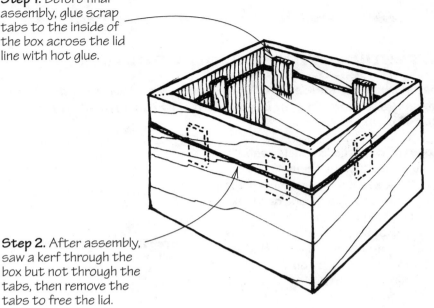

Step 1. Before final assembly, glue scrap tabs to the inside of the box across the lid line with hot glue.

Step 2. After assembly, saw a kerf through the box but not through the tabs, then remove the tabs to free the lid.

Strengthening Bracket Feet

PROBLEM: *I'm building a blanket chest with bracket feet, and I want the feet to withstand the weight of people sitting on the chest. How can I attach the feet so that they are their strongest?*

SOLUTION: The secret to a sturdy bracket foot isn't the bracket but rather the foot behind it. For a Colonial dovetailed chest, like the Pennsylvania five-board, screw and glue beefy mitered corner blocks to the bottom of the case, as shown at right. Use 8/4 (eight-quarter) stock if possible. The corner blocks carry the weight of the chest.

On a frame-and-panel chest, like those built in the Tidewater region of Virginia, the frame stiles extend to the floor to carry the weight of the chest. Glue corner blocks to the stiles and rails to reinforce the stile-to-case joints, as shown.

Your corner blocks should follow the grain direction of the casework. Once the corner blocks are attached, you can glue or brad the bracket to the case, trusting its strength.

To assemble the bracket itself, you can either miter it or dovetail it. Dovetailed brackets are a better choice to survive being kicked apart by shoes. Since the bracket is ornamental, leave it 1/16 inch above the floor. If the chest will be placed on a wooden floor, add felt pads to the bottoms of the corner blocks or stiles.

William Draper
Perkasie, PA

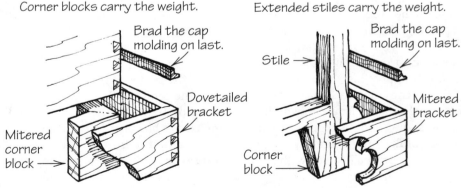

Corner blocks carry the weight.

Brad the cap molding on last.

Dovetailed bracket

Mitered corner block

Extended stiles carry the weight.

Brad the cap molding on last.

Stile

Mitered bracket

Corner block

To strengthen a dovetailed chest, screw and glue a heavy mitered corner block to the case, then glue and brad a dovetailed bracket to the blocking (above left). To strengthen a frame-and-panel chest, glue corner blocks to the stile, then glue and brad the mitered bracket around the corners (above right).

Gluing Long Edge Miters

PROBLEM: *I'm trying to assemble cabinet parts that are mitered along their edges. I cut a groove for a spline and the joint goes together fine when it's dry, but with glue and clamps the parts slip and refuse to close. What should I do?*

SOLUTION: My solution to gluing edge miters is effective, and simpler than it appears. It involves gluing triangular wooden strips along each side of the miter and then clamping across the glue blocks to close the miter, as shown.

I rip triangular hardwood strips from 1 inch stock by tilting the table saw blade to 45 degrees (plus or minus a degree won't matter). Then I glue the strips to the case sides with thin strips of brown grocery bag paper between the strips and the case. I find it's easiest to use spring clamps to clamp strips to the case. Hold the gluing strips back from the point of the miters about ⅛ inch because you want to see the edges of the two parts to be certain that the joint closes when you clamp it.

The triangular strips need to set for only an hour or so, then you are ready to glue up the joint. A spring clamp or small C-clamp every 8 or 10 inches will hold each case miter closed. After the assembly dries, remove the gluing strips by tapping a wide chisel gently under an end and pry upward. This will split the paper in half, leaving some paper glued to the cabinet. A sharp hand plane or hand scraper makes short work of removing the paper. If you use a scraper, wet the paper and it will come off easier.

David Page
Swarthmore, PA

Glue triangular strips to the edge of the case parts with a layer of paper between the parts so that you can easily remove the strips later.

The triangular glue blocks let you clamp perpendicular to the glue line and pull the miter joint together.

Building As You Go

PROBLEM: *I rely on the stated dimensions of project drawings and often end up with parts that won't go together. Are plans commonly full of mistakes?*

SOLUTION: The question of mistakes in project plans is one thing, and they no doubt do occur. Though it may seem everybody uses a different ruler to measure, that's not the problem. The problem more likely has to do with the fact that one small discrepancy—let's say in a cabinet dimension—affects the dimensions of so many subsequent parts, like doors, drawers, shelves.

The solution is to build tricky projects as a series of components and to cut and fit the rest of the project to what's been built already. In short, build as you go. When you have a project partly dry-assembled, you can scribe sizes of drawer openings directly off the piece or measure moldings to fit where they will actually go. You can determine whether a series of complicated measurements or angle cuts have truly added up to what the designer intended. Then, your project is bound to work out. Also, if there is an error in a plan, you'll likely spot it if you are focused on one part of the project at a time.

Jim Cummins
Woodstock, NY

Biscuit Joiner for Tabletop Fasteners

PROBLEM: *After I assembled my table, I realized I'd forgotten to cut slots in the aprons to fasten the tabletop. What can I do?*

SOLUTION: Z-shaped metal fasteners and a biscuit joiner provide a simple solution. The fasteners are slotted to allow solid wooden tops to move across the grain, and they're readily available. See "Sources," beginning on page 298. To cut the grooves, set your biscuit joiner at the #20 setting, then adjust its fence so that the tool will cut a slot about 1/32 inch lower on the rail. This offset ensures that the top will pull tight to the apron. Simply plunge the cutter into the apron without moving it sideways (one slot about every 10 inches works fine for most tops). Then insert the fasteners into the slots, align the top, and screw through the fasteners into the top.

An alternative solution is to rout the slots with a slot cutting bit. To steady the router on the narrow edge of the rails, clamp a block to the rail so that it is flush with the top of the rail at each slot.

Andy Rae
Lenhartsville, PA

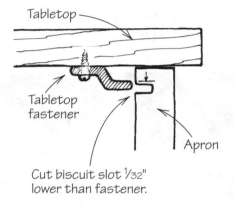

Tabletop

Tabletop fastener

Apron

Cut biscuit slot 1/32" lower than fastener.

One plunge with a biscuit joiner gives you a perfect slot for mounting a tabletop to the frame using Z-shaped fasteners.

Attaching a Tabletop Invisibly

PROBLEM: *I need to attach a solid wooden top to a leg-and-rail lectern base, but I don't want any hardware or blocking to show from underneath. What's a good technique for this?*

SOLUTION: Depending on your design, sliding dovetails may be a solution, but I came up with a much easier technique. The drawings on the opposite page show the method I used. It's very similar to hanging a picture frame in a routed "keyhole" slot, but in this case you don't need the special router bit.

My top was 7/8 inch thick and the frame was constructed with mortise-and-tenon joinery. To secure the top to the frame, I installed three #8 flathead wood screws into each of the two frame members that ran perpendicular to the grain direction of the top. I made sure that the screws were all aligned on the centerline of the frame members. I left the screw heads protruding 1/2 inch (you may have to reduce or increase this amount as well as the size of the screws for tops of a different thickness). Next I filed off the underside of each screw head with a fine mill file to form a sharp cutting edge.

Once this was done, I cut six keyhole-shaped mortises in the underside of the top so that they corresponded exactly to the position of the screws in the frame. The best way to do this is to rest the top on the screw heads and carefully check the overhang. When it's right, tap firmly on the top with a mallet so that the screws leave an impression on the underside of the top. Double-check that the impressions are aligned parallel to the edges of the top. To make the keyholed slots, I first drilled 1/2-inch holes on the drill press. Then I clamped a

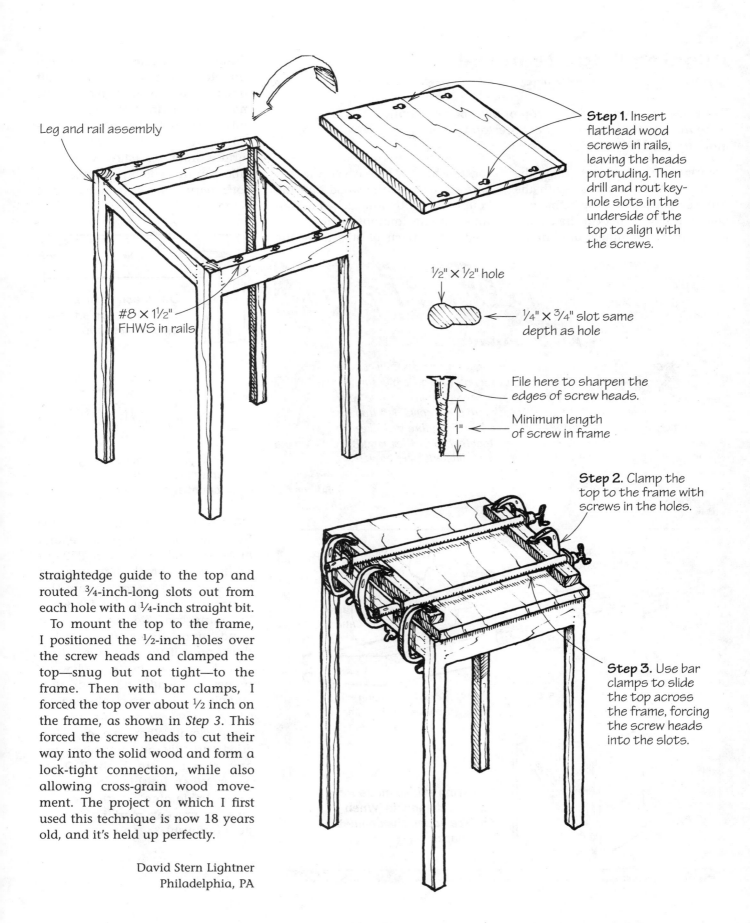

Leg and rail assembly

#8 × 1½" FHWS in rails

Step 1. Insert flathead wood screws in rails, leaving the heads protruding. Then drill and rout key-hole slots in the underside of the top to align with the screws.

½" × ½" hole

¼" × ¾" slot same depth as hole

File here to sharpen the edges of screw heads.

1"

Minimum length of screw in frame

Step 2. Clamp the top to the frame with screws in the holes.

Step 3. Use bar clamps to slide the top across the frame, forcing the screw heads into the slots.

straightedge guide to the top and routed ¾-inch-long slots out from each hole with a ¼-inch straight bit.

To mount the top to the frame, I positioned the ½-inch holes over the screw heads and clamped the top—snug but not tight—to the frame. Then with bar clamps, I forced the top over about ½ inch on the frame, as shown in *Step 3*. This forced the screw heads to cut their way into the solid wood and form a lock-tight connection, while also allowing cross-grain wood movement. The project on which I first used this technique is now 18 years old, and it's held up perfectly.

David Stern Lightner
Philadelphia, PA

Aligning Edge Material with Countertops

PROBLEM: *How can I get the top of my wooden edging to be flush with a laminated countertop without marring the laminate?*

SOLUTION: The trick is to align the edging so that it is flush with the surface of the countertop before you glue it in place. First cut the edging to size, including miters, and sand it for finishing. Then cover the top surfaces of both the wood and the countertop with low-tack masking tape. (If the laminate comes covered with stretch plastic, leave the plastic on and mask only the edging.) Rout a groove or use a biscuit joiner to cut slots in the pieces to be mated, registering your cuts off the masked surfaces. The tape (or plastic) on the laminate protects the surface from scratches, while the tape on the edging ensures that both parts register equally while being slotted.

Use biscuits or a spline to align edges on countertops.

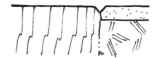

A V-joint disguises slight mismatches between a countertop and edging.

Before you glue, remove the tape from the edging and laminate, and make a single pass with 220-grit sandpaper to break the corners of the edging and the countertop. This creates a very slight V-joint when the parts come together, so that hands and elbows won't feel a sharp ridge if the edging is a fraction high or low. Then glue plywood splines or biscuits into your slots and glue and clamp on the edging, wiping any excess glue with a damp cloth. When the glue has dried, carefully sand any miters and any raised grain with 220-grit paper. When finishing the edging, cover the laminate with masking tape to prevent marking it with stain or finish.

Michael Knepp
Piscataway, NJ

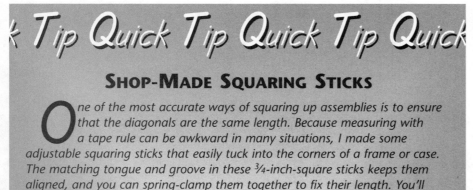
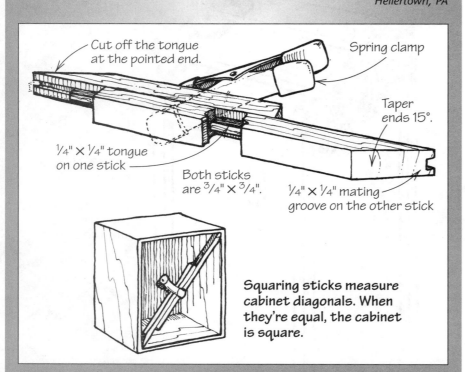

Assembling Doors, Drawers, and Frames

Making a Door That Fits

PROBLEM: *Every time I make frame-and-panel doors for a cabinet, I end up with too much of a gap between the door and the opening. I measure carefully. What else can I do?*

SOLUTION: I try to remember two things when I'm building and fitting a door. First I work with the actual opening rather than with the dimensions shown on my drawing. The door isn't going to hang on a drawing, and I've yet to build something that matches the drawing exactly. I also invoke the first law of cabinetmaking—if a part can possibly be the wrong size, it will be. Given that, I always make doors the exact size of the opening, without any gap. After assembly I fit each door individually so that there will be a consistent space between the door and the case.

To make the doors to the exact size of the opening, first measure the opening carefully. If there are multiple openings that are the same size, look for discrepancies and work to the largest opening. Then cut all the stiles to fit the full height of the opening. They should be snug when you put them in place.

Measure for the length of the rails by butting the stiles together on one side of the opening and measuring between them and the frame, as shown. This gives you the distance between tenons. Pick a tenon length that makes for easy math—1 or 1½ inch; then double it and add it to the distance between tenons. Cut all of your rails to this length. Be sure to cut two extra rails and stiles for setting up the mortise and tenon cuts.

Cut mortises and tenons on the test pieces. This allows you to gauge the fit of a door before you cut all the joints. Adjust the location of the tenon shoulders if necessary to get the fit you want; then cut all of your joints.

To trim the assembled doors, start by running each stile over the jointer with a light cut. Gauge the fit after each cut. Once the width is right, crosscut the door on the table saw, taking a light cut from each end. If the door is too wide for the table saw, trim the ends on the jointer.

Jeff Day
Perkasie, PA

RELATED INFO:
Jointing End Grain,
page 61

To accurately size door rails to an opening, fit both stiles into the opening and measure the remaining space. This gives you the distance between the tenon shoulders. Add the tenons to get the final length of the rails.

Assembling Flat Door Frames

PROBLEM: *My door frames rarely come out flat, and hanging twisted doors is a real nightmare. What am I doing wrong?*

SOLUTION: Poorly cut joints can result in a twisted door, and a warped panel will force a frame to warp. But the most common cause of twisted doors is poor clamping technique. Sometimes when gluing up a door I focus all my attention on getting the assembly square and overlook getting it flat.

I've used two similar techniques to assemble doors so that they come out of the clamps dead flat and stay that way. First, once the clamps are applied and the joints are pulled tight most of the way, I clamp down the assembly to the end of my bench, which I know is dead flat. Then I give the clamps on the door one final tightening.

An alternative approach, for situations when I can't clamp to my bench, is to create a flat plane by clamping the door to a pair of stout blocks, one under each rail. The blocks should be carefully planed and identical in thickness and width—I plane one long piece and then cut it in half. I position the blocks so that they are perfectly parallel and clamp the assembly against the blocks, as shown.

Tony O'Malley
Emmaus, PA

RELATED INFO:
Using Winding Sticks to Check Stock, page 68;
Flattening Twisted Doors, page 293

Clamping a door assembly onto a flat surface ensures that it will be flat when the glue dries. Here, a flat plane is created by using identical blocks of wood with square edges. You can use ³⁄₈"-thick acrylic (Plexiglas) cauls right over the joint (*inset*) so you can see the joint line and be sure it's closed.

Clamping Mitered Boxes

PROBLEM: *Even when I use a spline to align the joint, the corners of mitered boxes don't come out cleanly. What can I do?*

SOLUTION: Cut L-shaped pieces of scrap to fit the corners of the piece being clamped, and wrap a band clamp around the scrap, as shown. Crosscut the blocks from a longer length of stock after making the two partial rip cuts to create the L-shape. Cover the inside faces of the blocks with clear plastic packaging tape or coat them with wax to prevent their sticking to the box.

Graham Blackburn
Bearsville, NY

L-shaped blocks distribute the pressure from a single band clamp across the whole joint and help keep the assembly square at the same time.

Clamping Through-Tenons

PROBLEM: *Clamping through-tenons is tricky because the protruding tenon prevents the clamp from pulling against the mortised part of the frame. What's the best way to do it?*

SOLUTION: You might think that your best bet is to place the clamp beyond the tenon, but the pressure will not be enough to close the joint, and it will likely twist or bow the frame. Instead, make a set of blocks the length of the mortise and the same thickness as the stock you are working with. Cut a groove in the blocks that is slightly wider than the mortise width and a little deeper than the tenon protrudes, as shown. Coat the slot and edge of the blocks with a nonstick material (wax, finish, or plastic packing tape) so that the blocks will not be glued to the workpiece. Center the blocks over the mortise and pull the frame together with clamps. After you have pulled the piece together, temporarily remove the blocks and wipe off the squeezed out excess glue with a damp rag; then replace the blocks and reclamp.

Ben Erickson
Eutaw, AL

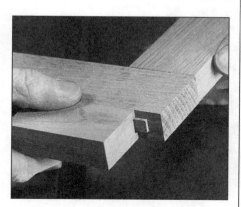

Using a clamping block with a groove cut in it simplifies assembling through-tenon joints.

Squaring Doors and Frames

PROBLEM: *How can I correct a door that's out of square when I initially clamp it together?*

SOLUTION: First be sure your method of checking for square is providing accurate information. A small try square, for example, will not detect out-of-squareness on a large door. Even a large framing square that suggests a corner is out of square may be indicating instead that one of the frame members is bowed.

The best method to check for square is to compare the length of the two diagonals. Any rectangle must have equal diagonals to be square. Diagonals can be measured by hooking a tape measure over one corner and measuring to the other corner. An alternative method is to compare the interior diagonals using two overlapping sticks with pointed ends. Hold or clamp the sticks together in one diagonal and then compare that length to the other diagonal.

If the diagonals are not the same length, pad the long corners with notched blocks and place a clamp diagonally across the door. Tighten the clamp and then remove it and check the diagonals again. Another method is to loosen the pipe clamps that are holding the door together and slant them slightly until the door is pulled square.

Ben Erickson
Eutaw, AL

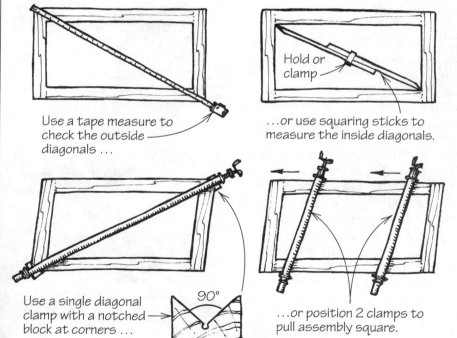

Use a tape measure to check the outside diagonals ...

...or use squaring sticks to measure the inside diagonals.

Hold or clamp

Use a single diagonal clamp with a notched block at corners ...

90°

...or position 2 clamps to pull assembly square.

Check for square by measuring diagonals (top).
Correct an out-of-square frame by clamping against the longer diagonal (bottom).

Assembling Shutters

PROBLEM: *I'm assembling a set of tall shutters with movable louvers, and it's really tedious getting all the little tenons lined up in order to pull everything together. How can I do this without throwing a clamp through the wall?*

SOLUTION: The process is similar for shutters which have either fixed or movable louvers. The trick is to be sure that the tenons on the louvers (slats) are at least ¼ inch shorter than the tenons on the rails. This will allow you to insert them partially into one stile. Then with the rails engaged in the second stile, pull the louvers partway into their mortises in the second stile.

With the stiles lying flat on a table or bench, first insert one end of all the louvers into one of the stiles. Also insert the rail tenons fully into the same stile. Then pull the other stile onto the rail tenons until the stile is almost touching the other end of the louvers. Now you can pull the louvers one at a time slightly out of their holes in the first stile and into their holes in the opposite stile. Once they are all in, pull the frame the rest of the way together.

Note: Before you assemble the shutters, you should attach the staples for the operator stick to the louvers. Also, use the same spacing that was used to drill the louver holes in the stiles to space the staples on the operator stick. When you assemble large shutters, your glue may start to set before you're ready to apply the clamps. Consider using a slower setting glue like polyurethane or epoxy.

Ben Erickson
Eutaw, AL

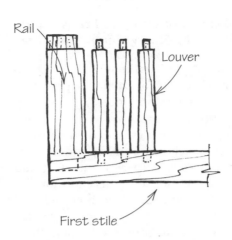

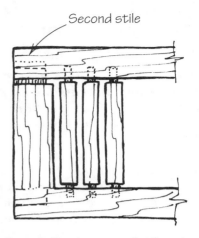

Step 1. Insert rails and louvers fully into first stile.

Step 2. Fit the second stile onto rail tenons until the louver tenons touch. Slide the louvers partway into the second stile, and then clamp the frame closed.

Quick Tip Quick Tip Quick Tip Quick

NO-MAR CLAMPING

Because of their low cost and adjustable length, pipe clamps are the clamp of choice in many shops. They have two drawbacks, though, that can mar your work. One is that the pipe tends to dent flat panels when the clamps are tightened during glue-up. The second is that, pressed against the panel, the iron pipe can cause a reaction between the moisture in the glue and the wood, leaving a dark stain on the wood.

To correct these problems, slide short strips of ⅛-inch-thick × 1-inch-wide acrylic (Plexiglas) between the clamp and the wood, as shown. The acrylic will act as padding to prevent denting and as a barrier to stop staining. It has two added advantages: It won't stick to glue; and because it is clear, you can see through it to the joint below.

Ben Erickson
Eutaw, AL

Short strips of acrylic (Plexiglas) keep pipe clamps from marring your glued-up panels.

Installing Doors, Drawers, and Hardware

Perfect Spacing on Flush Doors and Drawers

PROBLEM: *The face frames for some cabinets that I built are out of square, and fitting the drawer fronts and doors is a nightmare. Can I salvage the face frames, or should I start over?*

SOLUTION: If the openings in a face frame are not square, you can still fit the doors or drawers to conceal the error. Here are two options:

If the opening is not too far out, you can taper the edge of the drawer or door to fit the opening. First find the largest dimensions of the opening. Cut your drawer front or door to fit the largest measurement for the opening. Remember to allow for a consistent gap on all sides—I aim for $1/16$ inch. Then after fitting and marking your drawer front or door, taper it down to the shorter measurement to match the opening. I make tapered crosscuts on the table saw by angling the miter gauge (or angling the blade on a chop saw) $1/2$ degree or so. I make tapers along the length of a door or drawer on the jointer or with a hand plane.

If your drawer and door openings are so out of square that you can easily notice the problem just by looking at them, you should consider making overlapping drawers and doors. Sometimes, changing your design is the only way to conceal an error.

AVOIDING THE PROBLEM: Door and drawer openings can go out of square during the clamping process. You can prevent this in the future by using spacer sticks to define the openings in your face frame. The spacers should fit into the smaller dimension of the opening, typically horizontal for a door and vertical for a drawer, as shown

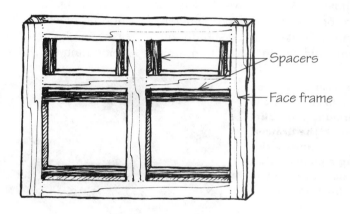

A pair of precut spacers in each face frame opening (above) will ensure a square assembly. Or work in reverse: Make the doors and drawer fronts first, then assemble face frames and drawers around them with shims in between (below).

at top. Use one spacer at each end of each opening.

Another effective approach, albeit unusual, is to make the drawer faces and doors before you glue the face frame together, then assemble the face frame around them with shims inserted to create consistent gaps, as shown above. Although it may seem "backward," it's actually a quick route to perfectly spaced doors and drawer fronts within a face frame.

Bill and Joanne Storch
Corvallis, OR

Mounting Metal Drawer Slides

PROBLEM: *I'm using side-mount metal drawer slides for a cabinet with a stack of drawers and am having trouble getting the drawers level and parallel to each other. What's a good way to do this?*

SOLUTION: This problem tends to be worse the deeper the drawers are. The solution is to mount both slides for each drawer using a spacer that locates them the same distance from the bottom of the cabinet—no matter how deep the drawer is. I use a piece of ¾-inch plywood. Different brands of slides call for slightly different calculations in determining exactly where each part needs to be located, but here are some general points that will minimize errors:

- Buy the slides before making the drawers and follow the specifications regarding space allowances for the slides.
- Level and plumb the cabinet before mounting the slides.

- With multi-drawer cabinets, always start with the bottom drawer and work your way upward.
- Attach the drawer-mounted part of the slide first, then the cabinet-mounted part.
- Mount the first drawer as a trial run, then if necessary make adjustments in your approach and mount all the slides the same way.

With some slides, you can mount the drawer part so that it is flush with the bottom edge of the drawer; other slides mount by wrapping the bottom corner of the drawer. Both types make this part of the job a lot easier. If you use a type of slide that doesn't mount in either of these ways, you'll need to mount the drawer part a specific distance up from the bottom edge. Use a combination square to strike a light pencil line parallel to the bottom edge of the drawer, as shown in the top photo. The line always locates the centerline of the slide, along which the mounting holes are aligned. Then mount the slide on the drawer.

The cabinet part is usually the culprit when drawer slides are unevenly mounted. It's just hard to get right because you're often squeezing halfway into the cabinet to mount the slides. The key to getting a drawer mounted evenly within a cabinet (level and plumb within its space) is to use the bottom and front edge of the case for reference. For a stack of drawers, start at the bottom using the bottom of the cabinet as the reference for mounting the cabinet part. With many slides, you mount the part right against the floor of the cabinet, which ensures that the drawer will be parallel with the bottom. Successive drawers will be kept parallel by using a spacer to mount the cabinet part, as shown in the bottom photo.

To ensure that the drawer slide is mounted parallel with the drawer, strike a line by riding a combination square against the bottom edge of the drawer.

Viewed from the rear, the slide for the bottom drawer is mounted, and a plywood spacer is used to locate the slide for the drawer above it. This ensures that successive drawers will be mounted parallel to the first.

Dennis Slabaugh
Naples, FL

Aligning Drawer Fronts

PROBLEM: *I've made drawers with separate fronts that get screwed to the drawer box. Since this has to be done with the drawers in place, how can I align them, hold them in place, and screw them on, all at the same time?*

SOLUTION: With a vertical bank of drawers, I always start by installing the front on the bottom drawer. I clamp a ledger to the face frame to receive the drawer front's bottom edge. I predrill my screw clearance holes in the drawer box, then place the drawer front on the ledger. I screw on the drawer front, accessing the screws from the drawer opening above. I then place thin plywood shims on the top edge of that drawer front and rest the next drawer front on top of the shims. I repeat the procedure, working my way upward. For the top drawer, I prebore my drawer box screw holes so that they are slightly undersized—just enough to hold a drywall screw in place with its tip slightly projecting out of the front of the drawer box. I press the drawer front in place against the protruding screw tips, then remove the drawer. I place the screw tips into their depressions, install a couple of screws, and check the fit with the drawer installed. I make any necessary fine adjustments before installing the final screws.

Paul Anthony
Hellertown, PA

ANOTHER VIEW: When hanging drawer fronts that get screwed-on handles, I use the handle screw holes to premount the drawer fronts to the drawer boxes. This way I can attach the front with the drawer in the closed position. Here's how: Decide on the location of your drawer handles and drill holes for the screws through all the drawer fronts. Also, predrill and countersink holes through the drawer box that will be used to permanently attach the fronts. See the top photo. Use clamps or double-sided tape to hold the drawer face in place against the drawer box. Now screw through the handle holes into the drawer box to attach the front temporarily to the drawer box, as shown in the bottom photo. You can now fine-tune the drawer front alignment by loosening or removing one of the screws. After all the fronts have been mounted and adjusted, open the drawers one by one and screw through the boxes into the drawer fronts for the final attachment.

Tony O'Malley
Emmaus, PA

> **RELATED INFO:**
> Mounting a Crooked Drawer,
> page 183

First drill screw holes in the drawer front for the handle and in the drawer box for mounting the front.

Then use drywall screws to mount the drawer front to the box. Loosened slightly, they allow you to fine-tune the location of the front before you mount it to the box permanently.

DRAWER-MOUNTING INSERTS

Mounting drawer fronts to drawer boxes is a finicky task, especially when you have several that have to align with each other and when you have inset fronts with a tight reveal around them. The attachment holes must be just right or you end up re-drilling them.

There's a simple piece of hardware that nearly eliminates the difficulty. These "adjustable drawer front inserts" (see "Sources," beginning on page 298) allow the drawer front to be mounted and then moved about ⅛ inch in any direction—just enough to fine-tune the location. A thin nut "floats" laterally inside the plastic insert.

Here's how to use the adjustable inserts: First drill ⁵/₃₂-inch mounting holes in the drawer box. Then position the drawer front against the drawer box in its desired location and transfer the hole location to the drawer front. If necessary, stick the drawer to the box using double-sided tape. Now drill 25-millimeter holes for the insert, as shown. A ⅞-inch Forstner bit can be substituted for the 25-millimeter bit, but check on a scrap first to ensure that the insert will fit tightly. Tap the inserts into their holes with a mallet. If they go in too easily, I first add a dab of cyanoacrylate glue (CA glue, also known as Super Glue). Mount the drawer front using the screws that have been supplied with the insert. Tighten the screws until the front is snug, then close the drawer. Adjust the drawer for even spacing and tighten the screws all the way.

*Dennis Slabaugh
Naples, FL*

When you use drawer-mounting inserts, the holes should be deep enough so that the inserts are just below the back surface of the drawer front.

The thin nut moves laterally within the insert. Once attached, the drawer fronts can be adjusted by loosening the mounting screws.

Making Drawer Stops

PROBLEM: *Now that I've gone to the trouble of carefully dovetailing the drawers in my cabinet, how can I keep the drawers from being accidentally pulled out and dropped?*

SOLUTION: There are a number of clever ways to keep a drawer from falling out of its cabinet. Which one works best for your project depends on the details of construction.

The easiest situation is when you have a front rail or horizontal divider directly above the drawer. It could also be the top of the cabinet. There are three stop mechanisms I use for this type of drawer. In the "bar-and-notch" method, shown in *Option 1*, I cut a rectangular notch in the center of the back of the drawer and mount a pivoting bar on the front rail. When the bar is turned parallel with the front of the drawer, it catches against the drawer back. By turning the bar 90 degrees, the bar slides through the notch, allowing the drawer to be removed. This method requires that the back of the drawer be high enough to catch against the bar.

If the back of the drawer is too low to use the bar-and-notch method, I employ the pivoting cam mechanism, shown in *Option 2*. I make the cam by screwing a 1-inch-diameter cam off-center onto the back edge of the rail above the drawer. Rotating the cam will cause it to catch the back of the drawer, preventing it from falling out. Because the cam is attached to the back edge of a rail divider, this method wouldn't work if the drawer rode directly under a cabinet top or a full panel divider.

The wooden spring stop, shown in *Option 3*, is another version I've used. I cut the spring on the band saw from a block of scrap wood and mount it to the underside of the cabinet top or the drawer rail. Depressing the spring lets the drawer slide out. Depending upon the drawer clearance, you may have to plan ahead for this one and mortise the base of the spring into the rail above the drawer.

Whatever solution you choose, bear in mind that it's best to plan the stop mechanism you'll use before you assemble the drawer and the cabinet. That way you can make any necessary modifications to the individual parts instead of wrestling with the assembled whole.

David Page
Swarthmore, PA

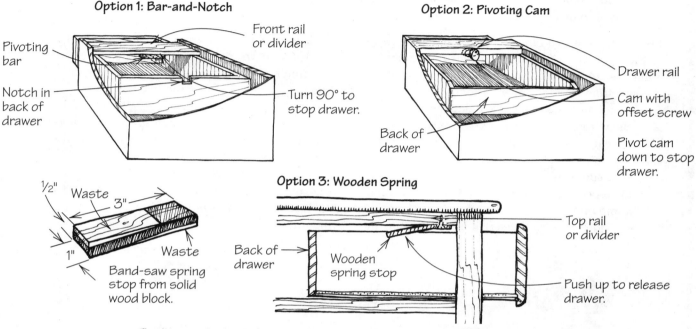

Option 1: Bar-and-Notch

Pivoting bar

Notch in back of drawer

Front rail or divider

Turn 90° to stop drawer.

Option 2: Pivoting Cam

Drawer rail

Cam with offset screw

Back of drawer

Pivot cam down to stop drawer.

½" Waste 3"

1" Waste

Band-saw spring stop from solid wood block.

Option 3: Wooden Spring

Back of drawer

Wooden spring stop

Top rail or divider

Push up to release drawer.

The bar-and-notch (top left) and the pivoting cam (top right) are two practical drawer stops that will work on most drawers. The more elegant wooden spring stop (bottom) works well when the drawer is under a solid panel.

Mounting a Crooked Drawer

PROBLEM: *I made a cabinet with three drawers and then found that one of the drawers is twisted. What can I do to get around this?*

SOLUTION: Twisted drawers can be caused by using crooked wood, but they can also be caused by one or more of the corners having been cut just slightly off square. In either case, you can knock the drawer apart and replace the offending part or parts. But that's a lot of work.

Here's a better approach. If you put the drawer together without noticing the problem, I'd assume that it's not twisted a lot. You probably realized it when you discovered that the drawer face didn't fit properly to the face of the cabinet. If that's the case, use the drawer as is, and adjust the drawer slides to make the face fit correctly. Commercial drawer guides are made with adjustable slots. You may need to use new holes if the twist is extensive. If you're using wooden runners, remove them from the cabinet and remount them at slight angles to accommodate the twisted drawer.

Fred Matlack
Vera Cruz, PA

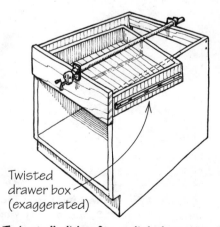

Twisted drawer box (exaggerated)

To install slides for a slightly twisted drawer, first clamp the drawer front flat against the cabinet face. Then from the rear of the cabinet, mark where the drawer slides will fall due to the twist.

USING EUROPEAN HINGES

European hinges, also known as concealed hinges, were developed for use on so-called "frameless" cabinetry. On this style of cabinet, the case parts themselves form the front edges, and there is no added face frame on which to hang the doors. The result is that doors and drawer fronts can be very tightly spaced, with a scant ¹⁄₁₆ inch between each. The look is generally sleek and modern.

This design requires a hinge that is both adjustable (to get the tight and consistent spacing) and concealed within the cabinet. Mounting these hinges is entirely different from mounting traditional style cabinet hinges. Though these hinges were designed for frameless cabinets, most manufacturers sell concealed hinges that can be used on face-frame cabinets as well. This is very useful on jobs that combine frameless and face-frame style cabinets.

All European hinges come in two parts—the hinge and the mounting plate, as shown below. The hinge fits into a large (32-millimeter) hole drilled into the back face of the door, and the plate mounts to the inside face of the cabinet side. So instead of mortising, you simply drill a precisely located hole for the hinge. The hinge plate is surface mounted.

Before you mount a door using European hinges, carefully read the specification sheet that comes with the hinges you purchase. Note that a different hinge (or hinge plate) is needed for an inset, overlay, or half-overlay door, so be sure to get the right hinge and plate combination. Additionally, each door-to-cabinet scenario will have slightly different specs for mounting the hinge.

A typical European hinge (see "Sources," beginning on page 298) has a body that fits into a hole drilled in the back of the door. The arm of the hinge attaches to the mounting plate, which gets screwed to the inside wall of the cabinet.

The assembled hinge uses different screws on the hinge arm to allow adjustments in any direction, including in and out from the cabinet face.

Using European hinges requires more forethought and planning than using conventional hinges. For example, if you intend to mount drawers in a case behind a door, you should know that the hinges may get in the way. You'll need to locate the drawers so that they slide out between the hinges, or build out the wall of the cabinet so that the drawers clear the hinges. Also, when you use frame-and-panel doors, make sure that the stiles are wide enough to receive the hinge hole without weakening the door.

To drill the holes for European hinges, you need a special 32-millimeter Forstner-type bit. They're expensive, but there are no good alternatives. Drill the holes on the drill press, as shown below left. The depth of the holes should be just sufficient for the hinge, so try the hole on a scrap first. The crucial specification is the distance between the door's edge and the edge of the hole—typically between ⅛ and ¼ inch. This distance determines the clearance between the edge of the door and the case. When first using a particular hinge, I always drill the holes and mount a dummy door. It doesn't need to be full width, just the full height of the real door.

To locate the mounting plate inside the cabinet, attach the plate to the hinge and position the door in place using shims. If you have access from the back of the cabinet, place the door in its closed position (I usually clamp or tape it into place temporarily) and simply screw the plate to the cabinet side. Otherwise, hold the door in its open position with the hinge edge of the door against the cabinet edge and attach the mounting plate, as shown below right.

Tony O'Malley
Emmaus, PA

Drilling the holes for European hinges couldn't be easier, but the location of the hole is crucial. Therefore, mount a dummy door panel first to test the hole's placement.

The easiest way to locate the hinge plate is to attach it to the hinge, position the door in place, and screw the plate to the cabinet. Note the horizontal divider below the hinge: Be sure to locate the hinge on the door so that it clears any obstructions in the cabinet.

Hanging Cabinet Doors

PROBLEM: *Whenever I hang a cabinet door using butt hinges, I get an uneven gap. Then I try (unsuccessfully) to move the hinges slightly. Isn't there a reliable way to do this job right?*

SOLUTION: Hanging a door on butt hinges is more demanding than it looks because there's no adjustability and therefore no room for error. So the first thing you want to do is adjust your thinking: Since you've got just one shot to get it right, slow down.

One approach that can avoid a badly hung door is to leave the door full in size, hang it, and then carefully trim the edges to get an even gap all around. This is tedious, but if have just one or two doors, you can get it just right without going back and moving the hinges.

If you want to trim the door to its final size and then hang it, first double-check the opening to make sure that it is square. Place the cabinet so it's sitting level and plumb. Position the door in place and mark the hinge side of the door. Then mount the hinges on the door edge.

For very small hinges, I cut the whole hinge mortise with just a mallet and chisel. But most of the time, I use a router in conjunction with a chisel.

To hang a door, first incise the edges of the hinge mortises with a chisel or razor knife, as shown in *Step 1*. Then use a small laminate trimmer with a straight router bit to rout away most of the waste, as shown in *Step 2*. This approach gives the mortise a consistent flat bottom. When the mortises are cleaned up, predrill for the screws and mount the hinges on the door.

To transfer the mortise locations from the door to the cabinet, position the door in place. Shim the door snugly in its opening and strike a razor mark at the top and bottom edges of each hinge, as shown in *Step 3*. Then remove the cabinet side hinge leaf to scribe the three edges of the mortise. Position the cabinet on its side, as shown in *Step 4*, and cut the mortises the same way that you cut them on the door. If you can't position the cabinet on its side, use the router with extra care to clean out the waste, or cut the whole mortise with a chisel. Mount the cabinet side hinge leaf and then mount the door.

Tony O'Malley
Emmaus, PA

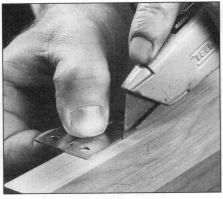

Step 1. Use the hinge itself to scribe the ends of the mortise, first with a razor knife, then with a sharp chisel. Use a light touch on the long edge of the mortise to prevent the thin lip from splitting out.

Step 3. With the door shimmed in its final location, strike a knife mark at the top and bottom edges of the hinges.

Step 2. A laminate trimmer and straight bit, guided freehand and with a careful eye, quickly removes most of the waste and gives the mortise a perfectly flat bottom.

Step 4. Use a hinge leaf to mark the three edges of the mortise; then cut the mortises as you did on the door.

> **RELATED INFO:**
> **Making a Door That Fits, page 175**

Clamping Difficult Assemblies

Gluing Up a Staved Column

PROBLEM: *Whenever I clamp up a multi-sided column, everything goes great in the dry run, but when I do the real glue-up, something always goes awry. What's the best approach to this job?*

SOLUTION: In my experience, time is of the essence when gluing up a staved column. If you spend too much time spreading the glue, fiddling with the alignment of the parts, and getting the clamps into position, the glue starts to tack up and that's what leads to trouble.

I use duct tape to speed the initial assembly of staved columns. It doesn't eliminate the need for band clamps, but it gives you a quick head start on the assembly and allows you to move more comfortably through the clamping process.

Place strips of duct tape that are long enough to go around your column so that they are parallel to each other on your bench, as shown. Place one at each end, and one every 10 or 12 inches. They need to be placed sticky side up with their ends turned under and stuck to the workbench. Position a framing square with the blade parallel to the duct tape and tongue over the ends of the tape.

Duct tape holds these beveled staves in perfect alignment as they are rolled together. The tape also prevents glue from gumming up your band clamps.

Lay out your column pieces, mitered sides up, with their ends snug against the blade of the framing square and the sides touching each other and parallel to the tongue. Roll up the column pieces carefully in a dry run and get the band clamps ready to go. Then unroll the assembly, spread glue on the miters, and roll it back up. The tape will pull the joints almost as tight as it did in the dry run. Apply the band clamps to bring the joints tightly together. The tape protects the wood from being dented by the band clamps, and keeps the band clamps free of glue squeeze-out.

Bill and Joanne Storch
Corvallis, OR

Clamping with Super Glue

PROBLEM: *I'm applying molding around the inside of a framed panel and I don't want to use nails, but my C-clamps don't reach. How can I do the job?*

SOLUTION: Because it bonds so quickly, cyanoacrylate glue (CA glue, also known as Super Glue) is my choice to "clamp" parts together when I glue with conventional polyvinyl acetate (PVA) white or yellow glues. When installing molding, I'll spread some PVA on the molding, then drop a couple of dabs of CA glue right on top of the PVA glue. I press the molding in place, then give the edges of the molding a couple of spritzes of CA accelerator. Presto! The molding is now clamped in place, and when the PVA glue dries, the bond is stronger than the wood itself. For jobs like this, you'll want to buy CA glue in larger 1- or 2-ounce bottles. See "Sources," beginning on page 298.

Andy Rae
Lenhartsville, PA

Fire Hose Column Clamp

FEW TASKS ARE AS FRUSTRATING as clamping a column or other large structure built with staves. If you use band clamps every 6 to 12 inches, as is commonly done, the process is slow and requires lots of clamps. And juggling many clamps before the glue has a chance to set is nerve-racking.

My solution is to use my air compressor and a section of fire hose to clamp the column together. I obtained a 1½-inch-diameter × 50-foot-long fire hose from an industrial supply company and capped both ends with standard galvanized pipe fittings, reducing one end down to a size that fits onto my air compressor.

I assemble the column and wrap the deflated fire hose tightly around it in a spiral, like a barbershop pole, as shown. I tie each end with an overhand knot and attach the threaded end to my air compressor. Turning on the air expands the hose and pulls the column together tightly and quickly. You can vary the air pressure to increase or decrease the clamping ability—just don't exceed the maximum pounds per square inch (psi) rating on the fire hose. I have found that about 40 psi is more than enough pressure; my hose has a 150 psi rating. Leave the hose hooked to the air compressor until the glue has fully set.

Besides being quicker, and cheaper over the long haul, air clamping with a fire hose has the added advantage of not denting the wood as band clamps often do.

Ben Erickson
Eutaw, AL

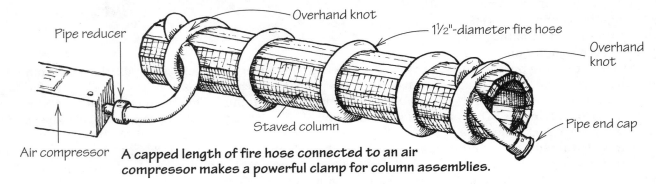

A capped length of fire hose connected to an air compressor makes a powerful clamp for column assemblies.

Labels: Pipe reducer · Overhand knot · 1½"-diameter fire hose · Overhand knot · Air compressor · Staved column · Pipe end cap

Deep Reach Clamping

PROBLEM: *I need to clamp a repair that's way out in the center of a wide tabletop. How can I get clamp pressure where my clamps won't reach?*

SOLUTION: You can extend a clamp's reach by clamping a pair of sticks against a pivot block. The longer the reach you need, the beefier the sticks should be. Make the pivot block thicker than the object you're clamping, more so if the sticks will flex under pressure. The key is to make the distance between the clamp and the pivot greater than the distance between the clamp and the repair.

An alternate approach is to clamp two sticks from both edges of the tabletop, with a block placed right over the repair.

Fred Matlack
Vera Cruz, PA

To apply pressure to a point beyond the reach of a clamp, position a pivot block between 2 sticks that do reach the point.

"Rubber Bands" for Hard-to-Clamp Glue-Ups

PROBLEM: *I'm trying to assemble a spindle chair with turned parts and odd angles. My bar clamps just slip off. How can I solve this problem?*

SOLUTION: I use "rubber bands" that have been cut from truck tire tubes for all sorts of clamping. For small jobs, I just crosscut circular bands from the tubes. For longer clamps, I cut 1-inch-wide spirals, producing a long length of rubber band.

On odd-shaped pieces, I will frequently place a small circular band around the object or wind a long band around the piece to help keep a regular bar clamp from sliding off the piece and to keep the clamps from marring the surface of the piece, as shown in the drawing.

The place where I use the rubber band clamp most is when I assemble new chairs or reassemble a chair that I have repaired or for which I have made new parts. It is often impossible to get a straight pull from a bar clamp because of the curved shapes that chairs often have. The most advantageous thing about the rubber band is that you can pull one side of a joint more than the other by putting differential stress on one side of a joint. In the same manner, you can square up a piece by putting more stress on one side of the joint than on the other.

E. E. "Skip" Benson
Camden, ME

Strips of old inner tubes make strong and versatile band clamps for glue-ups when conventional clamps won't work.

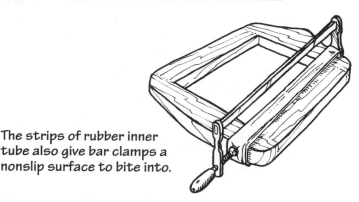

The strips of rubber inner tube also give bar clamps a nonslip surface to bite into.

Attaching Crown Molding without Clamps

PROBLEM: *I'm applying crown molding to the top of a cabinet, but I don't want to nail it. What other options are there?*

SOLUTION: Glue is the obvious alternative to nails, but unfortunately, the typical shape of crown molding makes it difficult to clamp as the glue dries. I suggest that you throw away the unwieldy clamps and use a few drops of hot glue. Of course, the hot glue won't squeeze the joint together tightly like clamps would, so instead of wood glue, I use epoxy, which fills any gaps.

First I spread the epoxy along the edge of the crown molding, leaving gaps every couple of inches for a dab of hot glue, as shown below. Then I apply the hot glue, quickly press the crown molding in place, and leave the cabinet alone until the epoxy has cured.

Rob Yoder
Quakertown, PA

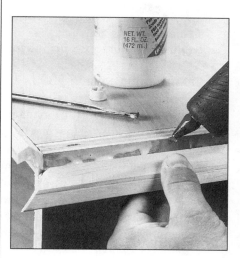

In a situation where clamps just can't do the job, you can use epoxy as the primary glue, then rely on hot glue to quickly "clamp" the molding in place.

CLAMPING ODD SHAPES

Clamping irregular shapes or square stuff at odd angles will try the patience of any woodworker. There's nothing more nerve-racking than knowing that the glue is drying as you are struggling to get clamps in place. Here are some suggestions for specific troublesome clamping situations.

CREATING PURCHASE POINTS

Sometimes you can save some lumber by cutting out specific shapes before gluing up to form a wider assembly for things like tabletops or headboards. However, the specific shape may prevent you from clamping the boards edge to edge. The answer here is to leave a few squared-off purchase points for the clamps rather than to cut out the shapes exactly, as shown below.

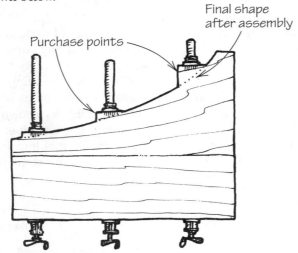

To clamp parts that are precut into shapes, leave squared off purchase points for the clamps.

CLAMPING TRIANGULAR WORK

Triangular pieces, like corner cabinets, are particularly difficult to clamp. The solution is to cut wedges and glue them in place using white PVA glue with a piece of paper in between, as shown above right. The wedges provide parallel points to clamp, and with the paper between the wood and the wedge, it is easy to split off the wedge once the glue is dry. Any leftover paper or glue can be removed with a scraper and some water. For less acute angles, it may be sufficient to line the face of the wedge with coarse sandpaper instead of gluing it onto the wood. The sandpaper often provides enough grip to prevent the wedge from slipping. You can also sometimes use another clamp as a purchase point, as shown.

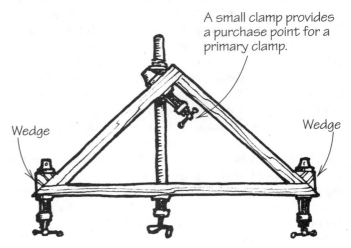

A glued-on wedge provides a square clamping surface. A strip of paper in the joint makes the wedge removable.

HAND SCREWS TO THE RESCUE

Hand screws, with their nonparallel jaws, excel at all sorts of jobs where other clamps fail. Cut a 90-degree notch in the face of the jaws, and a hand screw will securely grip a round or irregular shape, as shown at the top of the opposite page. Line the notch with sandpaper for added grip. The V-shaped notches will hold wedges, small and round workpieces, pieces of molding, and even lengths of dowel that need to be sanded, drilled, or worked on with chisels or files. The hand screw can be clamped at a convenient angle in the bench vise, or even in another hand screw, itself clamped in the bench vise, to present the workpiece at almost any angle you need.

Hand screws can also clamp segmented rounds, wheels, discs, or ovals that are too small for a band clamp, as shown on the opposite page. Notch two pieces of 1 × 2 for half their length so that you can slide them past the screws. At the ends that aren't notched, make shallow grooves that are large enough to contain narrow diameter cord or rope (½-inch sash cord is ideal). Wrap the cord around the workpiece and feed it into the hand screw. Tighten the back end of the hand screw first to secure the cord, then tighten the front end until the workpiece is sufficiently clamped.

CLAMPING EDGING

It's often convenient to profile an edge treatment before applying it to a counter or tabletop. But rounded profiles are difficult to clamp. The trick is to make clamp blocks that grip the rounded edge but give you a square edge to clamp against, as shown below. Channel out a long block and then cut it into short pieces. The blocks also protect the wood from being damaged by the clamps.

Edge molding also requires a large quantity of clamps. If you run out of long bar clamps for this job, use smaller C-clamps with wedges, as shown at bottom.

Tom Begnal
Kent, CT,
Graham Blackburn
Bearsville, NY,
and
W. Curtis Johnson
Corvallis, OR

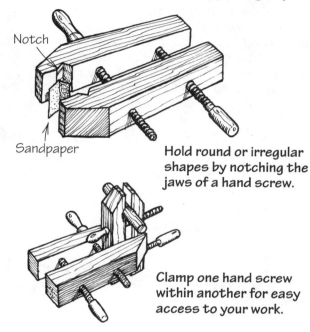

Notch

Sandpaper

Hold round or irregular shapes by notching the jaws of a hand screw.

Clamp one hand screw within another for easy access to your work.

Groove for cord

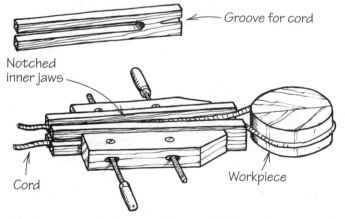

Notched inner jaws

Cord

Workpiece

To clamp round pieces, make notched inner jaws, and wrap a piece of cord around the workpiece and through the inner jaws. Tighten the back of the clamp first to lock the cord. Then tighten the front of the clamp to pull the cord tightly around the workpiece.

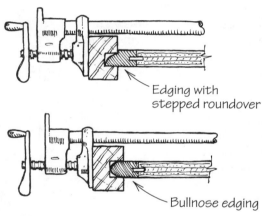

Edging with stepped roundover

Bullnose edging

Channeled-out clamp blocks allow you to clamp preprofiled edges.

To use a C-clamp for edge-gluing, clamp it to the table or counter and then drive a wedge between the clamp and the edging.

Clamping with Wedges and Pegs

PROBLEM: *I have a couple of nice scraps left over from a project, and I'd like to edge-glue them together to make one wider piece. But the edges of the scraps won't be parallel, and I'm afraid my clamps will slip during the glue-up. What can I do?*

SOLUTION: Borrow a trick that woodcarvers use to clamp irregular shapes. From a piece of ¾-inch plywood, cut a "table" that is big enough to hold the glue-up. Drill some holes around the edges of the shape's position on the table; these holes need to accept stub dowels that will act as anchor points. Then, between the dowels and the work, use paired wedges to apply even pressure all around the workpiece.

The reason to use paired wedges instead of just one wedge at each pressure point is that you want the edges to remain parallel, regardless of how tightly the wedges are driven. If part of your shape is concave, you can cut a plywood or other scrap filler to conform to the inside curve.

Jim Cummins
Woodstock, NY

You can clamp just about any shape imaginable by locating pegs in a plywood table and forcing paired wedges between the pegs and the edges of the workpiece.

"STRETCHING" YOUR CLAMPS

Here's a common woodworker's lament: "I never seem to have enough bar or pipe clamps, and the ones that I do have are often too short for the job."

I do, however, have more C-clamps than I ever seem to need. C-clamps are the least expensive and the most widely available clamps going. So I make them work harder for me in two ways: First I make matching pairs of hook bars and use a C-clamp to pull the bars together, as shown in the top drawing. This is a quick and convenient solution to those occasions when you need a really long clamp. I use lengths of 1 × 2 with the stop blocks screwed on securely.

The second trick is to convert a C-clamp into a more permanent bar clamp: Hacksaw a C-clamp in half and bolt or rivet each end into slots cut into the end of a stout solid wooden bar, as shown at bottom.

Graham Blackburn
Bearsville, NY

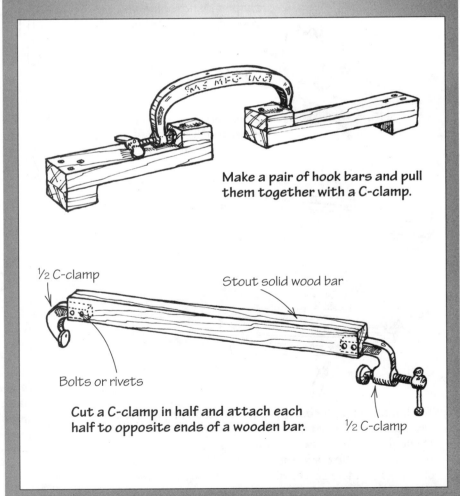

Make a pair of hook bars and pull them together with a C-clamp.

½ C-clamp

Stout solid wood bar

Bolts or rivets

Cut a C-clamp in half and attach each half to opposite ends of a wooden bar.

½ C-clamp

Using Fasteners

Improving a Screw's Hold in End Grain

PROBLEM: *I need to secure a cubby assembly to a desktop, but I'm afraid that screwing into the end grain of the vertical component will not hold or may split the wood. Is there a way to screw into end grain and avoid these problems?*

SOLUTION: Screws get their holding power by cutting threads *across* the grain. When driven into end grain, the screw threads act as wedges and split the fibers, producing a weak connection at best, and splitting the workpiece at worst. To improve holding power, I introduce cross-grain wood into the joint by adding a dowel, as shown. I locate the dowel so that the screw will be driven all the way through it. From the end grain of the board, I drill a clearance hole to the edge of the dowel and then drill the pilot hole through the dowel. In this way, the screw will cut threads across the dowel's long grain and hold tightly.

Robert Treanor
San Francisco, CA

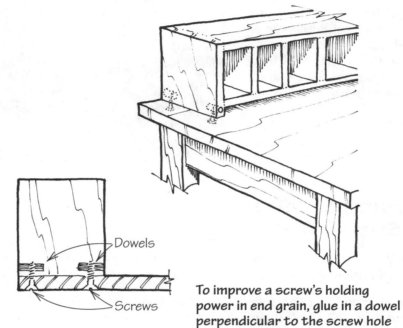

Dowels

Screws

To improve a screw's holding power in end grain, glue in a dowel perpendicular to the screw hole and screw through the dowel.

Dealing with Broken-Off Screws

PROBLEM: *Okay, I should have predrilled, but didn't. Now how can I remove the broken screw?*

SOLUTION: Every woodworker eventually has to deal with a screw that gets broken off in its hole. It usually happens when you're in a hurry and don't want to mess with drilling a pilot hole, and then the fix takes longer than the time drilling a pilot hole would have taken.

If the screw is being used for holding two pieces of wood together and you have the flexibility to relocate the hole, leave the broken screw in place and just patch that hole to make it look like a screw isn't there. The half-driven screw may actually have some holding power anyway. Once the wood is patched, move over half an inch, drill a pilot hole, and drive another screw.

If the screw is broken off in a hinge or handle where you can't relocate the hole, you have a couple of options. First, if you can make do without the screw, just epoxy the head of the broken screw in its hole and nobody will know the difference. After all, most hinge leaves will hold perfectly well with one fewer than their full compliment of screws.

Your second option is to move the hinge or handle ¼ inch to hide the old screw holes, and then to drill for some new screws. You may then have to repair the hinge mortise if there is one.

Avoid at all cost trying to drill out the broken screw. This rarely works. The new screw always ends up crooked and scarred by all the force you need to drive it. Or worse, the second screw pressing against the first will split the wood.

AVOIDING THE PROBLEM: To avoid breaking a screw follow these rules:

1. (repeat after me) "I will always drill a pilot hole in hardwood." Then drive your first screw slowly to make sure the hole is the right size.
2. If you are using brass screws to attach a hinge or handle, always predrill the screw hole and drive a matching steel screw into it first. Brass is just too soft to handle all that twisting.
3. Lubricate the screw. Rub some beeswax or Butcher's wax into the screw threads before you drive the screw into the wood.

Rob Yoder
Quakertown, PA

Wiping a screw's threads with some wax or a piece of bar soap will lubricate the screw, helping it cut into the wood without stalling and breaking off.

Removing Screws with Stripped Heads

PROBLEM: *The slot on a screw head stripped out as I was driving it. How can I remove the darned thing?*

SOLUTION: A friend of mine commented that he usually finds it best to throw the project into a roaring fire and then to dig the screw out of the ashes. A bit extreme, but it does highlight the difficulty in dealing with stripped screw heads.

If the head is still protruding above the surface of the wood, try clamping a locking pliers on it and gingerly turning it out. If that is not possible, try using a new screwdriver with a nice sharp factory tip. Put the driver into the screw head and then tap the driver smartly with a hammer or mallet to give it a purchase. Then, with lots of downward pressure on the screw, carefully try to turn it out of the hole.

If you can't remove the screw, cut off any part of the screw that protrudes above the surface of the wood, and file the shank flush with the surface of the wood or drive it below the surface of the wood with a punch.

AVOIDING THE PROBLEM: Okay, where did you go wrong? You should always make sure that you have the right driver for the screw and that the driver fits snugly in the crosshatch or slot in the screw head. Slotted drivers tend to get dull after a few years of use and then don't grip the screw properly, so touch them up on a grinding wheel every so often.

Square drive screws and drivers (see "Sources," beginning on page 298), as shown at left, are a good alternative to slotted and Phillips screws, and are less likely to strip out.

Rob Yoder
Quakertown, PA

Square drive screws are easier to drive, either by hand or with a power driver, and they're less likely to strip out than Phillips or slotted screws.

Driving Brads and Small Nails

PROBLEM: *How can I start and drive small brads and nails without getting sore thumbs and hammer dents in the work?*

SOLUTION: I insert the brad through a piece of thin cardboard and locate the point of the brad where I want it. Then I can hold onto the cardboard, which is safely away from the hammer, and drive the brad without fear of striking my fingers. An added plus to this method is that the cardboard acts as a guard against hammer blows that miss the target. When the brad is nearly home, a simple tug of the cardboard will free it from the brad, and a nail set can be used to finish the job.

Robert Treanor
San Francisco, CA

To start nails that are too small to hold by hand, insert the tip into a piece of cardboard.

GLUING WOOD SCREWS

Sometimes it's especially important for wood screws to stay permanently in place. For example, screws used to attach wheels to a toy train must remain firmly secured because a loose screw presents a choking hazard to small children.

To ensure that the screw stays put, add a drop of epoxy glue to the threads before driving the screw. The epoxy quickly bonds the screw to the wood. Before using the glue, however, check to make sure that the epoxy is the right type to join metal and wood.

Tom Begnal
Kent, CT

USING DRYWALL SCREWS

Drywall screws are the mechanical fastener of choice for many cabinetmakers, but as the name implies, they weren't designed for woodworking.

The fully threaded shank on these self-tapping screws works well if you are attaching a piece of predrilled hardware to a piece of wood. If, however, you are trying to screw one piece of wood to another, the threaded shank doesn't work to draw the pieces of wood together. That's because the threads on the upper portion of the shank don't allow the screw to spin freely in the top piece of wood, so the lower threads aren't able to draw the bottom board up tight. To remedy the problem, drill a clearance hole into the top piece of wood to allow the screw threads to spin freely.

If you're doing some rough carpentry with a soft wood like pine, you may not want to bother drilling clearance holes. In that case, drive the screw into the two pieces of wood, then back the screw out, and finally drive the screw back into its hole as you hold the pieces of wood together tightly with your free hand. When you initially drive the screw, it penetrates the first piece of wood, then tends to push the second piece of wood away slightly with its tip. By predriving, the screw cuts its path on the first pass, and this is no longer a problem.

Rob Yoder
Quakertown, PA

Tighter Shaker Pegs

PROBLEM: *How do I keep those shaker pegs in a shelf from loosening and falling out over time?*

SOLUTION: I borrowed this technique, called fox-wedging, from old chair assemblies where spindles are installed in arms and chair backs. Begin by cutting a saw kerf in the base of the peg, making the

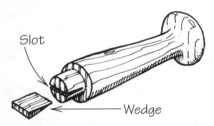

To keep shaker pegs tight, use a fox-wedge. First cut a slot perpendicular to the grain. Then glue in a wedge at assembly.

kerf perpendicular to the grain. This prevents the peg from splitting when a wedge is inserted and pressure is applied.

Cut a small wedge ½ inch long and about ¹⁄₁₆ inch at the widest end. Apply glue to the wedge and peg base, and insert the wedge in the peg slot. Insert the peg assembly into the hole and pat the peg into the hole with a wooden mallet.

An alternative method is to screw the peg into the hole from the back of the shelf. Countersink this hole from the back.

Rick Wright
Schnecksville, PA

Using an Air Nailer without a Compressor

PROBLEM: *I'd like to borrow a pneumatic brad nailer to install some molding, but I don't want to haul in a compressor. Is there any way to use an air tool without one?*

SOLUTION: Brad nailers use very little air volume, so you can use a portable air tank to drive this handy tool. These tanks cost a fraction of what a portable compressor does.

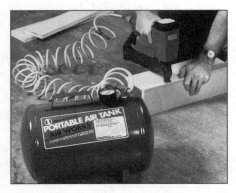

A portable air tank can supply enough pressure to drive a small job's worth of nails or staples.

Purchase a 25-foot coiled hose with the proper fittings for your gun and tank. To fill the tank, use one of the better electric inflater pumps, or just go to a full service gas station, and fill the tank to capacity. (Coin operated tire pumps won't work.)

You can drive dozens of nails before you will notice any loss of power in the gun. The other benefit of the portable tank is that you now have a portable nail gun you can easily take indoors for small jobs at home and in the field. Even though I have a large compressor, I keep my portable tank full for quick jobs that do not require the big machine.

Dennis Slabaugh
Naples, FL

Tip Quick Tip Q

AVOIDING PNEUMATIC NAILER MARKS

When I use my pin nailers to join soft woods, I find that they leave a distinct dent around the head of the nail that is too deep to sand out but too shallow to accept a filler.

To prevent this I place a sheet of thin noncorrugated cardboard on my board and shoot the nails through it. If I want to see where the nail is going, I find that a transparency sheet—the type that is used on overheads—works fine also. For vertical surfaces, I use a piece of masking or double-sided tape to hold the sheets for me. The nailer still countersinks the nails far enough so that I can fill the holes but doesn't leave the dents around the holes.

L. Jerry Hess
Tacoma, WA

Shooting pneumatic nails and staples through a piece of thin cardboard prevents denting.

Installation Solutions

Hanging Cabinets on a Bowed Wall

PROBLEM: *I was hanging a row of cabinets on my kitchen wall when I found that the wall has serious bumps and hollows. How can I hang the cabinets straight?*

SOLUTION: You'll have to shim the cabinets. I find that the fastest way to do a job like this is to preshim the entire wall rather than attempting to plumb and straighten each cabinet as I go along.

To preshim a wall, begin by drawing level lines on the wall that indicate the bottoms and tops of the installed cabinets. These will show you where the nailing cleats and hence the shims need to go. Next drive 8d nails into studs at each end of the run of cabinets. Align the upper nails with the cabinets' upper nailing cleats and set the lower nails a couple of inches up from the bottoms of the tallest cabinets. Now stretch strings between the nails.

Using a level, adjust the strings in or out on their nails until they're plumb to each other yet as close to the wall as possible. Nail shims where each string crosses a wall stud. The shims should just touch the back of the string. To make shims of varying thicknesses, use different thicknesses of plywood. As a final preparation for installation, you can nail temporary ledger strips to the wall to support the cabinets as you screw them into place.

If the run of cabinets abuts to a wall, install the corner cabinet first. Fasten it to the wall only through its top cleat. Then install the adjacent cabinet, fastening it through its top cleat and screwing its face frame to the first cabinet's face frame. Install each succeeding cabinet in the same fashion. After all of the cabinets are hung to the wall from their tops and screwed to each other through their face frames, remove the ledger strips and fasten the bottoms of the cabinets through the lower shims.

Paul Anthony
Hellertown, PA

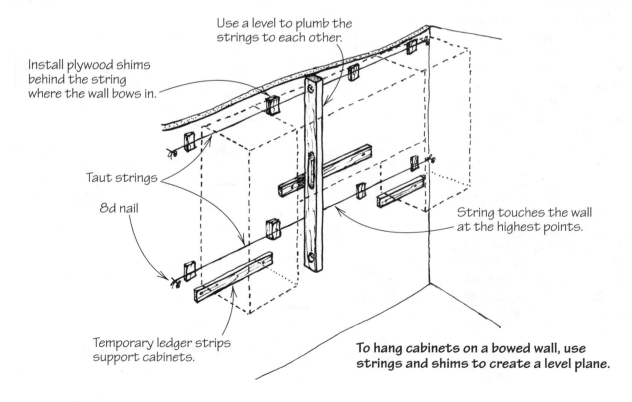

Use a level to plumb the strings to each other.

Install plywood shims behind the string where the wall bows in.

Taut strings

8d nail

String touches the wall at the highest points.

Temporary ledger strips support cabinets.

To hang cabinets on a bowed wall, use strings and shims to create a level plane.

Fitting a Counter into an Alcove

PROBLEM: *The alcove in which I'm installing a countertop is out of square. How can I get a good fit?*

SOLUTION: There's a trick called spiling that enables you to transfer the measurements of an oddly shaped area onto your workpiece. In a nutshell, spiling involves taping a piece of paper to the inside of the oddly shaped area, referencing measurements off the paper, then transferring the marks from the paper onto your workpiece. If the process is done carefully, you can create a workpiece that fits so tightly into place that there won't be any gaps. To fit your countertop, first create a temporary surface for the spiling paper. Nail ledger strips into the alcove, place an undersized piece of scrap plywood onto them, and tape a piece of paper to the plywood, as shown in *Step 1*. Next make a spiling stick, which is simply a straight, flat, narrow piece of wood with a point at one end.

To transfer the shape of the alcove to your workpiece, first place the spiling stick on the paper with its point touching a corner of the alcove. Then trace the outline of the stick onto the paper, as shown in *Step 2*. Repeat this at the other three corners. Now remove the paper and tape it onto your workpiece. Carefully align the spiling stick inside each tracing and mark the location of its point onto your workpiece, as shown in *Step 4*. If the walls of the alcove are flat, all you have to do is connect the points with a straightedge to create the outline of your finished piece. If a wall is bowed, scribe and fit a cardboard pattern against the wall, then use the pattern to trace the cutline between each set of points on the workpiece.

Paul Anthony
Hellertown, PA

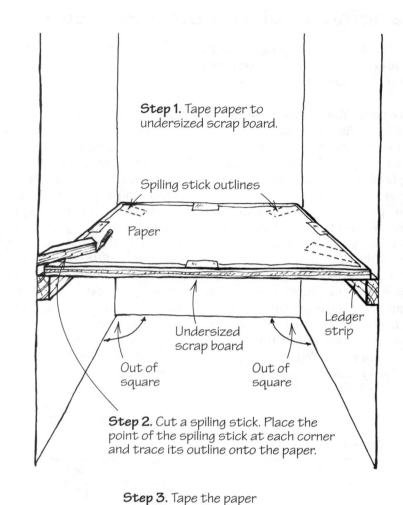

Step 1. Tape paper to undersized scrap board.

Spiling stick outlines

Paper

Ledger strip

Undersized scrap board

Out of square

Out of square

Step 2. Cut a spiling stick. Place the point of the spiling stick at each corner and trace its outline onto the paper.

Step 3. Tape the paper to the workpiece.

Workpiece

Step 4. Place the spiling stick inside the outlines and mark the corners of the finished workpiece.

Wall Cabinet Installation Support

PROBLEM: *I need to install a bank of upper wall cabinets by myself. How can I hold them in place and screw them to the wall at the same time?*

SOLUTION: There are "jack" systems available, but they can cost a bundle. For many years I have instead been using an adjustable painting extension pole for this purpose. They come in various lengths from 2 to 8 feet closed. I find that the 3-foot model works for most kitchen cabinet height installations. The aluminum extensions are light and easy to handle. They're quite strong when you lock them in place.

Extension poles come with a threaded plastic tip on the top end and a plastic tip on the bottom end. Purchase a suitably sized rubber furniture leg tip to give the bottom a nonmarring grip. You can add a rubber tip to the top to give it grip. You can also make a simple T support by cutting a 1-foot length of 2 × 4 wood and drilling a slightly undersized hole in it. Screw the extension pole into the hole. It works best if you can drill the hole at a slight angle. Since you will have the base of the extension pole a foot or so from the wall, the slight angle of the T will set the 2 × 4 base of the T so that it is parallel with the base of the shelf or cabinet.

An alternate method that works well but lacks adjustablilty is a length of 1 × 2 or a similar stick. Cut the stick to length so that when the bottom is about 12 to 15 inches from the wall at the floor, the top will support the cabinet at exactly the right height. Hold the stick in place with your foot; then hoist the cabinet against the wall and on top of the stick, as shown. Then screw the cabinet to the wall.

Dennis Slabaugh
Naples, FL

A length of 1 × 2 is just the right assistant when you are hanging wall cabinets by yourself. Position the stick and hold it in place with your foot while hoisting the cabinet against the wall.

SANDING

SOLUTIONS

USING SANDING TOOLS

Taming a Belt Sander	201
Belt Sanding across the Grain	202
Third-Sheet Sandpaper Cutter	203
Quieting a Noisy Belt Sander	203
Drum Sander Storage Tray	204
Improving Belt Sander Power	204
Pattern Sanding	205
Clamp-Free Planing and Belt Sanding	205
A Sanding Light Stand	206
Truing Up Miters on a Disc Sander	207
Sanding Edges on the Table Saw	207

SMART SANDING STRATEGIES

Keeping Sanded Edges Square	208

Sanding Small Wheels	208
Sanding Frame Joints	209
Sanding End Grain	209
Smoothing Small-Diameter, Inside Curves	209
Avoiding Sanding Flaws	210
Sanding Small Parts Safely	211
Making Sanding Blocks for Moldings	211
Sanding Coves	212
Curved Sanding Blocks	212
Cleaning a Shop-Vac Filter	212
Bench-Top Dust Collection	213
Improving Sandpaper Flexibility	213
Quick-Change Pad Sanding	213
Hand Scraping: A Good Alternative to Sanding	214

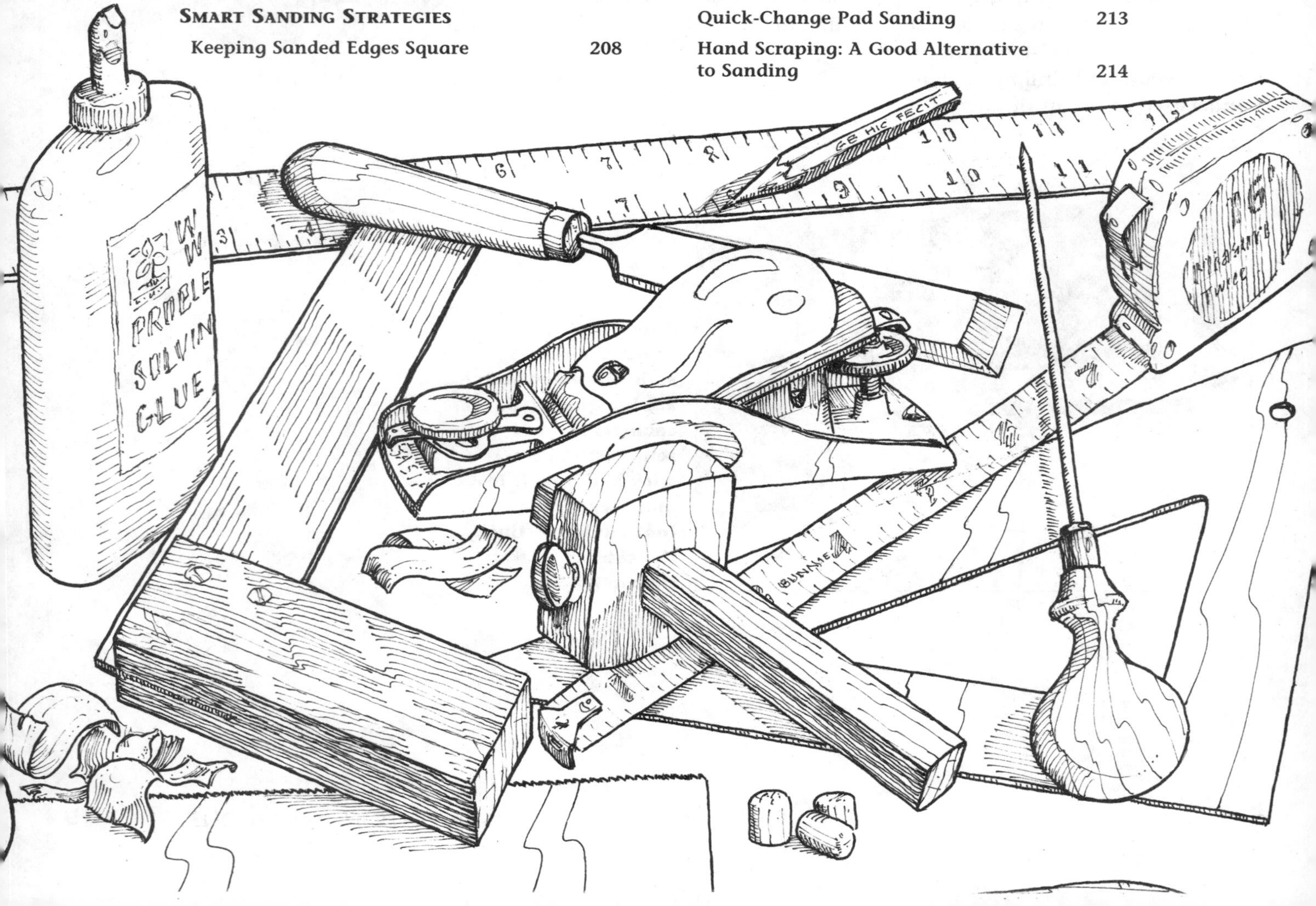

Using Sanding Tools

Taming a Belt Sander

PROBLEM: *I have a hard time controlling my belt sander. How can I use it more confidently and for doing fine work?*

SOLUTION: Belt sanders are aggressive stock removers. They're ideal for leveling the joints of glued-up panels if you don't have a planer. They can also do a lot of damage if you allow them to tip. Learning to control them is a matter of practice, but it's important that you form good habits while gaining the practice. Keep the following points in mind:

A sanding frame attached to a belt sander limits its aggressiveness and prevents gouging. The frame also makes the belt sander more suitable for finer sanding work.

- Keep the cord over your shoulder so that you won't have to worry about running over it with the sander. If you wear shirts with epaulets, button them down over the cord to keep it from slipping off of your shoulder.
- Never move the machine exactly in the direction it's pointed; that will cause it to "run." Instead, always move it at a slight angle. The slight sideways movement will minimize the risk of sanding a groove with the edge of the belt, but it will increase the tendency to tip, so be careful.
- Never, NEVER move the sander so that its center of gravity is off of the stock.
- Ignore advice to start the machine before putting it down on the stock—this is sure to gouge the wood. Instead, lift slightly to take

most of the weight off the belt but not enough to raise the machine; then turn the power of the machine on and allow the weight back onto the belt as you begin to move the machine forward.

- To avoid creating shallow areas, never concentrate your sanding in an area that is smaller than 3 times the length of the pad × 3 times the width of the pad.
- Consider equipping your belt sander with a sanding frame, as

shown. These attachments virtually eliminate the danger of tipping the sander. Properly adjusted, they prevent sanding a hollow if you sand too long in a small area. With a sanding frame, you'll confidently use the belt sander on finer work like veneered panels or hardwood plywood.

Bob Moran
Emmaus, PA

AGAINST THE GRAIN

Belt Sanding across the Grain

"ALWAYS SAND WITH THE GRAIN" *is an axiom well worth breaking—sometimes. For example, if you're belt sanding to remove planer marks and will follow this step with at least two finer grits, hold the sander at a 10- to 30-degree angle to the grain, as shown below left. This will remove stock more aggressively and make it easier to distinguish between the scratch marks of the current grit and the scratch marks of the next.*

Another case is when you are using the belt sander to sand an edge that is flush with an adjacent surface, such as when you are applying a wooden edge to a plywood countertop. If you sand the edge by holding the belt sander parallel with the length, you risk forming a trough that is equal to the width of the sanding belt. This is especially true with 2½- and 3-inch-wide belt sanders.

Instead, I hold the sander nearly perpendicular to the edge, with the front end of the belt over the edge,

as shown below right. It's easier to see the edge as you work it, and it's easier to control the sander.

I use 100- or 120-grit sandpaper for jobs like this even though it takes a little longer to get the job done. I then turn to an orbital or random-orbit sander and start with the same grit I used on the belt sander. Removing the cross-grain scratches is especially easy with a random-orbit sander.

On orbital and random-orbit sanders, by the way, the abrasive moves in every direction so you don't need to move the machine in the direction of the grain. But lower-quality versions of these tools will leave their telltale swirl marks no matter how carefully you use them, so spring for the better quality.

Tony O'Malley
Emmaus, PA

Belt sanding at an angle removes stock quickly and leaves scratches that are easier to see and remove when you switch to a orbital or random-orbit sander.

Belt sanding edges so that they are flush can be done more accurately by holding the sander almost perpendicular to the edge. Switch to the same grit on an orbital sander to remove the cross-grain scratches.

THIRD-SHEET SANDPAPER CUTTER BY ANDY RAE

A *standard sheet of 9 × 11-inch sandpaper that has been cut into thirds fits many orbital sanders, and that same size—one-third of the sheet—is perfect to fold four times on itself for hand sanding. But getting out your tape measure and a knife every time you need to cut a piece to size can quickly prove tiresome.*

This jig allows you to cut standard sheets of sandpaper into thirds without reaching for a tape, knife, or any other tool. To use the jig, lay a stack of sandpaper into the jig, grit side down, so that the edges of the paper butt tightly against the jig's two fences. Hold the plastic laminate tear guide firmly on top of the stack of paper and tight against the shorter fence, and tear off individual sheets one at a time to size.

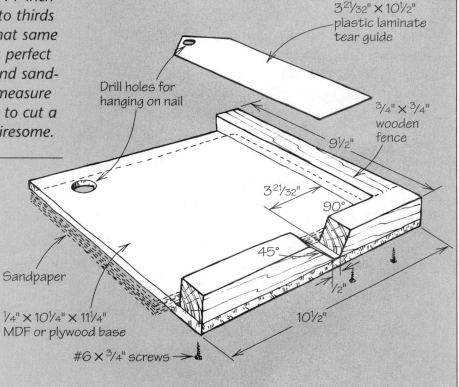

$3^{21}/_{32}" × 10^{1}/_{2}"$ plastic laminate tear guide

Drill holes for hanging on nail

$^{3}/_{4}" × ^{3}/_{4}"$ wooden fence

$9^{1}/_{2}"$

$3^{21}/_{32}"$

$90°$

$45°$

$^{1}/_{2}"$

$10^{1}/_{2}"$

Sandpaper

$^{1}/_{4}" × 10^{1}/_{4}" × 11^{1}/_{4}"$ MDF or plywood base

#6 × $^{3}/_{4}"$ screws

Quieting a Noisy Belt Sander

PROBLEM: *My portable belt sander now makes a thumping noise whenever I use it. What's the cause?*

SOLUTION: This is a common problem on belt sanders that aren't used regularly. The drive roller on your belt sander is slightly crowned (larger in diameter at its center) to keep the belt centered on the roller during use. The crown will deform the belt in one spot if the machine is idle for too long, resulting in a raised bulge that makes a thumping noise each time it passes over the workpiece.

AVOIDING THE PROBLEM: Rotate the belt occasionally so that the roller contacts different spots on the belt. If you won't be using the machine for a couple of weeks, you can simply relieve the tension on the belt or remove the belt until the next time you use the machine.

Walt Morrison
Northport, NY

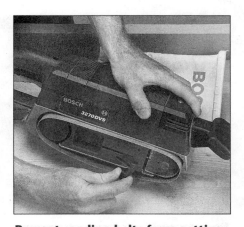

Prevent sanding belts from getting deformed by relieving the belt tension when the sander is not in use.

DRUM SANDER STORAGE TRAY BY ANDY RAE

Using a drum sander in the drill press is a great method for smoothing the edges of curved work, but where do you stow all those different-diameter drums so that they're handy—and not rolling around on the floor—when you need them?

My solution was to make the tray shown so that my drum sanders are available where they get used the most—at the drill press. I also keep a stick of rubber abrasive cleaner and accessories such as machine oil and oft-used drill bits on the tray.

Once you've made the tray, use a pair of pliers to bend the hook on one end of the metal banding. Then nail a briefcase latch, available at most hardware stores, onto the tray and secure the tray to the drill press column by wrapping the banding around the column and onto the latch.

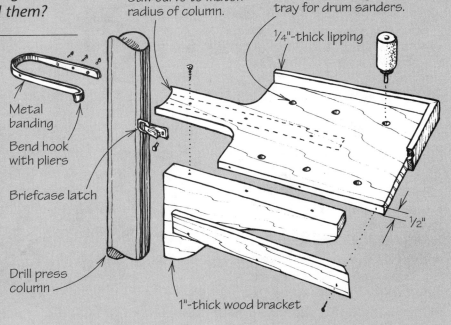

Saw curve to match radius of column.

Drill holes through the tray for drum sanders.

1/4"-thick lipping

Metal banding

Bend hook with pliers

Briefcase latch

Drill press column

1/2"

1"-thick wood bracket

Improving Belt Sander Power

PROBLEM: *My old 6 × 48-inch stationary belt sander seems underpowered. Whenever it starts sanding really well, it bogs down. Do I need a bigger motor?*

SOLUTION: When you put pressure on the work, friction between the belt and the platen beneath it increases greatly. You can reduce this friction and the load on the motor by covering the platen with a graphite cloth. When I did this on my old machine, it was like adding a half-horse to the motor. The graphite cloth (see "Sources," beginning on page 298) can be cut to fit the dimensions of the platen. Spray adhesive works fine to hold it in place. Then just tension and track the belt as usual. A piece of the cloth should last for years.

I've heard that some woodworkers even use this graphite cloth on portable belt sanders, and their only complaint is that if the cloth starts to fray, strings can wrap around the axles of the sanding drums. There's a simple solution to this: If you see a loose thread starting, just cut it off before it becomes long enough to be a problem.

Jim Cummins
Woodstock, NY

Pattern Sanding

PROBLEM: *I have a number of identical toy parts that were pattern routed, and now the edges need sanding. How can I keep the shapes perfectly consistent?*

SOLUTION: You can sand precise shapes with a drum-sanding accessory for a drill press. Cut a guide disc to be the same diameter as the drum sander and mount it to a sheet of plywood. Center the disc beneath the drum and clamp the plywood sheet to the drill press table. Adjust the height of the drum to about $1/16$ inch above the disc. Make a pattern template from stock that's about $1/4$ inch thicker than the guide disc, and attach it to the workpiece with double-sided carpet tape.

Nick Engler
West Milton, OH

Sanding multiple parts to the same precise shape is easy to do with a guide disc and a template. Attach the matching template to each workpiece with double-sided carpet tape; then sand the edge of the work by guiding the template against the disc.

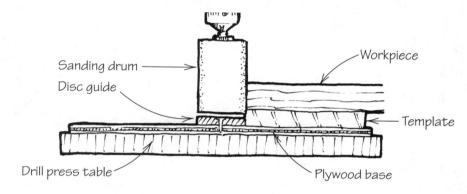

Sanding drum
Disc guide
Workpiece
Template
Drill press table
Plywood base

Clamp-Free Planing and Belt Sanding

PROBLEM: *Whenever I sand or plane stock on my bench, the clamps always get in the way. Is there an alternative?*

SOLUTION: Here's a simple jig for clamp-free planing or belt sanding. It saves a lot of clamping time, especially when you're taking only a few swipes off of a lot of pieces, such as when you're flattening the backs of face-frame joints prior to attaching them to cases. But it also works great for holding shelves and other boards when you're belt sanding.

To make the jig, attach two $1/4$-inch-thick stops along adjacent edges of a $1/2$-inch-thick hardwood plywood panel, as shown. Screw the plywood to your bench or make it long enough so that you can clamp the end that's opposite the stops to the bench. To use the jig, butt your workpiece against both stops. If your workpiece overhangs the panel, just shim it with $1/2$-inch-thick plywood scraps. The key is to position your workpieces so that the tool's force is directed against the stops.

Paul Anthony
Hellertown, PA

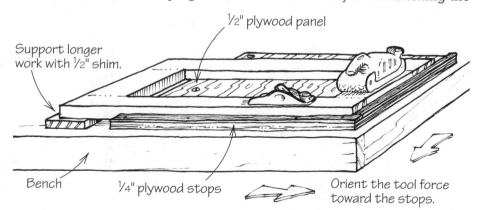

$1/2$" plywood panel
Support longer work with $1/2$" shim.
Bench
$1/4$" plywood stops
Orient the tool force toward the stops.

Sand or plane without clamps using this simple platform. The low profile stops keep the work from moving.

A SANDING LIGHT STAND BY KEN BURTON

The key to effective sanding is being able to see the sanded wood clearly as you work. That means removing the dust frequently between grits of sandpaper and using a light set to examine the wood carefully.

This light stand allows you to position a standard clamp-on utility lamp exactly where you need it to get just the right angle and amount of light for good sanding. The arm is counterweighted so you can really fine-tune the lamp's position. And it takes only a few minutes to cut the parts and put the light stand together.

You'll use it elsewhere in the shop, too—at the band saw or lathe or wherever you need that little bit of extra light to better see what you're doing.

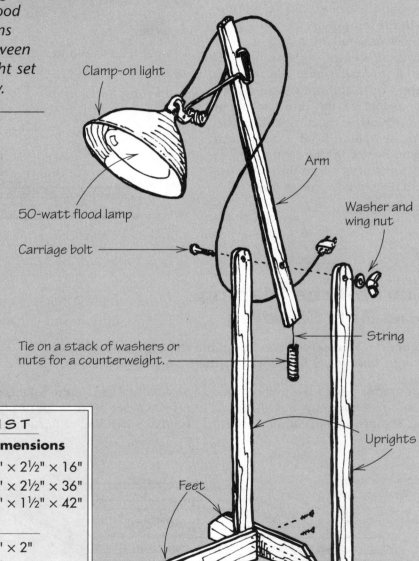

Clamp-on light

50-watt flood lamp

Carriage bolt

Arm

Washer and wing nut

String

Tie on a stack of washers or nuts for a counterweight.

Uprights

Feet

Glue and screw base together.

MATERIALS LIST		
Part	**Quantity**	**Dimensions**
Feet	2	¾" × 2½" × 16"
Uprights	2	¾" × 2½" × 36"
Arm	1	¾" × 1½" × 42"
HARDWARE		
Carriage bolt	1	½" × 2"
Wing nut	1	½"
Washers or nuts	Several	
Wood screws or drywall screws	4	#6 × 1⅝"

Truing Up Miters on a Disc Sander

PROBLEM: *I'd like to use my disc sander to true up miters and crosscuts. What's a reliable method for this?*

SOLUTION: Even if your disc sander came with an adjustable miter gauge, the gauge is probably inaccurate and doesn't fully support the workpiece. Instead of using the gauge, I made a sliding miter box for my sander. It has an 8 × 16-inch base, with a hardwood runner screwed to the underside. I screwed fences to the base at precise 90-degree, 60-degree, and 45-degree angles. Now I sand perfect miters every time.

Willard Anderson
Chapel Hill, NC

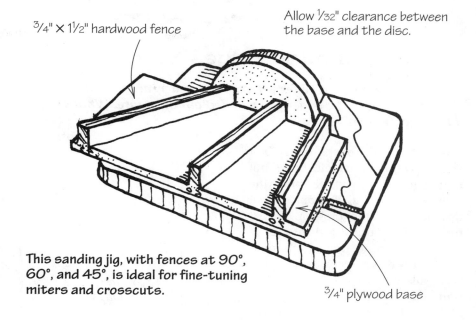

3/4" × 1 1/2" hardwood fence

Allow 1/32" clearance between the base and the disc.

This sanding jig, with fences at 90°, 60°, and 45°, is ideal for fine-tuning miters and crosscuts.

3/4" plywood base

Sanding Edges on the Table Saw

PROBLEM: *Can I safely and effectively joint edges using a sanding disc on my table saw?*

SOLUTION: If you mean jointing in the sense of straightening a crooked or bowed edge, I'd say you won't have good success with a table saw disc sander. Forcing a piece of bowed or crooked wood between the fence and a sanding disc won't straighten the edge, and it might cause a kickback. However, you can smooth straight edges that are rough.

Obtain a 9- or 10-inch sanding disk that mounts to the arbor of your table saw. Use 100-grit paper to avoid burning the wood. This technique requires two key steps. First you must set the fence just close enough to the disk so that the piece of wood is able to move past it with the least resistance possible. The idea here is to remove a little material at a time. Another important reminder is to move the wood past the disk at a fairly slow but consistent rate. Use a push stick and run the piece through against the fence. The effect that you will be creating is similar to taking very light passes with a 100-tooth blade.

Move the fence just a hair closer for each pass. Be sure to check the clearance with the sanding disk stopped. If you have multiple parts that are the same width, run them through before moving the fence. Usually after two passes, the edges will be smooth.

This system can also be used to remove burn marks caused by your saw blades. Use the same setup as you would for jointing, and keep the wood moving past the spinning disk at a consistant rate. If you stop, you will burn the wood.

Dennis Slabaugh
Naples, FL

You can smooth edges with a sanding disc on a table saw disc sander, using the saw fence to keep the parts consistent in width. But don't try to joint bowed pieces between the fence and disc.

Smart Sanding Strategies

Keeping Sanded Edges Square

PROBLEM: *I sand solid edges with a pad sander, but no matter how careful I am, the edges get rounded out of square. What's a better approach?*

SOLUTION: Sanding edges is best done by hand—after all there's not much area involved. Keeping the edge square is still a problem, but this jig solves the problem. I first ripped a length of 2 × 4 into an L-shaped section. I clamped the sanding strip with screws, as shown, but you could just as well attach it with spray adhesive or double-sided tape. Make a few of these in different dimensions to suit your needs.

J. D. McGary
Spring Valley, MN

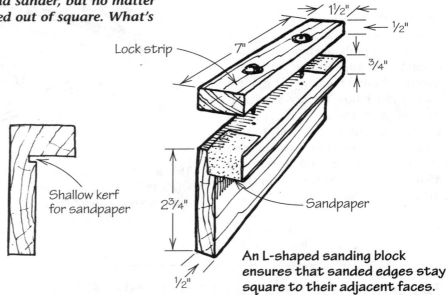

Lock strip

1½"

½"

7"

¾"

Shallow kerf for sandpaper

2¾"

Sandpaper

½"

An L-shaped sanding block ensures that sanded edges stay square to their adjacent faces.

Sanding Small Wheels

PROBLEM: *I need to true up some small wheels that were cut out on a jigsaw, but a belt/disc sander is too big and aggressive for the job. What should I use?*

SOLUTION: The setup I use will work on a stationary belt or disc sander, but you're right—these machines can easily send small wheels flying. I handle this situation by using this jig on a sanding drum in the drill press.

To make this jig, cut a ¾-inch-wide groove in the base and fit a sliding key into the groove. Predrill a hole and insert the end of a 4d nail about ½-inch from the end of the key. Install two small dowels, one at the other end of the key, and one in the end of the base, as shown.

To use the jig, position the centerpoint of the wheel on the nail tip. (I draw my circles with a compass and make sure that the compass tip leaves a distinct depression.) Clamp the base to the drill press table so that the edge of the wheel touches the sanding drum. Wrap a rubber band around the two dowels so that they act as a return spring mechanism. Pull the wheel away from the drum slightly, turn it on, and then push the wheel until it touches against the drum. The wheel spins as soon as it touches the sanding drum. Brake the wheel by gently pushing it against the drum, then spin the wheel by hand against the direction of the drum's rotation.

Wayne "Muggs" Storro
Wallace, ID

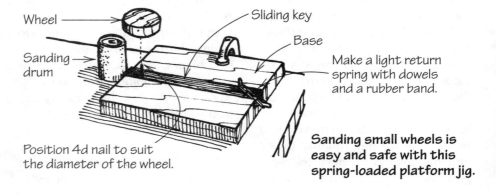

Wheel

Sliding key

Base

Sanding drum

Make a light return spring with dowels and a rubber band.

Position 4d nail to suit the diameter of the wheel.

Sanding small wheels is easy and safe with this spring-loaded platform jig.

Sanding Frame Joints

PROBLEM: *How can I hand-sand a frame joint without sanding across the grain or making the joint uneven?*

SOLUTION: You need to use a sanding block, as opposed to just holding the paper in your hand. If the joint needs to be leveled, do that first with a block plane or scraper. You can also sand the joint level by moving a sanding block in a circular motion to minimize cross-grain scratches.

To sand the frame, first sand the piece that has the end that forms the joint, usually the rail in a stile and rail door frame. Cross over the joint line and don't worry about cross-grain scratches at this stage. Then sand the other piece, taking care to remove the cross-grain scratches without adding new scratches to the first piece.

To sand a mitered frame joint, hold the edge of the sanding block parallel with the joint line and sand up to the line. As an alternative, try masking off one side of the joint while sanding the other.

Ken Burton
New Tripoli, PA

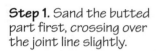

Step 1. Sand the butted part first, crossing over the joint line slightly.

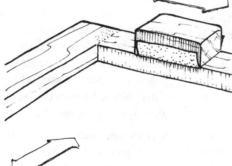

Step 2. Remove the crossover scratches by sanding the other part.

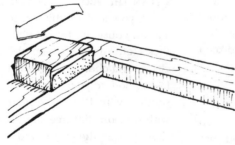

Sanding End Grain

PROBLEM: *How can I keep end grain from staining darker than face and edge grain?*

SOLUTION: End grain is more porous than edge or face grain, so it absorbs more stain and ends up much darker than the other surfaces of a project. This can be a problem if you're trying to achieve a very even-colored appearance. It's possible to use a sealer only on the end grain, but I don't always have sealer around. Instead, I take advantage of the fact that the more finely sanded a surface is, the less stain it absorbs. I sand end grain a grit or two finer than the face and edge grain. This offsets the end grain's greater porosity.

Walt Morrison
Northport, NY

SMOOTHING SMALL-DIAMETER, INSIDE CURVES

I recently made a chest of drawers with wooden drawer pulls. The pulls had some tight inside curves that needed to be sanded, but I couldn't find any commercial sanding drums that would fit. Rather than change the design, I stubbornly stuck to my original plan and looked for a way to sand the pieces quickly and efficiently.

I found a dowel that matched the curve and decided to use it as a sanding drum in the drill press. But how to attach the sandpaper? I finally found that if I slit the dowel lengthwise with a band saw kerf, the paper would stay in place just fine. As the drill press spins, the loose end of the paper wraps itself around the dowel. The paper gradually wears away, exposing fresh abrasive as you work.

Ken Burton
New Tripoli, PA

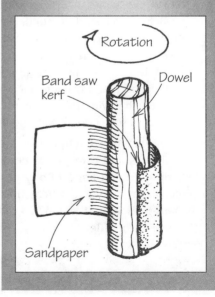

AVOIDING SANDING FLAWS

Of all the various processes that I go through as a woodworker, sanding is the task that I like the least. It has all the trademarks of being a chore, with precious little of the creativity and reward that comes with most other parts of a project.

Nothing helps in sanding more than experience, which you don't get except by sanding. So pay attention to your past mistakes.

A key point to remember is that surface preparation is ongoing from the moment you bring wood home from the lumberyard. Be careful when you handle the wood at every stage of construction: rough milling through final delivery. Nicks and dings that occur in the early going when you think it hardly matters can haunt you at finish time. It's a frame of mind that needs to become a habit. Here are some other guidelines to keep in mind:

SAND AS LITTLE AS POSSIBLE

We often choose to sand when planing or scraping would have been quicker and better suited to the job. Keep at least one of your smaller bench planes razor sharp and use it whenever possible for situations such as smoothing sawn edges and removing especially deep planer marks. Planing almost always gives a cleaner, crisper result than sanding. Use a hand scraper for jobs such as removing glue, leveling the wood around a dent or scratch, and removing finer planer marks. The scraper may be the simplest tool in your shop, but it's one that can give you magical results. Here, too, you need to keep at least one scraper sharp.

REPAIR DENTS AND DEFECTS FIRST

Before you start to sand, circle problem spots in white chalk and address these first. For example, fill deep holes, such as nail holes that you can't sand. If you spot a dent, let a few drops of clean water sit for 15 minutes on the dent, then lay a small square of moist cloth over it and touch it with the nose of a hot iron to swell out the dent. You'll save a lot of sanding time this way.

SAND ONLY IN THE DIRECTION OF THE GRAIN

This is and always has been the cardinal rule in sanding. I don't know of any typical exception to this rule. Even in places where this is difficult, such as where rails and stiles on a frame meet, you should adhere to the rule.

The cardinal rule holds even for the use of electric sanders. Move them back and forth with the grain. With orbital or random-orbit sanders, and even more particularly with belt sanders, be careful when you start and stop the sanding action—this is when damage to the wood surface is most likely to occur. Hit the ground running, so to speak, moving the sander forward as you set it down gently so that the entire pad or belt contacts the wood at the same time. Keep the sander moving. Take special care with portable belt sanders because they can remove wood quickly and unevenly, particularly with coarser grits.

I avoid 80-grit or coarser sandpaper on electric sanders because the scratches are too difficult to remove. If you have prepared and scraped the surface properly, such coarse sandpaper should not be necessary; if you think it is, sand by hand using a cork sanding block. Then, either by hand or with an electric sander, progress through successively finer grits: 120 to 180 to 220.

CLEAN THE WOOD BETWEEN GRITS

If you don't do this, the loosened grit mixed with the sanding dust will thwart your efforts. An air hose and a tack cloth are most helpful here. Keep your sandpaper clean, and change sandpaper when the paper begins to feel smooth to your touch. Here's a tip worth trying: After sanding with 180-grit sandpaper, wipe down the surface with a clean, lint-free slightly damp rag. This will very slightly raise the grain, and the final sanding with 220-grit sandpaper will produce a surface ready for the finish.

USE A BACKING BLOCK WHEN HAND SANDING

Otherwise, crisp edges get smudged. Wrap the sandpaper around a short length of dowel or buy a set of the small rubber contour sanding blocks. On convex surfaces, make a concave sanding block that mates to the surface, and vise versa.

David Page
Swarthmore, PA

Sanding Small Parts Safely

PROBLEM: *I need to sand a number of band-sawn animals that are both very rough and very small. What should I use?*

SOLUTION: I prefer a stationary belt sander for this kind of job; however sanding a small part on a stationary sander may bring your fingers uncomfortably close to the moving abrasive. To prevent this, attach the parts to a push block or a large wood scrap with double-sided carpet tape. Use the block or scrap to maneuver the part as you sand it.

Nick Engler
West Milton, OH

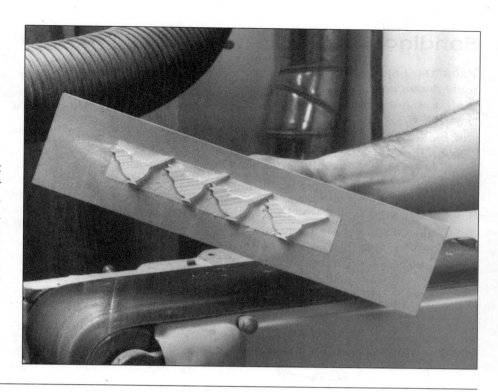

Making Sanding Blocks for Moldings

PROBLEM: *I've got a bunch of molding to sand and it's difficult to sand consistently into the tight corners of the profile. How should I handle this?*

SOLUTION: Make a sanding block that is custom-contoured to the exact counterprofile of your molding. You may be surprised at the material you can use to make such a sanding block: auto body filler. Just lay a piece of waxed paper over a section of the molding, and heap a generous glob of auto body filler onto the paper, as shown below. When the filler is completely hardened, pop it off the paper and trim the edges to a comfortable grip.

Mark Duginske
Merrill, WI

Many moldings are symmetrical and a scrap piece can be used as a sanding block.

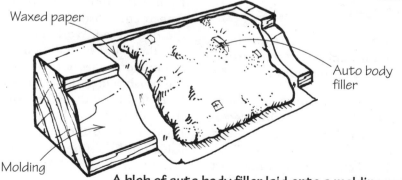

Waxed paper

Auto body filler

Molding

A blob of auto body filler laid onto a molding profile (with a piece of waxed paper in between) will form a perfectly shaped sanding block when dry.

Sanding Coves

PROBLEM: *I managed to cut some decent cove molding on the table saw, but how do I sand out the deep striations left by the saw blade?*

SOLUTION: Make a sanding block that fits perfectly into the cove. For very shallow coves, a band-sawn block of soft wood may do the trick. But most of the time, I use a piece of rigid foam insulation that can be sanded into an exact mirror image of the cove, as shown below.

Step 1. Stick 80-grit sandpaper into the cove.

Step 2. Sand a foam block to the shape of the cove.

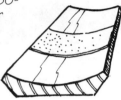

Step 3. Stick sandpaper to the foam and smooth the cove.

You can minimize the depth of the saw marks on a cove by using a good sharp blade and making a very light final cut.

Bob Moran
Emmaus, PA

> **RELATED INFO:**
> **Cutting Coves on the Table Saw, page 112**

Cutting Coves on the Table Saw, page 112

Quick Tip Quick Tip Quick Tip Quick

CURVED SANDING BLOCKS

Using a block to back up your sandpaper allows you to sand by hand more effectively, keeps the surface you're sanding flat, and makes sandpaper last longer before wearing out.

To handle sanding curves, I make two sets of four curved sanding blocks—one set for convex curves and one set for concave curves. Each block in the set has an increasingly smaller radius so that one of the blocks in the set will fit whatever curves I generate in my woodworking. To sand a curve, pick the block that is closest to the curve on your workpiece and wrap a piece of sandpaper tightly around the block with your hand. These blocks are sized to conveniently use one-sixth of a sandpaper sheet.

Andy Rae
Lenhartsville, PA

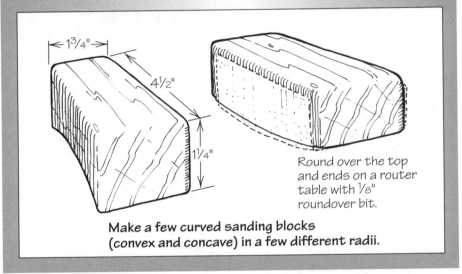

Round over the top and ends on a router table with 1/8" roundover bit.

Make a few curved sanding blocks (convex and concave) in a few different radii.

Cleaning a Shop-Vac Filter

PROBLEM: *How can I clean the filter on my shop-vacuum without getting a mouthful of dust?*

SOLUTION: Cleaning a shop-vacuum filter is a dirty but necessary job. The key is to do it in such a way that you don't end up inhaling a cloud of extra-fine dust and creating a mess in your freshly vacuumed shop. I always clean my filter outdoors, containing the dust in a clear plastic trash bag. I place the unit in the bag along with a stiff-bristled brush, and tie the bag closed. Working from outside the bag, I hold the unit off the ground and clean the filter with the brush. Once the filter is clean, I let the dust settle before removing the unit from the bag. When finished, I tie up the bag and set it aside until the filter needs another cleaning.

Walt Morrison
Northport, NY

Bench-Top Dust Collection

PROBLEM: *I spend a lot of time sanding small parts with an orbital sander. Is there a convenient way to reduce the dust in the air?*

SOLUTION: I made a vacuum sanding box with ¾-inch pine sides and a top and bottom surface of ¼-inch hardboard. The top surface is pegboard, the bottom one is solid. I find that enlarging the pegboard holes to ⅜-inch and countersinking them increases the effectiveness of the box.

To further improve suction, place a thin cardboard mask over the holes that are closest to your work. I made the top removable and provided a lip for clamping the box to my bench.

John Becker
Berwyn, PA

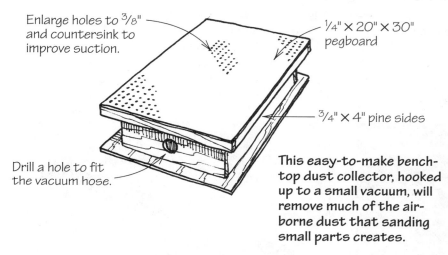

Enlarge holes to ⅜" and countersink to improve suction.

¼" × 20" × 30" pegboard

¾" × 4" pine sides

Drill a hole to fit the vacuum hose.

This easy-to-make bench-top dust collector, hooked up to a small vacuum, will remove much of the air-borne dust that sanding small parts creates.

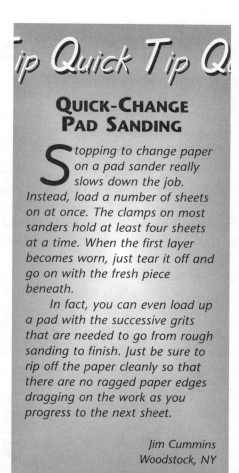

Improving Sandpaper Flexibility

PROBLEM: *Most of the sandpaper in my shop has a light A-weight paper backing, and it often tears in use. Yet the tougher papers with D-weight backings are very stiff and tend to crack when I use them on curves. Where can I get the same range of grits in a lightweight cloth backing that will be flexible yet tough?*

SOLUTION: Reinforce the paper you now use with fiberglass strapping tape. Just lay the sheet of sandpaper face down on a flat surface and cover the back of it evenly with strips of tape side by side. Then cut the paper into the shapes you need. You can buy strapping tape in two kinds: One has fibers running the length of the tape; the other has them in a crisscross grid pattern. Depending on how you plan to cut the paper and the forces it will encounter in use, choose the type of tape that will best resist the direction of pull. Reinforced paper is ideal for sanding small cylinders or other curved work. Just cut a narrow strip of paper and use it by pulling the ends back and forth the way you'd use a strip of cloth to shine shoes.

Jim Cummins
Woodstock, NY

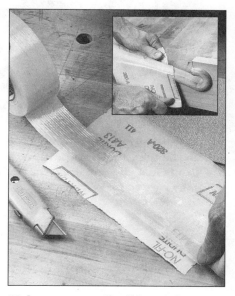

Make your own flexible sandpaper by reinforcing lightweight paper with fiberglass strapping tape.

HAND SCRAPING: A GOOD ALTERNATIVE TO SANDING

Sanding wood with abrasives can be described as the process of mashing the wood fibers. At the level of the wood surface, it's downright brutish. Only by using three or more progressively finer grits of sandpaper can you achieve satisfactory results. Scrapers, in contrast, cut the wood more like a plane—quicker and more cleanly.

A hand scraper is one of the simplest tools a woodworker can use, but it's also one of the most frustrating to sharpen. Once you get the sharpening right, using a hand scraper is as easy as brushing your teeth.

I think that most woodworkers start on the wrong foot by producing a mediocre edge on their hand scrapers. They get a taste of how well the tool can work, but it lasts only a few strokes before the edge breaks down.

What causes most edges to fail is the fact that they're formed roughly and are ragged and brittle.

You'll get the sharpest, longest-lasting edge if you take the time to sharpen it right in the first place. Start by filing the edge to both remove any trace of the old burr and square the edge to the faces of the scraper. I prefer to "draw file" the edge, holding the file with two hands and pulling it toward me, as shown below left.

Next remove the file marks from the scraper's edge with a fine india sharpening stone. Take care to hold the scraper perpendicular to the stone to keep the edge square to the face of the scraper. I also diligently use the entire surface of the stone to smooth

To file the edge of the scraper, hold the scraper firmly in a vise and draw the file toward you. Take care to make the edge square to the faces of the scraper.

After filing, remove the file marks with a fine india sharpening stone and remove any wire edge by stoning the faces of the scraper. Polishing the edge makes for a much smoother burr.

the edge of the scraper. After honing the edge, smooth the faces of the scraper on the stone as well, as shown at right on the opposite page.

After you finish stoning the edge, the next step is to consolidate it. This step, often neglected, strengthens the burr once it is turned with the burnisher. To consolidate the edge, hold the scraper flat on the bench and run the burnisher along the edge of the scraper nearly parallel to the face, as shown below left. This simple step builds up a stronger edge that will stay sharp longer. It is important to note that the burnisher must be kept nick-free and polished. Any nick in the burnisher will be transferred onto the sharpened edge of the scraper.

Now clamp the scraper in the vise to turn the edge, as shown below right. I turn the edge with three strokes of the burnisher. The first stroke is perpendicular to the face of the scraper, the second is about 7 degrees off perpendicular, and the third is 15 degrees from perpendicular. All the while I am careful to use the full length of the burnisher, so as to not wear a groove in the tool.

Preparing the edge of the hand scraper in this manner will provide a long lasting edge that will produce a smooth surface needing only a minimum of sanding.

Robert Treanor
San Francisco, CA

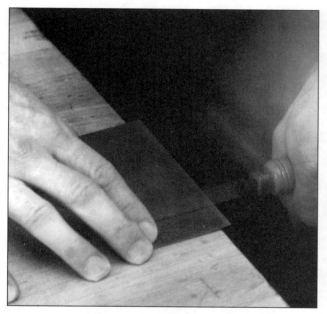

Burnish both faces of the scraper to consolidate the edge. Try to hold the burnisher at an angle that is just shy of being parallel to the faces.

To turn the burr, hold the scraper in a vise again and pull the burnisher across the edge. The burnisher should be well polished—any imperfections will be transferred into the burr.

FINISHING

SOLUTIONS

PREPPING FOR FINISH

Filling Defects on Open-Grained Woods 217

Making Patches That Absorb
Finish Evenly 218

Removing Rust Stains 218

Removing Iron Stains 218

Less Fuss Filler 219

STAINING WOOD

Avoiding Blotching 220

Staining End Grain and Face Grain 221

Staining Distressed Wood 221

Avoiding Bleed-Back When Staining 222

Dealing with Raised Grain 222

Matching New Pieces to Old 223

Staining Figured Wood 223

Staining Wood Jet Black 223

Blending Spots Left by Dye Stain 224

Staining Light and Dark
Woods to the Same Tone 224

Mixing Water-Based Dyes and Finishes 225

APPLYING FINISHES

Finishing Oily Woods 226

Dealing with Bubbles in
Water-Based Finish 226

Preventing "Fish Eye" 227

Reducing Bubbles in Polyurethane 227

Warming Wood to Prevent Bubbles 227

An Overview of Finishes 228

Building a Finishing Rack 230

Reducing Orange Peel
When Spraying Finishes 231

Dealing with Overspray 231

Brushing in Tight Spaces 231

A Quick Spray Booth 232

Reducing Shellac Brush Marks 233

Preventing Brush Marks
in Polyurethane 233

Avoiding Sags in Varnish 233

Finishing Exotic Woods 234

Building a Rich, Durable Finish 234

Building a Black Satin Finish 234

Good Lighting Is the Key to a Good Finish 235

Finding an Odor-Free Finish 236

Stopping Bleed-Back with an Oil Finish 236

Creating Fade-Free Outdoor Finishes 237

Dealing with Panel Shrinkage 237

Protecting Stains from Topcoats 237

Finishing Screw Heads 237

One-Day Spray Finishing Strategies 238

Producing a Flaw-Free Spray Finish 240

FIXING FINISHES

Fixing a Lacquer Finish That "Blushes" 241

Preventing Shellac from Clouding 241

Dealing with Dust in a Finish 242

Dealing with Cracking Lacquer 242

Keeping Dust Off of Your Work 242

Helping Tacky Varnish Cure 243

Colored Waxes 243

Smoothing and Waxing in One Step 243

Removing Glue Residue 243

Hiding Glue Spots after Finishing 244

Scraper Shavers 244

Shortcuts to a Hand-Rubbed Look 245

Fixing Color Variations in Cherry Projects 245

Improving Gloss on a Low-Sheen Surface 245

PAINTING WOOD

Sealing Medium-Density
Fiberboard (MDF) 246

Hiding Unsightly Pine Knots 246

Dealing with Cedar Oil Bleed-Through 247

Coating Decorative Accents 247

Keeping Brass Shining Brightly 247

Painting Pressure-Treated Pine 247

Prepping for Finish

Filling Defects on Open-Grained Woods

PROBLEM: *I want to fill the surface defects in some oak wall paneling that I intend to paint, but I don't want the patches to show. How can I blend the repair with the open-grained wood around it?*

SOLUTION: When you apply wood putty to a ding or defect on a piece of ash or oak—or any other open-grained wood—the putty fills the grain in the surrounding area as well as the defect. Your attempt at concealment sticks out like a sore thumb. To hide the repair, you need to work the putty to mimic the surrounding wood grain.

First place a few pieces of masking tape around the defect to keep the putty from filling the wood grain around the repair. Then apply your wood putty as you would normally, as shown above right. While the putty is still wet, remove the tape. If you wait until the putty dries, the tape may pull the putty out of the defect.

When the patch is thoroughly dry, sand it flush, then use a dental pick or sharp awl to connect the fine lines of grain that are broken by the defect, as shown below right. The fine scratch lines may seem nearly invisible, but when you finish the piece, the repair will blend in much better with the surrounding wood than it would without the lines.

Mark Romano
Gibbstown, NJ

When patching open-grained woods, prevent filler from getting into surrounding wood grain by masking off the area to be patched.

After sanding the patch, carve in some of the grain lines with a dental pick or awl to give it a more realistic texture.

Making Patches That Absorb Finish Evenly

PROBLEM: *I made a glue-and-sawdust patch to fix a damaged tabletop, but the sheen varies between the patch and the surrounding wood. Can this be corrected?*

SOLUTION: Making a putty from glue and wood dust solves the problem of color matching, since the putty contains wood from the project you're working on. But as you've discovered, often the mixture is denser than the wood surrounding it, so it will absorb less finish and take on a different luster. You can see the same effect when you have a very tight, dense knot in softwood, such as pine. The wood will absorb the first coat of finish and look matte, while the dense knot will often look shiny.

There are two solutions to this problem. First, you can make a putty mixture that contains a higher percentage of wood dust. One of my favorite putty formulas is to add a few drops of 3-pound-cut shellac to wood dust until a thick paste is formed. This mixture dries quickly and is invisible under the first sealer coat, especially if you use shellac as the sealer.

Your second choice is to make the finish thicker by applying either thicker coats or more coats. Sealing the wood with two coats of varnish and then sanding before the third coat will most likely give you a uniform sheen, even on areas that absorb differently.

Michael Dresdner
Puyallup, WA

Removing Rust Stains

PROBLEM: *I spilled some water on an unfinished table and by the time I saw it, there were rust stains from finish nails I'd left on the wood. How can I remove the stains?*

SOLUTION: You can remove the rust stains with oxalic acid (available at better paint stores). Make a solution by stirring at least two heaping tablespoons of oxalic acid crystals into a pint of warm water. Brush the solution over the entire tabletop, not just over the stain. Otherwise, you might create lighter spots. Let the wood dry until only the oxalic acid crystals remain. Thoroughly wash off the crystals with a hose or with a well-soaked sponge or cloth. Then add a mild alkali like baking soda or a small amount of household ammonia to some clean water and wash the tabletop again to neutralize any remaining acid. If traces of the stain remain, repeat the procedure or lightly sand to remove them.

Bob Flexner
Norman, OK

Removing Iron Stains

PROBLEM: *My oak table has black stains on it from my bar clamps. What caused the stains, and how can I remove them?*

SOLUTION: The stains are formed when iron comes in contact with woods that are high in tannin. The iron and tannin react to form ferric tannate, which happens to be bluish black. You can remove the stains without affecting the original oak color by using an oxalic acid wash (oxalic acid crystals are available at better paint stores). The oxalic acid will reduce the stain from bluish black ferric tannate to colorless ferrous oxalate.

Make your oxalic acid wash by adding about an ounce of oxalic acid crystals to a pint of warm water. This will produce a 6 percent solution. Wear a dust mask while mixing and be careful: The dry oxalic acid is toxic and irritating. Sponge the solution liberally onto the sanded raw wood, covering the whole surface, not just the area that is stained. Let it dry overnight. The next day you will notice a white crystalline residue on the surface of the wood. Wash off the residue with plenty of clean water, wipe off the piece with a clean cloth, and let the wood dry. The stains should be gone, and the oak will retain its original color. If any stains remain, simply repeat the process until they are all gone.

Michael Dredsner
Puyallup, WA

Avoid iron stains like these by keeping your clamps from contacting the wood during glue-ups.

Less Fuss Filler

ONE OF THE BEST WAYS TO GIVE A PROJECT A HIGH END LOOK *is to fill the wood pores and apply a high-gloss finish. But working with paste wood filler can be difficult. Even if you follow the instructions on the can exactly, you may end up with a chalky mess. What's the solution?*

Many manufacturers of paste wood filler suggest that you apply it with a brush and remove it with balled-up burlap just as the surface "flashes" dry but before the filler dries completely. This leaves you with a narrow time window to complete what ends up being a strenuous process. The larger the surface you're trying to fill, the more exasperating the task becomes.

On large flat surfaces, you can speed application substantially by using a paint roller equipped with a sponge rubber cover, like the kind used for applying varnishes. To work the filler without wearing yourself out, forget the burlap. Instead, rub the filler into the wood pores with a soft felt block, a felt chalk eraser, or a wood block wrapped in a piece of sturdy cloth, like denim. Then scrape off the filler with a wide plastic or metal putty knife that has well-rounded corners. These

filler scrapings, if soft enough, can even be dropped back into a separate can to be rejuvenated with naphtha and reused later if you're running low on filler. For small, curved, or carved areas I rub off the filler with #00 steel wool. However, make sure that any steel wool fibers are removed after the filler cures properly.

*Mark Romano
Gibbstown, NJ*

Step 2. To force the filler into the wood pores, rub it across the grain with a firm cloth like denim wrapped around a softwood block or a thick block of felt.

Step 1. After pouring the filler onto a tabletop, spread it quickly with a standard foam paint roller.

Step 3. Forget the burlap! Once the surface of the filler starts to flash dry, scrape off the excess with a putty knife. Make sure that the edge of the knife is smooth and the corners are rounded.

Staining Wood

Avoiding Blotching

PROBLEM: *I stained the doors on my pine hutch and ended up with a blotchy mess that has ruined the look of the piece. How can I fix it?*

SOLUTION: Blotching is the most common and frustrating stain problem. It occurs when stain penetrates different depths in the wood. It's most likely to be a problem in fir, pine, poplar, aspen, birch, and cherry—all very popular woods. There is no way to remove blotching except to sand, scrape, or plane to the depth below which the stain has penetrated.

AVOIDING THE PROBLEM: To prevent blotching in the future, you have to keep the stain from penetrating unevenly. There are two easy ways to do this: Use a gel stain or a stain controller. Gel stains don't flow unless moved by a rag or brush, so they barely penetrate into the wood. The thicker the gel stain, the less it penetrates and the more effective it is at keeping blotching to a minimum.

Stain controllers fill the pores and prevent a liquid stain from penetrating unevenly. To get the best possible result with a stain controller, apply it liberally with a brush or rag until all parts of the wood are wet. Keep applying more controller until no more dry spots appear. Then wipe off all of the excess liquid and apply your stain as soon as possible—within 30 minutes is best. If you wait too long, enough of the stain controller will have evaporated or soaked deeper into the wood so that the stain will again penetrate and cause blotching.

Stain controllers are advertised specifically for reducing blotching. Gel stains are more predictable, however, because variables, such as the number of coats applied or the time elapsed before the stain is applied, are not a consideration.

Bob Flexner
Norman, OK

Blotching occurs when stain unevenly penetrates woods with swirly grain or varying density, such as this pine board. The only way to deal with it is to sand, scrape, or plane below the stained surface.

Gel stains penetrate less than liquid stains and blotch less too.

If you must use a liquid stain, and if you expect blotching by doing so, apply a stain controller first.

Staining End Grain and Face Grain

PROBLEM: *When I stained my new coffee table, the end grain came out much darker than the rest of the wood. How can I even the color?*

SOLUTION: One solution is to make the lighter areas the same color as the darker end grain by restaining only the lighter parts with another coat of stain, perhaps even a darker tone. If you choose this route, first seal the end grain carefully with two coats of finish so that you won't accidentally darken it while you are restaining the rest of the table. Shellac works well for this operation, but you also could brush on whatever finish you are planning to use on the entire project.

Another approach is to seal the entire piece with two coats of your chosen finish, then glaze those areas you want to darken. Make your glaze by mixing japan color with boiled linseed oil and mineral spirits. (Japan color, a pigmented varnish, is available through professional finishing suppliers; see "Sources," beginning on page 298.)

If you want to lighten the stain on the end grain, you may be able to remove some of it by scrubbing with a stiff bristle brush and lacquer thinner, followed by some judicious sanding. Once you get the table as light as you can, restain as described below.

AVOIDING THE PROBLEM: The easiest way to get even color between end grain and face grain is to use a water soluble dye stain. Dyes tend to stain more evenly and may make end grain SLIGHTLY darker than flat wood surfaces, but not as much as pigmented stains. Besides, if you do not like the color, you can remove it completely with a wash of household laundry bleach. The bleach will not affect the wood color. Unfortunately, this trick does not work with pigmented stains, nor with dyes that are dissolved in oil.

If you must use a pigmented stain, pre-seal the end grain with either 2-pound cut shellac or a coating of glue size (a thin mixture of white or yellow glue and water). This will mitigate the stain absorption and will help keep all of it closer to one color. Brush or wipe the solution into the end grain, and wait until it is dry before you apply the stain.

Please remember that any time you finish, you should first test the stain on a scrap of the SAME wood that has been sanded to the smoothness of your piece. When in doubt as to the color you will get, start with a stain that is lighter than the color you want (by diluting the stain with extra solvent) and "creep up" on the color with several applications. It's much easier to go darker by applying more stain than to go lighter.

Here's one final old cabinetmaker's trick: If you're going to use a pigmented stain, sand the end grain with garnet sandpaper (as opposed to silicon carbide or aluminum oxide). As it wears, garnet gets dull. When this happens, the dull garnet will burnish the end grain and reduce the amount of pigmented stain the wood will absorb.

Michael Dredsner
Puyallup, WA

Staining Distressed Wood

PROBLEM: *I'm using a chain to add distress marks to a table that I made so that it looks like an antique. What I want to know is: Should I stain the table before I make dents with the chain or afterward?*

SOLUTION: There aren't exact steps for doing anything in finishing; it always depends on what you are trying to achieve. In this case, everything is very logical. If you apply the stain and maybe one or two coats of finish before you dent the wood, the dents will be the same color as the surrounding wood. The table will look like it still has its original finish and the damage occurred after that finish was applied. If you dent the wood and then apply a stain, the stain will be darker in the dents because the wood fibers will be broken and will absorb more stain. The table will look like it was stripped, stained, and refinished after it was damaged.

One note of caution: The trick to achieving believable distressing is to make the damage random, as it would be if it had occurred naturally. If the dents you make are fairly uniform in size and shape, as they probably will be if you use a chain, the distressing won't look natural. Try using many different-shaped metal objects instead. You will find countless possibilities in your tool box and kitchen utensils drawer. It's best to practice on a scrap board before scarring up your table. That will also help you determine whether to do the distressing before or after the finishing and which tools are best to use.

Bob Flexner
Norman, OK

Avoiding Bleed-Back When Staining

PROBLEM: *The oil stain I applied to my new hutch bled back out of the pores and has hardened on the surface of the wood. What can I do to fix this mess?*

SOLUTION: Oil-based stain, when applied to certain open-pored woods, has a tendency to bleed out as it dries. This seems to be a problem particularly in hot, humid weather. If your stain has dried completely, you have little recourse other than to remove the drips by scraping or sanding and then to restain the piece. However, if the droplets are still tacky, you can wipe the piece with a rag dampened with stain. The solvent in the stain should redissolve the spots so that you can remove them.

AVOIDING THE PROBLEM: To prevent bleed-back, apply the stain as you usually would and wipe off any excess with a cloth. Then check every 15 or 20 minutes for the first hour or two to see if bleeding is occurring. If it is, wipe the piece with a clean rag while the droplets are still wet to remove them.

Ben Erickson
Eutaw, AL

Dealing with Raised Grain

PROBLEM: *I just stained a project with a water-based stain and the wood is now all rough and fuzzy. What went wrong and what can I do to remove the raised grain?*

SOLUTION: Water- and alcohol-based stains, including some labeled NGR (non-grain-raising), can make even your most finely sanded wood very rough. The problem occurs when the wood fibers swell as they absorb the liquid in the stain. You can sand the surface smooth, but when you restain, the wood absorbs color unevenly, and the result is a vicious cycle of resanding and restaining.

You can try to work around this problem in two ways. First, try to remove the raised grain by burnishing the wood using a large handful of thin shavings from your hand plane. This technique works best on flat surfaces like tabletops.

If this doesn't work, try covering the wood with two thin coats of lacquer, polyurethane, or another finish that builds up on the surface. When the finish cures, smooth the surface with fine sandpaper to level the finish and remove the raised grain. Then wipe the wood with a tack cloth and apply another coat of finish.

AVOIDING THE PROBLEM: There are a couple of ways to avoid raised grain, or at least control it. The first is to intentionally raise the grain before you stain. Sand the project as you normally would, but before you apply the stain, rub the wood all over with a clean, wet cloth. The cloth should be more than damp but not soaking. This will raise the grain just slightly. Once the wood is thoroughly dry, sand off the nubs of raised grain. This will lessen the raised grain when you apply the stain.

The second method is to apply a wood conditioner, a thinned coat of white shellac, or a sanding sealer to the wood. Wood conditioners and shellac go on before the stain. The conditioner will help even out the color, while the shellac will seal the wood, preventing the stain from raising the grain. Sanding sealers generally are applied over the stain to seal in the stain so that you can sand lightly without affecting the color. When you use any of these three products, always test a small, inconspicuous area first to make sure that the product you have chosen is compatible with your stain.

David Page
Swarthmore, PA

If the stain you've used raises the grain, try burnishing away the rough wood fibers using thin shavings from a hand plane. This technique works best on flat surfaces.

Matching New Pieces to Old

PROBLEM: *I'm making a maple table that I need to stain to match the very dark color of the antique chairs it will go with. Nothing I can find will get the wood dark enough. Any suggestions?*

SOLUTION: Hard maple is so dense that pigmented stains tend to wipe off as fast as they wipe on. To get maple really dark, you need to resort to dyes and sometimes to layered staining techniques. Here's how to do it:

Prepare the wood by sanding, but use no finer than 220- or 320-grit sandpaper. Finer sandpapers will burnish maple and make it resist stains even more. I would also avoid garnet paper, which tends to dull more quickly and is more likely to burnish the wood than aluminum oxide or silicon carbide. Choose a dark, water-soluble dye stain that matches the color of your chairs. Mix it into some very warm water using the heaviest concentration that the manufacturer allows. Flood the warm stain liberally onto the wood, and wipe off any excess before it dries. This will give you the darkest color you can get in one step.

If the wood is still not dark enough after the first application of dye stain has dried, apply a coat of dark pigmented stain directly onto the wood. The raised grain will help the maple absorb the stain. If you want to make the wood darker still, you can reapply the pigmented stain after the first coat has dried. Or, if you prefer, you can seal the table after the first coat and then glaze it. Make your glaze by mixing japan color with boiled linseed oil and mineral spirits (see "Sources," beginning on page 298).

Depending on the color you are seeking, you might want to try some asphaltum (fiberless roofing tar) stain. Be sure to test it on a scrap of the same wood first. Make the stain by cutting asphaltum 50/50 with toluene or naphtha. This stain will take well even on maple and will give you a dark blackish brown color. It might be just the ticket, either alone or on top of your first dye stain.

Michael Dresdner
Puyallup, WA

Staining Figured Wood

PROBLEM: *I'm making frame-and-panel doors out of quilted maple. How can I stain the wood without obscuring the figure?*

SOLUTION: While pigmented stains tend to obscure quilted maple, pure water-soluble dye stains will let the figure shine through.

Mix the dye powder in warm water, then stain by flooding the surface and wiping off all of the stain before it dries. This will yield the clearest and most even stain. Remember that you control the color by using more or less dye powder in your mixture, not by the way you apply it.

To enhance the grain even more, try this trick. Stain the wood with a very diluted black dye. When it dries, resand the wood with 220- or 320-grit paper. This will remove the dye from the "flats" but leave some of it in the deeper recesses of the curls or quilts. Now restain with water-soluble dye in the color of your choice. The black "highlights" will add even more depth and dimension to your fancy wood.

Michael Dredsner
Puyallup, WA

Staining Wood Jet Black

PROBLEM: *I want to stain a project pure black, but none of the stains I've tried have worked. What's the best way to stain wood pure black?*

SOLUTION: The technical term for staining things black is ebonizing, and the most common way to ebonize is with an aniline dye stain. These dyes come in two types of powders: one mixes with alcohol; the other with water. The alcohol-based dye has a reputation for being not quite as colorfast as the water-based dye—I've seen the black turn blue after a few years in the sunlight. The water-based dye penetrates deeper and is more colorfast; however, the water raises the grain, so you have to sand lightly after the stain dries.

My coworkers and I have used both types of aniline dye in our shop and no one was really crazy about either. The problem is that once you start mixing things, you get a lot of inconsistencies in color. You'd think that with water-based dyes, everything would be pretty straightforward. But in Philadelphia, where I live and work, the tap water comes out of the murky Schuylkill River and nobody has any idea what chemicals are in it.

The best coloring agent I've come across for ebonizing wood is leather dye, used by belt makers and leather workers. If you don't have a ready source, go visit a shoemaker and talk him out of a little bottle.

Leather dye is aniline-based, but it's premixed, so you always get the same results. Because it is produced for the large, competitive shoe market, a lot of research is involved in developing it, and the quality control is excellent. The dye is easy to apply, it's colorfast, it doesn't raise the grain, and it comes in a wide range of colors in addition to basic black.

To use this dye, apply two coats of dye to wood that has been well sanded. Be sure to remove all the wood dust. After each coat has dried, you'll find a light, powdery residue; wipe it off with a clean cotton or wool rag. Allow at least a day after the second coat of dye before you apply your finish. We've found that, otherwise, the finish pulls off some of the color.

Jack Larimore
Philadelphia, PA

Blending Spots Left by Dye Stain

PROBLEM: *While applying a water-soluble aniline dye to the side of desk, I dripped some of the dye onto the lower parts. When I stained the spotted areas, the spots remained. How can I fix them?*

SOLUTION: The spots show the places where the dye penetrated deeper than the rest of the wood—this happens when dye remains on the surface longer. The fix is to apply the dye to the entire surface again and keep the surface wet so that the dye penetrates equally everywhere. If the surface is then too dark, wipe over everything with a damp or wet rag to remove excess stain until you get the color that you want.

Bob Flexner
Norman, OK

Blend unintended dark spots of stain by restaining the entire area.

Staining Light and Dark Woods to the Same Tone

PROBLEM: *I tried to even out the tone of light and dark boards by using pigmented gel stain and leaving it on the lighter parts longer. It just left the wood looking muddy. How can I stain the light and dark woods on a project so that they come out an even color?*

SOLUTION: You need to "tone" the different shades of wood to be more even in color, and the best way to do this is with spray toner. A toner is simply a tinted lacquer applied over the stain. By carefully applying more toner to the lighter areas, you can blend a large area to a more consistent color or tone.

Toners can be tricky to apply at first, but if you are dexterous, you'll find that a spray gun is invaluable for blending light and dark woods. For small jobs, you can use aerosol cans of tinted lacquer, but because you can't adjust the spray nozzle on a can, the blending action is more difficult to control than it is if you use a spray gun.

The procedure is the same for both spray types: First apply your gel stain, then spray on a sanding sealer. (If you don't have a spray gun, use an aerosol can of lacquer sanding sealer.) Once the sealer is dry, sand the surface, apply one light coat of clear lacquer, and let it dry overnight. The next day, carefully mask off the darker boards with painter's masking tape, which has adhesive on just one edge. Then tone the wood.

To make my toners, I tint lacquer with NGR (non-grain-raising) dye stains. See "Sources," beginning on page 298. These stains are premixed in a solution that can be added to clear lacquer, and they are available from finishing suppliers like Mohawk or Behlen. After thinning the lacquer, I add NGR stain to the mixture sparingly. A good rule of thumb is to add the NGR so that it accounts for no more than 5 percent of the total mixture. In any case, when you dribble some of the toner off of the mixing stick onto a piece of white cardboard, the toner should have a color that appears strong enough to successfully tint the wood but be fairly translucent.

Spray the toner onto the exposed wood in thin coats until the color is the desired depth. Above all, take your time. It's easy to inadvertently go overboard when applying toners. If you need to, temporarily peel back some of the masked area to see what kind of progress you're making in blending the wood tones. When the color is evened out and the toner is dry, remove the masking tape. To further blend your panel, apply a quick dusting coat of toner to the entire panel. Finish up by locking the color in with two coats of clear lacquer.

Mark Romano
Gibbstown, NJ

The top rail on this cherry door looks like a different wood. The difference in tone between heartwood and sapwood is greater after staining.

After sealing the entire project with a light coat of lacquer, mask off the darker wood and spray very light coats of toner onto the light wood.

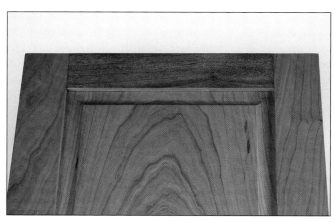

After the toner dries, apply two or more coats of clear lacquer to give the entire piece an even sheen.

Mixing Water-Based Dyes and Finishes

PROBLEM: *I made a hall table with a veneered top of Honduras rosewood, and I want to stain it and finish it. Can I use a water-based aniline dye with a water-based topcoat, or will the topcoat loosen the dye?*

SOLUTION: You can apply a water-based topcoat over a water-based dye stain, but I recommend that you apply a shellac barrier coat between the two. While water-soluble dyes are undeniably the best material for this type of staining, some may bleed if they are coated directly with a water-based topcoat. However, a thin wash coat of fresh shellac will seal in the dye and make an ideal foundation for the water-based coating. In fact, the shellac will reduce contamination problems, provide excellent adhesion, and improve the appearance of the wood.

Here's how to do it: Buy several colors of water-soluble dye powder from your supplier and mix them in warm water to get the color you want. Flood the wood with the dye stain; then wipe it off immediately to get even coloration.

Next, dissolve dewaxed blonde shellac flakes in denatured alcohol (to twice the height of the shellac flakes) in a lidded glass jar. Shake the jar frequently, and wait until the next day to use the mixture. Using a clean rag, flood the surface with the shellac mixture. Wipe off any excess immediately, and let the wood dry for about two hours. After that, you can proceed with the water-based topcoat.

Michael Dresdner
Puyallup, WA

Applying Finishes

Finishing Oily Woods

PROBLEM: *I tried to finish a cocobolo box with polyurethane, but the finish won't dry. What's the reason?*

SOLUTION: The oily resins in some exotic woods, such as cocobolo, teak, rosewood, ebony, padauk, and kordia, get into the polyurethane as you apply it and act like paint thinner that doesn't evaporate. This slows the curing significantly, but it doesn't stop it.

The best thing you can do after you have applied the finish is to warm the air around the object. A warmer environment speeds the curing of all finishes.

AVOIDING THE PROBLEM: In the future, wipe the surface of the wood with naphtha or lacquer thinner to remove the oily resin before finishing. Then apply the polyurethane relatively soon, before the oily resins that are still in the wood can rise back to the surface.

The resins in oily woods retard the curing of oil, varnish, and polyurethane finishes. While the oily resins won't slow the curing of shellac, lacquer, or water-based finishes, they may weaken the bond of even these finishes, especially lacquer and water-based. So, it is wise to wash the oily resin from the surface of the wood before applying any finish.

Bob Flexner
Norman, OK

ANOTHER VIEW: The trick to finishing oily woods is to first seal in the natural oils before topcoating. If you are finishing with lacquer, spray on several thin coats of vinyl sealer or shellac and allow the light coats to dry thoroughly before you apply a topcoat. If you are finishing with a varnish, spray on several thin coats of shellac and allow to them to dry thoroughly before you add a topcoat. Spraying rather than brushing is important—brushing will mix the oil with the sealer coat and allow continued problems.

Ben Erickson
Eutaw, AL

You'll get better results when finishing oily woods like this teak if you wipe off the surfaces with lacquer thinner before you finish.

Dealing with Bubbles in Water-Based Finish

PROBLEM: *I always get bubbles on the surface when I brush on water-based finishes. How can I prevent this?*

SOLUTION: Most people immediately suspect that bubbles are caused by the type or quality of brush they're using, but the brush is probably not the problem. The particular water-based finish you use and the weather determine whether or not you'll get bubbles.

Most water-based finishes brush smoothly in ideal weather conditions (70°F, 40 percent humidity). But many have bubbling problems when it's colder or hotter—the kind of weather we usually get when it's time to lay down that perfect finish. If you get bubbles when the temperature is below 70°F, dry off your brush with a clean cloth and run your brush back over the finish to pick up as much of the excess as possible. The idea is to make the finish as thin as possible. Do the same when the temperature is above 80°F, although in hotter weather the finish tends to dry so fast that it becomes difficult to go back over it with a brush. If this happens, thin the finish in the can by adding 10 percent water. If you're still getting bubbles, switch to another water-based finish. I've had good results under most weather conditions with Zar, Benjamin Moore, General Finishes, and Hydrocote Brushable.

Bob Flexner
Norman, OK

Preventing "Fish Eye"

PROBLEM: *When I spray lacquer or brush varnish, I often get "fish eye" on the surfaces. What causes it and how can I prevent it?*

SOLUTION: Fish eye is the term for small craterlike indentations that sometimes appear in a just-applied coat of finish. Most fish eye is caused by the presence of oily contaminants (mainly silicone oil) in the wood. The main culprits are furniture polishes that contain silicone and silicone sprays that may have been used as a lubricant on machines in the shop. Both varnish and lacquer finishes can exhibit fish eye. Since oil finishes do not build up on the surface, they will not show fish eye even though contaminants may be present.

If you notice fish eye when the first coat of finish is applied, remove the finish before it dries by wiping it off with the suitable solvent. Clean the surface thoroughly with lacquer thinner followed by mineral spirits or naphtha in a well-ventilated area. This will remove much of the silicone.

AVOIDING THE PROBLEM: There are two ways to prevent fish eye from recurring. The most reliable method is to spray on several thin coats of shellac, which acts as a sealer between the wood and the finish. After the shellac has dried thoroughly, apply the topcoat of varnish or lacquer. The other method is to spray on several very fine mist coats of your finish, let them dry, and then apply a heavier wet coat. This last wet coat traps the silicone in the finish and keeps it from floating to the surface. Spraying is important in both of these methods because brushing will drag the silicone back to the surface again.

Ben Erickson
Eutaw, AL

Reducing Bubbles in Polyurethane

PROBLEM: *I can't seem to apply polyurethane without getting bubbles in the finish. Sometimes they pop out before the finish cures, but sometimes they cure in the finish. I don't shake or stir the can at all. What is the trick?*

SOLUTION: The trick is to get the bubbles to pop out of the finish as soon as possible after applying it and before the finish "skins" over or cures. As you have discovered, it's not the shaking or stirring of the can that causes the bubbles. It's the brushing, and you can't keep the brush from causing bubbles.

To get the bubbles to pop out, you need to apply the finish thinly. Do this by stretching the finish out with your brush or, in the case of polyurethane, by thinning the finish with mineral spirits (paint thinner). Stretching out the finish with your brush makes a thinner film, so there is less film for the bubbles to travel through. By thinning the finish with mineral spirits, you create more time for the finish to "skin" over, so the bubbles have a longer time to get out. Keep in mind that the more you thin the finish, the more coats you will have to apply to get the same total film thickness.

Bob Flexner
Norman, OK

Warming Wood to Prevent Bubbles

PROBLEM: *I'm having a devil of a time spraying a cherry chest of drawers because no matter what I do I get bubbles. I've tried thinning the finish and adding anti-fish eye, but the bubbles still appear. Any ideas?*

SOLUTION: One thing you haven't mentioned is the temperature of the wood when you finish it, and that alone could be enough to cause your finishing problem. Here's why: If you magnify a raw wood surface enough, it resembles a kitchen sponge, with lots of open cells and air spaces. If you bring wood from a cold storage place into a heated finishing room, the air inside the wood expands as the wood warms. Bubbles of expanding air then escape from the wood, and can become trapped in a finish film. Such bubbles are quite mysterious and vexing, because they don't come from solvents in the finish or from air trapped in the brush or applicator pad; they're in the wood itself. The same problem can occur if you let your workspace get cold overnight and then turn the heat up to start finishing when you get there in the morning. The cure is to warm up the wood thoroughly before applying the finish.

The problem is most evident with water-based rather than solvent finishes. A solvent finish evaporates rapidly, cooling the surface in the same way that rubbing alcohol cools skin. Water evaporates more slowly, so the bubbles have time to escape from the warming wood.

Jim Cummins
Woodstock, NY

AN OVERVIEW OF FINISHES

Finishes can be confusing, but really they are nothing more than liquids that change to solids. Soon after you apply a coat of finish to wood using a rag, brush, or spray gun, the finish solidifies and seals the wood.

The first coat of finish is called the sealer coat. Each additional coat of finish is called a topcoat. There are six common finishes used on wood: wax, oil, varnish, shellac, lacquer, and water-based. Sometimes, several of these are mixed and called by a different name. For example, "Danish oil" is usually a mixture of oil and varnish. Sometimes, a finish is called by a different name when it is thinned. For example, many of the finishes marketed as "tung oil" are really just varnish thinned by half with mineral spirits (paint thinner). Mixtures of finishes take on some of the characteristics of each finish. Thinned finishes perform the same as the unthinned finish; they just produce thinner coats. Here's an overview of the common finishes:

Wax. Most waxes are natural products, either refined from petroleum, secreted by insects, or scraped from plants. Some waxes are synthetically made to imitate the characteristics of natural waxes. When you buy a commercial wax in paste or liquid form, it could be a single wax, or it might be a blend of waxes. Manufacturers often blend waxes to achieve special application characteristics or keep costs down.

All wax products perform about the same after they have been applied and the excess has been removed. But they apply differently, primarily due to the evaporation rate of the solvent used; solvents used include turpentine, mineral spirits, naphtha, and toluene.

A wax finish adds shine to wood without darkening it. But wax is too soft and porous to be scratch or water resistant. Wax is a good finish for decorative objects that aren't handled much, and it is excellent as a polish on top of another finish.

Oil. Oils used for finishing are also natural products. The two common oils that cure to a solid are linseed oil and true tung oil. Other oils like mineral oil, vegetable oil, and motor oil don't cure.

Linseed oil is pressed from the seeds of the flax plant. Tung oil is pressed from the nuts of the tung tree, which is native to China. Linseed oil cures very slowly, so metallic driers are commonly added to speed the curing. When this is done, the oil is called boiled linseed oil, and it is much easier to use than raw linseed oil for finishing

Different finishes make the wood look different. Clockwise from top right, wax doesn't darken the wood at all. Choose it when you want to keep the wood looking unfinished but with a little sheen. Boiled linseed oil darkens the wood and yellows it. So does polyurethane, but less so than linseed oil. Orange shellac adds a warm orange color to wood. Lacquer adds very little color. And water-based finish adds no color but darkens the wood.

indoor furniture or woodwork. Tung oil cures faster than raw linseed oil, but slower than boiled linseed oil. Driers are not added to tung oil. This oil is rarely used to finish wood because it cures so slowly, and it takes five or more coats to achieve a nice looking and nice feeling surface.

Oil finishes don't cure hard, so you have to wipe off all the excess after each coat. They are easy to apply and are therefore popular. But since they don't "build," these finishes are suited only for nonwear surfaces like entertainment centers and curio shelves.

Varnish. Varnish is made by cooking an oil, such as linseed oil, tung oil, or modified soy bean (soya) oil with a resin. Natural resins like amber and copal were once used, but they have been replaced by synthetic resins like polyurethane and alkyd.

Spar varnish is made with a higher ratio of oil to resin, so the varnish is softer and more flexible, making it better suited for outdoor furniture. Indoor varnish is made with a higher ratio of resin to oil which makes the varnish harder. When built up to three coats, varnish is a very protective and durable finish. It is excellent for floors, tabletops, and kitchen cabinets.

Shellac. Shellac is a natural resin secreted by insects that inhabit certain trees in South Asia. The resin is collected, strained to remove twigs and bug parts, spread into thin sheets, and broken up into flakes. You can buy the flakes and dissolve them in denatured alcohol yourself, or you can buy the shellac already dissolved in cans.

As soon as the shellac is dissolved in alcohol, it begins to deteriorate; the result is that it takes longer to harden and never gets as hard as it does when it is new. Though the process occurs slowly, it's wise to always use shellac that is as freshly made as possible.

Natural shellac has an orange dye tint, which makes it an excellent finish for adding warmth to wood. Bleached (clear) shellac has had the orange color removed. Shellac is an excellent finish for all furniture and woodwork except that which receives a lot of wear.

Lacquer. Lacquer is made from nitrocellulose, which is derived synthetically from cellulose in cotton and wood. To make nitrocellulose more flexible and full-bodied, manufacturers add additional resins, like alkyd and maleic. This blend is then dissolved in lacquer thinner, which is a combination of several solvents. When the solvents evaporate, the lacquer hardens.

Because lacquer dries very quickly, it is usually sprayed. Lacquer is fairly protective and durable, but more importantly, it dries quickly enough that it is already dry before dust has a chance to settle. Lacquer is therefore the finish most commonly used by people who own spray guns, and it is used for all surfaces.

Water-based. Think of water-based finish as latex paint without the pigment. It is made by dispersing droplets of already-cured acrylic or polyurethane resin into a mixture of water and a small amount of solvent. As the water evaporates, the droplets come together; the solvent makes them sticky so that they join to make a film. Then the solvent evaporates as it does in lacquer.

Water-based finishes provide about the same protection and durability as lacquer, and they have less solvent odor and fire risk. They don't yellow and they make brush clean-up easy. On the other hand, they are more difficult to apply because they raise grain, dry very quickly, and don't penetrate very deeply, which causes a washed-out appearance on darker woods. Also, the water in the finish causes metal cans to rust, and the rust can get into the finish.

Bob Flexner
Norman, OK

COMMON FINISHES COMPARED

Here's how the 6 most popular finishes stand up to the most common forms of abuse.

	WAX	OIL	VARNISH	SHELLAC	LACQUER	WATER-BASED
Water resistance	0	1	5	2	3	3
Wear resistance	1	1	5	2	3	4
Solvent resistance	0	2	5	1	3	3
Heat resistance	0	3	5	2	3	3
Acid & alkali resistance	0	1	5	2	3	3

0 = very poor, 1 = poor, 2 = fair, 3 = good, 4 = very good, and 5 = excellent

BUILDING A FINISHING RACK BY BEN ERICKSON

The surest way to prevent runs in a finish is to deal with what causes them: gravity. This finishing rack keeps flat surfaces in a horizontal position while they dry so that the finish can't run or sag.

The rack has a 2 × 4 frame, with 1 × 2 supports to hold the finished parts. Screw on the top brace and base members so that you can easily undo them to vary the width of the racks if necessary. Leave plenty of space between the dividers to insert the finished pieces. If you want, you can add casters so that you can move the rack around the shop.

When using the rack, finish one side of your doors, tabletops, and other parts at a time, and slide them into the rack to dry before finishing the other side.

MATERIALS LIST		
Part	**Quantity**	**Dimensions**
Uprights	2	1½" × 3½" × 46½"
Bases	2	1½" × 3½" × 41"
	2	1½" × 3½" × 30"
Top	1	1½" × 3½" × 30"
Cross braces	2	¾" × 1½" × 60" (cut to fit)
Rack supports	28	¾" × 1½" × 44"
HARDWARE		
Casters	4	3" dia. or larger
Wood screws	As needed	#8 × 1½" and #8 × 3"

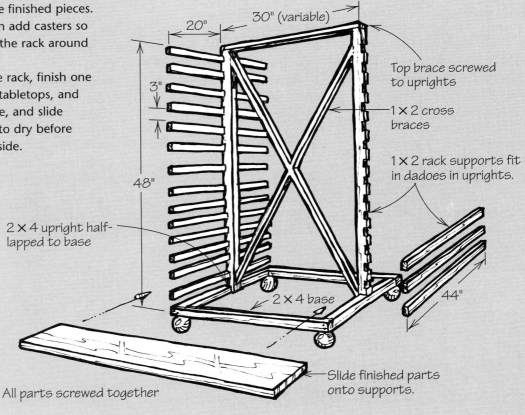

20"

30" (variable)

Top brace screwed to uprights

3"

1 × 2 cross braces

1 × 2 rack supports fit in dadoes in uprights.

48"

2 × 4 upright half-lapped to base

2 × 4 base

44"

All parts screwed together

Slide finished parts onto supports.

Reducing Orange Peel When Spraying Finishes

PROBLEM: *I just bought a new HVLP (high volume, low pressure) spray gun and I can't seem to spray either lacquer or water-based finish without getting a rough surface that looks like the peel of an orange. What am I doing wrong?*

SOLUTION: The condition you're describing is commonly known as orange peel, and it may not be you but the spray gun that is causing the problem. Generally, the more you pay for a spray gun, the finer the atomization the gun can achieve. Finer atomization produces less orange peel and a more level surface. Cheaper spray guns leave more pronounced orange peel.

To remove the orange peel that you have created, you will have to strip it off or sand it so that it is level. In the future, if you're using lacquer, try thinning the finish more to achieve the minimum orange peel possible with your spray gun. Thin it with between two and three parts of lacquer thinner and see if this helps. If you're using a low pressure spray gun, thinning the finish is your only option. But if your spray gun runs off of a high pressure air line, you can try turning up the air pressure to between 30 and 40 psi (pounds per square inch) to reduce orange peel. Thinning the finish and increasing air pressure are the only ways to reduce orange peel in lacquer.

If you're using water-based finish, try spraying several thin coats rather than one or two thick coats. Thin coats of water-based finish result in less orange peel than do thick coats. Allow each coat to cure for at least an hour. Most of the orange peel should disappear.

Bob Flexner
Norman, OK

Dealing with Overspray

PROBLEM: *Whenever I spray the insides of cabinets or drawers with lacquer, I get a lot of overspray that lands back on the surface and makes it feel sandy. Is there any way to prevent this from happening?*

SOLUTION: Add lacquer retarder to the lacquer. This will slow the drying of the lacquer enough so that when the overspray lands on the lacquer, it dissolves into the lacquer. You may have to experiment a little to find the optimum percentage of retarder to add. Retarders from different manufacturers vary significantly. Too much retarder and the lacquer may sag and take so long to dry that it collects dust. Mix too little retarder with your standard lacquer thinner and the problem won't be corrected.

Bob Flexner
Norman, OK

Quick Tip Quick Tip Quick Tip Quick

BRUSHING IN TIGHT SPACES

When I need to apply stain or finish in a really narrow space, I create a custom brush with a right-angle handle. I take a wooden-handle brush that is matched to my finish requirements, and I cut off the handle just above the metal ferrule. Then I glue a piece of scrap so that it is perpendicular to the brush end, creating a low profile brush. Curving the handle and holding it as you would a butter knife gives you better leverage and is easier on the wrist. I like to carve or sand the scrap before gluing it on so that it is comfortable in my hand.

Dennis Slabaugh
Naples, FL

This shop-made brush fits in tight spaces that are hard to reach with a regular one. The curved handle makes it more comfortable to use.

A QUICK SPRAY BOOTH BY KEN BURTON

Spraying is a fast and accurate way to stain or finish your work, but it's also messy. If you don't work in a spray booth, you end up with sticky stain and finish on everything around the project. Fortunately, there's a simple way to solve this problem.

MATERIALS LIST		
Part	**Quantity**	**Dimensions**
Mounting strips	4	1" × 2" × width of plastic
Filter racks	2	1" × 2" × width of window fan
6-mil polyethylene sheets	2	Cut to fit
Furnace filter	1	Size according to window and fan
HARDWARE		
Wood screws	As needed	

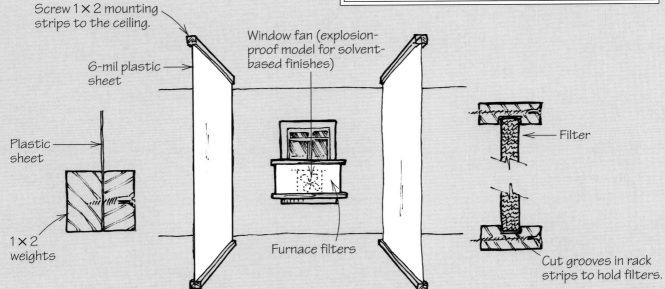

Screw 1 × 2 mounting strips to the ceiling.

6-mil plastic sheet

Window fan (explosion-proof model for solvent-based finishes)

Plastic sheet

1 × 2 weights

Furnace filters

Filter

Cut grooves in rack strips to hold filters.

As the drawing shows, you can make a low-cost, knockdown spray booth with some plastic film, a few furnace filters, and a fan. If you're spraying water-based stains or finishes, you can use a standard window fan. However, since the furnace filters won't catch the solvent in the overspray, if you're spraying any other type of stain or finish, you should use a fan with an explosion-proof motor (available from industrial suppliers).

To make the booth's plastic walls, use 6-mil polyethylene, which is sold through hardware stores and home improvement centers. Screw 1 × 2 mounting strips to one end of the plastic sheets and attach the strips to the ceiling. Add a 1 × 2 "weight" to the other end of each sheet to hold it in position.

The furnace filters are sure to clog, so change them frequently. Also, don't allow the finish to build up on the fan blades. Clean them periodically if necessary. Add more filters if too much finish is getting through.

Reducing Shellac Brush Marks

PROBLEM: *When I use shellac, the brush marks are very visible after the finish dries. Is it the brush, the shellac, or my technique?*

SOLUTION: It could be any one or all of the three. Better quality brushes with a chiseled tip rather than a cutoff, flat tip usually leave less-pronounced brush marks. You can also reduce brush marking by thinning the shellac with denatured alcohol, but the more you thin the shellac, the slower the build and the more coats you will have to apply to get an equivalent film thickness. You need to experiment until you achieve a balance between reduced brush marking and an effective build.

As far as technique goes, keep in mind that shellac dries very fast, so you don't have much time to spread it onto the surface before it starts to become tacky. Once tackiness sets in, any overbrushing will drag the finish and leave more severe brush marking.

Bob Flexner
Norman, OK

Shellac is a quick-drying finish, which means that you can end up with noticeable brush marks if you don't apply it carefully. For best results, apply thin coats and use a good quality brush.

Preventing Brush Marks in Polyurethane

PROBLEM: *When I was finishing a table recently, the oil-based polyurethane I was using tacked up so quickly that I was left with brush marks. What can I do to slow the drying time?*

SOLUTION: Most oil-based polyurethanes are formulated to be too thick to brush right out of the can. Try thinning your finish about 10 to 15 percent with mineral sprits or turpentine. Brush the finish on thinly, applying it in the direction of the grain, not across it. Cover one narrow section entirely with finish, then "tip it off" by holding the brush nearly vertical and lightly dragging its tip in long strokes to evenly distribute the finish. If you tip off as you go, it won't matter if one side of the table is dry before you complete the rest of it. Working in a cool room and out of direct sunlight will also help decelerate the drying time.

Michael Dresdner
Puyallup, WA

Avoiding Sags in Varnish

PROBLEM: *When I finish with varnish, it seems that no matter how carefully I brush, I can't seem to keep it from sagging on vertical surfaces. What's the trick?*

SOLUTION: The trick is to always position your work, or a light, so that you can see a reflection in the surface you are brushing. If you can't see a reflection, you might as well be working blindfolded because you can't see what is happening.

When you can see what's happening, keeping sags from curing in the finish is easy—with any finish. Simply brush over the sagging to pick up some of the finish and spread it out more evenly. Or, you can drag the brush over the lip of a jar to remove the excess. Continue rebrushing until you have removed enough of the finish to stop the sagging.

Bob Flexner
Norman, OK

Lighting that reflects off the surface of your work will highlight sags in the finish (*left*). Without the reflection, the same sags are not visible (*right*).

Finishing Exotic Woods

PROBLEM: *I am building a display case out of curly maple and bubinga. What's the best finish to use and the best technique for applying it?*

SOLUTION: My first choice would be an oil-based exterior polyurethane varnish with UV blockers. It brings out the chatoyance, or changing luster, in wood, has plenty of flexibility to deal with the different rates of wood movement between the maple and bubinga, and the UV blockers will help the bubinga hold its color a bit longer.

How you apply it is up to you. I'll offer you some tips for both brushing and spraying. If you are brushing, first apply a wipe-on coat of thin finish. Cut the varnish in half by adding the recommended solvent, then wipe the finish onto the wood with a clean rag, wipe off any excess, and let it dry. Next thin the varnish by adding 10 to 15 percent thinner and brush on several coats. Sand lightly and leave plenty of drying time between coats.

If you prefer to spray, first cut the varnish with 10 to 15 percent acetone and spray a VERY light fog coat onto the wood. Let it dry for about ten minutes and then spray a thin wet coat. The tacky base coat will help the varnish hang and help prevent sag. Let the finish dry overnight, sand lightly, and repeat the fog/spray procedure for each coat.

Michael Dresdner
Puyallup, WA

Building a Rich, Durable Finish

PROBLEM: *I want the rich color of an oil finish, but also the protection and ultraviolet resistance of lacquer. Can I use oil under lacquer and get both?*

SOLUTION: Oil under lacquer will give you a rich, durable finish but it won't resist ultraviolet radiation. To use the oil-lacquer combination, apply boiled linseed oil or an oil-varnish blend (often sold as "Danish" oil), let it cure, and then apply lacquer. It's critical, though, that you allow the oil to cure fully—it needs a week or so in a warm, dry room. Otherwise, the lacquer will wrinkle when you apply it.

Lacquer will provide you with more protection for the wood than oil alone, but the only commonly available finishes that are UV resistant are boat varnishes.

Bob Flexner
Norman, OK

Applying oil finish under lacquer (*left*) results in a richer looking finish than lacquer alone (*right*).

Building a Black Satin Finish

PROBLEM: *I am finishing some large tabletops with black lacquer. What's the best way to apply this to achieve a satin finish?*

SOLUTION: The best way to apply any lacquer finish, colored or clear, is by spray gun.

I like to start by staining the raw wood with a black dye so that if the finish ever chips, it will show black. Next use a black lacquer primer for the first two coats to seal the wood. Then spray black satin lacquer for as many coats as you need to get the build you want. Because black will show any scuffs or scratches, I like to wet sand before the last two coats with 600-grit sandpaper just to make sure that I have a perfectly smooth surface for the final coats. Satin is best as a "straight-from-the-gun" finish as opposed to one that requires rubbing out. Try to get the last coat perfectly smooth by thinning it slightly with lacquer thinner and do not try to rub it out.

Michael Dredsner
Puyallup, WA

Good Lighting Is the Key to a Good Finish

If you want to get superior results when you finish, you have to be able to see what you're doing, and that means you need light—the right types and properly placed.

Inspecting the finish quality itself calls for stationary lights and a portable light to provide good reflection. When you're inspecting for surface imperfections like "orange peel" (a dimpled-looking finish) or dust nibs, you need to position a portable light so that you're viewing its reflection at about a 60-degree angle away from you. On the other hand, when you're inspecting for inclusions (junk suspended within the finish), the light should be coming from your direction, so that reflections don't obscure your view into the finish.

Inspecting for color correctness is a more difficult process. A color can appear quite different when viewed under different lights. This can mean problems if you want to match the color of a new piece to an existing one under all conditions. The best solution is to outfit your finish area with incandescent lights, cool white fluorescents, and 6,500-degree color-corrected fluorescents, which simulate daylight. That way you can see how the piece will react under all types of lighting.

To match a new project to an old one, inspect a part from the existing project in the room where the piece will reside. Note the type of lighting in the room, including daylight. Then bring the part back to your shop and match it, working under lighting that is similar to the piece's final home.

If you can get the existing part and the new piece to match under all three types of lighting separately, you won't have to worry about color changes due to lighting later on, even if the piece is moved to different lighting conditions. When this isn't practical, just make sure that your work matches under the type of lighting in which it will be viewed.

Tom Brown
Puyallup, WA

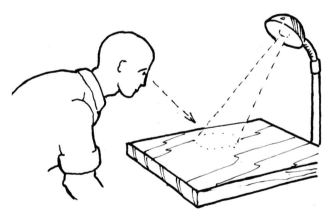

Light set at 60° and pointing toward you reflects on a surface, revealing imperfections such as brush marks and orange peel.

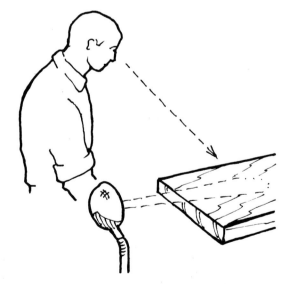

Light set behind you reveals dust and other particles suspended in the finish.

Finding an Odor-Free Finish

PROBLEM: *I finished a set of bureau drawers with an oil finish and it makes my clothes smell. What finish won't cause this?*

SOLUTION: I generally finish drawers with shellac because it's simple to apply, it seals the wood adequately, and it's natural looking. Shellac will give you a smooth finish with just light sanding, and, unlike oils and varnishes, it won't smell bad when trapped in an enclosed space.

You can make your own shellac by dissolving shellac flakes, which are available in orange or blond colors, in denatured alcohol. For sealing wood, I recommend a "1-pound cut"—1 pound of shellac flakes to 1 gallon of alcohol. Most canned shellac is prepared as a 3-pound cut, so you'll have to dilute it: Two parts of denatured alcohol to one part of shellac will make a 1-pound cut.

Brush two coats of this mixture onto all the drawers' interior surfaces, sanding lightly with 220-grit stearated sandpaper after each coat dries. Rub the final surface with a soft cloth to remove any dust and to produce a satiny luster. If you want, you can apply a coat of paste wax for more protection against smudges and dirt.

A note about shelf life: Most canned shellac has a shelf life of 18 months to 2 years from the manufacture date that is stamped on the can. When shellac is initially dissolved in alcohol, it begins a process of "esterification" that makes it dry slower and softer the more it ages. If you plan to apply a topcoat, your shellac should be as fresh as possible, preferably less than 6 months old. A soft shellac sealer coat can cause subsequent topcoats to develop tiny cracks, known as alligatoring. For drawer finishing, freshness is of less concern.

Ellis Walentine
Coopersburg, PA

Stopping Bleed-Back with an Oil Finish

PROBLEM: *The oil finish I used bled back out of the wood, where it dried as shiny spots. What happened, and what can I do now to fix it?*

SOLUTION: There are two causes for bleed-back. The finish is either pulled back out of the pores by the thinner as the thinner evaporates, or the finish is warmed in the pores and comes back out as it expands. Warming occurs if you rub the finish vigorously, or if you take the wood out into the sun or from a cool garage into a warm house.

Bleeding can occur on any wood. But it's more likely on large-pored woods, such as oak, and on any parts of wood that have unusually large pore or cell cavities. Once these pores or cavities have been sealed (usually by the first or second coat of finish), bleeding will no longer occur.

The only way to deal with bleeding is to wipe it off as it occurs. Apply the finish early enough in the day so that you will have time for removing all the bleeding. Wipe the wood with a dry cloth every hour or so until the bleeding stops. If the bleeding has already cured, you can remove the shiny spots of finish either by abrading or stripping. Try abrading with fine steel wool before you resort to stripping. Either way, apply another coat of finish to replace the finish you have removed.

Bob Flexner
Norman, OK

This piece of ash shows the telltale signs of bleed-back: shiny spots of finish that dried on the surface a few hours after the wet finish had been wiped off.

Creating Fade-Free Outdoor Finishes

PROBLEM: *The clear exterior finish that I used on my front door didn't prevent the wood from turning gray when it was exposed to the elements. What finish will do the job?*

SOLUTION: Two-part polyurethanes are your best bet. Marine supply stores sell several two-part polyurethanes that work well. See "Sources," beginning on page 298. One is WEST SYSTEM 1000 Varnish and another is Interthane Plus. Though expensive, these finishes are nonyellowing and will keep the sun from fading your woodwork. That said, all exterior finishes on wood require maintenance, meaning that you'll need to refinish the door annually or twice-yearly in order for the finish to last. (Check the label of the product you're using.) The good news is that the finishes mentioned here are designed to wear from the outside first—not at the wood line—so regular scuffing and recoating is all that's necessary. If you want to preserve the colors further, keep the door out of direct sunlight.

Michael Dresdner
Puyallup, WA

Dealing with Panel Shrinkage

PROBLEM: *My frame-and-panel doors looked fine when I finished the project, but now a strip of unfinished wood shows along the long grain edges of all the panels. What went wrong and what can I do?*

SOLUTION: I suspect that you used solid wood to make your panels and that you finished the doors after you assembled them. So, when the panels shrank in response to changes in the moisture content of the surrounding air, a strip of unfinished wood appeared at the edges of the panels.

To blend, apply the same stain and finish treatment to your unfinished strip of wood as you did to the rest of the panel. If you sprayed on the topcoat, however, it will be easier if you wipe on a varnish or oil finish to the newly stained strip. **AVOIDING THE PROBLEM:** I finish my panels before gluing up the doors. In this way, should the panel shrink, the newly exposed wood will have a coat of finish on it and no one will notice a thing.

Robert Treanor
San Francisco, CA

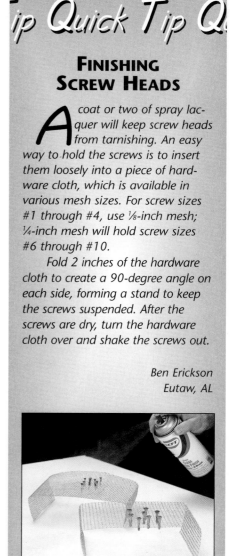

Quick Tip Q

FINISHING SCREW HEADS

A coat or two of spray lacquer will keep screw heads from tarnishing. An easy way to hold the screws is to insert them loosely into a piece of hardware cloth, which is available in various mesh sizes. For screw sizes #1 through #4, use ⅛-inch mesh; ¼-inch mesh will hold screw sizes #6 through #10.

Fold 2 inches of the hardware cloth to create a 90-degree angle on each side, forming a stand to keep the screws suspended. After the screws are dry, turn the hardware cloth over and shake the screws out.

Ben Erickson
Eutaw, AL

Protecting Stains from Topcoats

PROBLEM: *I applied a clear topcoat over a project that I'd stained, and the topcoat muddied the look of the stain. What happened?*

SOLUTION: Sometimes the solvents in a clear finish partially dissolve the stain. As the two materials mix, the resulting mess looks cloudy and uneven. Also, when you apply one finish over another, the chemicals in the bottom layer sometimes keep the top layer from drying properly.

To prevent these problems, seal one layer of finish with a coat of white shellac (a 1-pound cut) before applying a different material. Shellac is compatible with almost all other finishes. When applied between coats of incompatible materials, it keeps them from reacting with each other.

Nick Engler
West Milton, OH

ONE-DAY SPRAY FINISHING STRATEGIES

It used to take me a minimum of two days to apply a spray finish to my projects. I would completely finish one side, first coat to last, and then have to wait for that finish to dry thoroughly before I could flip the project over and finish the other side.

Then I came up with a "one-day" approach. It's not only faster than the way I used to finish, it also minimizes overspray by keeping both sides of a panel wet during each application. And less overspray means less rubbing out after the finish is dry.

The basic thrust of my methods is shown in these drawings. It will help you get whole spray jobs done quickly and it also will make handling project parts more convenient.

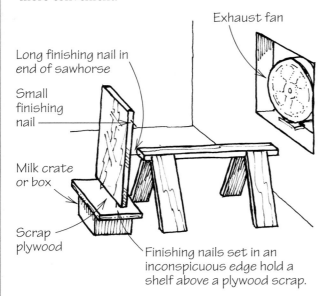

Exhaust fan

Long finishing nail in end of sawhorse

Small finishing nail

Milk crate or box

Scrap plywood

Finishing nails set in an inconspicuous edge hold a shelf above a plywood scrap.

To spray shelves, insert small nails in the 3 edges that are not visible (above). **The nails support the shelves and are used as handles to rotate them. On cabinet doors** (below), **locate the support nails in the least visible edge and use a screw in the hinge mortise as a handle.**

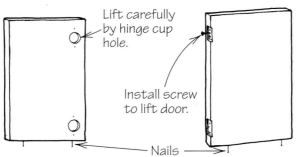

Lift carefully by hinge cup hole.

Install screw to lift door.

Nails

SMALL DOORS AND SHELVES

Since these are usually light parts, the key here is to hold them so that they won't be blown around when you spray. The drawing at top left shows how I use 6d or 8d finish nails to support a workpiece for spraying. The nails are always placed in the least conspicuous edge—typically the back of a shelf and the bottom of a door. In shelves, I also put a small nail in the sides of the panel to serve as a handle for picking up the panel. The holes can be filled if necessary after finishing. For cabinet doors, where I don't want a nail hole in the edge, I put the nail (or a screw) in the hinge mounting screw holes, as shown at bottom left.

I spray the less important face first, then flip the shelf or door around, holding it by the nails in the edges. Next I can spray the edges and the good face. Then I lift the door by the nails and stand it up against a wall, leaning it on one of the corners to dry.

LARGE DOORS

Large entry and passage doors can also be finished entirely in one day by screwing lag screws into the top and bottom edges, as shown at the top of the opposite page. After you spray one side, you and a helper can flip the door over and rest it once again on the screws so that you can finish the second side.

HEADBOARDS

To finish bed parts like headboards, I nail or screw braces to the bottom of both headboard posts. The braces act as skis that allow the headboard to stand up, which keeps the bottom of the posts clean during the finishing process.

CABINETS

I'm a big fan of using dollies to finish cabinets. They raise the project off of the ground enough that you don't stir up dust as you spray. In most cases, the dolly can be rotated while you spray, so you don't have to walk around it and risk dragging the spray hose across the wet finish. Also, you can simply roll the dolly out of the way if you have something else to finish. I often complete my staining, sealing, topcoat, rubbing

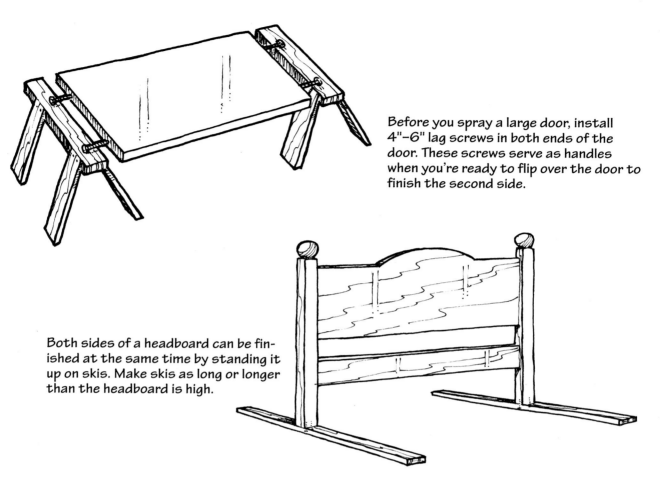

Before you spray a large door, install 4"–6" lag screws in both ends of the door. These screws serve as handles when you're ready to flip over the door to finish the second side.

Both sides of a headboard can be finished at the same time by standing it up on skis. Make skis as long or longer than the headboard is high.

out, and sometimes assembly procedures with the cabinet remaining on the same dolly at all times.

Before you employ these procedures, check the drying time on the finish you're using. Not all finishes are suitable for a one-day job. Lacquer dries and is ready for recoating within 30 minutes, so up to five coats can be applied in one day, as long as the humidity is low. Water-based finish will cure in about two hours, if the weather is warm and dry. And if you are spraying shellac, you can apply two coats per day. Varnish is the exception: It takes quite long to dry, and it's more likely than lacquer or shellac to sag on vertical surfaces. All varnishes, no matter how they are applied, dry slowly, so you'll be limited to one coat per day.

Mark Romano
Gibbstown, NJ

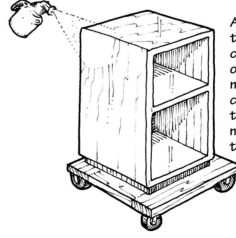

A dolly allows you to rotate the cabinet instead of you having to move around the cabinet. Spray the inside of cabinets first, then the outside.

PRODUCING A FLAW-FREE SPRAY FINISH

Spraying a finish is a messy process, but it's fast and it produces the most level finish possible. The physical act of spraying is very simple, but it is important to keep a few things in mind as you work:

Keep square to the work. Always hold the gun perpendicular to the piece you're spraying, as shown at right. If you tilt it vertically or swing it in an arc, it will distribute the finish unevenly. It helps to keep your wrist locked and to use your elbow and shoulder to direct the gun.

Work smoothly. Move the gun at a steady, even pace. If you move it at irregular speeds, the finish will build up unevenly.

Ease up at the edges. At the end of each stroke, ease up on the trigger so that only air or nothing at all passes through the nozzle. This reduces waste and overspray, and it cuts down on finish buildup on the nozzle. Also, if you work this way, you'll get less puddling on horizontal surfaces and fewer runs and sags on vertical ones.

Overlap your strokes. When spraying a large flat surface, overlap each stroke by about 50 percent. This way, as you move across the surface, you will deposit an even thickness.

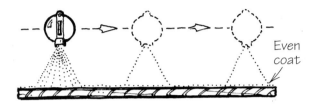

Spray gun, held 6"–10" from surface

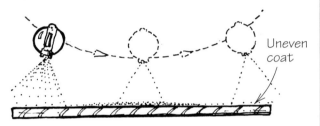

To produce an even coat, move your gun parallel with the surface when spraying (top), not in an arc pattern (bottom).

Sequence for Spraying a Table

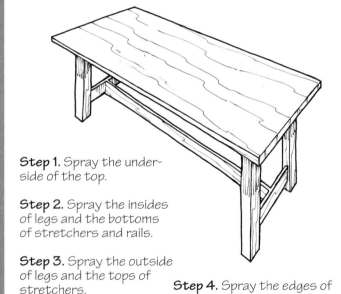

Step 1. Spray the underside of the top.

Step 2. Spray the insides of legs and the bottoms of stretchers and rails.

Step 3. Spray the outside of legs and the tops of stretchers.

Step 4. Spray the edges of the top and the sides of rails.

Step 5. Spray the top, overlapping each stroke by 50%.

Spray the perimeter first. When spraying an item that has a broad, flat surface, like a tabletop or cabinet door, spray the edges before spraying the surface. This will reduce the likelihood of overspray on the surface, which causes roughness.

For more complicated assemblies, spray the least important parts first. You want to reduce the possibility of overspray landing on visible parts after they have been sprayed, so spray the least important surfaces before starting on the ones that will be seen. The drawing at left shows how you can apply this idea to a table and base.

Don't douse the corners. If you spray directly into inside corners, you're likely to get sag and runs. Instead, spray each side right up to the corner. This will produce the most even buildup with the least overspray.

Bob Flexner
Norman, OK

Fixing Finishes

Fixing a Lacquer Finish That "Blushes"

PROBLEM: *I just sprayed lacquer on a small tabletop and the dry finish has a milky look in some areas. What should I do?*

SOLUTION: This condition is called blushing. It is caused by moisture in the air condensing on the lacquer, where it gets into the film and can't evaporate before the film cures. The blushing may go away by itself within a couple of hours. If it doesn't, there are several ways to remove it.

- Wait for a drier day and spray some lacquer thinner onto the surface. The thinner will redissolve the lacquer and allow the moisture to evaporate.
- Spray lacquer retarder, or a mixture of lacquer retarder and lacquer thinner, onto the surface. The more humid the weather, the higher the percentage of retarder you'll need. The lacquer retarder will redissolve the lacquer and allow enough time for the moisture to evaporate.
- Rub the surface with an abrasive, like fine steel wool. The blushing is usually right at the surface of the film. By removing a little of the film, you remove the blushing.

Lacquer finishes can "blush," or turn milky, if the lacquer is applied under humid conditions. To remove the blushing, spray lacquer thinner or lacquer retarder over the finish to redissolve the finish and let the moisture escape.

AVOIDING THE PROBLEM: The way to prevent blushing from occurring in humid weather is to add some lacquer retarder to the lacquer before applying it. You will need to experiment a little to get the most effective combination of lacquer retarder and lacquer thinner. If you add more retarder than necessary, you slow the drying of the lacquer more than necessary, which allows time for more dust to settle and stick to the surface.

Bob Flexner
Norman, OK

Preventing Shellac from Clouding

PROBLEM: *Whenever I use shellac I get a cloudy sheen. What am I doing wrong?*

SOLUTION: Humid weather is often the culprit when a shellac finish clouds over. As the alcohol in the shellac dries, it cools the finished surface, causing moisture in the air to condense on the finish. This prompts the clouding, or blush.

The only way I know to avoid shellac blush is to add a compatible retarder to your shellac mixture. One such retarder, intended for lacquer, is ethylene glycol butyl ether (EB), also called butyl cellosolve; it's available at Sherwin Williams and James B. Day stores. Add 10 to 15 percent EB by volume to the shellac. The trade-off is that the extended drying time also gives floating dust more time to settle into your finish.

One way to get rid of blush in an existing shellac finish is to French polish the surface. The heat created in the polishing process will remove the blush and prevent it from returning.

Michael Dresdner
Puyallup, WA

Dealing with Dust in a Finish

PROBLEM: *Whenever I use polyurethane on my woodworking projects, I end up with dust curing in the finish. What can I do to prevent this?*

SOLUTION: Start reducing dust before you apply the finish. For example, you should keep your brush wrapped up between uses to reduce dust contamination, and wipe the surface of the project with a tack cloth just before you apply the finish. It may also be helpful to strain the varnish if you have used it previously, and wet mop the floor just before finishing to keep down the dust. But you will probably still have some dust settling in the finish. To remove this, sand between coats and after the last coat.

Sand between coats with very fine sandpaper—320-grit or finer. After your last coat, sand with 600-grit sandpaper and add water or oil as a lubricant.

Finally, rub the surface with #0000 steel wool, pumice and oil, rottenstone and oil, or a commercial rubbing compound to get the sheen you want. You should be very pleased, then, with the way the finish looks and feels.

Bob Flexner
Norman, OK

If dust mars your finish despite your best efforts to control it, smooth the surface with fine-grit sandpaper, then rub it to the sheen you want.

Dealing with Cracking Lacquer

PROBLEM: *I sprayed a catalyzed lacquer on an entertainment center and as the finish cured it developed cracks. What caused this and how can I fix it?*

SOLUTION: You did not mention whether you sprayed the lacquer over an existing finish or built it up from raw wood. Spraying catalyzed lacquer on top of a noncatalyzed finish will often cause such cracking. So if you're spraying over an existing finish and you're unsure of exactly what it is, stay away from catalyzed lacquer.

Assuming that you built up the finish from the raw wood using only catalyzed lacquers and sealers, the cracking may be due to one of two factors. The first is "violating the window." These coatings generally have a recoat window— a period of time during which it is safe to recoat. This should be clearly spelled out on the technical data sheet that most companies make available with their coatings.

If you recoat too soon, or in some cases too late, the finish can crack as it cures.

The other possibility is a faulty mixture. The lacquer catalyzes due to the action of an acid that you must add to the lacquer prior to spraying. The acid must be measured out exactly and not estimated, since putting in the wrong amount can cause anything from a minor change in sheen to the cracking you describe.

Now for the bad news. The only way to repair the condition is to strip off the coating and refinish the piece. Unfortunately, there is no way to chemically "re-knit" catalyzed lacquer.

Michael Dredsner
Puyallup, WA

KEEPING DUST OFF OF YOUR WORK

*I*f you've just carefully finished a project, the last thing you want to do is expose it to the dust that may settle out of the air in your shop. To protect the piece, build a dust "umbrella" using scrap wood for the feet and scrap plywood or cardboard for the top.*

Nick Engler
West Milton, OH

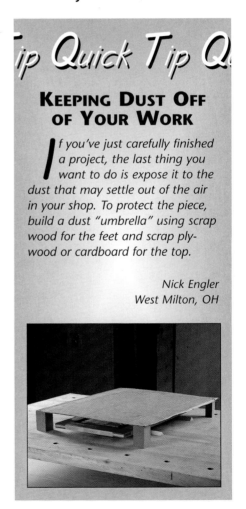

Helping Tacky Varnish Cure

PROBLEM: *I brushed varnish onto my oak table two days ago and the varnish is still tacky. The table is in my basement workshop where the temperature gets down to about 40°F at night. But the room temperature is in the 60s most of the day. Isn't that warm enough to allow the varnish to dry?*

SOLUTION: Temperature in the 60's is borderline; in the 40's is much too cold. Cool, damp conditions slow the curing of varnish and most other finishes significantly. Usually the finish cures eventually, but it collects a lot of dust in the meantime. Take the table upstairs and put it in a room where the temperature is 70°F or warmer and remains that way overnight. The finish should then cure quickly.

Bob Flexner
Norman, OK

Removing Glue Residue

PROBLEM: *While gluing up my ash coffee table, I left a little glue on the surface of the wood. I didn't notice it until I applied the stain. Now I have some light spots where the glue is. What can I do to fix it?*

SOLUTION: You will have to remove the glue from the wood and restain. There are two ways to remove the glue: Abrade it or dissolve it. You can remove the glue mechanically by scraping it off with a hand scraper or sanding it. Either way, you should then finish-sand the wood with exactly the same final-grit sandpaper you used to sand the table originally.

You can also soften the glue with water (hot water or water mixed with white vinegar works fast), or a solvent like toluene or xylene, and then scrub the glue off of the surface. You will need to use a toothbrush or brass-wire bristle brush to remove the glue if it is in the grain. Again, finish by sanding with the final-grit sandpaper you used originally on the wood.

Both of these methods will remove the stain from the area you are working on, so you will have to replace the stain. Because it's not likely that you will get exactly the same stain effect after you remove the glue, you should do the same removal steps over an entire part (top, leg, rail) or even on the entire table. As long as you've done everything the same on an entire part, that part should stain evenly, but it may be lighter than other parts. If it is too light, or if the staining is uneven on that part, apply more stain and sand the part while it's wet using the same final-grit sandpaper or one grit lower. Then remove the excess stain. If you can't get the coloring even, you will have to strip the table with paint-and-varnish remover and begin again. You don't have to remove all of the stain from the wood if you strip, just make the coloring even.

AVOIDING THE PROBLEM: If you're concerned that glue spots may affect your stain, you can find the spots before applying stain by wiping the wood with water or paint thinner. The liquid will make the areas that are coated with glue look lighter.

Bob Flexner
Norman, OK

With some help from an old tooth-brush, a mixture of hot water and vinegar will dissolve yellow glue that has dried in the pores of an open-grained wood like this oak.

Hiding Glue Spots after Finishing

PROBLEM: *When I applied stain to a jelly cupboard I'm finishing, I noticed a few glue spots that are too obvious to ignore. Is there a way to hide them, or do I have to resand and restain the spotted areas?*

SOLUTION: It would be rather inefficient to sand down large areas of a project for the sake of a couple of unsightly glue spots. Instead, coat these spots with a special touch-up stain, like Mohawk Blend-all. Just dissolve a small amount of the touch-up powder (see "Sources," beginning on page 298) in French padding lacquer or thinned down clear shellac; then apply it with an artist's brush. It dries in 30 minutes or less and is compatible with lacquer or shellac topcoats. As long as the glue spots don't cover more than a half inch or so of space, they can be coated over with varnish.

Mark Romano
Gibbstown, NJ

To disguise glue spots, blend your own touch-up stain from powdered stains and clear shellac, and use it before applying the topcoat of finish.

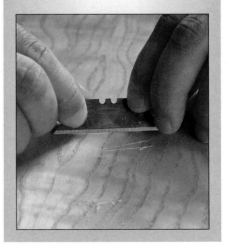

Shortcuts to a Hand-Rubbed Look

PROBLEM: *Can I get a hand-rubbed look without all that rubbing?*

SOLUTION: Yes, if you carefully prepare the surface for the finish. To prepare the wood, sand with successive grits, working from 80-grit to 100-grit and then to 120-grit sandpaper. After this, wet the surface with a damp cloth to raise the grain. When the surface is dry, sand again using 150-grit or finer sandpaper. This removes the rough wood fibers and leaves a smooth and level surface.

After sanding, if you intend to apply a stain, lay the stain in two coats, allowing good drying time between coats. If the stain raises the grain a little, go over the surface lightly with #00 steel wool.

Next apply some kind of sealer—I've found that shellac works great. It can be thinned down with denatured alcohol and applied very liberally. If necessary go over the surface again with #00 steel wool.

At this point apply a good finish in light coats, again allowing each coat to dry completely before applying the next. I find that tung oil gives me the best hand-rubbed look. I apply three coats, rubbing the wood with steel wool between each coat.

Lastly, apply a good furniture paste wax. Allow the wax to dry completely and buff with a soft cotton cloth (old bath towels work great). When you are finished, you'll have a very smooth and velvety feeling finish that was achieved with minimal hand rubbing.

Rick Wright
Schnecksville, PA

Fixing Color Variations in Cherry Projects

PROBLEM: *I made two end tables out of cherry a year ago. I finished one of them right away with Formby's tung oil, but I didn't get the other one finished until last week. Even though I used the exact same container of tung oil, the table I just finished is lighter than the other. What happened, and how can I make the two tables match?*

SOLUTION: There are several possible causes for the color difference. First, cherry darkens with age. So if you finish-sanded the second table before you applied the finish, that table would be lighter than the first table which has darkened for an entire year.

Second, the product you used, Formby's tung oil, is not tung oil but rather varnish thinned with paint thinner. All varnishes darken as they age, so the varnish on the first table will have darkened some during the year.

At this point you can either live with the difference, which will become less noticeable as both tables age, or you can strip, sand, and refinish the first table using the same finish.

Bob Flexner
Norman, OK

Improving Gloss on a Low-Sheen Surface

PROBLEM: *I finished a coffee table with three coats of satin polyurethane. Now my wife tells me that she wants the table to be shinier. I tried waxing it, but that wasn't enough. Is there any way to raise the gloss without having to start over?*

SOLUTION: Yes. The flattening agents in the satin polyurethane cause the surface of the film to be rough. This is what produces the satin effect. To raise the sheen, just sand the surface with very fine sandpaper (1,000-grit or finer), then rub it with rottenstone and mineral oil or a commercial rubbing compound.

Bob Flexner
Norman, OK

Using ultra-fine abrasives, you can change a satin polyurethane finish into a glossy one.

Painting Wood

Sealing Medium-Density Fiberboard (MDF)

PROBLEM: *I'm painting cabinets and cabinet doors made of medium-density fiberboard (MDF), but the raw edges keep soaking up the paint. What can I do?*

SOLUTION: You need to seal the edges before painting, and the best product is pigmented shellac-based sealer, which is available at most paint stores under brand names like Kilz and BIN. You can apply numerous coats in one day because it dries in about 30 minutes, and it's easy to sand between coats. I like to load up a paint brush and spot seal the end grain first, as shown. Once the edges are fully sealed, I prime everything with the shellac-based sealer. It can be brushed, rolled, or sprayed. I apply two sealer coats before topcoating with paint. I usually use three sealer coats under lacquer.

Mark Romano
Gibbstown, NJ

The porous edges of an MDF panel need to be sealed thoroughly, or they'll sop up the paint. Just brush on a sealer, like shellac, and sand after 30 minutes or so. With the edges sealed, you can paint the faces and edges at the same time.

Hiding Unsightly Pine Knots

PROBLEM: *I painted my new pine hutch recently, and ever since then, the knots and sap streaks have been bleeding through. What can I do to hide them?*

SOLUTION: The resins in pine are used to make turpentine, so it's not surprising that knots will bleed through paint. To prevent knots from bleeding through paint, you need to seal them thoroughly. Make sure that the paint you applied is completely dry, then spot-prime the knots and streaks with two coats of a pigmented shellac-based sealer, like Kilz or BIN. These are commonly available at paint stores and home centers. Once the sealer is dry, apply a topcoat of paint.

AVOIDING THE PROBLEM: Next time, after you sand your cabinet, scrub it down with a rag saturated with naphtha. Then apply at least two coats of pigmented shellac-based sealer as a primer. Spot-sand the primed areas; then apply the topcoat.

Mark Romano
Gibbstown, NJ

Pine knots will stubbornly bleed through regular paint no matter how many coats you apply. To hide them, seal the wood first with a shellac-based sealer.

Dealing with Cedar Oil Bleed-Through

PROBLEM: *I painted the outside of a cedar chest with a good quality latex paint, but it looks like the oils from the wood have bled through the paint. How can I hide them?*

SOLUTION: Some woods, like cedar, fir, mahogany, and redwood, have oils in them which tend to bleed through paint, leaving a stain on the surface. To prevent bleed-through, you have to prime with an oil-based primer or a primer that is formulated to stop bleeding. Two coats of primer are often recommended. Before priming, you should seal knots with pigmented shellac-based sealer. To fix your chest, you'll have to seal the affected areas with the shellac-based sealer and repaint.

Ben Erickson
Eutaw, AL

Coating Decorative Accents

PROBLEM: *I painted some decorative accents on a blanket chest with oil-based paint, then applied clear lacquer over the whole thing. The painted accents bubbled up and crinkled. What went wrong?*

SOLUTION: Oil-based paints and lacquer coatings are not compatible. Next time use latex or water-based paints for your accents. When they are sufficiently dry (allow them to dry overnight preferably), you can apply the clear coat. If you must accent with oil-based paint, use varnish to coat over it.

Mark Romano
Gibbstown, NJ

Keeping Brass Shining Brightly

PROBLEM: *The brass hardware on my new wall cabinet has already started to tarnish. What can I do to keep it bright?*

SOLUTION: To keep brass looking new, apply a coat of spray lacquer to the hardware before you install it. First, though, wash the hardware in mild soap or detergent, then dry it thoroughly. To avoid getting fingerprints on the brass, which can show after the lacquer is applied, you should wear a pair lightweight gloves when you handle the hardware.

Tom Begnal
Kent, CT

Painting Pressure-Treated Pine

PROBLEM: *I painted a deck that I built from pressure-treated pine, and the paint is peeling after just a few months. What went wrong and how can I get the paint to stick?*

SOLUTION: Pressure-treated pine lumber is usually sold without being dried after treatment, so the pressure-treated wood that you bring home from the building supply store has a much higher moisture content than the outside air has. If the wood is painted, the interior moisture will try to equalize itself with the outside air, but the paint film will prevent it from doing this. In its bid to escape confinement, the moisture will cause the paint film to blister and peel.

The best remedy for your deck is to strip the old paint, then recoat the wood with a breathable latex primer and topcoat. The moisture will be able to escape through the paint rather than around it, preventing blistering and peeling.

AVOIDING THE PROBLEM: To build a deck, buy the wood well in advance, sticker it in a covered location like a shed, and allow enough time for the moisture content to equalize with the outside air. Fans blowing through the stack will greatly decrease drying time. You can also install the wood and let it dry in place (be prepared for some warping as it dries), then paint it.

Ben Erickson
Eutaw, AL

TOOL MAINTENANCE AND SHARPENING SOLUTIONS

TABLE SAW SOLUTIONS

Adding a Table Saw Kill Switch 249
Using Saw-Blade Stabilizers 249
Dust Collection on a Contractor's Saw 250
Keeping Scraps Away from the Blade 250
Auxiliary Fence for the Table Saw 251
Preventing Rust on Machine Tables 251
Twenty-Minute Tune-Up: The Table Saw 252

BAND SAW SOLUTIONS

Correcting a Wandering Band Saw Blade 253
Keeping Band Saw Blades Resin-Free 253
Cutting Small Stock on the Band Saw 254
Choosing Band Saw Speeds 254
Avoiding a Burned Cut 255
Supporting Large Work on the Band Saw 255
Twenty-Minute Tune-Up: The Band Saw 256

JOINTER SOLUTIONS

Diagnosing Common Jointer Woes 258
Skewed-Up Jointing 258
Twenty-Minute Tune-Up: The Jointer 259

OTHER STATIONARY MACHINES

Preventing Dents When Thickness Planing 260
Dealing with Chipped Planer Knives 260
Turning Ovals on the Lathe 260

Maintaining a Lathe Bed 261
Routing on the Drill Press 261
Leveling a Drill Press Table 261

ROUTER SOLUTIONS

Preventing Bit Creep 262
Easy-On, Easy-Off Router Fence 263
Freeing Stuck Router Bits 263
Grinding Custom Router Bits 264

HAND TOOL SOLUTIONS

Resharpening a Dovetail Saw 265
Tuning a New Hand Plane 266
Securing Japanese Chisel Hoops 268
Preventing Clogged Hand Planes 268
Keeping Files and Rasps Sharp 268

SHARPENING SOLUTIONS

Grinding with a Belt Sander 269
Taming a Vibrating Grinder 269
Keeping Your Temper 270
Sharpening with Waterstones 270
Choosing Grinding Wheels 270
Making Slip Stones for Gouges 271
Making Sharpening "Stones" for Gouges 271
Hand-Holding a Sharpening Stone 272
Flattening Gouged Waterstones 272
Sharpening Chisels and Plane Irons 273

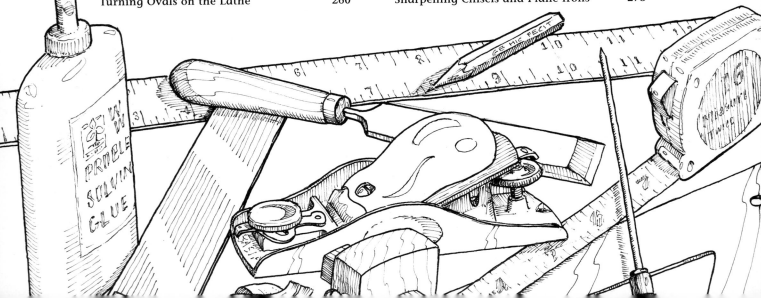

Table Saw Solutions

Adding a Table Saw Kill Switch

PROBLEM: *How can I install a kill switch on my table saw so that I can turn it off without letting go of a work piece?*

SOLUTION: You can install a knee- or foot-operated shut-off, often called a panic switch, on your table saw by hinging a piece of wood or plywood from the top of the switch box so that it hangs in front of the push buttons. Drill a hole in the board for access to the "on" button and you can then turn the saw off by pressing the lever with either your knee or the tip of your foot.

Andy Rae
Lenhartsville, PA

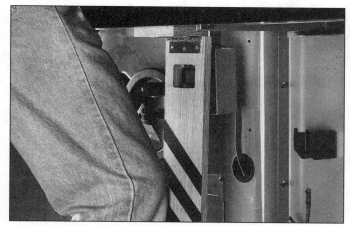

This knee-operated kill switch is easy to get used to. It makes using the table saw safer, especially when you want to switch the saw off without letting go of the workpiece.

Using Saw-Blade Stabilizers

PROBLEM: *I'm thinking of adding saw-blade stabilizers to my table saw to improve the quality of the cuts. Do they really work?*

SOLUTION: Saw-blade stabilizers dampen vibrations in a running blade, reducing noise and improving cut quality. Although they won't give you a miracle cut on a badly warped blade or reduce arbor runout, they can improve cutting with a blade in good condition. Normally, I use stabilizers only when cutting with thin-kerf blades. A stabilizer helps stiffen these blades, which tend to deflect slightly during cutting. I use a stabilizer on a standard 1/8-inch-kerf blade when I'm cutting veneer plywood because it gives me the least chipping.

I usually mount a single stabilizer on the left side of the blade. However, when using an "ultra-thin" (0.064-inch-kerf) blade, I sandwich the blade between two stabilizers for maximum rigidity. If you sandwich the blade, remember to reset your saw fence cursor if you have one: A stabilizer on the inside of the blade changes the blade's reference to the fence.

Depending on their diameter, stabilizers will limit your depth of cut, so you may want to buy a couple of sizes. I use several stabilizers with diameters ranging from 3 to 6 inches.

Matt ver Steeg
Johnston, IA

RELATED INFO:
Cutting Veneered Plywood without Tear-Out, page 77

Dust Collection
on a Contractor's Saw

PROBLEM: *I want to connect a dust collector to my table saw, but it has an open base. How can I do it?*

SOLUTION: After years of sweeping under my contractor-type table saw, I finally devised a way to collect most of the sawdust *before* it hits the floor.

I made a bridle-jointed frame out of 1 × 2s with inside dimensions matching those of the opening in the table saw base. Then I drilled holes for machine bolts in the frame and base. I epoxied the machine bolts in the base holes. Four washers and wing nuts and a standard kitchen garbage bag were all it took to complete the job.

Stephen R. Drummer
Kasota, MN

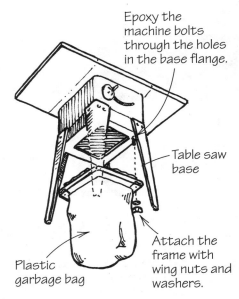

Epoxy the machine bolts through the holes in the base flange.

Table saw base

Attach the frame with wing nuts and washers.

Plastic garbage bag

A plastic garbage bag attached to a wooden frame makes for convenient dust collection on a contractor-type table saw.

ANOTHER VIEW: If you close in the bottom of your saw with a panel that has a vacuum port and plug any small holes around the saw body, you can collect about 80 percent of the sawdust. That's pretty good for the table saw because some dust inevitably gets thrown upward with the blade rotation. But keep in mind that a table saw requires a dust collector capable of inhaling at least 300 cubic feet per minute (cfm), so a properly sized collector is a must. To seal the base, you can buy an accessory panel that fits most contractors' saws, or you can make one from plywood scrap. To catch as much of the remaining dust as possible, you'll have to close off the back of the saw with a panel. To do this, cut a piece of plywood to fit around the motor support and belt, and attach it to the saw with a few sheet metal screws. While this won't allow the blade to tilt, it's easy to remove the panel for those occasional angled cuts.

Kelly Mehler
Berea, KY

Quick Tip Quick Tip Quick Tip Quick

KEEPING SCRAPS AWAY FROM THE BLADE

The kids in my beginning woodworking class were making some small puzzles the other day. Everything was going well until we started cutting the pieces to final length on the table saw. The cutoff from the first piece vibrated into the blade and—"PING"—it sent everyone ducking for cover.

Not a good situation—the kids were scared enough of the table saw as it was. To have each student shut off the machine in between cuts so that they could recover their scrap would have taken next to forever (or at least into lunch period). So I reached for the blow gun we keep hooked up to our air compressor. We clamped the gun in position so that it blew each cutoff away from the blade, as shown. This kept everyone safe and added a little lesson about problem-solving and efficiency to boot. Who could ask for more?

Ken Burton
New Tripoli, PA

A blow gun from an air compressor (or the backwash from a shop vacuum) can keep scraps or small parts away from your saw blade. For better control of the air stream, you can hook up a tap valve with a length of ¼" copper tube and a quick-release air fitting (inset).

SHOP-MADE SOLUTIONS

AUXILIARY FENCE FOR THE TABLE SAW BY ANDY RAE

When cutting very thin strips or when rabbeting with a dado blade, you need to add a wooden fence to whatever stock table saw fence you use. Otherwise, you risk damaging both your fence and your blade.

I use this drop-on plywood fence over my table saw's fence for these situations. Make the parts from good-quality hardwood veneer plywood so that you'll have a flat, smooth surface for your work to ride against. Glue the sides and the top into dadoes cut into the end pieces. Aim for a sliding fit over your existing fence. To use the fence, just drop it over your table saw's fence—no hardware or clamps are necessary. When one side gets used and abused, simply turn the fence around and use the other side.

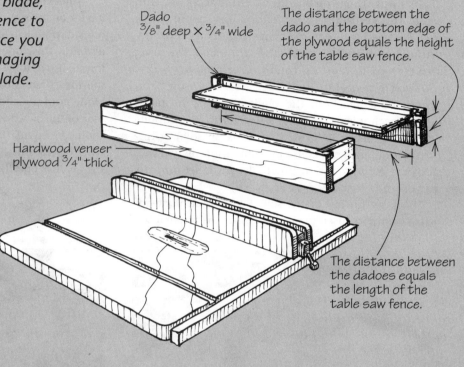

Dado
³/₈" deep × ³/₄" wide

Hardwood veneer plywood ³/₄" thick

The distance between the dado and the bottom edge of the plywood equals the height of the table saw fence.

The distance between the dadoes equals the length of the table saw fence.

Preventing Rust on Machine Tables

PROBLEM: *No matter how carefully I clean and wax my machine tables, eventually spots of rust appear. How can I prevent rust altogether?*

SOLUTION: Rust typically appears as spots because corrosion begins in small pits in the surface. The only way to prevent rust is to prevent moisture from reaching the cast iron.

A film of wax applied to machine tables can serve as a good moisture barrier. But not all paste waxes are the same. I've had good success with Minwax. Avoid products that contain silicone, like automotive waxes and talcum powder, because the silicone can migrate into your workpiece and cause finishing problems.

Before waxing, do some prep work on the surface you're trying to protect. It should be as smooth as possible. The goal is to remove most of the small pits in the metal because corrosion will recur rapidly in these areas. To smooth a surface, use silicon carbide paper, polishing to 600 grit. I suggest that you beef up your waxing regimen to once a month, and for a surface that gets daily use, once a week.

Finally, check the shop for any source of chlorine (bleach, swimming pool additives, and sidewalk salt) and relegate it to the shed outside. Chlorine in the atmosphere can accelerate the corrosion reactions that cause rust.

Carl Dorsch
Pittsburgh, PA

TWENTY-MINUTE TUNE-UP: THE TABLE SAW

A little TLC can go a long way toward keeping your table saw in top running condition. The photographs here show the routine that I go through every month or two with my saw.

A smooth table is an undervalued component of an accurate table saw. I start off by rubbing down the table, the fence, and the fence rail with fine steel wool dipped in paste wax. Then I buff all the waxed surfaces well with a rag. This keeps rust at bay and makes running stock over the saw much easier. Granted, this is a bit controversial, but in over 16 years of woodworking, I've never seen the wax interfere with either glue or finish.

Next I clean out the underside of the saw thoroughly and give both the blade tilt and the blade height mechanisms a shot of a dry lubricant (graphite or silicone, depending on which was on sale). While I'm under there, I check to make sure that the bolt that stops the blade square to the table still is set properly and doesn't have any crud on it.

Back up on top of the saw, I hold a straightedge across the throat insert to make sure that the throat insert is flush with the table surface. If it is not, I adjust the setscrews to make it so. Every once in a while, I'll check the alignment of the table extensions this way also.

After cleaning the blade with oven cleaner, I mount it back on the saw and check that the fence and the blade are still parallel. To do this, you lock the fence in place and raise the blade all the way. Choose a tooth and rotate it until it is at table level toward the front of the saw. Note the measurement from tooth to fence. Then rotate the blade until the chosen tooth is at table level toward the rear of the saw. Measure again. The two measurements should be equal. If they aren't, adjust the fence. Once or twice a year, I use the same technique to make sure that the blade is parallel to the miter gauge slots.

Ken Burton
New Tripoli, PA

Step 1. Wax the table regularly to prevent rust and allow the work to move smoothly across the metal.

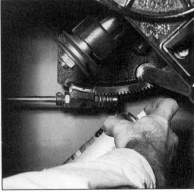

Step 2. Clean and lubricate the blade height and angle adjustment mechanisms for smooth operation.

Step 3. Adjust the throat plate so that it is level with the table surface.

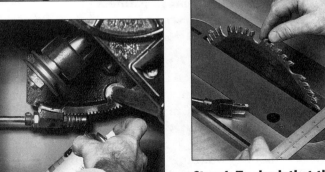

Step 4. To check that the fence is parallel to the blade, measure between a specific tooth and the fence, first at the front (*left*) then at the rear (*right*).

Band Saw Solutions

Correcting a Wandering Band Saw Blade

PROBLEM: *I have trouble following a line when cutting on my band saw, particularly at places where the cut meets the edge of the stock at an acute angle. The blade wants to jump in or out of the stock, leaving a big sidestep. Do I need a new saw?*

SOLUTION: Yes! Everyone "needs" a new band saw, but you'd better concentrate on the basics of saw adjustment and cutting technique so that you can show some improvement when you get the new saw. It should come with instructions for proper tracking, tensioning, and guide adjustment, but most manufacturers won't tell you anything about the proper use of side pressure to improve cutting accuracy.

Let's start with an exercise. With the saw running, ease a piece of scrap wood against the side of the blade so that it just touches the heel of the blade and not the teeth, as shown. Exert just enough pressure to make the blade run consistently against the inside guide. Now ease the stock around until the teeth start to make a mark on the side of the wood. Feed the stock forward and use the heel contact to control the amount of stock that the teeth remove. With a little practice, you

Dragging the heel of the blade lightly against the workpiece is a good way to guide the cut.

can take half of the thickness of the blade off of the edge of the stock.

Once you've mastered that, try dipping into and back out of the stock. With that light side pressure, you'll be able to enter and exit the wood without creating sidestep. This also works when you cut

through knots or other inconsistent spots in the wood. In fact, I find that I tend to drag the heel of the blade against the workpiece almost all of the time.

Fred Matlack
Vera Cruz, PA

Keeping Band Saw Blades Resin-Free

PROBLEM: *I'm constantly getting a resin buildup on my band saw blades. How can I prevent it?*

SOLUTION: The key is to reduce the amount of friction—and thus heat—on the blade because heat causes the buildup. One source of friction is the speed at which the blade travels through the wood.

The solution is to slow the saw blade down from its normal speed of 3,000 feet per minute (fpm) to about 1,200 fpm by installing a smaller diameter pulley on the motor and a larger pulley on the

saw's arbor. A second source of friction is wood binding against the blade, which may occur if a workpiece twists during the cut or if wood movement closes the kerf behind the blade. To prevent twisting, make sure that the bottom of your workpiece is flat. If the kerf is pinching the blade, wedge it open as you cut. You can reduce friction by spraying a vegetable shortening, like "PAM," onto the blade or by rubbing a block of paraffin against the blade.

To clean a blade, remove it from the saw, coil it, and put it in the sink. Then spray the blade with a foaming oven cleaner. After 10 minutes, simply rinse away the residue with cold water and towel-dry the blade. Before you reinstall the blade, clean your band saw's wheels and guides with a brass brush.

Jim Cummins
Woodstock, NY

Rubbing a block of paraffin against your band saw blade will reduce resin build-up.

CUTTING SMALL STOCK ON THE BAND SAW

*A*llowing your hands to come near the blade while you band saw small stock is not a good idea. If the blade catches the work, it could force your hand into the blade. But standard push blocks are too big to accurately handle such small pieces.

The answer is to use a small push stick fitted with brads to hold the work while keeping your hands clear of the blade. Cut a ½-inch-thick stick to about 6 inches long and drive two brads through one end, as shown. Drill a shallow, flat-bottomed hole in the handle end of the stick with a Forstner bit; then epoxy a magnet into the hole. Store the push stick by sticking it to the steel wheel casing of your saw where it's within easy reach.

Andy Rae
Lenhartsville, PA

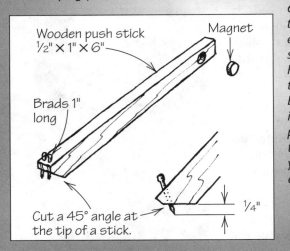

Wooden push stick ½" × 1" × 6"

Magnet

Brads 1" long

Cut a 45° angle at the tip of a stick.

¼"

Choosing Band Saw Speeds

PROBLEM: *How do I choose the correct band saw speed for resawing?*

SOLUTION: The simple answer is to run the saw at the fastest speed that won't bog the motor down. But if you're having trouble resawing, it may not be caused by using the wrong speed. Several variables can affect how a band saw cuts. Blade configuration, motor torque, feed rate, and blade speed must all work together in a delicate balance. Getting this just right means making the correct choice of blade and motor and developing an intuitive sense of how fast to feed the stock.

First select the widest blade with a hook-tooth pattern that fits your band saw—about six teeth per inch (tpi) with a ½-inch blade, and four tpi with a ¾-inch blade. The coarse teeth have a bigger gullet to clear out the waste without clogging. Make sure that the blade is sharp, clean, and degummed.

The motor's power is what really pulls the blade through the cut, so if you have the option of different motors with your saw, always go for the bigger one. This will ensure enough power to keep the feed rate up without taxing the motor. The secret to clean, straight resawing is that you should feed the stock at an optimum rate of speed—hard or thick woods should be fed more

slowly than soft or thin woods. As a rough guide, I feed about 4 to 6 feet per minute (fpm) in 6-inch pine, and 2 to 3 fpm in 6-inch maple. If you're feeding too quickly (pushing too hard), the blade will buckle and wander in the cut. If the wood is scorched, then you're feeding too slowly or the blade is dull. If you can't maintain a satisfactory feed rate without bogging the motor down, switch to a slower blade speed. This acts like "shifting gears," which changes the balance of the above variables. The blade has more power at a slower speed—like a car in a lower gear going up a hill. Again, feed as quickly as the motor will allow.

Charles Harvey
Berea, KY

Avoiding a Burned Cut

PROBLEM: *My band saw leaves a lot of black burn marks on the cut surface. What's the cause?*

SOLUTION: If burning happens mostly on curves, you may be trying to cut curves that are too tight with a blade that is too wide. That forces the heel of the blade to rub the already cut surface with a great deal of pressure. If you're burning all of the time, it probably means that the blade is dull or gummed up. And unless you've been cutting particularly sticky stock, the gum on the blade probably is due to the heat created by a dull blade. Try a new blade.

Using a fine-toothed blade to cut thick stock also can cause heat. Essentially what happens is that the gullets between the teeth get packed full of sawdust before they get through the thickness of the stock. Another surprisingly common problem that few people admit to is that they put the blade on inside out, which means that the teeth are pointed up instead of down. Even a brand-new blade won't cut worth a darn this way.

Fred Matlack
Vera Cruz, PA

Supporting Large Work on the Band Saw

PROBLEM: *I've tried using a roller stand to support large pieces that I'm band-sawing to shape. But for some reason, I feel like I'm always fighting for control of the direction of cut. Is there a better way?*

SOLUTION: Roller stands are great for straight cutting jobs like table sawing, where the stock rolls over them in a straight line. They're "directional" in that they want to move the stock in a specific direction perpendicular to the axis of the roller. Except for resawing, band saws aren't usually used for making directional cuts. Band saws are most often used for cutting curves and irregular shapes. So, no matter what direction you face the roller, it's going to be pulling against you a good bit of the time.

What you need is a nondirectional support. A smooth, flat surface is often an adequate nondirectional support. Or make a support using full motion ball bearings trapped in sockets, as shown. This type of bar unit can be purchased ready to use, or you can buy the bearings individually and make your own version.

Fred Matlack
Vera Cruz, PA

Ball bearings like the ones on this roller stand are nondirectional, so they'll help move and support large workpieces without moving the stock in a specific direction.

TWENTY-MINUTE TUNE-UP: THE BAND SAW

How often should you tune up your band saw? That depends on how much you use the machine. Every time you change blades, you have a good opportunity for a quick tune-up. Provided you don't let the blade get painfully dull, that kind of timing should keep your saw running quite well.

Let's say that you've already turned off the power and removed the blade. The covers are open and the wheels are bare. Brush or blow out as much of the inevitable collection of dust as you can. Take a look at the tires. If they're cracked or badly chewed up, plan to replace them. Spin the wheels to see if they're running freely and true. Check for play in the bearings. Don't forget that the upper wheel is on a hinge-like arrangement that allows tracking adjustment.

If everything is normal, throw a blade on the wheels and bring up the tension. Make sure that the blade is running clear from wheel to wheel on both sides. I like to hand turn the wheels slowly as I bring up the tension. That allows me to check the tracking and, at the same time, to make sure that the blade is clear. There's been a lot of stuff written about tension—how the engineers don't know anything and how the built-in gauges are always wrong. Personally, I prefer to start by setting the tension to the built-in gauge.

It is true that tension gauges are designed for general purpose work and may not suit all of your needs. For instance, if you decide to resaw one piece of wide stock and don't want to change to a bigger blade just for that cut, you can often get by with a little increase in tension to keep the blade stable. And some older saws may lose spring tension and read incorrectly. But those are special cases. In general, it's best to start with the gauge.

Most band saws are designed to have the blade running roughly on the center of the wheel. But don't forget that there are some saws that use an uncrowned (flat) wheel and that run the blade with the teeth hanging off the front of the wheel. Check your manual if you're in doubt. In either case, the blade guide system should not be needed to keep the blade in place when you turn the wheels. The guides are there only to keep you from pushing the blade off of the wheels when you start to cut.

Now it's time to set those guides. If you're still using the old steel block guides, you need to set them

Set the blade guide blocks with a feeler gauge or so that you can see just a thin line of light between the blade and guides.

about .005-inch from the blade on either side. If you don't happen to have a feeler gauge handy, a dollar bill is close enough. I generally set my blocks about as close as I can get them and still see light on both sides of the blade, as shown on this page. If you set them that tight, turn the wheels by hand until the splice in the blade goes through the guides. You may have to loosen them a bit if the splice sticks.

If you have roller guides or lubricated composite blocks, you can set the guides right against the blade. Just remember that you don't want to change the free-running position of the blade with the guide system. Also note that you can rotate or turn guide blocks end for end to come up with a surface that will accurately guide the blade. If all of the surfaces are grooved or out of square, you can square up the blocks on a stationary belt sander.

Adjust the guide assembly so that the teeth of the blade, plus ¹⁄₁₆" or so, are forward of the guide blocks.

Set the thrust bearing so that it just clears the blade. When you make a test cut, it should spin immediately.

Set the guide assembly so that the teeth, plus about ¹⁄₁₆ inch of the blade body, run proud of the guide, as shown above left. Now bring the thrust bearing up behind the blade until it almost touches, as shown above right. The idea is that the thrust bearing should be clear of the blade until you start to cut, but then it should catch the blade well before the teeth contact the side guides. Hand turn the wheels a couple more times.

Replace the wheel covers, throat plate, and table stabilizer pin, as shown at right. This pin keeps the halves of the table in flat alignment. Without it, the table is likely to warp over time. Finally, adjust the table so that it's square to the blade. Then power up the saw and try it out. After a few times through this procedure, you'll make it the standard blade-change tune-up.

Fred Matlack
Vera Cruz, PA

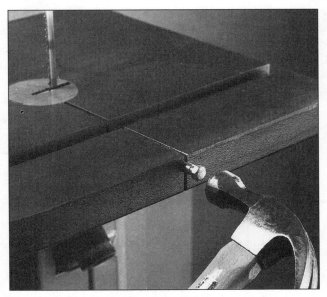

Don't forget to replace the stabilizer pin in the table. Otherwise, the table may warp over time.

Jointer Solutions

Diagnosing Common Jointer Woes

PROBLEM: *When I joint long edges, they usually have two or three facets instead of a single straight edge. What am I doing wrong?*

SOLUTION: When a jointer is properly set up, the cutting path of the knives is exactly level with the outfeed table, as shown. This allows the freshly jointed edge to ride flat on the outfeed table and sets up the rest of the board to be cut to that level. So the critical relationship is between the height of the jointer knives and the height of the outfeed table.

When the relationship is off, you can end up with all kinds of nonstraight edges—convex and concave, as well as faceted. It all depends on how you adjust your technique in response to the machine being out of adjustment.

The only solution is to correct this critical adjustment. Assuming that the knives are installed so that they are parallel with the outfeed table, you may simply need to adjust the table's height. See "Twenty Minute Tune-Up: The Jointer" on the opposite page.

Once the height has been set, you should keep it there, adjusting only the infeed table for normal usage.

You should check the height of the outfeed table periodically. Here's a simple way to do it: Take a piece of stock that's about 2 feet long and joint the first few inches. Reverse the piece and joint the entire length, but slow down and observe the cut as you approach the previously jointed end. If the outfeed table is correctly adjusted, the cuts will meet perfectly and the edge will be dead straight. If the outfeed table is too low, the stock will bite more deeply into the end that already has been jointed. If the outfeed table is slightly high, the board will gradually rise away from the cutterhead and stop cutting before it reaches the already jointed end.

Jim Cummins
Woodstock, NY

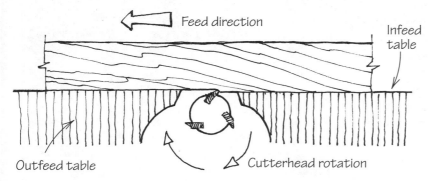

On a properly adjusted jointer, the cut surface rides directly onto the outfeed table.

(labels: Feed direction, Infeed table, Outfeed table, Cutterhead rotation)

Quick Tip Quick Tip Qu

SKEWED-UP JOINTING

Even with sharp knives, your jointer may have difficulty planing woods with contrary grain structure. Birds-eye, quilted, or curly maple are common culprits. A trick I learned while hand planing is to hold the blade askew to the direction of travel. The fence on some jointers can be set at an angle to the blades, thus providing the same kind of skew cut. Since I can't do this on my jointer, I made a tapered fence that can quickly be clamped to the jointer fence. It's just four pieces of scrap plywood assembled into a trapezoidal box.

Make the taper angle as large as possible, depending on the width of your jointer.

Mark Torpey
Madison, NJ

Jointing edges at a skew angle with this auxiliary fence reduces tear-out on figured stock.

Twenty-Minute Tune-Up: The Jointer

A jointer is designed to produce flat faces and straight edges. If the machine is not properly set up and adjusted, it will do neither.

There are two common misalignments that cause jointer frustrations: The infeed and outfeed tables are not parallel to each other, and the outfeed table is not correctly aligned with the cutterhead. Either one will prevent you from getting the flat faces and straight edges needed for all subsequent joinery and shaping.

To tune a jointer, start by checking that the tables are parallel, as shown in *Step 1*. Unplug the jointer and lay a long straightedge along the tables from end to end. Lower the infeed table and use a shim or a feeler gauge to see if the gap is the same from one end of the infeed table to the other. To correct tables that are not perfectly parallel, loosen the setscrews that hold the gibs on the outfeed table (these are the strips of metal that ride in the dovetail ways which connect the tables to the jointer base). Insert some shim material between the outfeed table dovetails and the base dovetails; then tighten the gibs and check the tables with the straightedge. You may find it useful to hold the outfeed table in position with a small hydraulic jack while making these slight adjustments. I prefer to make all my adjustments on the outfeed side; once they are done, I rarely move my outfeed table.

While you're looking at the tables, check to be sure that there is no twist across the width: Place a 2-foot-long straightedge across each table and sight down the tables from a few feet away, as shown in *Step 2*. The edges of the straightedges should be parallel. Again, if you find that the tables are out of parallel across the width, you can try to tease them into alignment with shims under the ways. In this situation, however, you'll shim only one side.

Next check that the blades at the peak of their arc are at exactly the same height as the outfeed table . Hold a straightedge on the outfeed table so that it protrudes past the blades. Rotate the blades by hand past the straightedge, as shown in *Step 3*. The blades should just tick the straightedge as they pass it. Check both ends of the blades to be sure that they are installed parallel with the table.

Ben Erikson
Eutaw, AL

Step 1. Check that the infeed and outfeed tables are parallel by extending a straightedge (or taut string) across the outfeed table and over the infeed table. The gap should be even at the front and back of the infeed table.

Step 2. Check that the tables are free of twist by sighting across a pair of straightedges, one laid across each of the tables.

Step 3. Adjust the knives so that they are perfectly parallel with the outfeed table and cut at exactly the same height as the outfeed table.

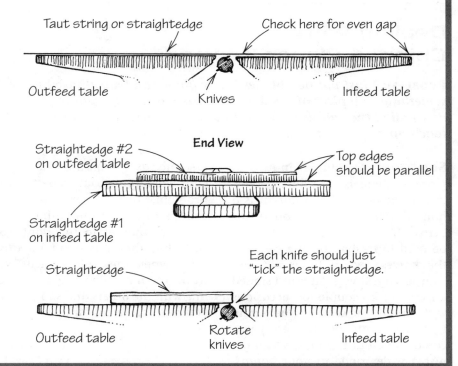

Taut string or straightedge   Check here for even gap

Outfeed table   Knives   Infeed table

End View

Straightedge #2 on outfeed table   Top edges should be parallel

Straightedge #1 on infeed table

Straightedge   Each knife should just "tick" the straightedge.

Outfeed table   Rotate knives   Infeed table

Other Stationary Machines

Preventing Dents When Thickness Planing

PROBLEM: *Wood shavings sometimes stick to my planer's outfeed rollers like flies to flypaper. The chips cause dents in the planed surface. What's going on?*

SOLUTION: Planer chips should never reach the outfeed roller because they can mar the surface of your stock even if they don't stick to the roller. Your problem results from poor evacuation of the chips. The chips should be funneled up and out through the dust opening by the chip breaker. If there's no dust collector attached, chip removal depends solely on the chips being thrown by the cutterhead, and some chips don't make it. They can easily wind up pressed into the wood as it passes under the outfeed roller. You can minimize the number of chips left behind by taking shallower cuts, using slower feed rates, keeping the knives sharp and properly adjusted, and checking that there are no obstructions in the exit opening. Some machines require a dust collector for proper chip removal. My 20-inch planer needs a collector that moves about 1,200 cubic feet of air per minute.

Kelly Mehler
Berea, KY

ANOTHER VIEW: Raise the humidity in your shop. Shavings from resinous wood can be so tacky that they require much more than normal air flow from a collector for proper removal. I gave up on one batch of pine because shavings stuck to everything and left a resinous residue on all my tools. I've also had problems in especially cold, dry weather when static buildup caused every stray shavings to cling tenaciously to the nearest surface of the machine. After a few minutes of operation, I couldn't see the planer under its plumage of wood shavings. A pan of water on the wood stove raised the humidity enough to solve the static problem.

Bob Moran
Emmaus, PA

Dealing with Chipped Planer Knives

PROBLEM: *I just put new blades in the planer and must have hit something in a piece of wood because there is a ridge running down all of the boards that I just planed. Is there any way to touch up a spot on the blades?*

SOLUTION: On large industrial planers, there is usually a "jointing" attachment. Essentially it is a honing stone that runs on a bar across the cutterhead so that it can be used to freshen up the edges of the knives several times between sharpenings. I've even hand stoned knives on a couple of occasions with limited success, but generally I don't recommend it. Even if you could stone out the nick, you'd get just a wider ridge in your boards.

It sounds as though this might be a case where you could sidestep the problem. Just loosen the blade clamps and slide one knife to the left and another to the right. (Be sure that the ends don't hit anything when they rotate.) This will throw the nick in each blade out of line with the others and should give you a passable cut for awhile.

Fred Matlack
Vera Cruz, PA

Turning Ovals on the Lathe

PROBLEM: *I want to turn ovals on my lathe. Although it's a heavy machine, I'm afraid that even at the slowest speed (340 rpm), the ovals could shake the lathe off of its mounts. Should I put in a DC motor with a speed control?*

SOLUTION: Whenever you turn a large diameter or out-of-round piece, a slow speed and secure lathe are of utmost importance. Some of the new "custom" lathes with DC drives have a variable speed that goes down to one revolution per minute (rpm). This may sound like overkill, but even at this speed, the surface speed on the rim of a large piece is quite high.

You can do several things to steady the lathe. Bolt it to the floor. If the lower portion of the lathe has an empty enclosed cavity, fill it with sand or put sand bags on the bed. If the lathe is located under a beam, wedge a 4 × 6 timber from the beam to the bed, sandwiching the bed between the floor and ceiling.

You may find that steadying the lathe is all you need to do. If not, you will have to slow down the speed at which you turn. Instead of changing the motor, change the pulley on either the motor or the lathe. To cut the lathe's speed in half, put a pulley that is half the diameter of the original on the motor, or double the size of the pulley on the lathe.

A DC motor with speed control is an excellent idea. The worst problem then is uneven wear on the bearings over time.

Mark Sfirri
New Hope, PA

Maintaining a Lathe Bed

PROBLEM: *I keep all my metal machine surfaces clean and waxed to protect the metal. I'm finding, though, that the wax on my lathe bed causes the tailstock to creep. What can I use to protect the metal so that this won't happen?*

SOLUTION: On the surface of a lathe's bed, or ways, you don't want the clean slick surfaces that work so well on a jointer or table saw. As a matter of fact, I find that a slightly pocked surface on the ways helps to prevent the tailstock from sliding when locked. Here's my approach to maintaining the ways of a lathe:

First clean off the wax with mineral spirits. Then cover the ways with freshly cut oak or walnut shavings and leave them overnight. The tannins in the shavings will quickly produce a light coat of rust on the ways. The next day, spray the ways with WD-40, wipe off the rust with fine steel wool, then wipe off the bed with a clean rag. This leaves a rust-free but slightly pocked surface that provides traction for the locked tailstock and tool rest while allowing them to slide easily when unlocked. Repeat this as often as seems necessary. As radical as this method might seem, I've been doing it for 25 years and it works.

David Ellsworth
Quakertown, PA

Routing on the Drill Press

PROBLEM: *Can I get acceptable results running router bits in my drill press?*

SOLUTION: Attempting to run router bits in your drill press will damage your project and may also damage the drill press. Router bits are designed to operate at speeds as high as 25,000 revolutions per minute (rpm). A drill press develops a maximum speed of less than 5,000 rpm. Running a router bit at such a slow speed results in an extremely rough cut, with lots of chipping and tear-out.

The bearings in a drill press are usually designed to take only vertical loads. Putting a lateral load on the bearings during routing may wear them out prematurely. My advice is to buy a router. In my shop, we use the router for shaping, cutting grooves, mortising, and cutting edge profiles. It is a much more versatile machine than a drill press.

You can also mount a router in a table for those jobs where it's more practical or safe to move the workpiece instead of the router. This gives you two router tools from a single router.

James Van Etten
Perkasie, PA

Leveling a Drill Press Table

PROBLEM: *How can I quickly and accurately reset my drill press table to be perfectly perpendicular to the quill after it has been tilted for an angled cut?*

SOLUTION: Bend a scrap piece of wire (such as a length of wire coat hanger) into a Z shape. Chuck one end into the drill press and adjust the table until the other end just touches the table continuously as you rotate the chuck by hand.

Graham Blackburn
Bearsville, NY

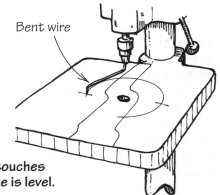

Bent wire

When the wire just touches at all sides, the table is level.

Router Solutions

Preventing Bit Creep

PROBLEM: *Every so often, one of my router bits creeps out of the collet as I'm cutting. The last time this happened, it ruined a drawer front I was just finishing. What can I do to keep this from happening again?*

SOLUTION: Presumably you didn't neglect to tighten the collet. (If you *didn't* tighten the collet, well, you know the solution to the problem.) So ask yourself a key question to start. Does the problem occur with just a particular bit, or does it occur with all bits? Inspect your bits for signs that the bit shank is spinning inside the collet, as shown above right.

If just one bit causes the problem, it may have a slightly undersized shank. Measure the shank of that bit with a micrometer or precision dial caliper, as shown below right, doing this several places along the shank. If the shank is more than 2 or 3 thousandths undersized, or if it tapers, it's not worth the risk of using it.

If the problem occurs with several bits, you probably have a bad collet. Replace the collet, and the problem is likely to go away. However, if you were using a sleeve to fit a ¼-inch shank bit to a ½-inch collet, look at that sleeve as the potential culprit before tossing the collet. (It is always better to use a ¼-inch collet for ¼-inch shanks, but it isn't always possible.) With the router unplugged and the collet tightened, lock the armature and try twisting the bit. If the bit does turn, does it twist in the sleeve, or does the sleeve also twist? In either case, it is probably wise to replace the sleeve. If you cannot twist the bit by hand, test how the setup works in use. Use a felt-tip marker to draw a line down the bit shank and onto the collet. Make a cut with the

The score marks around the shank of this bit are the result of the bit's spinning in a slightly loose collet. The scoring can probably be removed with some emery cloth, but that could make the shank too undersized to use.

To determine if a bit shank is the proper diameter, measure it with a micrometer or precision dial caliper. If the shank is undersized by more than 3 thousandths, it is probably too small to be gripped securely by a collet and the bit should not be used.

router, then check the mark. If the bit has twisted—if the mark on the shank no longer is aligned with the mark on the collet—replace the sleeve and/or the collet.

Remember that you shouldn't have to "muscle" the collet wrench or wrenches to tighten the collet. If each bit change presents a major tussle, it might be worthwhile to buy a new collet.

Bill Hylton
Kempton, PA

SHOP-MADE SOLUTIONS

Easy-On, Easy-Off Router Fence BY ANDY RAE

I mounted my router under my table saw's outfeed table to save space. That left me needing a router fence that I could set up quickly and then remove when it got in the way of ripping and crosscutting operations.

I installed threaded inserts into the top of my plywood outfeed table, then made an L-shaped router fence with open-ended slots in the base. The fence is held tight to the table with plastic knobs that have threaded studs to match the inserts. See "Sources," beginning on page 298. To remove the fence, I loosen the knobs about a turn, then slide the fence off of the table.

Knob with ⅜" stud

Table saw

Outfeed table/router table

7/16"

⅜" threaded insert

Freeing Stuck Router Bits

PROBLEM: *I often have a hard time removing router bits from my router. Are the bits bad, or is the collet?*

SOLUTION: Clean the bit shanks *and* the collet. Often router bits stick because pitch and wood resins have built up inside the collet. Cleaning the collet with #0000 steel wool and oven cleaner should help reduce sticking. While it's a good idea to place a drop of oil on the outside of the collet to keep it from sticking, don't oil the inside of the collet, or you risk the bit loosening during routing. A bit will also stick if it has a galled or scored shaft. To remedy this problem, remove any burrs or high spots with a mill file.

If these steps don't solve your problem, you can usually use one of the following methods to remove a bit without damaging the carbide: If the head of the bit is larger than the shank, cut a V in a thin piece of scrap wood and use this "fork" to lever between the nut and the top of the cutter's flute, as shown. If this doesn't loosen the bit, or if the head of the bit isn't big enough to apply a lever, clamp the bit in a wooden-jawed vise and turn the router shaft with a wrench until the bit loosens. (On routers with shaft locks, simply engage the lock and rotate the router.) Finally, if you lightly tap the collet nut or the shank of the bit where it exits the collet, you can usually get the bit out.

Pat Warner
Escondido, CA

Most stuck bits can be freed with the gentle application of a shop-made "router fork."

Grinding Custom Router Bits

I NEEDED TO DUPLICATE A TABLETOP MOLDING, and I couldn't find a router bit to match the shape. I couldn't afford to have a bit custom-made for just one molding. So I decided to grind one myself.

I was pleased to find that it's surprisingly easy and inexpensive. I frequently grind my own custom bit on my standard 6-inch bench grinder, which I have equipped with a couple of narrow (¼-inch and ½-inch) grinding wheels. (For really tight areas, I use an abrasive cutoff wheel.) I round the corners of the wheels with a diamond dressing stick (see "Sources," beginning on page 298), so that I can grind fluid curves.

For small profiles, I use high-speed-steel (HSS) two-wing rabbeting bits, available at hardware stores and home centers. For large profiles, I use HSS ½-inch-shank industrial bit blanks (see "Sources," beginning on page 298). These have 1½-inch-long flutes and diameters from ¾ to 3 inches. Caution: With the largest of these, you'll need to use a variable-speed router mounted in a table. Also, I never grind the bit smaller than the shank diameter. So, for profiles that require fairly deep cuts into the flutes, you'll need a fairly large bit.

When you start to grind the bit, there are two things to keep in mind. The first is the actual profile you want, which I'll get to in a minute; the second is the bevel angle. I usually follow the blank's original bevel angle—usually 70 degrees, as shown in Top View—when I grind. This leaves a clearance angle of 20 degrees, which is necessary to keep the heel of the bevel from rubbing the workpiece. On very deep parts of a profile, you'll need a little more clearance because the cutting radius is smaller. In these areas, I usually make the bevel slightly convex (as opposed to hollow-ground) to avoid weakening the cutting edge. Set the bevel angle by angling the tool rest on your grinder in relation to the wheel.

To grind the profile, you first have to draw it on the bit. Coat the face of each flute with layout dye (see "Sources," beginning on page 298), and let it dry. Next use an awl to scratch the desired profile onto one of the dyed surfaces. Hold the blank on the toolrest and slowly grind the steel down to the layout lines, working away at the deepest sections first. To avoid overheating the bit, I dip it in water regularly. Once you've completed the profile on the first flute, trace it onto paper and use this pattern as a reference for the second. For complex designs, I use a cardboard template or a sample of the molding as a reference for both flutes.

Once both flutes are ground, I hone the edges with a small slip stone. Then I'm ready for a light test cut. I chuck the bit, set my router to 15,000 rpm or less, depending on the bit diameter, and take it for a spin.

Lonnie Bird
Gallipolis, OH

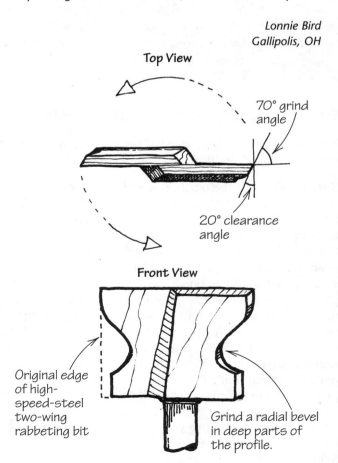

Top View

70° grind angle

20° clearance angle

Front View

Original edge of high-speed-steel two-wing rabbeting bit

Grind a radial bevel in deep parts of the profile.

Hand Tool Solutions

Resharpening a Dovetail Saw

PROBLEM: *Whenever I try to start a dovetail cut, my western dovetail saw skips off the line. Is it me or could it be the saw?*

SOLUTION: When a western dovetail saw skips off the line as you're starting the cut, it may be the saw's fault rather than your own. There are two problems. First, when you cut dovetails, you're actually making a rip cut, but dovetail saws are generally sharpened for crosscutting. Second, the teeth on most dovetail saws have a lot of set—meaning that the teeth are bent out to make a fairly wide kerf in relation to the thickness of the blade. The more set a saw has, the harder it is to start a cut.

Resharpening your saw can solve both problems. To start with, the teeth should be filed for ripping, rather than for crosscutting, as shown in the drawing. You can do this fairly easily yourself, as shown in the photo. You could also take your saw to a local sharpening shop and explain what you'd like to have done. Make sure it's a professional shop and that they know how to do the job.

Reshaping the teeth will also reduce the set. If the saw still skips, you can reduce the set even further by putting the blade between two pieces of hardboard and squeezing it in a vise. You'll want to keep a little set so that the kerf is slightly wider than the thickness of the blade. Otherwise the saw will bind as it cuts.

W. Curtis Johnson
Corvallis, OR

To sharpen a saw, hold it in a vise between two pieces of wood with only the teeth showing. File each tooth with the same number of strokes from a small triangular file.

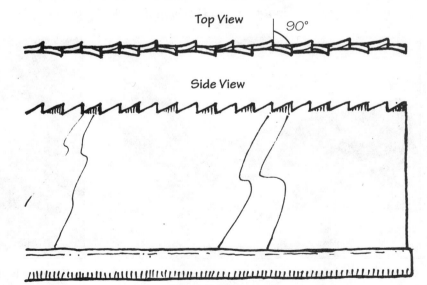

Top View

90°

Side View

To refile a saw for better dovetail cuts, file the face of each tooth so that it is square to both the face and the back of the saw.

TUNING A NEW HAND PLANE

More than one woodworker has pitched a hand plane across the shop in disgust, proclaiming "I just can't make that bleepin' thing work. Guess I'll just use my belt sander instead."

If this sounds like an experience you've had, take heart. While it is true that learning to hand plane takes some practice, it is also likely that your plane needs a good tune-up before it will whisk away shavings with a swoosh.

Given the cost of a new plane, you'd think you'd be able to use it right off the store shelf, but this is rarely the case. Even very expensive specialty planes need to be tuned up before use. Medium cost planes need even more work.

You should check out a new (or secondhand) plane before parting with your money. Using a good straightedge, check the sole of the plane for flatness. Hold the straightedge on the sole at each side and at the center, as shown below left. Chances are good that the straightedge will touch at the heel and toe of the sole, and possibly around the throat, but will reveal gaps in between. As long as the gaps are less than 1/32 inch, the plane is tunable. Larger gaps will require too much effort to flatten.

Once you have a plane that you want to tune, the main task will be to flatten the sole—a job that can take the better part of an afternoon. This lengthy task isn't particularly difficult, just time-consuming. To start, use duct tape to attach two sheets of 80-grit emery paper end to end onto a flat metal surface, like a table saw table or a jointer bed. Be careful not to overlap the pieces of abrasive paper. Run the tape along the sides only, leaving a long stretch of uninterrupted abrasive.

Set up the plane as if you were going to use it, but retract the blade well above the sole. With the blade in place, the plane body is under the same tension it will be in use—meaning that the flattening you do should be accurate. Grasp the plane as if you were using it and move it across the abrasive, as shown below right. Try to maintain uniform downward pressure throughout each stroke. After a few passes, inspect the sole. You should see shiny areas where the plane was in contact with the abrasive. These are the high spots and they will gradually enlarge as the sole of the plane becomes flat. Eventually the entire plane bottom should become uniformly shiny. Once you reach this point, switch to 150-grit emery paper and keep going. Note that because this process is slow and repetitive, it is easy

Check the sole with a straightedge to see how flat it is. Test several places across the width of the sole as well as the diagonals. If the diagonals show significantly different gaps, the sole is likely to be twisted and is probably not worth trying to flatten.

A flat sole is the result of a lot of scrubbing across a couple of sheets of abrasive paper.

The front of the throat opening must be square to the sides of the plane as it forms, in conjunction with the plane iron, the opening through which the shavings pass.

Another critical adjustment is to make sure that the frog seats perfectly on the plane body. The mating surfaces should be free of paint, burrs, and other imperfections.

to rock the plane without being aware of it. This will create a twisted sole, so try to concentrate on holding the plane flat.

When the bottom is true, check the front of the throat opening with a square, as shown above left. In all likelihood, it will be a little off. Mark the discrepancy with a scribe and file the opening so that it is true. Try to remove as little metal as possible.

Next disassemble the plane, removing the handles as well as the plane iron and frog. On the underside of the frog, there are two pads which seat on two small platforms cast into the plane body. All of these surfaces will probably have paint on them. Using acetone and a small shop knife, scrape the paint off completely. Next very carefully file down any high points or rough edges from the casting and machining processes, as shown above right. This will ensure that the frog seats properly on the plane and does not rock.

The plane handles may have some finish on their undersides, and the cast iron mount in the plane body will probably be painted too. These all should be given the same cleaning process with acetone and scraping to make sure that the handles seat securely. Reattach the handles.

Sharpen the plane iron, then check the fit of the chip breaker (see "Sharpening Chisels and Plane Irons" on page 273). It should mate to the back of the iron without any gaps. If necessary, file it to fit.

Place the freshly sharpened iron and chip breaker on the frog, aligning them with the throat opening. For fine work, the throat opening should be about $1/64$ inch wide. If it is not, carefully move the frog forward or backward as necessary. When this is done, tighten the frog permanently. Reassemble the plane and adjust the plane iron to take a fine cut. You should be able to make a continuous shaving that curls up and lays in the plane when you plane down the length of a board.

David Stern Lightner
Philadelphia, PA

Securing Japanese Chisel Hoops

PROBLEM: *The hoops keep slipping off the handles of my new Japanese chisels. How can I fasten them securely?*

SOLUTION: Remove the hoop from the chisel and examine its inside surface. It should be smooth and free from any burrs that might keep the hoop from seating all the way. File away any imperfections and, while you're working, file the inside surface of the hoop to a slightly convex shape. This slight convexity will provide room for the wood fibers when you hammer the end of the chisel to hold the hoop in place.

Slip the hoop back on the chisel. It should seat slightly below the end of the handle with no more than $1/16$ inch of wood projecting. If the hoop doesn't go on that far, file a little more off of its inside surface. Next, with the hoop pushed onto the handle, dip the end of the handle into warm water for a few seconds to soften the wood. Then hammer the end of the handle to mushroom the wood over the hoop, thus securing it in place.

Robert Treanor
San Francisco, CA

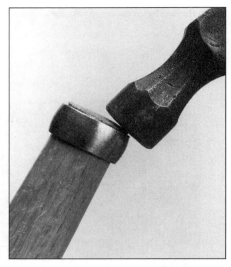

After wetting the end of the handle, hammer over the edges to mushroom the wood over the hoop.

Preventing Clogged Hand Planes

PROBLEM: *Splinters of wood keep jamming between my plane iron and the chip breaker. How can I correct this?*

SOLUTION: This is a fairly common problem, which occurs when there is some sort of gap between the plane's iron and chip breaker. To solve this problem, you need to make sure that your iron's back is well flattened, and then you need to make sure that the edge of the chip breaker meets the back of the iron perfectly. Hold the two up to a light to check. If necessary file or stone the edge of the chip breaker until the gap disappears. You may need to regrind the chip breaker first so only its leading edge contacts the blade.

Rob Yoder
Quakertown, PA

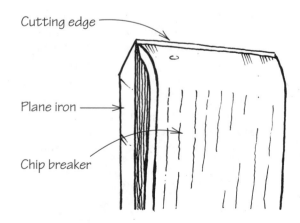

Cutting edge

Plane iron

Chip breaker

The chip breaker should contact the plane iron across its entire width.

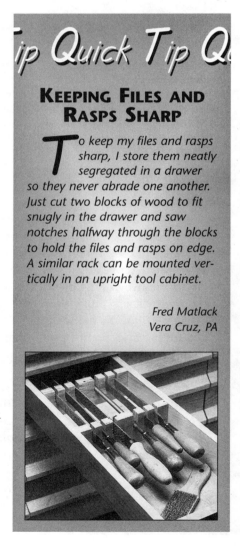

Sharpening Solutions

Grinding with a Belt Sander

PROBLEM: *How can I grind my small plane irons accurately without a grinder?*

SOLUTION: Saw a block of wood at the angle you want the bevel. Then secure the plane iron with a wing nut and washer to the block, as shown. Clamp a belt sander upside down in a bench vise and hold the block with the plane iron attached against the running belt.

If the iron is badly nicked and needs reshaping, start off using a coarse belt, like 60-grit. When the desired shape of the cutting edge is attained, change to a finer belt, like 120-grit, and continue until the scratches left by the coarse belt have been removed. Use sharpening stones to remove the scratches left by the 120-grit.

Since the wood block is liable to be worn away almost as fast as the cutting iron, take care to hold it square to the belt and watch the edge of the iron carefully to ensure that the grinding proceeds the way you want it to.

Graham Blackburn
Bearsville, NY

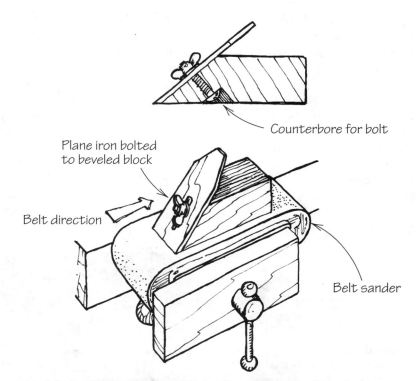

Counterbore for bolt

Plane iron bolted to beveled block

Belt direction

Belt sander

A belt sander is a good substitute for a bench grinder when regrinding plane irons. Just bolt the iron to a block of wood that has been beveled to the desired angle.

Taming a Vibrating Grinder

PROBLEM: *My bench grinder vibrates so much that I can't keep a tool against the wheel, and it's gotten progressively worse since I first purchased it a year ago. Is there a fix?*

SOLUTION: Something—either the wheels or the rotor, or both—is out of balance. To figure out which, first dress both wheels with a carbide, star, or diamond wheel dresser—they may be slightly out of round. If the problem persists, either the rotor is out of balance or one or both grinding wheels are. To check the rotor, remove the abrasive wheels and run the rotor without them. If the machine runs smoothly, the trouble is in the wheels. If not, have the grinder serviced by a repair shop, or return it if the warranty is in effect.

To check the wheels, mount one at a time on the machine and turn on the power (replace the guard first). If you find that either of the wheels is grossly out of balance, replace it. If both wheels are slightly out, draw reference lines, then spin one wheel 15 degrees in relation to the other. See if the vibration is better or worse. Continue until you find the orientation with the least vibration.

Simon Watts
San Francisco, CA

Keeping Your Temper

PROBLEM: *How can I prevent burning the edge when sharpening tools on a bench grinder?*

SOLUTION: You'll get off to a good start if you dress the wheels regularly. As you grind, the space between the abrasive particles fills up with metal. The wheel becomes "glazed," which creates a lot of heat but little material removal. Running a wheel dresser lightly over the face of the wheel brings up fresh, sharp abrasive particles.

I'd suggest you switch to an aluminum oxide grinding wheel. It's better than a silicon carbide wheel for tool steel because it runs cooler.

Also, in grinding, finer is hotter, but not necessarily better. Your wheel may be too fine. I use a 46- to 60-grit wheel on my left arbor, where I do most of my grinding, and an 80-grit on the right. Since you'll be removing the grinding marks with a sharpening stone anyway, a finer wheel doesn't give you any significant advantage.

Finally, you may be grinding your tools to an edge that's too thin. A 30-degree bevel angle is right for just about all woodworking tools. A thinner edge (less angle) will build up heat quickly when grinding and could burn the edge. I like to grind just shy of the edge, leaving a flat of $1/64$ inch or less. This means slightly more work at the whetstone, but I never burn an edge.

Ernie Conover
Parkman, OH

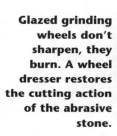

Glazed grinding wheels don't sharpen, they burn. A wheel dresser restores the cutting action of the abrasive stone.

Sharpening with Waterstones

PROBLEM: *Whenever I flatten the back of a plane iron with waterstones, suction causes the iron to stick to the stone. How can I prevent this?*

SOLUTION: The answer is to keep the stones' pores open. Suction occurs when a wet paste of stone and steel is created during sharpening. The water in the paste is sucked into the stone, and the dry paste glazes the stone's surface. This happens more often with man-made waterstones because they're more porous than natural stones. To overcome the suction, you need to keep the pores of the stones clean. First, before you use them, submerge man-made stones in water for about 20 minutes to fill the pores with water. (Natural stones don't need soaking.) Then as you sharpen initially, keep the stone well washed with water to prevent paste buildup. On the final strokes, when you're ready to move to the higher-grit stone, reduce pressure and allow the paste to remain on the stone. This will make the scratches on the tool shallower, which makes for less work as you hone on the finer-grit stone.

Toshio Odate
Woodbury, CT

Choosing Grinding Wheels

PROBLEM: *My grinding wheels seem to get glazed quickly, causing the tools to burn. Am I doing something wrong?*

SOLUTION: Your problem may be caused by the grit and grade of your grinding wheels. This information is generally found on the paper surrounding the wheel's hub. "Grade" refers to the strength of the bonding agent that cements the grains together. Grades A-H are considered soft, I-P are medium, and Q-Z are hard. For grinding most woodworking tools, I prefer 60-grit. On a 3,500 rpm grinder, use an H grade wheel, and on a 1,750 rpm grinder, an L or M grade is standard. The slower speed grinders are a better choice for woodworkers.

Grinding wheel manufacturers (see "Sources," beginning on page 298) will provide advice and the name of a local supplier who carries their products. Also, you can check the Yellow Pages under "Abrasives," or contact catalog sales companies that carry a variety of grinding wheels.

John Grew-Sheridan
San Francisco, CA

Making Slip Stones for Gouges

PROBLEM: *I occasionally need to use gouges in my work and would like them to be sharp. However, I don't want to buy a bunch of different slip stones to keep them honed. Is there another option?*

SOLUTION: You can make your own slips in a variety of sizes with dowels and adhesive-backed, silicon carbide sandpaper. This paper comes in rolls and is sold for use on random-orbit sanders. I usually use 320-grit sandpaper, but for an even keener edge, you can purchase finer paper. If you can't find self-adhering paper, you can use spray adhesive with regular sandpaper instead.

Cut a short length (3 to 4 inches long) from several different diameter dowels. Use a utility knife to cut strips of paper. Wrap a strip around each dowel. Select the dowel that best matches the curve of your gouge and use this to hone the inside edge. I prefer to use the slip dry, without any oil or water as a lubricant.

Mike Dunbar
Hampton, NH

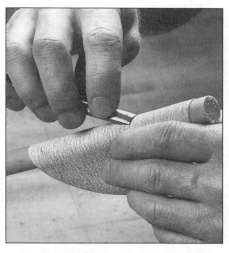

Instead of buying a bunch of different gouge slips, make your own from dowels and silicon carbide sandpaper.

Making Sharpening "Stones" for Gouges

PROBLEM: *I've finally mastered sharpening chisels, but sharpening gouges on flat stones seems impossible. Is there a simpler way, other than buying slip stones?*

SOLUTION: First use the gouge you want to sharpen to cut a groove in a piece of scrap wood. Then fill the groove with abrasive compound or slurry from a waterstone, as shown. You now have a sharpening "stone" perfectly matched to the edge you want to sharpen.

The first time you do this, the tool will probably be dull, so I suggest you make the groove in a piece of softwood, like pine. After sharpening the tool, you may want to make a second groove in a piece of hardwood, like oak or maple, which will last longer.

Abrasive compounds can be purchased in paste form in various grits at automotive parts stores or tool shops. For tool-sharpening purposes, the coarsest of these "pastes" is ideal. The finer grades, such as #000, will take longer to cut although they will leave your tool with a brighter polish.

If you use waterstones to sharpen your plane irons and other cutting edges, use the mud that accumulates in the bottom of the water container that you soak or wash your stones in as a slurry. Even if this mud is a mix from the various grit stones that you use, it will still work adequately.

Graham Blackburn
Bearsville, NY

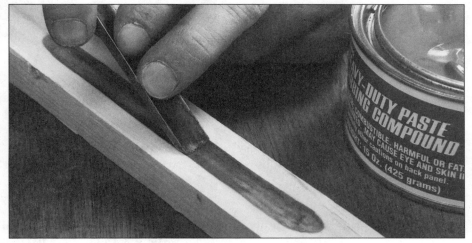

To make a sharpening "stone" that matches the curve of your gouge perfectly, cut a groove in a piece of scrap with the gouge itself. Dab a little abrasive in the groove and you'll have a first-rate sharpening system.

Hand-Holding a Sharpening Stone

IT SEEMS THAT EVERYONE AND HIS BROTHER HAS A DIFFERENT WAY TO SHARPEN. *Some people rely on special jigs, while others use sandpaper, plate glass, and other such things. To this tangle, I offer my simple system. While I won't claim that it's perfect, it works for me, and it does offer several advantages over some of the more complex methods I've seen.*

Instead of laying your stone on a bench, where it is apt to make a mess, hold it lengthwise in the palm of your hand, as shown at right. Hold your chisel lengthwise in your other hand with your index finger centered behind the cutting edge (for wide chisels and plane irons, use two fingers). With your elbows at your side, hold your hands out in front in a praying position, so you can see the angle at which the chisel is touching the stone.

Keeping your elbows at your side and your wrists almost rigid, move your hands back and forth with a slight left-right-left-right roll (almost like the motion you'd use to roll out snakes of pretzel dough). I find that the stone and chisel keep their proper angle almost automatically. If you watch the angle carefully, you'll see that subtle changes in your wrist position will be needed during different parts of the stroke. But it doesn't take much practice to get it right.

I like to sharpen while sitting down. It's easy to control the length of stroke because that depends on how far left and right you move your hands. I don't get a perfectly flat bevel, but it's darn close to flat and quite smooth. Microbevels can be made by adjusting your wrist angle slightly.

Mark Popp
Seattle, WA

Holding a sharpening stone vertically in one hand and the tool in the other gives you a bird's-eye view of the contact between the stone and the tool's bevel.

Flattening Gouged Waterstones

PROBLEM: *My Japanese waterstones are dished out in the center. How can I flatten them?*

SOLUTION: When drastic measures are called for, I dress my stones on wet-or-dry sandpaper that has been laid on a sheet of plate glass. Water sprinkled on the glass will hold the paper in place. Lubricate the paper with water as you rub the stone on it.
AVOIDING THE PROBLEM: I try to keep my waterstones as flat as possible at all times by dressing them every time I use them. This is easily accomplished by rubbing them against each other—the coarse stone against the medium and the medium against the fine. If you rotate the faces as you rub, you won't transfer irregularities from one face to the other. You can recognize the flattened areas of the stones by the clean, even slurry the rubbing produces.

Paul Anthony
Hellertown, PA

To keep waterstones from getting seriously out-of-flat, rub two of them together until both faces are flat.

Sharpening Chisels and Plane Irons

PROBLEM: *I must have tried a dozen techniques, but my chisels and plane irons never get really sharp. What's the secret?*

SOLUTION: Regardless of whose system you use, sharpening a chisel or a plane blade involves three key steps: flattening the back, honing the bevel, and adding a slight secondary bevel, or microbevel. These steps are the same whether you use oil stones, waterstones, buffing wheels, or even sandpaper to do the actual sharpening. With that said, here is the sharpening method I use:

Flattening the back is the easiest step, though it's often disregarded. Take a look at the back (or flat) side of your tools. If you can't see yourself looking back, you may have discovered your problem. The backside of a chisel or plane iron should be polished to a near mirror-like surface—the last inch or so is sufficient. The nice thing about polishing the back of a tool is that, once you've done it, you should never have to do it again. During routine sharpening henceforth, the back is only honed with your finest stone. To polish the back

To sharpen a tool, you must polish both of the surfaces that intersect to make the cutting edge. Many woodworkers spend a lot of time polishing a tool's bevel and forget all about the second surface—the tool's back.

initially, hold your tool flat on a coarse or medium-grit stone (which one depends on how dull the tool is to begin with) and slide it back and forth repeatedly. Once the back has an even sheen to it, repeat the process with your finest stone, working toward that bright mirrorlike polish. Take care to keep the tool dead flat on the stone, as shown below left. Also make sure that the stone itself is flat or you'll be wasting your time.

With the back polished, you can turn your attention to the bevel. Contrary to popular opinion, you don't need to use a honing guide to produce a sharp bevel and microbevel. Most chisels and plane irons come with a flat grind, so that's your likely starting point. Begin by holding the chisel with the bevel flat on the stone, as shown above right. Move it forward and backward several times. Use whatever stones you have, starting with a medium-grit stone, like an india stone or a 1,200-grit waterstone. Check your progress from time to time by looking at the edge in a strong light. Move the tool under the light to see if you can spot any reflection off the edge—a dull edge will appear as a white line of reflected light. No light will reflect off of a sharp edge. This process gives you a sharp, flat bevel.

Once you've got a sharp edge using the medium-grit stone, switch to a fine-grit stone, like a hard Arkansas or a 6,000-grit waterstone. Find the bevel angle again, then lift the back end of the tool a fraction of an inch. The exact angle isn't important—just raise the back of the handle roughly ¼ inch or so—and continue the back and forth sharpening motion. This second step creates a smaller bevel right at the cutting edge. This

Hold the tool in your hands with two fingers on its back opposite the bevel. Rock the tool back and forth slightly until you find the bevel angle, then move the tool over the stone, maintaining that angle.

microbevel is much easier to polish than the whole bevel would be. Five or six strokes should create a fine microbevel and a very sharp edge. Future sharpenings will require only that you repolish the microbevel.

As a final step, turn over the tool and polish the back with a stroke or two. Sharpening often creates a slight wire edge that must be polished away. Breaking off this little bit of metal will create a small flat at the tool's tip.

A stroke or two on the back followed by a final stroke or two on the microbevel should leave you with a truly keen edge. If you use a wheeled sharpening gauge, the microbevel will be very distinct. Without one, it will be less distinct but can be made just as a sharp. Obviously you want to hold the blade at a constant angle to the stone as you sharpen the microbevel so that you don't round the edge. But it's more important that the cutting angle formed by the microbevel isn't too severe. That's why you need to raise only the back of the tool very slightly to go from the flat bevel to a microbevel.

Jeff Day
Perkasie, PA

REPAIR

SOLUTIONS

FIXING DENTS AND GOUGES

Repairing Large Gouges	275
Ironing Out Dents	276
Filling and Staining Gouges	276
Fixing Small Gashes	277
Disguising Veneer Sand-Through	278
Fixing Scratches	279
Repairing a Splintered Edge	279

SOLVING GLUING PROBLEMS

Softening Old Glue	280
Fixing a Failed Glue Joint	280
Regluing Bubbled Veneer	281
Cleaning Off Old Glue	281

DEALING WITH STRUCTURAL PROBLEMS

Replacing a Broken Spindle	282
"Stretching" Short Rails	282
Splicing Together a Busted Spindle	283
Repairing a Dowel Joint	284
Making a Drawer Front Fit	284
Correcting Shelf Support Holes	285
Repairing a Split Tabletop	286

Repairing an Inlay Groove	286
Retrofitting Sagging Shelves	286
Repositioning Hinges	287
Rebuilding a Profiled Edge	288
Leveling Legs on Chairs and Tables	289
Cures for Cracked Case Sides	290

REPAIRING TWIST AND WARP

Flattening a Bowed Panel	291
Removing Twist from a Panel	292
Flattening a Warped Tabletop	292
Fitting a Cabinet to an Uneven Wall	292
Dealing with a Twisted Box	293
Flattening Twisted Doors	293

FIXING IMPERFECTIONS IN WOOD

Disguising Mismatched Boards	294
Concealing Pitch Pockets	294
Filling Knotholes	295
Patching Veneer Flaws	295

REPAIRING FINISHES

Eliminating Water Rings	296
Repairing a Burn Hole	297
Repairing a Softened Finish	297

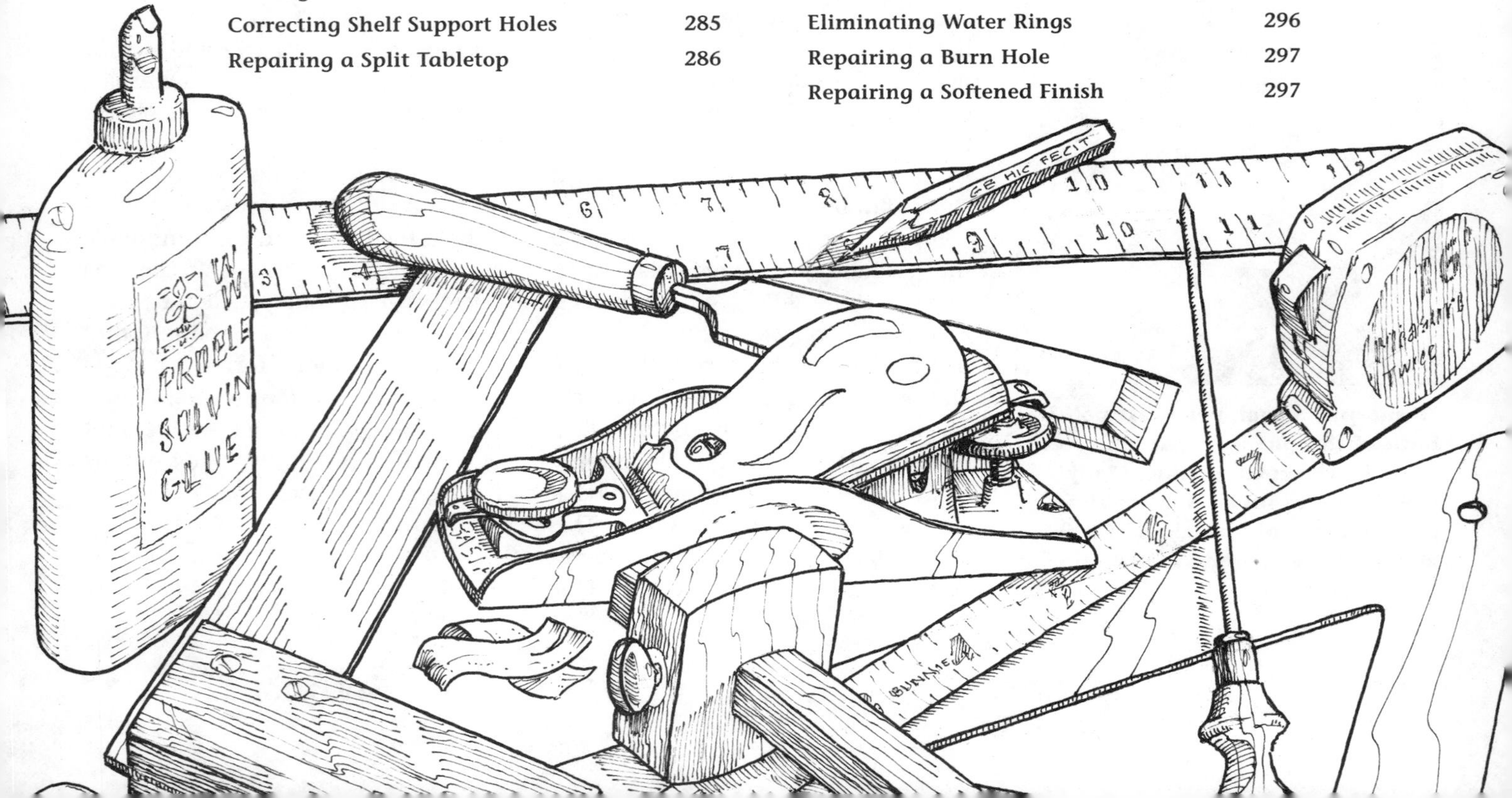

Fixing Dents and Gouges

Repairing Large Gouges

PROBLEM: *I dropped a big chisel onto a tabletop, leaving a wide gash in the wood. It's too big to fill with putty. What else can I do?*

SOLUTION: Gashes, gouges, and deep dents can be repaired by gluing in a wood patch from a piece of similar wood, ideally a cutoff from the same board. Use a small carving gouge to create a concave cavity that can be filled with a convex piece of wood, as shown in the middle below. Carve gently in the direction of the grain so that you are forming crisp edges along the opening. Taper the opening to rounded points at its ends, like a canoe or elongated football. This shape avoids abrupt end grain joints between the patch and the workpiece.

To shape the patch, file the edge of a piece of scrap so that its cross section is convex and it approximately matches the concave shape of the opening. Then cut the patch from the edge of the board and file or sand it to fit the overall shape of the opening. It doesn't need to fill the entire depth of the opening, but it should be at least ⅛ inch thick. In hardwoods, fit the patch so that it matches the opening cleanly. With softer woods, pressure from the clamp will mold the patch somewhat to the opening. Glue the patch into the opening with epoxy. Then hand plane the patch so that it is even with the surface. Sanding alone usually leaves an obvious mound.

W. Curtis Johnson
Corvallis, OR

RELATED INFO:
Deep Reach Clamping,
page 188

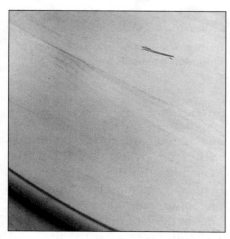

To repair a deep gouge like this one from a dropped chisel you need to make a wood patch.

Use a carving gouge to fashion the defect into a canoe-shaped trough, and then carve a patch to fit the opening.

Once the patch is glued in, you can plane and sand it level with the surface. Done well, the patch is indistinguishable from the surrounding wood.

Ironing Out Dents

PROBLEM: *I dropped my sander onto my freshly sanded tabletop. Is there a way to remove the dent without having to start over?*

SOLUTION: Nothing lifts up little dents like a little steam. Steam softens and expands the wood fibers, allowing them to return to their original shape. For raising a dent, you have a choice of tools. Woodburning pens and clean soldering guns are commonly used and are good for supplying heat right where you want it. When using these tools, puddle a few drops of water on the dent. After allowing the water a couple of seconds to sink in, touch the tip of the pen or gun to the water and steam away the puddle. The trick with this technique is to not touch the wood with the heat element—you don't want to scorch the wood.

Another tool, and one I prefer, is a small travel iron. Although it tends to raise the grain more around the surrounding surface, an iron is easier to hold and you can adjust the temperature, which reduces the chance that you'll burn the wood. I set the iron to "cotton," apply a damp cotton rag over the dent, and iron away. Don't let the iron touch the wood itself; it's not as likely to burn as the woodburning pens and soldering guns, but it can stain certain woods like oak. After steaming the wood, allow the piece to dry overnight. Then lightly sand the surface with 220-grit or finer grit sandpaper to knock off any whiskers raised by the extra steam.

Joe Wajszczuk
Jersey City, NJ

Dents in wood are inevitable. But if the wood fibers are not severed, dents can be raised with heat and moisture.

Hold a hot iron against a wet cloth laid on the dent for a few seconds at a time.

Resand the raised grain and the dent will be much less visible.

Filling and Staining Gouges

PROBLEM: *I am refinishing a blanket chest that appears to be made of walnut. One piece has some gouges that I would like to fill before staining. Is there a filling material that will accept stain to match the rest of the piece?*

SOLUTION: Sad to say, most fillers do not accept stain in quite the same way that wood does. However, some are better than others. The best I've found is 3M's Just Like Wood filler.

To prevent problems, get the filler as close as you can to the lightest value in the walnut. Let it dry on a sample scrap first, then stain it to see how it takes stain. (Some may end up too dark). If you are happy with the results, go for it. Remember that if you stay on the light side, you always have the option of putting in some grain lines or darkening the patch with a touch-up brush after the first coat of finish has dried.

Michael Dresdner
Puyallup, WA

Fixing Small Gashes

PROBLEM: *I just discovered a small gash in my new hall table. The wood fibers are torn, so I can't steam it out. How can I disguise the damage?*

SOLUTION: If the table has a film-type finish, the best bet is to use a burn-in stick (see "Sources," beginning on page 298) to fill the gash; then touch up the spot with paint to simulate the grain of the wood. Burn-in sticks are made from solid, colored shellac or lacquer. To use one, just heat the end with a special burn-in knife (a heated screwdriver will do in a pinch). This melts the finish so that you can puddle it into your gash.

To make your job simpler, mask off around the gash with 3M Fineline tape, a very thin tape that will not damage the finish. It is available from auto supply stores. Choose a burn-in stick that corresponds to the LIGHTEST background color you can find in the wood. Melt the burn-in stick into the hole, overfilling slightly, as shown at top right. If the blade of your knife has a flat end, let the knife cool a bit and then scrape across the burn-in lightly to level the burn-in to the tape. Otherwise, sand the burn-in flat to the tape.

Now remove the tape and sand the last bit of raised burn-in using 600-grit wet/dry paper wrapped around a small block, as shown at middle right. Be careful not to sand the surrounding finish too much or you will penetrate the finish.

When the surface is level, you can touch up the spot, as shown at bottom right. I like to use finely ground touch-up powders (see "Sources," beginning on page 298) mixed into shellac or padding lacquer. Since you already established the background color by using a light burn-in stick, you need only

add the darker grain lines to make the spot all but disappear. After the touch-up has been completed, finish the surface with French polish or a light topcoat to blend it with the area you worked on. Buff or steel wool the final surface (depending on whether it is gloss or satin) and you are back in business.

Incidentally, although you may do a good enough job on the spot so that no one else notices it, you will always see your own touch-up. You might want to place something artistically on or near the spot after it has dried, just to distract your eyes, if no one else's.

Michael Dresdner
Puyallup, WA

ANOTHER VIEW: While your first thought probably is of making an invisible repair of that gash, it's not your only option. As a woodworker, you've probably admired work with inlay designs or edgebanding. Any chance you could incorporate such treatment to enhance the look of that hall table instead of patching the gash?

Prepared inlay bandings are available by the foot in various woodworking catalogs, and such sources usually have larger pictorial designs as well. Routing the depression to accept an inlay is not difficult work.

Sometimes "accidents" offer a hidden opportunity to expand your woodworking repertoire.

Jim Cummins
Woodstock, NY

To hide a gouge or gash, fill the void with a colored shellac burn-in stick.

Once the burn-in has hardened, lightly sand the surface.

After finishing the work, paint in grain lines to disguise the repair.

Disguising Veneer Sand-Through

PROBLEM: *I was a little too aggressive in sanding the surface of some ash plywood, and I cut right through to the layer below. How can I hide the damage?*

SOLUTION: You have two choices: You can fill the damaged area and paint in the wood grain, or you can actually install a new strip of veneer along the whole length of the board. Filling in works best for small repairs, while replacing the veneer is the best cure for high-quality projects or for those that have straight grain or quarter-sawn material where there is a linear figure to the graining.

To fill the damaged area, first use a sharp chisel and very carefully remove the veneer around the sand-through down to a depth of ⅛ inch. Mix a small amount of Bondo, a fairly course auto body filler, and with a firm putty knife fill the damaged area until it's just proud of the surrounding surface. Allow this to dry overnight, then sand the surface so that it is flush. Next apply a light coat of Nitro-san. This is another form of auto body filler, only finer in substance. (Both are available at auto supply stores.) Then lightly sand with 400-grit sandpaper wrapped around a cork block. Dust off the sandings and reapply the Nitro-san. Allow this coat to dry overnight and then sand again with 400-grit sandpaper, but this time wrap the sandpaper around a firm sponge. This will help you feather the edges of the repair so that they blend into the veneer without the risk of sanding through the surrounding area.

Now you can color the repair. Many companies sell touch-up paints for furniture, but for a small-scale repair, several tubes of artist's oils will do. All you need are the basic colors that match your wood and some drying agent to help the oils dry quickly. Mix the colors to match the wood tone as closely as possible, then apply a very thin coat and allow it to dry. The coat will change tone when it's dry, and it usually won't be as bright as when it was wet. Apply a thin second coat, and when this is dry, you should be closer to the right color. Lightly sand the repair with 400-grit paper, then paint in the fine grain lines with a darker color to suggest the graining. A paint brush with only one hair can work well to grain the repair. After the graining dries, spray lacquer sealer over the paint and proceed with the finishing.

To install a new strip of veneer, first rout away the damage. Clamp two uniformly sized pieces of wood of similar thickness to the board and use them as guides for the router base. Set the depth of cut to the exact thickness of the veneer and carefully rout the entire length of the board. When you're done, cut a piece of replacement veneer that is just a hair larger than the size of your opening, then finely plane the edges to fit. Apply glue to the routed area and the veneer and press the veneer in place. If necessary gently use a small hammer and a smooth hardwood block to tap down the edges of the veneer. Then clamp the veneer overnight. I like to place waxed paper between the new veneer and my scrap clamping blocks so that the two don't stick together if glue seeps through.

David Stern Lightner
Philadelphia, PA

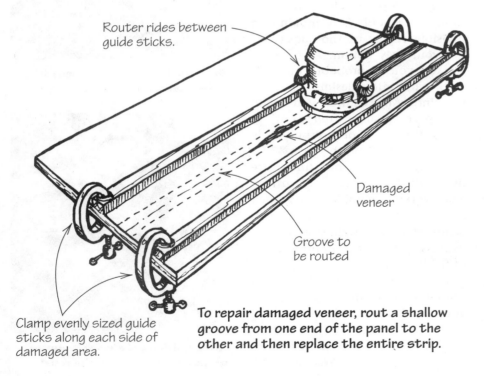

Router rides between guide sticks.

Damaged veneer

Groove to be routed

Clamp evenly sized guide sticks along each side of damaged area.

To repair damaged veneer, rout a shallow groove from one end of the panel to the other and then replace the entire strip.

RELATED INFO:
Two Dado Routing Jigs, page 153

Fixing Scratches

PROBLEM: *As I was moving a coffee table from my shop to the house, I bumped into the door frame and scratched the top. Can I fix this without resanding and refinishing the entire top?*

SOLUTION: Surface scratches may look slightly white from abrasion, but that doesn't mean that they have gone deep enough to remove the color from the wood. If that's the case with your scratch, you may be able to rub it out. Sand the area carefully with 600-grit wet/dry sandpaper using either mineral spirits or soapy water as a lubricant, as shown below left. You want to abrade the surface just enough to remove the scratch but not enough to cut through the entire finish. If this removes the scratch, you then can bring back the original sheen by rubbing out the surface. Use steel wool and paste wax for a satin finish or automotive polishing compound for a gloss finish.

If the scratch did not go down to the wood but is too deep to sand out, use a toothpick or a fine brush to carefully lay more finish into the scratch, as shown below right. Let it dry and repeat the process several times until the finish on the scratch is slightly proud of the finish on the rest of the surface. This process is called doping in. When the last coat of finish is dry, sand the proud area with 600-grit sandpaper and a lubricant, and rub out the surface as described above.

If the scratch is in a thin, penetrating oil finish, you can usually resand the spot, starting with 220-grit sandpaper and moving up to 600-grit, then reapply the oil finish to the area. If the finish is fairly new, reapplied oil finish should hide the spot well.

Michael Dresdner
Puyallup, WA

To repair minor scratches in a finish, sand them lightly with very fine sandpaper and a lubricant.

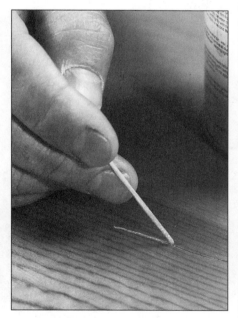

If the scratch is too deep to sand out, use a toothpick to apply finish directly to the scratch, then sand it level with the surrounding surface.

Repairing a Splintered Edge

PROBLEM: *A piece splintered up on the front edge of my tabletop. What can I do to fix it so that it won't show?*

SOLUTION: If the piece hasn't completely split off the board, you can glue it back to make an invisible repair. Use a thin piece of paper, thread or dental floss to work glue into the crack. For this kind of work, I prefer to use polyvinyl acetate (PVA) glue because it tacks up quickly. I just hold the piece in place with my finger or with masking tape until the glue sets.

If I'm fixing a split that is so tight that I can't work glue in with paper or floss, I like the self-spreading action of polyurethane glue. I apply a small amount of glue to the crack, then seal the outside edge with packing tape. As the glue cures, it will foam and work its way deep into the joint.

Joe Wajszczuk
Jersey City, NJ

To work glue under a splintered edge, use dental floss or the edge of a thin paper strip. Then use clear tape or a small spring clamp to press the splinter in place.

Solving Gluing Problems

Softening Old Glue

PROBLEM: *I glued up a chair recently and have since discovered that the legs aren't square. I know that I'll have to disassemble it and reglue, but how can I get the glue joints apart without damaging the chair?*

SOLUTION: Since the glue is fresh, you can probably resoften it enough to pull apart the chair back. I have found that a hot mixture of vinegar and water squirted into the joint will soften hide glue, white glue, and yellow glue. Be patient, apply the mixture frequently, and give it time to work.

In extreme cases, I've used steam. Using hose clamps, I attach a basketball air pump needle to one end of an automotive radiator overflow hose and put the other end of the hose on the steam stem of a cappuccino maker. Then I drill a small hole in the joint and push the nozzle of the fill pin into the hole. The steam softens the glue quickly.

With either method, once the glue starts to soften, you should wiggle apart the chair, and then clean all the glue off of the joints before it hardens.

If by chance you glued up the chair with epoxy, learn to live with it crooked. You will destroy the chair before you will convince epoxy to let go.

You usually can loosen a badly assembled glue joint by applying a mixture of hot water and vinegar; however if that fails, try steam. Drill a small hole in the joint and use a basketball air pump needle to direct steam into the hole.

Michael Dresdner
Puyallup, WA

Fixing a Failed Glue Joint

PROBLEM: *It looks like I didn't get enough glue on one of the mortise-and-tenon joints in a frame-and-panel door. Is there a way to reglue it without tearing apart the whole frame?*

SOLUTION: There's very little space in a properly cut mortise-and-tenon joint, so even if there isn't any glue, the joint should have very little play except for a straight pullout. I would just drill and pin all of the joints in that frame and be confident that the geometry of the joint will do its job. Timber frame barns and other buildings have been standing as solid as rocks for hundreds of years without a drop of glue in them, and I've seen solid antique furniture built the same way.

I made a small and sturdy trestle table without glue about ten years ago, and if I drive out a few pins, it will knock down into all of its parts with no problem. Pin it and nobody will ever know. Even if somebody takes your door apart 50 years from now to repair it, it's unlikely that the absence of glue in that joint will ever be noticed.

Of course, if you're one of those people who wears suspenders and a belt, you could try drilling a series of holes in the back of the door and using a high pressure glue injector to fill the joint with glue.

Jim Cummins
Woodstock, NY

Regluing Bubbled Veneer

PROBLEM: *My prized table has a spot where the veneer has bubbled up. How can I fix it?*

SOLUTION: If the table was made before 1950, it's probably held together with hide glue, which can be reactivated. Usually applying a medium hot, dry iron to the wood is enough to revitalize the glue and restore the glue bond. Make sure that you put a cloth between the iron and the veneer so that you don't damage the veneer surface. Get the veneer good and hot without burning it and then clamp a block of wood over the trouble spot for a couple of hours to hold the veneer flat while the glue dries.

If the hot, dry iron does not work, you need to get some moisture down under the veneer to where the hide glue dried out. Again use a medium hot, dry iron, but this time place a damp cloth under the iron. If the offending piece of veneer can be lifted, spray a little water under it to help reactivate the glue. Clamp the veneer down with a block and let it dry.

If the hide glue has deteriorated so much that there is nothing there to revitalize or if the piece was assembled with a modern glue such as yellow or white wood glue, you can inject glue under the veneer. If possible, lift the veneer with a razor to get the glue underneath. If the veneer is bubbled and you can't get under it, cut a slit through the bubble with a razor and inject the glue with a hypodermic needle made for this purpose, as shown below. Then use blocks and clamps to hold the veneer in place until the glue dries.

Bill and Joanne Storch
Corvallis, OR

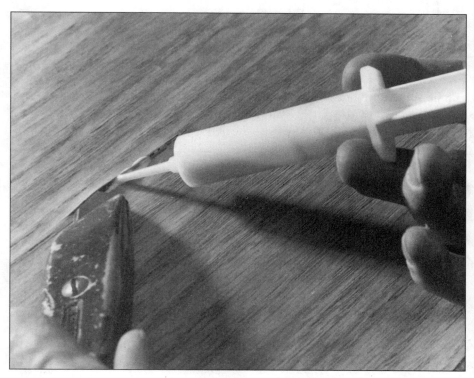

If your veneer bubbles up due to failed glue, cut a slit in the area that's bubbled, insert fresh glue, then clamp the area down.

CLEANING OFF OLD GLUE

When regluing a repaired joint, if you don't remove the old glue, the joint is likely to fail in the future. The usual solution is to scrape away the glue with a sharp chisel, but this quickly dulls the tool. To save my chisels, I use 3M's Safer Stripper to take off old glue. I've found that this paint stripper works well on yellow and white glue. To use, carefully brush the stripper onto the wood, wait a few hours, then rub everything off with an abrasive pad. Clean any glue or stripper residue from the joint with a damp rag before regluing the joint.

To avoid this problem entirely, I prefer using old-fashioned hide glue. Nothing is easier than repairing joints with this stuff—new glue melts the old glue to form a cohesive bond. You can choose to cook up a batch yourself, or use the bottled version. And should you need to make another repair sometime in the future, you can open the glue joints with a little water and heat.

Randy Wilkenson
Baltic, CT

Hide glue can be reactivated with heat and water, making it an excellent choice for repairs.

Dealing with Structural Problems

Replacing a Broken Spindle

PROBLEM: *One of the arm spindles was broken off of my Windsor chair when it was being moved. Is there any way to replace it without disassembling the chair?*

SOLUTION: There are a couple of ways to tackle this one. First, you could extend the mortise in the seat so that it goes all the way through the seat, as shown below. This should allow the bottom tenon of the replacement spindle to slip far enough into the new hole that the top tenon has clearance to enter the mortise in the arm. Once the spindle is glued in place, you can install a plug from below to keep it from dropping down.

Or, if you're willing to give up a little structural integrity, you could make a replacement spindle with a short stub tenon on the bottom and flex the chair arm until the spindle pops into place.

Finally, here's how I repaired a Boston rocker that had a couple of back spindles broken off right at the crest rail. I removed the crest rail, drilled out the broken stubs, then cut down the other spindles by ½ inch. The rail then went back on with no problems. Nobody would ever notice that it's ½ inch lower than it used to be.

Jim Cummins
Woodstock, NY

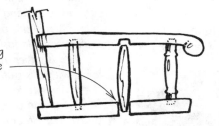

The new spindle drops deep into the extended mortise, creating clearance for the top tenon.

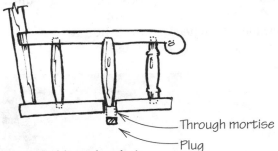

Through mortise

Plug

To replace a chair spindle without disassembling the chair, drill the seat mortise all the way through. Position the new spindle, then install a plug from below to hold it in place.

"Stretching" Short Rails

PROBLEM: *I misread the marks on some mortise-and-tenon door frames I'm making and now the rails are too short. Can I fix this without starting over?*

SOLUTION: It depends on how short the rails are and how the fix will affect your design. If they are short by a distance that is the same as the combined length of the tenons (a mistake we all make at least once), then mortise both the rails and the stiles and connect the parts with separate tenons. If they're a little shy of a good fit between the stiles, you could glue a contrasting wood to the ends of the rails or the edges of the stiles and then join the parts with loose tenons.

Kevin Ireland
Wescosville, PA

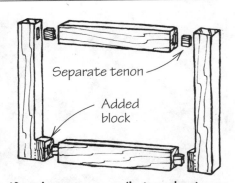

Separate tenon

Added block

If you've cut your rails *too short*, use separate tenons instead of cutting tenons on the rails (*top*). Or add a contrasting block of wood to compensate for short rails (*bottom*).

Splicing Together a Busted Spindle

PROBLEM: *I'd just finished turning a rather complex spindle and I was removing the toolrest to sand it. In my impatience, I slipped with the wrench and broke the spindle. Is there any way I can fix it?*

SOLUTION: In most cases, it's easier and better to make a new one. But if you really want to save and use the one you've already turned, here's one way to do it. Let's say that the turning was about ¼ inch in diameter where it broke. Cut a couple of ½-inch-long pieces of ½-inch-diameter hardwood dowel. Drill a ⁵⁄₁₆-inch hole about halfway through each dowel piece, centering the holes on the dowels. Now shoot a little hot glue into these caps and press them onto the broken ends of the spindle parts.

Drill a small center hole into the exposed end of each cap and remount the spindle in the lathe. Check the centering at low speed or even by hand turning the piece; reposition the part as necessary until the spindle turns without wobbling. Now you can finish sanding the spindle.

Once you have completed the sanding, leave the caps in place and use the center holes in the caps as guides to follow when you drill a hole into each broken spindle. Make the holes to fit an appropriate nail, say an 8d, and drill about an inch into each broken end. Now pop the caps off and pick out any bits of glue from the broken parts. Test fit the pieces, lining up the original break as well as you can. If the parts won't fit, you may need to trim some slivers; be careful to cut away as little as possible to make them the proper proportion.

Mix up some epoxy and work it into the nail holes as well as onto the mating surfaces of the spindle parts. Push the parts together with the lathe centers, hand turning the parts to make them as straight as possible. Leave the parts clamped until the glue dries.

Fred Matlack
Vera Cruz, PA

In a pinch, you can sand and repair a broken spindle with the help of temporary "caps." First hot-glue each half of the spindle to a cap (*far right*).

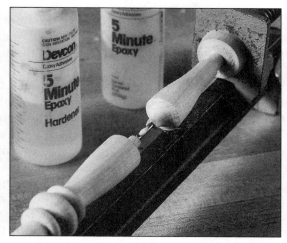

Locate the center of the caps (*left*); then remount the spindle halves and sand them. Next drill through the caps to create a mortise in the broken end of each spindle. Finally epoxy a nail into the mortises to strengthen the reconnected spindle (*right*).

Repairing a Dowel Joint

PROBLEM: *The dowel joint in the seat of a favorite chair has broken. How can I replace the dowels so that the two halves of the seat meet flush at the surface?*

SOLUTION: The simplest solution is to use dowel centers, but first you'll need to establish a flat surface on which you can work. Trim the broken ends of the dowels with a sharp chisel or plane so that they are flush with the edges of both boards. Then in the edge of one board bore holes for a dowel center that is larger in diameter than the original dowel. Locate the holes exactly over the broken ends of the dowels if necessary or, if you have the space, move them a little farther along the edge. Fit your dowel center into the board and clamp the boards together. Use the marks left by the dowel centers in both edges to position your drill bit for boring the dowel holes.

Use a spade bit to bore the hole to the required depth (using a depth stop, depth gauge, or simply a

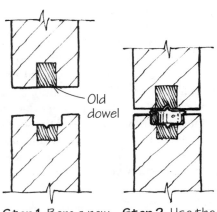

Step 1. Bore a new hole in one side of the joint.

Step 2. Use the dowel center to mark the other side at the joint.

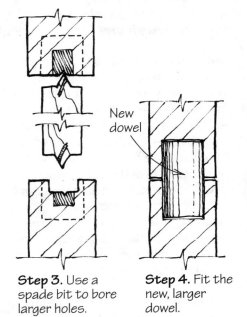

New dowel

Step 3. Use a spade bit to bore larger holes.

Step 4. Fit the new, larger dowel.

piece of tape wrapped around the spade bit's shank to indicate the depth you need). Test fit your larger replacement dowels to make sure that the two halves of the chair seat are flush. Then glue the dowels in place.

Graham Blackburn
Bearsville, NY

Making a Drawer Front Fit

PROBLEM: *Murphy's Law was in effect when I made the two drawers for my new stepback cupboard—each one is a little too small for the opening. How can I salvage this project?*

SOLUTION: Unless you busted your buns making those drawers, the easy solution is to make new ones and save the undersized ones for the next piece. But if you absolutely must use them, here are some ideas:

Install beading. Cut the drawers down on all sides to make a uniform gap of between 1/8 and 1/4 inch around them. Then make edge strips as wide as the drawer is thick. If the drawer front is plywood or a veneered panel that won't expand and contract substantially, you can

apply the bead to the front itself. If the drawer front is solid wood, apply the bead to the edges of the case to make the opening smaller.

In either situation, round the front edge of the strips to disguise the glue line. Miter the strips to fit, and glue them on. This look imitates "cock beading," which is a feature on many antiques. Cock beading is usually the same wood as the rest of the drawer, but it could be a contrasting wood. You might like the look of the modified drawer so much that you

want to add the same feature to the cupboard's doors. In that case, it's easier to rout a rabbet to accept the cock beading than it is to glue the strip to the full width of each board.

Build out the opening. If the drawer front is too small by more than 1/2 inch or so, adding a bead won't work. But you can use the same technique to build out the drawer opening to make it smaller. Instead of a bead though, glue in square build-out blocking. As with beading, miter the corners and consider using a contrasting wood to make the feature look intentional.

Build up the divider. If a pair of drawers is too narrow, and they are separated by a center divider, add cock beading to the divider on both sides. If the divider absolutely must be replaced instead of shimmed, cut out the old one and, instead of disassembling the case to get the new one in, dovetail the new one into place. If you cut the dovetails on the divider and then scribe them onto the cabinet, the joint is not difficult to cut. People seeing the dovetails will marvel at your craftsmanship and never think to ask why you picked the "hard way" to do it.

Jim Cummins
Woodstock, NY

RELATED INFO:
Adding Molding to Enhance Plain Projects, page 19

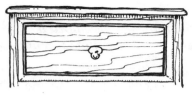

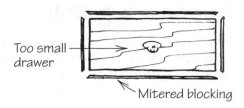

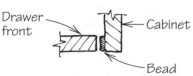

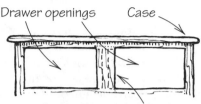

To correct a drawer front that's *too* small for the opening, add beading around the opening or the drawer (above left). Or build out the opening with mitered blocking (above right). Or replace the divider with a thicker one on side-by-side drawers (bottom right).

Thicker dovetailed divider reduces the width of the opening on side-by-side drawers.

Correcting Shelf Support Holes

PROBLEM: *When I was halfway through the process of drilling shelf support holes in a set of bookcase sides, I realized that the fence on my drill press had slipped. Now the shelf holes don't line up. Is there any way to fix this, short of starting over?*

SOLUTION: Assuming that you found the problem before you assembled the shelves, you have a couple of options. First, you could rout grooves where the holes are, then glue in strips of contrasting wood and drill new holes, as shown. Or, if you're worried that you may run into the same hole alignment problems a second time, you could rout grooves that are wide enough to accept standard metal shelf pilasters and install them in the grooves instead.

If the mismatched holes are off by more than the diameter of a hole, you have a third option: Drill double the number of holes in both case sides and pretend that the extra holes are there for greater adjustment opportunities.

If you discovered the problem after you glued together the bookshelves and the error is small, you could try to disguise it. Carve your own shelf support pins and make the pins on one side taller than those on the other.

Kevin Ireland
Wescosville, PA

You can salvage a bookcase that has mislocated shelf holes by routing grooves over the old holes, inserting contrasting strips of wood, then redrilling new holes into the strips. Use a template block to locate the holes.

Repairing a Split Tabletop

PROBLEM: *I built a beautiful dining table that has developed a nasty split in the top after just a few weeks inside my home. What went wrong and how I can fix it?*

SOLUTION: Boards shrink and expand in width as they lose and absorb moisture from the air. Even a stable wood like mahogany can shrink up to ¼ inch per foot of width when the moisture level in the wood decreases from 12 to 6 percent. You'd encounter such a swing if during the winter you brought your table into a heated home from a cold garage or unheated shop. The same wood movement can occur if the wood used to build the project was not properly kiln-dried.

A tabletop splits at the edges when the wood loses moisture. Moisture is released much more readily along the end grain of the wood, so the ends of the boards in a tabletop dry before the middle parts do. When this occurs, the table splits. If your edge joints are less than perfect, the split may occur there. If the glue bond is sound, the wood itself will split.

The fix, once the table has fully acclimated to indoors and the boards have stopped moving, is to rip the top along the glueline, then joint or plane the edges and reglue the boards. (If you just squeeze some glue into the open joint, it will eventually split again.) Most often, the top will still be wide enough to use on the piece. If it's not, rip out more than you need to, then add a board that's wide enough to get the tabletop to size again.

You'll occasionally see a piece of art furniture with a split that is held together with a dovetailed "butterfly." The main job of such a patch is to catch the eye and make the viewer wonder at how rare and special that piece of wood must be, to require a Band-Aid. On more commonplace furniture, such a repair is out of place and looks about as glamorous as a piece of tissue stuck onto a shaving cut. It's more a distraction than a feature to be proud of.

Jim Cummins
Woodstock, NY

Repairing an Inlay Groove

PROBLEM: *While I was cutting a slot for a strip of inlay on a tabletop, the router moved off of the fence slightly and left a bulge in the groove. How can I fix it?*

SOLUTION: You have several options. First, consider whether or not a wider strip of inlay would look okay. If so, rout the groove with a wider bit, or move the router fence and widen the groove with a second cut. Second, if the mishap occurred in a groove that runs with the grain of the tabletop, saw the top along its length at the groove, joint the parts, reglue them and recut the groove. You sacrifice a bit of the width this way, but not much. Finally, small imperfections can be filled with wood filler or glue mixed with sanding dust after the inlay has been glued in place.

Ben Erickson
Eutaw, AL

Retrofitting Sagging Shelves

PROBLEM: *After making and installing some plain plywood bookshelves, I found out that they would have to support medical encyclopedias. Is there a good way to counteract the now sagging shelves?*

SOLUTION: There are several approaches to consider, and the best one will depend on the details of your cabinet's construction. You might also combine more than one of these approaches.

Back edge support strips. The technique least obtrusive to the existing shelves, and the easiest to accomplish, is simply to nail or screw a strip of wood onto the bottom of the shelf along the back edge. The strip should be a minimum of ⅝ inch square. A similar but stronger measure is to attach the new strips to the cabinet back. This works only if the shelves are nonadjustable, and if you can get behind the cabinet. Both versions of this fix will maintain the vertical capacity of the shelves, which may be important. However, these approaches may keep the back edge from sagging while the shelf continues to sag along its front edge.

Front edge support strips. You could install the support strips along the front edge of the shelves. This approach is quite visible but can be accomplished so that the strips look like they're part of the original design. The easiest method is to screw on the strips. If you want to conceal the screws, consider screwing from under the strip on the lower shelves, and from above on the higher shelves. Or use biscuits and glue instead of screws or nails to reinforce the joint. Also, to conceal the joint between the two parts, prefinish the strips, and rout or plane a small chamfer along the joined edge. If the shelves are removable, chamfer their edges as well. This fix reduces the clearance for the books by the thickness of the supports.

Vertical supports. The third and most effective solution is to add vertical supports between the shelves. These supports can be full depth, stepped back somewhat from the shelf edges, or canted at an angle. They should be screwed or nailed in place from above and below. You'll have to offset these supports enough to access the screws or nails, or you could offset them a lot to create a symmetrical pattern.

David Stern Lightner
Philadelphia, PA

RELATED INFO:
Avoiding Sagging Shelves,
page 11

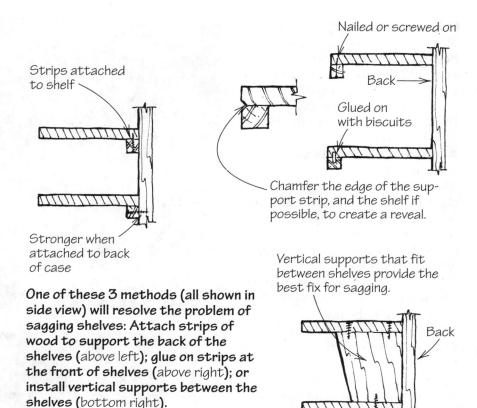

One of these 3 methods (all shown in side view) will resolve the problem of sagging shelves: Attach strips of wood to support the back of the shelves (above left); glue on strips at the front of shelves (above right); or install vertical supports between the shelves (bottom right).

Repositioning Hinges

PROBLEM: *One of the butt hinges on a door is not properly located. It needs to move only 1/16 inch or so. How can I move it to the right place?*

SOLUTION: For best results, enlarge the mortise on the door or the cabinet and move the hinge as needed. Then patch the gap that's left along the edge of the hinge. Depending on the size of the gap, use a piece of matching veneer or solid wood that's been cut to fit. Match the grain direction of the wood around the patch, as shown at right. Let the patch extend above the wood; then sand or plane it flush when the glue has dried.

That takes care of the mortise, but if you already drilled the holes, the hinge will pull its way back to the previous location. That's why it's best to mount hardware with one or two screws only, leaving the others undrilled in the event of repositioning. If the drilled holes are off by more than half a hinge hole, fill the holes with a tapered plug whittled with a sharp knife or chisel, as shown on page 288.

Wait for the glue to dry, then trim the plug flush with the mortise. Put the hinge in place and punch a centered starting hole with an awl for each screw. Then drill starter holes for the screws. Better yet, drill with a Vix Bit, which automatically centers the screw hole in the hinge hole. Don't redrill the hole until you first fix the mortise.

For drilled holes that are off by less than half a hinge hole, try to

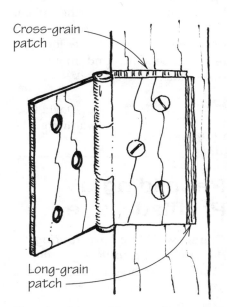

To reposition a hinge, enlarge the mortise, remount the hinge, and then patch the gap.

fudge the situation by inserting the other screws first (assuming you haven't misaligned them all), then ream out the last hole with an awl in the direction you need it to go. If the screw still sits too cockeyed in the countersink, remove the hinge, plug the hole, and redrill it.

AVOIDING THE PROBLEM: When you install hardware—especially hinges—always make sure that the chest or cabinet sits on a flat and level surface. Otherwise you may wonder why your carefully aligned doors fit so poorly when the project is installed.

Also, don't choose and apply hardware as an afterthought. Plan for it as you do the rest of your design, and buy it ahead of time so that you'll have it in hand as you build the piece.

When positioning hardware to mark a mortise, use a little hot glue to hold it in place. Use hot glue also when you are locating mating parts, like the strike for a ball-bearing catch. After mounting the catch on the door, position the strike plate and apply a dab of hot glue. Then quickly close the door so that the strike is in its desired position. When the glue sets, you can mark the location, remove the glue, and mount the strike plate.

David Page
Swarthmore, PA

When screw holes are off by more than half a hinge hole, fill them with a tapered plug (*left*) then form a centered starter hole with an awl or Vix Bit and re-drill (*below*).

Rebuilding a Profiled Edge

PROBLEM: *While I was routing the profile on a table edge, some blow-out destroyed an inch or so of the edge. How can I repair this?*

SOLUTION: You can patch the mistake with new wood, and the job is easy if you use a guide block and a chisel that's been properly sharpened. It's not enough that the chisel be sharp enough to shave with; the main thing is that the back of the chisel be honed down until it is dead-flat right up to the cutting edge. This will allow the chisel to cut flat, instead of riding up like a ski as it works. Once the chisel is ready, saw a guide block at an angle (45-degree or shallower) and clamp it to the work, as shown at top right on the opposite page. Using the block to guide the chisel, shave the ends of the cutout. Then flatten the bottom of the repair area. If the blow-out isn't too deep, you can probably cut away the damage with just your chisel. For more significant repairs, set up your router and a fence, and rout to a uniform depth. Once the damaged area is prepared, make a patch from wood that closely matches the grain and tone of the damaged area and cut the same angle on the ends of the patch. Glue in the patch, then plane or chisel the surfaces so that they are flush with the existing edge and re-rout the profile.

Jim Cummins
Woodstock, NY

The router is a perfect tool for cutting profiles, but it can also cause blow-out when the high-speed cutter meets troublesome grain in the wood.

To repair a blow-out, use an angled guide block to trim each end of the damaged area, then flatten the area in between.

Cut a patch and glue it in place. The angle of the ends of the patch should match the angle of the guide block.

Rout the profile on the patch. If possible, deepen the profile slightly and re-rout the entire edge.

Leveling Legs on Chairs and Tables

PROBLEM: *I made a chair that will not sit level. I need to trim the legs, but I am afraid of ending up like the guy in the old cartoon—sitting in a chair with legs only inches high. What should I do?*

SOLUTION: There is a very simple solution to this old problem, and it will work for tables as well as chairs. As you may remember from high school geometry, three points describe a plane. That's why a three-legged stool will not rock, while a four-legged chair will. To fix your chair, first place it on a flat surface. The top of your table saw is more reliable than a workbench. Allow the longer leg to hang over the edge. The chair sits level on the three legs and does not rock. Push the overhanging leg against the edge of the table. Mark where the surface and the leg meet, as shown below. When you cut on

If one leg on a chair is too long, stand the chair on a flat surface with the long leg overhanging and mark where the leg meets the surface. This is the amount you need to remove.

this mark, the four chair legs will all be in the same plane.

If you discover that more than one leg is uneven, you can use the following solution, although it is more complicated than fixing just one leg. Begin on a surface that is not only perfectly flat but also level. If you use the top of your table saw, make sure it is level first. Using the chair seat to check for level, place shims under the ends of the legs. When the seat is level, set a pencil compass to the maximum amount you need to trim.

Place the point of the compass on the level surface and use the pencil to draw a line around each leg. Cut on these marks and the four legs should again lie in a plane.

Mike Dunbar
Hampton, NH

If all four legs are uneven, stand the piece on a surface that is level and flat, then shim the legs. When the chair seat is level, use a compass to mark off the amount to be trimmed.

CURES FOR CRACKED CASE SIDES

When the side of a chest or case develops cracks, you can usually blame the problem on another piece of wood in the case.

Wood expands and contracts in width, but not in length. So anytime the width of one board is attached to the length of another, movement will be restrained, and the tension can build up until one board splits or the attachment fails.

On a case side, a molding applied across the grain will pop off in time because the side is shrinking and expanding constantly while the molding's length remains the same. For example, if the cross-grain piece is an attached drawer runner on the inside, the runner will loosen, or, if the glue is really good, the side may split.

The cure for such problems is to attach wood so that the restrained piece can still move. The drawings show a few methods I've run into over the years.

If a case develops cracks, you have a few options for repairing it. The most elaborate requires that you disassemble the case, saw the sides apart along the crack line and reglue the wood. There aren't many people who would find this practical. A second option is to rout a 3-inch-wide shallow groove along the entire length of the side. You then can inlay matching wood and pass it off as a three-board side. However, my inclination would be to leave the crack alone. It's part of the delight of woodworking to know that the material we use is still alive and moving long after it's been cut from the tree.

Jim Cummins
Woodstock, NY

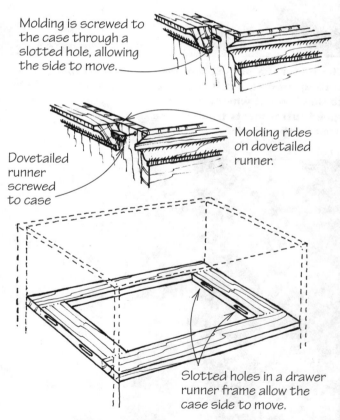

Molding is screwed to the case through a slotted hole, allowing the side to move.

Molding rides on dovetailed runner.

Dovetailed runner screwed to case

Slotted holes in a drawer runner frame allow the case side to move.

Chests and other wide cases can crack if the wood is restrained from moving due to changes in the moisture content of the air. These construction methods will prevent the problem.

Repairing Twist and Warp

Flattening a Bowed Panel

PROBLEM: *I thickness planed some figured boards to use as panels in frame-and-panel doors, but they bowed severely. Is there a reliable method of flattening them?*

SOLUTION: If the bow isn't too severe, you can try wetting the wood and then clamping it flat until it redries. To be sure the panels won't bow again, or bow further, I'd install sliding dovetail battens in the back of each one, as shown.

When making the battens, cut them from a length of stock, so that the grain in the batten runs perpendicular to the grain in the panel. The battens can't be glued in place; they rely instead on a tight mechanical fit to hold the wood flat. A setscrew at the center of each batten keeps the battens in place permanently, while allowing the panel to expand and contract. Locate each batten at least a few inches in from the end of the panel. When done with precision and care, this method can lend an interesting detail to a project. I've used it on tabletops and have left the batten protruding slightly, chamfering the ends as you would a through-tenon joint.

When using this technique, always make the dovetail slot first and then fit the batten to the slot. Make the depth of the slot about two-thirds the thickness of the top. Remember that a dovetail slot has to be routed in a single pass. However you should first remove most of the waste by sawing or routing a dado. You then can rout the dovetail with minimal resistance. If possible, rout the slots on the router table; then all you need to do is adjust the fence to rout the

A dovetailed batten made of contrasting wood can add an interesting design detail while keeping the panel flat.

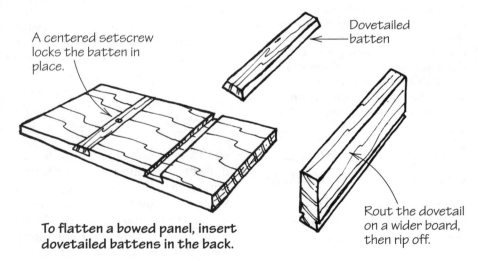

A centered setscrew locks the batten in place.

Dovetailed batten

To flatten a bowed panel, insert dovetailed battens in the back.

Rout the dovetail on a wider board, then rip off.

shoulders on the battens. For safety, rout each batten from a wider piece of stock, then saw it off.

When you fit the batten to the dovetail slot, it should be tight enough that you have to tap it in with a mallet or draw it into the slot with a clamp. To install the battens,

clamp the panel flat and insert the battens and the center setscrew. If possible, leave the panel clamped flat for a day so that the wood fibers can relax in their new position.

David Stern Lightner
Philadelphia, PA

Removing Twist from a Panel

PROBLEM: *I glued up a panel and when I removed it from the clamps, I found that it was twisted. Is there a way to straighten it?*

SOLUTION: If you have sufficient thickness, you can hand plane the panel straight. Or if you can't spare that much wood, you can rip the

You can sometimes remove twist from a board by clamping the high corners (thus reversing the twist), then using a wet cloth and an iron to steam the wood and relax the fibers. Allow the panel to cool for an hour before unclamping.

panel into narrower pieces, plane the twist out of each one, and then reglue them. Relieving a little of the twist in each segment reduces the amount of wood you'll lose, though you'll still sacrifice a little thickness and a little width.

There's also a last-resort technique that's worked occasionally for me. Lay the panel on a flat, sturdy surface and check how far the opposing corners lift off the table. Find a strip of wood that's as thick as this gap or a little thicker and lay it under the panel diagonally between the low corners. That should double the height of the raised corners. Now clamp down the raised corners to the table so that you've reversed the twist.

Next saturate a piece of cloth—say a hand towel—and lay it across the face of the panel. Rub a hot iron over the towel until it is dry and the wood is about as hot as you can get it without it becoming scorched. Leave the clamps on until the panel is cool to the touch—at least an hour. Results vary, but this could remove most of the twist.

Fred Matlack
Vera Cruz, PA

Flattening a Warped Tabletop

PROBLEM: *The top has cupped on a 5-foot-diameter table that I just built. Can I reflatten it?*

SOLUTION: The prevailing wisdom on straightening a warped top like this is to place it in the sun, concave side down, until it returns to its original flatness. A few woodworkers claim that wetting the underside helps to speed up the process. After the wood has straightened out, check its moisture content. If it's fairly high,

say 12 percent or so, clamp the top flat with cauls and store it in a warm, dry place until it drops to around 8 percent. After the top is dry, apply a finish to the top's upper and lower surfaces. This way, seasonal movement will occur at an even rate.

AVOIDING THE PROBLEM: When building a large surface such as a tabletop, you can prevent warping by using quarter-sawn stock and by making sure that the underside gets as much finish as the top, show side.

Ellis Walentine
Coopersburg, PA

Fitting a Cabinet to an Uneven Wall

PROBLEM: *I made a wall cabinet square and true, but when I tried to hang it on a plastered wall, it wouldn't lay flat. What can I do to mount it so that it lays flat against the wall?*

SOLUTION: Sounds like your wall is the culprit here, but you'd face the same problem if the cabinet were slightly twisted. There are two solutions to consider: First, glue strips of wood to the back edges of the cabinet, then scribe the strips to the wall; or second, apply a thin strip of wood over the back edge of the cabinet to cover the gap. The first solution will be cleaner and look less like a fix—if you can get a clean glue joint between the cabinet and the added scribe strip. The second solution is easier but may not look as satisfactory as the first. Both solutions require that you scribe new strips of wood to the contour of the wall.

To add glued-on scribe strips, first determine the maximum gap between the wall and the back of the cabinet when the cabinet is correctly positioned level and plumb. Mount the cabinet temporarily to the wall with screws to do this. Rip strips of wood that are slightly wider than the gap and glue them to the back edges of the cabinet parts. (You need to work on only the sides of the cabinet that are visible.) Again, secure the cabinet level and plumb to the wall and scribe the curvature of the wall onto the new scribe strips. Use a saber saw, block plane, or spokeshave—whatever works best—to trim the scribe strips to the lines traced off the wall. Once the cabinet fits satisfactorily, finish the scribe strips to match the rest of the cabinet and permanently mount the cabinet to the wall.

To cover the gap with applied scribe strips, attach the cabinet to the wall using shims to keep it level and plumb. Rip strips that are at least ¼ inch wider than the widest gap and as thin as practical. Scribe the strips as described above and attach them to the cabinet with brads or hot glue.

AVOIDING THE PROBLEM: Always build cabinets that will be mounted to the wall so that the edges can be scribed. That usually means recessing the back ½ inch or so in from the sides, top, and bottom.

Fred Matlack
Vera Cruz, PA

Dealing with a Twisted Box

PROBLEM: *A jewelry box that I made from mahogany has twisted so that it rocks on all corners. I joined the sides with box joints and sealed the wood inside and out. What's the problem?*

SOLUTION: My hunch is that it may have to do with how accurately you machined your box joints. It's not sufficient for the interlocking fingers to fit perfectly into each other; they must be square in both directions, too. If they're off by just a little bit, you'll be introducing twist into the assembly. You wouldn't notice this when gluing up because the weight of the clamps tends to counteract the twist.

I'm assuming here that the top and bottom panels are veneered or floating in grooves. If they are solid and glued onto or into the sides, differential shrinkage or expansion could be the source of your problem. You might be able to make the box side level by planing some of the twist out of the bottom of the box, but the best option for a quality job is to start over.

Ellis Walentine
Coopersburg, PA

Flattening Twisted Doors

PROBLEM: *The frame-and-panel doors that I just assembled are twisted and won't hang right in the cabinet. Can I get rid of the twist?*

SOLUTION: Flattening a twisted frame-and-panel door has a low probability of success. Before making the door over from scratch, however, consider this technique: On the table saw, cut a kerf through the joint lines on the back of the doors. The kerf should be in the rail stock and go as deep as the tenon in the rail. The kerfs will allow the joints to flex slightly without breaking the bond between the mortise and tenon. Now clamp the door to a flat surface and glue slips of wood into the kerfs, as shown. The grain in the slips should run lengthwise. The kerfs may vary slightly in width once you clamp the door flat, so make the slips fit the narrowest kerf. Use epoxy and it will fill any gaps where the shims are slightly loose. Let the epoxy cure thoroughly and, with some luck, the door should be flatter than when you started. One final note: Large doors made from ¾-inch-thick stock will twist AFTER you've glued them up if you don't keep them flat. I stack doors on a flat surface or stand them vertically against a flat wall.

QUICK FIX: When you're stuck with a twisted door, you can sometimes force it to lie flat in its opening by installing stops and then fitting a latch on the corner that protrudes.

Tony O'Malley
Emmaus, PA

To flatten a twisted door, saw kerfs along the glue line on the back of the door to allow the joints to flex slightly. Then clamp the door flat and glue slips of wood into the kerfs to help hold the door flat.

Fixing Imperfections in Wood

Disguising Mismatched Boards

PROBLEM: *When I glued up the sides of a cabinet that I'm building, the color of all the wood looked like a good match. But now that I've applied stain, the difference in color is just screaming. How can I disguise this?*

SOLUTION: You can remedy this problem and create an attractive design effect with some simple inlay placed along the glue line. Use a nice contrasting wood to maximize the effect. First rout or saw a groove along the seam where the two pieces of wood are glued. I make mine about ¼ inch wide × ¼ inch deep. Then cut your inlay stock on the table saw and plane it down to fit snugly in the groove. Sand the bottom edges of the strips slightly if necessary to get them in the grooves. I shoot for a tight fit and I don't mind if I have to tap them into place after I have applied some wood glue to the groove.

When the glue is dry, use a hand plane or sander to trim the inlay so that it is level with the face of the boards. You now have a more attractive and interesting glued-up panel. The inlay prevents the eye from seeing the mismatched boards, creating instead a segmented view of the individual boards. Of course, you can use the technique anytime you want to add some contrasting lines to a solid panel.

Dennis Slabaugh
Naples, FL

When you need to disguise a mismatch between the color or grain of glued-up boards, rout a groove on the glue line and inlay a strip of contrasting wood.

Concealing Pitch Pockets

PROBLEM: *I have a few pitch pockets on the surface of an otherwise beautiful board. How can I best fill and conceal them?*

SOLUTION: Clean the resin out of the pocket with lacquer thinner and a toothbrush. Let the wood dry thoroughly. Fill the pocket with a mixture of epoxy and sanding dust. Let this dry and plane the repair so that it is flush with the surface of the wood.

Ben Erickson
Eutaw, AL

You can hide an ugly pitch pocket by filling it with a mixture of epoxy and sanding dust. The repair will be nearly seamless.

Filling Knotholes

PROBLEM: *An otherwise perfect board has a knothole. How can I best fill it without detracting from the beauty of the board?*

SOLUTION: If you want to conceal the knothole, look for an area on a scrap piece of wood where the grain forms circles or has a pleasing irregular shape that will blend with the wood around the knothole. You might even find a tight knot in a similar piece of wood. If you just want to fill the hole without concealing it, choose a very dark piece of scrap that resembles the color of the missing knot. Saw and file a plug that fits well at the surface. The fit won't be perfect in any case, but the surface fit is the most important. The trick is to glue in the plug with a filler made from sanding dust and epoxy glue. The epoxy will glue the plug in place, while the sanding dust will fill any imperfections. Of course, if you have the missing knot, you can just glue it in with the epoxy filler.

W. Curtis Johnson
Corvallis, OR

A knothole like this in an otherwise attractive board can be plugged with a piece of wood from a board with similar grain.

First use a rat-tail file to smooth the edges of the hole. Then cut a plug on the band saw and sand it until you can force fit it into the hole.

The finished result looks like a tight knot, but stands out much less.

Patching Veneer Flaws

PROBLEM: *I veneered a panel with burled veneer and there are a few voids where the veneer simply broke off during handling. How can I fill these holes?*

SOLUTION: Because the figure on burl veneer is convoluted and irregular, patches are easier to conceal than on plain-sawn veneers. I'd fill small voids (¼ inch or less across) with a shellac burn-in stick. See "Fixing Small Gashes" on page 277. Larger voids will be better concealed with a veneer patch. Depending on the location and size of the patch needed, you may be able to cut out a triangular- or diamond-shaped area around the void and fit a veneer patch to match.

But the best patch for burl is an irregularly shaped one with curved edges—think of the amoeba from high school biology class. Cutting and fitting such a patch can be done, but it'll take some time and patience to get good results. Or, if you work with veneer a lot, consider buying a veneer punch, like the one shown. It cuts the shape around the defect as well as the perfectly fitting patch.

Tony O'Malley
Emmaus, PA

A veneer punch cuts an irregularly shaped area around a defect or void, as well as a perfectly fitting patch.

Repairing Finishes

Eliminating Water Rings

PROBLEM: *After our annual New Year's Day party, we noticed some light water rings on several pieces of furniture. Is there any way to remove them without stripping and refinishing?*

SOLUTION: Water marks appear in a finish when moisture gets into the film, reducing its transparency. To remove the marks, you need to either pull the moisture out of the finish film or cut the film back below the damage. There are four ways to do this, and I suggest you try them in the following order (the easiest and least destructive ones first) until you develop a feel for the process. Success is unpredictable because of variables such as the kind of finish and its age, how long the water mark has been in the finish, and how deeply the water damage has penetrated.

One way you can remove water rings from a surface is to wipe the area with a rag dampened with alcohol. The rag should be just damp enough to leave the appearance of a comet's tail as you wipe.

- Apply an oily substance, such as furniture polish, petroleum jelly, or mayonnaise, to the damaged area and allow it to remain overnight. The oil is more easily absorbed by the finish than water, so the oil will sometimes replace the water if the damage is superficial.
- Heat the finish with a hair dryer or heat gun to dry out the moisture. Be careful not to get the finish so hot that you can't touch it: If it gets too hot, the finish may blister.
- Dampen a cloth with any commonly available alcohol (denatured alcohol is best) and wipe it gently over the damaged area. Begin with a very slight dampening and add more alcohol if necessary, observing closely what happens each time you wipe. Your cloth is damp enough when the

evaporating alcohol looks like a trailing comet's tail as you wipe. Because alcohol absorbs moisture, this procedure will pull out most water marks. But proceed slowly and carefully: Too much alcohol on your cloth will wet the surface enough to draw moisture from the air into the finish and make the water mark worse.

- Cut through the damage by rubbing with a mild abrasive. Use toothpaste or make a paste of cigarette ashes and a light oil, such as mineral oil or furniture polish.

Fine #0000 steel wool lubricated with a light oil is more effective, but it scratches the surface more severely. Use steel wool only as a last resort. Rub the damaged area until the water damage is gone, being careful not to rub through the finish. Then, rub the entire finished surface with the same abrasives to even the sheen, or use finer abrasives if you want to raise the sheen.

Bob Flexner
Norman, OK

Repairing a Burn Hole

PROBLEM: *A candle fell over on the oak dining table I just made and finished with lacquer. We caught it quickly, but not before it melted a dime-sized hole in the finish. It didn't seem to char the wood, since the color has not changed. How can I repair the hole without refinishing the entire table?*

SOLUTION: Spray light coats of lacquer through a hole in a card until you have built up the finish so that it is level. Make the hole in the card about the same size as the crater in the finish, and hold the card just above the finish so that the card doesn't stick to it. Use lacquer with the same sheen (gloss, satin, flat) as the one you used originally. Work slowly, allowing each coat of lacquer to cure hard.

After you've filled the hole, let the lacquer harden for several days. Then sand it level, backing the sandpaper with a small flat cork or felt block. Rub the area with an abrasive, such as steel wool, pumice, rottenstone, or commercial rubbing compound, so that it matches the sheen of the rest of the table. If you can't match this sheen, you'll have to rub out the entire tabletop to an even sheen, which is still a lot less work than refinishing.

Bob Flexner
Norman, OK

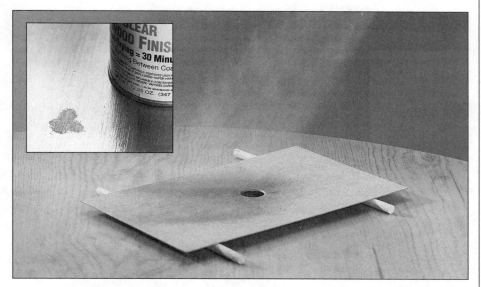

You can fix small burn holes in a lacquer finish as long as the burn hasn't damaged the wood. Cut a hole about the size of the damaged area in a card; then spray the finish through the opening until the finish is level with the surrounding surface. Rub out the repair to blend it in with the rest of the surface.

Repairing a Softened Finish

PROBLEM: *I used Murphy's Oil Soap to clean a side table that was finished with linseed oil. Now the finish is very sticky and seems to be ruined. Do you have any suggestions on how to repair this?*

SOLUTION: Excess buildup of dirty wax or sebaceous oil (the oil that comes from our skin) can leave a sticky film on a table, and strong alkalines, which some cleaners contain, can break down cured oil and turn it into a sticky mess. However, it is rare that any wax will harm cured linseed oil, and there is nothing in Murphy's Oil Soap that will harm any finish, including a linseed oil finish.

Whatever has caused your problem, the cure is fairly simple. Scrub down the table with a fine Scotchbrite pad or #0000 steel wool and plenty of naphtha or mineral spirits. This should remove all of the sticky film and leave the wood clean. Then reapply one or more coats of boiled (not raw) linseed oil. Wipe on the oil, and then wipe off any excess with a clean cloth. Let it dry overnight, and repeat the process until the table once again looks as it did before. To maintain an oil finish, just wipe it with a damp cloth when it needs it; twice a year, clean it with naphtha and refurbish it with another wipe of boiled linseed oil.

Michael Dresdner
Puyallup, WA

SOURCES

Adjustable drawer front inserts
[Page 182]
The Woodworker's Store
4365 Willow Dr.
Medina, MN 55340-9701
(800) 279-4441

Anchorseal *[for sealing ends of boards when air drying]*
[Page 58]
U.C. Coatings
P.O. Box 1066
Buffalo, NY 14215
(716) 833-9366

Burn-in sticks
[Page 277]
Mohawk Finishing Products, Inc.
Rt. 30 N
Amsterdam, NY 12010
(518) 843-1380
(800) 545-0047

Cyanoacrylate (CA) glue
[Pages 52, 187]
Craft Supplies USA
1287 E. 1120 S
Provo, UT 84606
(800) 551-8876

DE-STA-CO Industries *lever-action clamps*
[Page 86]
P.O. Box 2800
Troy, MI 48007
(800) 245-2759
Web site: http://www.destaco.com

Diamond dressing sticks *for grinding wheels*
[Page 264]
MSC Industrial Supply Co.
151 Sunnyside Blvd.
Plainview, NY 11803
(800) 645-7270

End-grain balsa *for compound curved forms*
[Page 38]
RP Associates
Minturn Farm Rd.
Bristol, RI 02809
(800) 343-3030

Epoxy
[Page 38]
Gougeon Brothers, Inc.
P.O. Box 908
Bay City, MI 48707
(313) 684-7286

European hinges
[Page 184]
Woodworker's Warehouse
For the nearest location, call:
(800) 827-5632

Gatorfoam *[rigid foam panels]*
[Page 43]
International Paper
6400 Poplar Ave.
Memphis, TN 38197
(901) 763-6000

Graphite cloth *for belt sanders*
[Page 204]
Woodworker's Supply, Inc.
1125 Jay Ln.
Graham, NC 27253
(800) 645-9292

Grinding wheels
[Page 270]
Norton Co. Coated Abrasives
    Division
1 New Bond St.
Box 15008
Worcester, MA 01615-0008
(800) 543-4335

High-speed-steel router bit blanks
[Page 264]
DML Industrial Products
For the nearest dealer, call:
(704) 322-4266

Hygrometers *for measuring relative humidity*
[Pages 12, 53]
Edmund Scientific Co.
101 E. Gloucester Pike
Barrington, NJ 08007
(609) 573-6250

Japan color
[Pages 221, 223]
Mohawk Finishing Products, Inc.
Rt. 30 N
Amsterdam, NY 12010
(518) 843-1380
(800) 545-0047

Knobs for jigs and fixtures
[Page 263]
Reid Tool Supply
2265 Black Creek Rd.
Muskegon, MI 49444
(800) 253-0421

Layout dyes
[Page 264]
MSC Industrial Supply Co.
151 Sunnyside Blvd.
Plainview, NY 11803
(800) 645-7270

Medex [formaldehyde-free wood paneling]
[Page 38]
For the nearest dealer, write or call:
Medite Corp.
P.O. Box 4040
Medford, OR 97501
(541) 773-2522

NIDA-CORE [honeycombed plastic cores for hollow-core tabletops, doors, counters, etc.]
[Page 39]
3240 S.W. 42nd Ave.
Palm City, FL 34990
(561) 287-6464
fax: (561) 287-5373
e-mail: sales@nida-core.com

NGR (non-grain-raising) stains
[Page 224]
Woodworker's Supply, Inc.
1125 Jay Ln.
Graham, NC 27253
(800) 645-9292

Mohawk Finishing Products, Inc.
Rt. 30 N
Amsterdam, NY 12010
(518) 843-1380
(800) 545-0047

Picture framer's vise
[Page 130]
AMT
400 Spring St.
Royersford, PA 19468
(800) 435-8665

Polyethylene glycol (PEG)
[Page 58]
Constantine's
2050 Eastchester Rd.
Bronx, NY 10461
(212) 792-1600
(800) 223-8087

Polyurethane, two-part
[Page 237]
West System 1000 Varnish
Gougeon Brothers, Inc.
P.O. Box 908
Bay City, MI 48707
(313) 684-7286

Interlux Yacht Finishes
2270 Morris Ave.
Union, NJ 07083
(800) INTRLUX

Shareware programs for laying out plywood
[Page 94]
Sheet Layout for Windows
Don Michelotti
707 Sunlight Dr.
Rochester Hills, MI 48309
DPMIC@aol.com
Web site: http://members.aol.com/dpmic/sheetlay.htm

Spacers and **shims** for table saw tenoning
[Page 145]
Delta International Machinery, Inc.
For dealer location, call:
(800) 438-2486

Square drive screws
[Page 194]
McFeeley's
P.O. Box 11169
Dept. AW6J
Lynchburg, VA 24506
(800) 443-7937

Touch-up powders
[Pages 244, 277]
Mohawk Finishing Products, Inc.
Rt. 30 N
Amsterdam, NY 12010
(518) 843-1380
(800) 545-0047

USDA Forest Products Laboratory
[Page 42]
1 Gifford Pinchot Dr.
Madison, WI 53705
Web site: http://www.fpl.fs.fed.us/

Veneer: peel-and-stick veneers
[Page 43]
Constantine's
2050 Eastchester Rd.
Bronx, NY 10461
(212) 792-1600
(800) 223-8087

Woodsealer [to slow wood drying and reduce checking]
[Page 58]
Craft Supplies USA
1287 E. 1120 S
Provo, UT 84606
(800) 551-8876

Z-shaped fasteners for attaching tabletops to aprons
[Page 172]
Woodworker's Supply, Inc.
1125 Jay Ln.
Graham, NC 27253
(800) 645-9292

CONTRIBUTORS

Marc Adams has been a professional woodworker for over 17 years and currently runs the Marc Adams School of Woodworking in Franklin, IN.

Willard Anderson is a research scientist and a passionate hobbyist woodworker. He's especially interested in collecting and using antique woodworking tools.

Paul Anthony, an associate editor of *American Woodworker* magazine, ran his own custom woodworking business for 20 years in California.

John Becker is a hobbyist do-it-yourselfer who is spending his retirement fixing and refinishing things for his family, friends, and church.

Tom Begnal was the managing editor of *The Woodworker's Journal* magazine for 15 years. He has written or edited woodworking and how-to books for several publishers, including Betterway Books, McGraw-Hill, and Sterling Publishing.

E. E. "Skip" Benson has been a woodworker since obtaining an M.I.A. degree from The School for American Craftsmen at Rochester Institute of Technology in 1972. He has taught at the California College of Arts and Crafts and the Artisans College while maintaining a shop in his home, where he has made one-of-a-kind contemporary furniture and sculpture.

B. William Bigelow is a woodworker who teaches high school in Peterborough, NH.

Lonnie Bird operates a small shop in southern Ohio where he specializes in 18th-century reproductions. He is the head of the woodworking program at the University of Rio Grande, OH, and is a contributing editor for *American Woodworker* magazine.

Graham Blackburn is a prolific writer and illustrator of books on woodworking and other crafts. He is a regular contributor to various magazines in the crafts field. He has also been the editor of *Woodwork*, and a contributing editor for *Fine Woodworking* and *Popular Woodworking* magazines.

Dick Boak has worked for the Martin Guitar Company in Nazareth, PA, for more than 20 years. In his spare time, he is a musician, lathe turner, guitar maker, and graphic artist.

Allan J. Boardman is a retired aerospace executive and lifelong woodworker and puzzle maker.

Tom Brown is a professional finishing consultant.

Ken Burton is a woodworker, teacher, and writer. A former Rodale Press book editor, he now teaches technology education during the school year and woodworking at the Yestermorrow School in Warren, VT, during the summer. In his spare

time, he operates Schocary Ridge Woodworks, which is located in a building that he built from straw bales.

Ernie Conover, along with his wife, Susan, operates Conover Workshops, a company which offers intensive hands-on classes in all types of woodworking.

Jim Cummins has been a professional woodworker for more than 30 years. His career includes work as a writer, editor, and instructor for magazines, books, and videos. These days you'll find him on-line as host of *American Woodworker* magazine's forum on America Online.

Jeff Day is a woodworker and writer in Bucks County, PA.

Carl Dorsch is a tool steels research engineer and a hobbyist woodworker. He is a contributing editor for *Woodwork* magazine.

William Draper has been a professional cabinetmaker since 1976, and is currently president of William Draper—DBS Custom Cabinetry, where he produces original designs and reproduction furniture that is sold in showrooms throughout the United States.

Michael Dresdner is the author of *The Woodfinishing Book, The Woodfinishing Video, Restoration Clinic,* and the "Just Finishing" column in *American Woodworker* magazine. In addition to having a long career in guitar making, musical instrument design, writing, and finishing, he is a specialist in production manufacturing engineering.

Stephen R. Drummer is a retired professional woodworker.

Mark Duginske is an inventor, woodworker, and author of woodworking books, including *Band Saw Handbook* and *Mastering Woodworking Machines.* He has developed many innovative products for woodworking, including Cool Blocks band saw blade guides. He demonstrates his techniques regularly at seminars across the country.

Mike Dunbar has been a professional woodworker for 27 years. He is a contributing editor for *American Woodworker* magazine and author of seven woodworking books. Along with his wife and son, he runs Dunbar Workshops in Hampton, NH. There, he and his staff teach chairmaking and woodworking classes.

David Ellsworth is a pioneer of thin-walled hollow turnings using the bent tool. He was the first president and is a lifetime member of the American Association of Woodturners.

Nick Engler is the author of *The Workshop Companion,* a best-selling series of books on woodworking. He has taught wood technology and craftsmanship at the University of Cincinnati and holds several patents for woodworking tools.

Ben Erickson has been a professional woodworker for the past 20 years. He lives and works in a restored antebellum house in Eutaw, AL, where he specializes in custom furniture and millwork.

Bob Flexner has managed his own furniture making and refinishing shop since 1976. He is the author of *Understanding Wood Finishing* and has made instructional videos on repairing and refinishing furniture. He also writes for a number of magazines and teaches seminars and workshops around the country.

Robert G. Flower, of Applied Science Associates, develops test methods for evaluating products used in building construction and woodworking.

John Grew-Sheridan has been a furniture maker and teacher since 1975 and is still active at both.

Ric Hanisch works on architecture and furniture design in Quakertown, PA.

Greg Harkins has made chairs for 20 years. Using techniques passed down from the mid-1800's, Greg is preserving the all but dead aspects of chair making. His hand-turned parts make for extremely durable and fine quality chairs.

Charles Harvey has specialized in Shaker furniture and oval boxes since 1984.

Rick Hearne is a professional lumberman and logger whose four children all work in the family business, Hearne Hardwoods, Inc.

L. Jerry Hess is a physics professor at Pierce College in Tacoma, WA. The oldest son of a cabinetmaker, he has never quite been able to shake off all of the shavings and sawdust. He makes small chests, boxes, and wooden ballpoint pens and remodels houses during the summer.

Bill Hylton has written numerous books on woodworking, including *Router Magic, Woodworking with the Router,* and *Country Pine.*

Kevin Ireland is managing editor of Woodworking Books for Rodale Press and a part-time woodturner and woodworker.

Bob Jardinico was a sales manager at Colonial Saw Co. in Kingston, MA, from 1984 to 1996. He has been a woodworker for more than 30 years, and his experience includes professional furniture restoration and period furniture reproductions. Since 1996, he has been a Machinery Sales Manager at Louis & Co., Brea, CA.

W. Curtis Johnson is a professor of Biophysics at Oregon State University and part-time professional woodworker. He uses a blend of power and hand tools to make custom furniture at his small shop in the heart of the Willamette Valley, OR. He is a longtime contributor to *American Woodworker* magazine.

Frank Klausz is a master cabinetmaker who owns and operates a cabinet shop in Pluckemin, NJ. He is a contributing editor for *American Woodworker* magazine.

Michael Knepp has been involved in woodworking for over 20 years and currently works for an architectural millwork company.

Peter Korn is the director of the Center for Furniture Craftsmanship in Rockport, ME.

Jack Larimore has been a professional furniture maker for 15 years and exhibits his work nationally.

David Stern Lightner trained at the Leads Design Workshops in furniture making and has taught furniture making at Bucks County Community College in Newtown, PA. He writes about and photographs architecture and fine art.

Jeffry Lohr is a professional woodworker who specializes in Arts and Crafts furniture.

Salvatore Marino is a technical consultant for Constantine's. He also writes, lectures, teaches, and serves as a consultant to various woodworking companies.

David J. Marks is a self-employed professional furniture maker who has maintained his shop/studio in Santa Rosa, CA, since 1981. He has been a Master Craftsman member of the California Contemporary Crafts Association since 1989 and teaches apprentices at his studio.

Fred Matlack is head of the woodworking design shop at Rodale Press.

J. D. McGary is a 79-year-old woodworker who has tried it all: home building, crafts, carving, furniture making, antique restoration. He also enjoys teaching woodworking to children.

Kelly Mehler has been a custom furniture maker for 20 years in Berea, KY. He is a teacher and author of *The Tablesaw Book* and has created 2 videos: *Build a Shaker Table* and *Mastering Your Tablesaw*.

Michael Mode is a self-taught and self-employed lathe artist with more than 20 years of experience. His work can be seen in individual, corporate, and museum collections.

Bob Moran is an editor of woodworking books at Rodale Press and

author of *Woodworking: The Right Technique.*

Walt Morrison is an engineer and woodworker. He has contributed material for several Rodale Press woodworking books, and his work has appeared in *American Woodworker* magazine since its inception. His writing concentrates mainly on furniture design and freelance projects.

Toshio Odate is a teacher, sculptor, and woodworker.

Michael O'Donnell is a professional woodturner in Scotland.

Tony O'Malley began his woodworking career in Philadelphia in 1984. After 10 years of working in a variety of architectural millwork and furniture shops, he joined Rodale Press, where he is currently an associate editor of woodworking books.

David Page has been a full-time professional woodworker for 16 years. He specializes in building custom contemporary furniture on commission. He holds an M.F.A. degree in Woodworking and Furniture Design from the Rhode Island School of Design.

Mark Popp is a do-it-yourselfer with a strong interest in using hand tools.

Andy Rae began his woodworking career in the workshops of George Nakashima in 1980. In 1992, after running his own woodworking design and building business in Princeton, NJ, he joined the editorial staff of *American Woodworker* magazine. He continues to design and build furniture in his home shop in Pennsylvania.

C. E. "Chuck" Ring is a professional woodworker who lives near Albuquerque, NM. His articles about woodworking can be found on the internet at http://www.theoak.com/chuck/index.htm1.

Mark Romano became involved in wood finishing in 1980 by learning the craft of piano finishing and antique restoration. He worked for several years as a production finisher, and he is currently employed as a furniture refurbishing specialist by a major interior design firm in southern New Jersey.

Mark Sfiri is primarily a spindle turner who incorporates turned parts into furniture and sculpture. He teaches woodworking and turning at Bucks County Community College in Newtown, PA.

Jonathan S. Simons has been making beautiful and functional wooden spoons since 1978. His spoons can be found throughout the United States as well as in other countries, including the United Kingdom, Canada, Japan, and France.

Dennis Slabaugh, a hospital risk manager, began woodworking as a hobby in 1990. Focusing on the Arts and Crafts style, he makes quarter-sawn white oak his wood of choice. His shop is a two-car garage that mostly contains reconditioned tools.

Tim Snyder is currently the executive editor of *American Woodworker* magazine. He has written two books: *Shelving and Storage* and *Decks*, both published by Rodale Press.

Bill Storch, following his dream, started his custom woodworking business in 1975. He specializes in truly custom furniture, often matching pieces in a client's home or designing a piece for a particular space or function.

Joanne Storch built her first woodworking project—an eight-harness floor loom—in 1975. She is now a professional woodworker whose specialty is the production of heat registers for hardwood floors. Joanne particularly enjoys intricate projects that require precision.

Wayne "Muggs" Storro is a retired building contractor in Wallace, ID.

Jim Sunderland has been the owner/operator of a small harvesting/sawmill/planermill operation for 15 years. He spent 10 years in boat and house construction.

Mark Torpey works full time as a mechanical engineer developing alternative energy technologies, and in his spare time is a woodworker developing alternative furniture designs.

Robert Treanor is a former woodworking teacher. He currently works as a furniture maker and freelance writer with a particular interest in Shaker and American Windsor furniture.

James Van Etten has been a professional designer and craftsman of custom furniture and architectural woodworking since 1982.

Matt ver Steeg operates a professional tool sharpening and treatment business in Johnston, IA.

Joe Wajszczuk is a writer and woodworker whose recent move to a two-bedroom apartment has presented the opportunity to get reacquainted with the simple pleasures of hand tool woodworking. Presently, he is an editor for Creative Homeowner Press, writing books for people who still think that a chisel is the best tool for opening paint cans.

Ellis Walentine has been working wood professionally since 1971, specializing in architectural woodworking and custom furniture. He joined *American Woodworker* magazine in 1992 and is currently Executive Editor for New Ventures.

Pat Warner is the author of a trilogy of router books. His books, *Getting the Very Best from Your Router* and *Router Joinery,* are currently available. His third book, *Routers, Jigs and Fixtures,* is forthcoming (all are published by Betterway Publications).

Simon Watts is *American Woodworker* magazine's West Coast editor and the codirector of the Arques School, a new school of traditional wooden boat building.

Randy Wilkenson specializes in the reproduction of 18th-century furniture. He is a student in the Smithsonian Institution's Furniture Conservation Training Program.

Gene Wengert is an Extension Specialist in Wood Processing at the University of Wisconsin-Madison, and has 30 years of experience in the drying, gluing, and machining of wood.

Rick Wright taught industrial arts for 23 years. Before retiring, he taught photography, graphic arts, drafting, woodworking, plastics technology, and metal working.

Rob Yoder worked as a cabinetmaker for several years before joining the Rodale Press woodworking book team. In his free time, Rob enjoys building and playing stringed instruments.

INDEX

Page references in *italic* indicate tables.

A

Anchorseal, 58
Angles. *See also* Bevel angles; Shop math and geometry
    compound, cutting, 88–89, 133
    cutting with templates, 27
    how to determine odd, 23
Apple Ply plywood, 44
Architect's rule, 21
Arcs, finding center or radius of, 32
Assembly techniques
    for door frames, 175–76
    for large cabinets, 169
    for stave columns, 187, 188

B

Baltic Birch plywood, 44
Band saws
    adjusting for blade drift on, 72
    burn marks caused by, 255
    cutting techniques
        delicate material, 97
        milling logs, 74
        resawing, 72, 254
        tight turns, 106, 109
    making small push stick for, 254
    preventing resin buildup on, 253–54
    skill exercises, 253
    tuning, 256–57
    work support stands for, 255
Bar gauges, 26
Bark, preserving, 46
Belt sanders
    cross-grain sanding with, 202
    guidelines for using, 201
    reducing motor load of, 204
    reducing noise of, 203
    sharpening plane irons with, 269
Bench grinders
    guidelines for using, 270
    substitutes for, 269

vibrations in, 269
wheel selection for, 270
Bending wood. *See also* Steam bending
    kerf bending technique, 114
    making quick forms for, 114
    table for, 118–19
Bevel angles
    calculating, 30–31, 155
    of router bits, 264
    for woodworking tools, 270
Beveled stock
    cutting biscuit slots in, 155
    ripping, 83
BIN (sealer), 246
Birch, preserving bark on, 46
Biscuit joints
    in beveled edges, 155
    fastening tabletops with, 172
    fixing misplaced slots for, 156–57
    stacking, 155–56
    visible after finishing, 157
Blades and knives
    for band saws, 72, 253
    dealing with chipped, 260
    for table saws, 80, 249
Blemishes and defects in stock. *See also* Dents and gouges; Repairs; *specific problem*
    in pine, 52
    iron and rust, 218
    mold and mildew, 52
    removing sticker marks, 50
Blow-out, repairing, 288–89
Bondo (auto body filler), 278
Bowing
    defined, 53
    flattening, 71
    straightening, 53
Boxes
    dealing with twisted, 293
    sawing lids safely, 170
Brads and small nails, driving, 195, 196
Brass, tarnish prevention, 247
Brushes, modifying, 231
Burl, defined, 49

Burns, in finish repairing, 297
Burn marks, router
    preventing, 80–81
    removing, 99
    repairing in lacquer finish, 297
Butterfly keys, using for repairs, 51, 286

C

Cabinets. *See also specific part*
    cracks in, 290
    designs, modifying, 8, 19
    doors
        hanging, 186
        hinge alignment on, 15, 288
        sizing and fitting, 5, 175
    gap-free case joint miters in, 130
    hanging
        on an uneven wall, 197, 292
        techniques and tips for, 199
    spray finishing strategies for, 238–39
Case hardening, explained, 53
Cedar, painting, 247
Centerpoints, finding, 32
Chair legs, leveling, 289–90
Chair rungs, turning multiple, 109
Checks, cracks, and splits
    in case sides, 290
    evaluating surface, 39
    saving stock with, 51
    in tabletops, 286
Cherry, fixing color variations in, 245
Chests
    cracks in, 290
    design modifications for, 9
    strengthening feet on, 170
Chipboard, characteristics, 45
Chisels, securing the hoops on Japanese, 268
Chlorine, rust prevention and, 251
Clamping
    alignment jig for, 168
    deep reach, 188
    door frames, 175–76
    with glue or epoxy, 187, 189

irregular shapes and pieces, 189, 190–91
long edge miters, 171
mitered boxes, 176
no-mar, 178
notched glue blocks for, 47
panels, 164, 166, 167
rubber band, 189
stave columns, 187, 188
through-tenons, 177
with wedges and pegs, 192
Clamps
aligning, 168
De-Sta-Co lever-action, 86
stretching, 192
Climb-cutting, explained, 104
Cock beading, 19
Columns, stave construction and glue-up, 30–31, 155, 187, 188
Combination-core plywood, 44
Compound curves, 38
Compound cuts, mitering, 88–89, 90–91, 133
Contractor saws, dust collector for, 250
Contrast, as a design element, 18
Contributors, 300–303
Cope-and-stick frames
router bit setup for, 136–37
simplified, 135–37
Countertops
aligning edge material with, 174
fitting into an alcove, 198
Coves, cutting on a table saw, 112–13, 212
Cracks. *See* Checks, cracks, and splits
Crosscutting
acute angles, 92
with a miter saw, 85
with a sled, 86
delicate or small stock, 86, 88
long or unwieldy stock, 84, 87
narrow stock, 92
wide stock, 93
Cupping
defined, 53
flattening, 71, 73, 101
straightening, 53
Curved parts, planing jig for tapering, 115
Curves
compound, 38
tight, cutting on a band saw, 106, 109
layout lines for, 24, 25
routing profiles along, 104

sanding, 209, 212, 213
technique for matching, 107
Cutting multiple parts, 27, 105. *See also specific machine*
Cyanoacrylate glue (CA or Super Glue), 52, *163*, 187
Cylinders
dividing into equal segments, 31
sanding, modifying paper for, 213
turning, 110

D

Dadoes
aligning multiple, 154
back-to-back, 151–52
making perfect, 151
routing jigs for, 153
Dado joints
combining with sliding dovetails, 125
concealing, 152
Deflection, in shelving, 11
Dents and gouges. *See also* Blemishes and defects in stock; Repairs; *specific problem*
filling and staining, 276
fixing scratches, 279
fixing with burn-in sticks, 277
ironing out, 276
preventing, while thicknessing, 260
repairing a splintered edge, 279
repairing large gouges, 275
Design. *See also specific aspect of*
how grain and figure affects, 33
mock-ups and models for, 10
modifying, 8–9
planning details, 15
repetition and contrast in, 18
site-built projects, 14
with scale models, 3
wood movement, as a factor in, 12
Desks, standard dimensions, *7*
De-Sta-Co lever-action clamps, 86
Dimensional changes in wood. *See* Stability
Dimensions, standard furniture, *6, 7*
Dining tables, standard dimensions, *6*
Disc sanders, truing miters on, 207
Distressing wood, tips for, 221
Dividers, half-lapped, 154
Doors
assembling flat frames, 175–76

design modifications for molding, 19
flattening twisted, 293
hanging cabinet, 186
sizing and fitting, 5, 175, 179
spray finishing strategies, 238–39
squaring, 177
Dovetails
curing loose, 122
cutting clean, 123
filling gaps at the base, 123–24
fitting too-tight, 121
guide block for, 124
half-blind, removing waste from, 127
mock, 127
sliding
combined with dado joints, 125
routing, 124, 126
Dovetail saws, resharpening, 265
Dowel joints
grooving dowels for better, 148
repairing, 284
techniques for making, 150
Dowels
cutting mortises in, 142
routing tenons on, 142
Drawers
adding detail with molding, 19
aligning fronts, 181, 182
lock joints for, 128, 129
making fronts fit, 284–85
mounting crooked, 183
mounting metal slides for, 180
spacing problems, 179
stops for, 182–83
Drawings. *See also* Layout lines
from photos, 21
making quick changes to, 5
Drill presses, leveling, 261
Drop-leaf tables, edge treatment for, 17
Drum sanders, storage tray for, 204
Drying lumber
in a microwave, 58
conditioning, 53, 55
outdoors, 50
stumps, 58
Dust collection
bench-top, 213
cleaning shop-vac filters, 101
contractor saw, 250
for freehand routing, 101
Dye stains, finishing with, 221

E

Edge-jointing. *See* Jointing
Edge treatments
    aligning with countertops, 174
    clamping, 191
    for drop-leaf tables, 17
    mitering veneer edge banding,
      132
Ellipse or oval shapes
    layout lines for, 25
    turning, 260–61
End grain
    finishing, 221
    jointing, 61
    sanding, 209
    screwing into, 193
End-grain balsa, making compound
   curves with, 38
Epoxy
    characteristics, 160, *163*
    gluing wood screws with, 195
    using, 189, 280
European hinges, using, 184–85
Exotic woods, finishing, 234

F

FAS (firsts and seconds) lumber grade,
   defined, 40, *41*
Featherboards, using with thin
   stock, 79
Feet on furniture
    design modifications with, 8
    strengthening, 170
Fences
    auxiliary for a table saw, 251
    easy-mounting router, 263
    for resawing on a band saw, 72
    saving settings, 82–83
Fiberboard, types of, 44–45
Figure. *See also* Grain
    creating the effect of quarter-
      sawn, 47
    detecting curly, 37
    handling veneer with, 49
    jointing stock with, 258
    milling a stump for, 49
    staining, 223
Files and rasps, storing, 268
Fillers
    applying paste, 219
    shop-made, 218
    using wood putty, 217
Finishes. *See also specific type*
    bubbles in, 226, 227

controlling wood movement
    with, 12–13
    fade-free outdoor, 237
    mixing water-based dyes and, 225
    odor-free, 236
    overview of, 228–29, *229*
    protecting stains from topcoats,
      237
    repairing damaged, 296–97
    spraying tips and strategies, 231,
      232, 238–39, 240
Finishing
    avoiding bleed-back, 222, 236
    blending dye stain spots, 224
    distressed wood, 221
    drying rack for, 230
    dust problems, 242
    ebonizing, 223–24
    equalizing light and dark boards,
      224–25
    exotic woods, 234
    figured wood, 223
    hand-rubbed look, shortcut to, 245
    hiding and removing glue
      residue, 243–44, *244*
    lighting for, 235
    matching existing stains,
      223, 235
    oily woods, 226
    panel shrinkage and, 237
    peel-and-stick veneer, 43
    prepping tips and techniques,
      217–19
    preventing blotching, 220
    preventing fish eye, 227
    raised grain, 222
    reducing brush marks, 233
    richness and durability, 234
    screw heads, 237
    staining end grain, 209, 221
    in tight spaces, 231
    for ultraviolet resistance, 234
    wood filers, 276
    wood temperature and bubbles,
      227
Finnish Birch plywood, 44
Fire hose column clamp, 188
Fish eye, preventing, 227
Flakeboard, characteristics, 45
Flatness, gauging, 68
Flat-sawn wood, movement in, 12,
   13, 48
Fluorescent lighting, color-corrected,
   235
Foam panels, working with, 43
Food utensils, wood selection for, 42

Formaldehyde, limiting exposure to,
   37–38
Formulas. *See* Shop math and
   geometry
Frames
    concealing uneven joints, 145
    cope-and-stick, 135–37
    determining odd angles for, 23,
      90–91
    picture, 90–91, 134
    squaring, 177
Furniture, standard dimensions, *6*

G

Gang cuts, how to make, 27
Gashes. *See* Dents and gouges
Gatorfoam, 43
Gel stains, using, 220
Glue. *See also specific type*
    choosing, 160, *162–63*
    cleaning off old, 281
    general purpose, *162*
    softening old, 280
    special purpose, *163*
    temperature and strength, 159
    water-resistant, *163*
Glue-up
    in a cold shop, 161
    avoiding glue creep, 160–61
    avoiding out-of-square, 169
    cleaning squeeze-out, 168
    cross-grain inlays, 34–35
    dowel joints, 148
    glue lines
      avoiding stepped, 48
      preventing depressed, 161
    grain matching issues, 33
    hard-to-clamp items, 189
    long edge miters, 171
    notched and L-shaped blocks for,
      47, 176
    oily woods, 160
    panels, techniques for, 164, 166,
      167
    stave columns, 187, 188
    veneer registration for, 76
Golden Section (system for calculating
   proportions), 4
Gouges (tools), sharpening, 271
Gouges to wood. *See* Dents and
   gouges
Grades, lumber, 40
Grain. *See also* Figure
    arranging boards for best match,
      33, 34–35

contrast in book-matched
  panels, 33
inlaying wood against the, 34–35
Grinding wheels, 270. *See also* Bench
  grinders

H

Half-laps, cutting, 154
Hambridge Progression (system for
  calculating proportions), 4
Hand planes
  jointing edges with, 65
  preventing clogs, 268
  reducing tear-out, 70
  sharpening irons, 269, 273
  surface planing with, 71
  tuning, 266–67
Hand scrapers
  sharpening, 214–15
  using razor blades for, 244
Hand screws, clamping with, 190–91
Hardboard, 45
Hardware
  inserts, for mounting drawer
    fronts, 182
  placement of finish, 15
Hardwood
  lumber grades, 40, *41*
  plywood, 44, 45
  price, 40–41
  reducing planer tear-out in, 67
  size conventions, 40
Headboards, spray finishing, 238–39
Hexagon, laying out a, 29
Hide glue, reactivating, 281
Hinges
  concealed, 184–85
  drop-leaf, 17
  mortises for, 186, 288
  no-show, 16
  placement recommendations, 15
  repositioning, 287–88
Honing. *See* Sharpening
Hot glue, using with epoxy, 189

I

Inlays
  cross-grain, 34–35
  repairing, 286
  using for repairs, 277, 294
Inserts, for mounting drawer fronts,
  182
Interthane Plus, 237
Iron stains, removing, 218

J

Japanese chisels, securing the hoops
  on, 268
Jigs
  for clamp-free planing and belt
    sanding, 205
  for drilling perpendicular holes,
    149
  for loose tenon joints, 146–47
  for routing dadoes, 153
  routing end-grain mortises,
    146–47
  to save fence settings, 82–83
  tapering, 111
  for cutting sandpaper, 203
Joinery. *See also specific type*
  mock-ups, full-scale, 10
Jointers
  common problems, 258
  tuning, 259
Jointing
  on a planer, 63
  on a router, 62, 64
  edge jointing
    with a hand plane, 65
    on a planer, 64
    avoiding tear-out, 62
    for tight and flat panels, 63
  end grain, 61
  figured stock, 258
  small pieces, 62
  veneer, 75
  wide boards on a narrow jointer,
    66
Joints. *See also specific type*
  drawer locks, simplifying, 128, 129
  interlocking three-stick, 140–41
  offset, 138
  remaking bad edge, 168
Just Like Wood (filler), 276

K

Kerf bending, spacing for, 114
Kilz (sealer), 246
Kitchen cabinets
  pull and knob placement, 15
  sizing doors for, 5
  standard dimensions of, *7*
Knife hinges, 16
Knives. *See* Blades and knives
Knobs. *See* Pulls and knobs
Knotholes
  filling, 295
  hiding in pine, 246

L

Lacquer
  applying, 234
  blushing problems, 241
  characteristics, 229, 239
  cracking problems, 242
  repairing damaged, 297
  using with paint, 247
Laminating
  curved parts, 115
  dissimilar woods, 46
Lathes
  bed maintenance on, 261
  duplicating technique for, 109
  re-turning a spindle, 108
  turning long posts on short, 110
  turning ovals, 260–61
  turning round tenons, 148–49
Layout lines. *See also* Patterns; Shop
  math and geometry
  for curves, 24, 25
  mortise-and-tenon work, 21–22
  for polygons, 28–29
  removing, 23
  for sign making, 24
Layout, planning, 34–35
Leather dye, 224
Leveling techniques
  chairs and tables, 289–90
  drill press tables, 261
Lighting
  for applying finishes, 233, 235
  for sanding, 206
Light stand, for sanding and finishing, 206
Lightweight materials, for counters
  and tabletops, 39, 43
Lines, scribing, 21–22
Linseed oil, 228, 297
Load, shelving, 11
Logs and stumps
  assessing for curly figure, 37
  drying, 58
  milling for figure, 49
  milling with a band saw, 74
  preserving bark on, 46
Loose tenon joints, jigs for, 146–47
Louvers, assembling, 178
Lumber. *See also* Drying lumber;
  Storage
  basic terms, 40–41
  hardwood grades, *41*
  recycled, detecting metal in, 42
  "stretching" special, 97
Lumber-core plywood, 44

M

Marking gauges
  adding a pencil to, 22
  using, 26
Marking knife, using, 21–22
Masonite, 45
MDF. *See* Medium-density
  fiberboard
Measuring, tips for, 26–27
Medex (paneling product), 38
Medium-density fiberboard (MDF)
  characteristics, 44–45
  sealing, 246
Microwave ovens, drying wood in, 58
Minwax, 251
Mismatched boards, disguising, 294
Miter gauges
  adjusting, 131–32
  alternatives to, 86
Mitering. *See also* Splined miters
  on a table saw, 90–91
  case joint, 130
  crown molding, 133
  guide block for, 135–36
  setting up compound cuts, 88–89
  small parts, 85
  veneer edge banding, 132
Miter joints
  clamping, 176
  fixing and preventing gaps,
    130–31
  moisture content and, 13
Miters
  gluing long edge, 171
  truing on a disc sander, 207
Miter saws, using, 85
Mock dovetails, 127
Mock-ups and models, 10. *See also*
  Design
Mohawk Blend-all, 244
Moisture content
  checking, 59
  miter joints and, 13
  recommended, 12, 59
Mold and mildew, 52
Moldings
  clamping with glue and epoxy,
    187, 189
  as cover-ups, 20
  cutting large cove, 112–13, 212
  as design elements, 8–9, 19
  matching or duplicating profiles,
    100, 133
  mitering, 85, 90, 133
  routing narrow, 101–2

sanding with custom blocks,
  211, 212
Mortise-and-tenon joints. *See also*
  Mortises; Tenons
  basics of, 143
  concealing uneven, 145
  fixing a failed glue joint, 280
  large, 139
  offset, 138
  with round stock, 142
  "stretching" short rails, 282
  using loose (separate) tenons,
    146–47
Mortises. *See also* Mortise-and-tenon
  joints
  basics of, 143
  cutting in end grain, 146–47
  cutting in round stock, 142
  for hinges, 186, 288
  laminating for large, 139
  laying out, 21–22
  offset, 138
  removing chips, 138
  squaring, 140–41
Mullions, 101–2
Multiple cuts, making, 27, 105. *See
  also specific machine*
Murphy's Oil Soap, 297

N

NIDA-CORE, 39
Nitro-san (auto body filler), 278
No. 1 Common (wood grade),
  defined, 40, *41*
No. 2 Common (wood grade),
  defined, 40, *41*

O

Oak, stains in, 50
Occasional tables, standard
  dimensions, 6
Octagon, laying out, 29
Oil finishes
  avoiding bleed-back, 236
  characteristics, 228, *229*
  maintaining, 297
Oily woods
  finishing, 226
  gluing, 160
Orange peel, reducing, 231
Orbital sanders, dust collection device
  for, 213
Oxalic acid wash, for removing iron
  stains, 218

P

Pad sanders, quick paper changes,
  213
Painting, tips for, 246–47
Panels
  cutting cupped, 101
  cutting large, 95
  finishing, 237
  flattening bowed, 291
  foam, 43
  glue-up techniques, 164, 166, 167
  jointing tips, 63
  making from salvage, 48
  manufactured, 44–45
  removing twist from, 292
  routing raised, 103
  sawing odd-shaped, 94–95
  straightening warped, 53
Particleboard, characteristics, 45
Patching dents and gouges. *See* Dents
  and gouges
Patterns. *See also* Layout lines;
  Templates
  transferring and changing,
    23–24
  transferring odd shapes, 198
Pegs
  clamping with, 192
  Shaker, 196
Pencils
  for iron-on transfers, 23–24
  removing lines with alcohol, 23
  using with a marking gauge, 22
Pentagon, laying out a, 28
Photos, drawing plans from, 21
Picture framer's vise, 130–31
Picture frames, 90–91
Pine
  coping with stained, 52
  hiding knots and sap streaks, 246
  painting pressure treated, 247
Pitch pockets, concealing, 294
Pivot hinges. *See* Knife hinges
Pivot pins, 16
Planers. *See also* Hand planes
  avoiding snipe, 68
  chipped knives on, 260
  preventing dents, 260
  reducing tear-out, 67
  using for jointing, 63, 64
Planing
  short stock, 69
  surface planing with hand
    planes, 71
  thin stock, 69–70

warp after, 70
Planning
    cut layout, 34–35
    cutting and fitting as you go,
        96, 171
    replacing spoiled parts, 70
Plinths, design modifications with,
    8–9
Plywood
    cutting for best yield, 94
    cutting veneered, 77
    hardwood types, 44, 45
    restoring warped, 54
    salvaging cutoffs, 48
    for shelving, 11
    vertical rack for storing, 57
Pneumatic nailers
    avoiding marks from, 196
    using without a compressor, 196
Polygons
    cutting on a table saw, 96
    laying out, 28–29
Polyurethane
    fade-free, 237
    preventing brush marks, 233
    raising the gloss of, 245
    reducing bubbles in, 227
Posts, joining, 150
Posts, turning. *See* Turning
Power, table saw requirements, 81
Pressure-treated pine, painting, 247
Profiled edges, repairing, 288–89
Proportions
    altering drawings, 5
    mathematical systems for, 4
    visualizing with scale models, 3
Pulls and knobs, placement recom-
    mendations, 15
Puzzles, wood selection for, 41–42

Q

Quarter-sawn wood
    creating the effect of, 47
    movement in, 12, 13, 48

R

Rabbeting, without tear-out, 157
Radial movement, rule of thumb, *13*
Radius
    finding an arc's, 32
    laying out, 24
Recycled lumber, detecting metal in, 42
Repairs. *See also* Blemishes and
    defects in stock; Dents and gouges;

Stains
    bubbled veneer, 281
    failed glue joints, 280
    structural problems, 282–90
Repetition, as a design element, 18
Resawing
    band saw, 72, 74, 254
    keeping boards flat after, 73
    table saw, 73
    warp after, 70
Resorcinol glue, 159, *163*
Rift-sawn boards, wood movement,
    48
Ripping
    beveled stock, 83
    crooked or wavy-edged stock, 83
    table saw safety tips, 80
    thick stock, 80–81
    thin stock, 79
Router bits
    for cope-and-stick joinery,
        136–37
    fit guidelines, 262
    grinding custom, 264
    stuck, 263
Routers
    dust collection tips, 101
    easy-mounting fence, 263
    jointing with, 62, 64, 76
    preventing bit creep, 262
    starting pin, making and using,
        104
Routing
    burn marks, removing and pre-
        venting, 99
    dadoes, 151–52, 153
    narrow moldings, 101–2
    preventing tear-out, 102, 104
    profiles along curved edges, 104
    raised panels, 103
    repairing blow-out damage,
        288–89
    sliding dovetails, 124, 126
    small workpieces, 104
    splined miter, grooves for, 134
    thick stock, 106
Rubber band clamping, 189
Rust
    preventing on machine tables,
        251
    removing stains from wood, 218

S

Safety tips
    crosscutting small stock, 88

cutting large sheet goods, 95
formaldehyde, limiting exposure,
    37–38
metal in sawed logs, 42
pattern cutting, 96
resawing with table saws, 73
ricochets off a moving blade, 250
ripping thin stock, 79
routing raised panels, 103
routing small workpieces, 104
sawing box lids, 170
walnut sawdust, 53
for making puzzles, 42
Sagging shelves
    factors that affect, 11
    retrofitting, 286–87
Sanding. *See also* Belt sanders; Disc
    sanders; Drum sanders; Orbital
    sanders; Pad sanders
    on a table saw, 207
    burnishing with garnet sand-
        paper, 221
    clamp-free, 205
    curves, 209, 212, 213
    end grain, 209
    frame joints, 209
    guidelines for, 210
    keeping edges square while, 208
    light stand for, 206
    molding with custom blocks,
        211, 212
    pattern, 205
    small parts, 211
    wheels, 208
Sanding frame, using, 201
Sandpaper
    burnishing with garnet, 221
    improving flexibility, 213
    jig for cutting, 203
Sawdust and wood shavings, disposal
    tips, 53
Sawhorses, adjustable, 165
Scale models, making, 3
Scorch marks. *See* Burn marks, router
Scotchbrite pads, 243
Scratches, fixing, 279. *See also* Dents
    and gouges
Screws
    dealing with broken-off, 193–94
    drywall, using, 195
    gluing wood, 195
    preventing tarnishing, 237
    removing, with stripped heads,
        194
    using in end grain, 193
Select (wood grade), defined, 40, *41*

Shaker pegs, tightening, 196
Sharpening
    chisels and plane irons, 273
    dovetail saws, 265
    gouges, 271
    hand scrapers, 214–15
    plane irons, 269, 273
    stone techniques, 272
    with waterstones, 270
Sheet goods. *See also specific type*
    cutting for best yield, 94
    cutting large, 95
    manufactured panels, 44–45
    for shelving, 11
Shellac
    as a finish, 236
    characteristics, 229, 239
    clouding, 241
    reducing brush marks, 233
Shelves
    hole alignment problems, 285
    maximum spans recommended,
        12
    sagging, factors that affect, 11
    sagging, retrofitting, 286–87
    spray finishing strategies,
        238–39
    support pins, rounding over, 109
Shop math and geometry. *See also*
    Layout lines
    arcs, finding center and radius, 32
    determining stave angles, 30–31,
        155
    dividing a cylinder into equal
        segments, 31
    dividing a line, 30
    proportions, mathematical
        systems for calculating, 4
Shop-vacs, cleaning filters in, 212
Shutters, assembling, 178
Sign making, layout lines for, 24
Site-built projects
    designing, 14
    fitting, 198
Sketching, 15. *See also* Drawings
Slip stones, making, 271
Snipe, defined, 68
Solid-core plywood, 44
Sources for materials, 298–99
Spalted wood
    encouraging, 58
    salvaging, 52
Spans
    maximum recommended for
        shelves, *12*
    tabletops, 39

Specialty tables, standard dimen-
    sions, *7*
Spheres, drilling, 108
Spiling sticks, using, 198
Spindles
    joining, 150
    replacing and repairing, 282–83
    re-turning on a lathe, 108
Splined miters
    cutting on a table saw, 134
    routing grooves for, 134
Splits. *See* Checks, cracks, and splits
Splitters
    using for safe ripping, 80–81
    using with thin stock, 79
Spray booths, shop-made, 232
Spray guns, tips for using, 231
Spraying finishes. *See* Finishes
Squaring, method for, 177
Squaring off
    odd-shaped workpiece, 93
    unwieldy stock, 87
Squaring sticks, shop-made, 174
Stability, moisture content as a factor
    in, 12, 13
Stain controllers, using, 220
Stains. *See also* Finishes; Finishing
    iron, 218
    from mold and mildew, 52
    in oak, 50
    in pine, 52
    rust, 218
Standard furniture dimensions, *6, 7*
Stave construction and glue-up,
    30–31, 155, 187, 188
Steam bending. *See also* Bending
    wood
    avoiding breaks while, 119
    shop-made steamer, 116, 117
Steamer, shop-made, 116, 117
Sticking, explained, 135, 136
Stop blocks, using, 27
Storage
    burled turning blanks, 58
    files and rasps, 268
    tips for, 56
    using stickers for, 55
    veneer, 59
    vertical rack for, 57
Story sticks, 26
String-and-Pins Technique, for
    drawing an oval, 25
Structural problems, joint
    mock-ups, 10
Super Glue (CA glue), 52, *163*, 187
Support pins, 109, 285

T

Tables. *See also specific type*
    legs, leveling, 289–90
    for making multiple bends,
        118–19
    spray finishing sequence, 240
    standard dimensions, *6, 7*
Table saws
    auxiliary fence, 251
    blade stabilizers, 249
    cutting
        coves, 112–13, 212
        large panels, 95
        miter splines, 134
        odd-shaped panels, 94–95
        tenons, 145
        plywood veneer, 77
        polygons, 96
    burn marks and glazes, 80–81
    crosscutting
        acute angles, 92
        delicate or small stock, 86,
            88
        long or unwieldy stock, 84, 87
        narrow stock, 92
        wide stock, 93
    kill switch, 249
    mitering, 90–91
    preventing ricochets, 250
    resawing with, 73
    ripping safely, 79, 80
    sanding with, 207
    tuning, 252
Tabletops
    attaching invisibly, 172–73
    deep reach clamping for, 188
    fastening with biscuit joints, 172
    lightweight, 39, 43
    repairing a split, 286
    warped, 292
Tangential movement, rule of
    thumb, 13
Tapers
    cutting, 111
    jig for planing tapered
        laminating, 115
Tear-out
    avoiding
        with edge jointing, 62
        in jointing end grain, 61
        when cutting veneered ply-
            wood, 77
        when routing, 102, 104
        when routing rabbets, 157
    hand planes and, 70

minimizing with a marking
knife, 22
planer, reducing, 67
Templates
making multiple cuts with, 27,
105
pattern routing thick stock, 106
Tenons. *See also* Mortise-and-tenon
joints
adjusting
correcting ill-fitting, 144
fine tuning, 138
tightening through-tenons,
144
basics of, 143
clamping through-tenons, 177
cutting tapered, 139
fox-wedging, 196
laying out, 21–22
offset, 138
one-pass, 145
routing on round stock, 142
turning round, 148–49
tusk, 10
Thicknessing
with a hand plane, 71
preventing dents while, 260
short stock, 69
tapered laminations, 115
thin stock, 69–70
3M Fineline tape, 277
3M Safer Stripper, 281
"Tone woods," 40
Trammels, drawing an ellipse with,
25
Trestle table feet, cutting, 109
Triangles
clamping and gluing, 190
laying out, 28
T-square, double-bladed, 152
Tung oil, 228
Tuning
band saws, 256–57
hand planes, 266–67
jointers, 259
table saws, 252
Turning
duplicating technique, 109
long posts on a short lathe, 110
out-of-round pieces, 260–61
perfect cylinders, 110
Tusk tenon, 10
Twisted wood
defined, 53
flattening, 71, 73
mitering, 91

repairing, 291–93
straightening, 53

U

U.S. Department of Agriculture
(USDA) Forest Products Laboratory,
42

V

Varnish
avoiding sags in, 233
characteristics, 228, *229*, 239
curing, 243
VC (veneer-core) plywood, 44
Veneer
on a compound curved surface, 38
bubbled, 281
cutting plywood, 77
disguising sand-through, 278
handling figured, 49
jointing, 75
mitering edge banding, 132
patching flaws, 295
peel-and-stick, 43
protecting edges with
cock beading, 19
registering for glue-up, 76
removing ripples, 54
routing seams, 76
storing, 59
Veneer-core (VC) plywood, 44
Vises, picture frame, 130–31

W

Walnut, sawdust disposal, 53
Warping
after planing or resawing, 70
panels, straightening warped, 53
plywood, restoring warped, 54
preventing, 55
removing with a planer, 63
repairing, 291–93
Water-based finishes
bubbles in, 226
characteristics, 229, 239
Water rings, eliminating, 296
Waterstones
dressing, 272
sharpening with, 270
Wax
characteristics, 228, *229*
colored, 243
finishing with, 243

Ways, maintaining lathe, 261
Wedges
clamping with, 192
fox-wedging, 196
WEST SYSTEM 1000 Varnish, 237
West System epoxy, 38
Wheels, how to sand, 208
Winding sticks, using, 68
Woestemeyer, F. B., 88
Wood movement
as a design factor, 5, 12–13
chamfering to conceal, 145
construction techniques, 290
how flat-, quarter-, and rift-
sawing affects, 48
stress-related, 80–81
when laminating, 46
Wood putty, using, 217
Wood selection
for food utensils, 42
for puzzles, 41–42
recommended for shelving, 11
for speaker cabinets, 40–41
Wood species, using contrasting for
design, 18

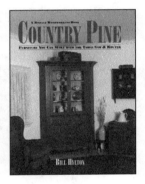

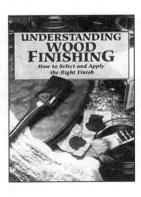

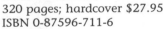